Imaginary Conversations and Poems
Walter Savage Landor

Contents

- IMAGINARY CONVERSATIONS ... 7
- MARCELLUS AND HANNIBAL ... 7
- QUEEN ELIZABETH AND CECIL ... 13
- EPICTETUS AND SENECA ... 18
- PETER THE GREAT AND ALEXIS ... 25
- HENRY VIII AND ANNE BOLEYN ... 35
- JOSEPH SCALIGER AND MONTAIGNE ... 44
- BOCCACCIO AND PETRARCA ... 51
- BOSSUET AND THE DUCHESS DE FONTANGES ... 64
- JOHN OF GAUNT AND JOANNA OF KENT ... 74
- LEOFRIC AND GODIVA ... 80
- ESSEX AND SPENSER ... 88
- LORD BACON AND RICHARD HOOKER ... 94
- OLIVER CROMWELL AND WALTER NOBLE ... 101
- LORD BROOKE AND SIR PHILIP SIDNEY ... 107
- SOUTHEY AND PORSON ... 113
- THE ABBE DELILLE AND WALTER LANDOR ... 120
- DIOGENES AND PLATO ... 123
- ALFIERI AND SALOMON THE FLORENTINE JEW ... 142
- ROUSSEAU AND MALESHERBES ... 151
- LUCULLUS AND CAESAR ... 165
- EPICURUS, LEONTION, AND TERNISSA ... 183
- DANTE AND BEATRICE ... 224
- FRA FILIPPO LIPPI AND POPE EUGENIUS ... 235
- THE FOURTH ... 235
- TASSO AND CORNELIA ... 266
- LA FONTAINE AND DE LA ROCHEFOUCAULT ... 279
- LUCIAN AND TIMOTHEUS ... 302
- BISHOP SHIPLEY AND BENJAMIN FRANKLIN ... 368
- SOUTHEY AND LANDOR ... 377
- THE EMPEROR OF CHINA AND TSING-TI ... 386
- LOUIS XVIII AND TALLEYRAND ... 392
- OLIVER CROMWELL AND SIR OLIVER ... 406
- CROMWELL ... 406
- THE COUNT GLEICHEM: THE COUNTESS: ... 416
- THEIR CHILDREN, AND ZAIDA ... 416
- THE PENTAMERON; OR, INTERVIEWS OF MESSER GIOVANNI BOCCACCIO ... 427
- FIRST DAY'S INTERVIEW ... 427
- THIRD DAY'S INTERVIEW ... 441
- FOURTH DAY'S INTERVIEW ... 464
- FIFTH DAY'S INTERVIEW ... 477
- TO MY CHILD CARLINO ... 491
- POEMS ... 508

IMAGINARY CONVERSATIONS AND POEMS

BY

Walter Savage Landor

IMAGINARY CONVERSATIONS

MARCELLUS AND HANNIBAL

Hannibal. Could a Numidian horseman ride no faster? Marcellus! oh! Marcellus! He moves not--he is dead. Did he not stir his fingers? Stand wide, soldiers--wide, forty paces; give him air; bring water; halt! Gather those broad leaves, and all the rest, growing under the brushwood; unbrace his armour. Loose the helmet first--his breast rises. I fancied his eyes were fixed on me--they have rolled back again. Who presumed to touch my shoulder? This horse? It was surely the horse of Marcellus! Let no man mount him. Ha! ha! the Romans, too, sink into luxury: here is gold about the charger.

Gaulish Chieftain. Execrable thief! The golden chain of our king under a beast's grinders! The vengeance of the gods hath overtaken the impure----

Hannibal. We will talk about vengeance when we have entered Rome, and about purity among the priests, if they will hear us. Sound for the surgeon. That arrow may be extracted from the side, deep as it is. The conqueror of Syracuse lies before me. Send a vessel off to Carthage. Say Hannibal is at the gates of Rome. Marcellus, who stood alone between us, fallen. Brave man! I would rejoice and cannot. How awfully serene a countenance! Such as we hear are in the islands of the Blessed. And how glorious a form and stature! Such too was theirs! They also once lay thus upon the earth wet with their blood--few other enter there. And what plain armour!

Gaulish Chieftain. My party slew him; indeed, I think I slew him myself. I claim the chain: it belongs to my king; the glory of Gaul requires it. Never will she endure to see another take it.

Hannibal. My friend, the glory of Marcellus did not require him to wear it. When he suspended the arms of your brave king in the temple, he thought such a trinket unworthy of himself and of Jupiter. The shield he battered down, the breast-plate he pierced with his sword--these he showed to the people and to the gods; hardly his wife and little children saw this, ere his horse wore it.

Gaulish Chieftain. Hear me; O Hannibal!

Hannibal. What! when Marcellus lies before me? when his life may perhaps be recalled? when I may lead him in triumph to Carthage? when Italy, Sicily, Greece, Asia, wait to obey me? Content thee! I will give thee mine own bridle, worth ten such.

Gaulish Chieftain. For myself?

Hannibal. For thyself.

Gaulish Chieftain. And these rubies and emeralds, and that scarlet----?

Hannibal. Yes, yes.

Gaulish Chieftain. O glorious Hannibal! unconquerable hero! O my happy country! to have such an ally and defender. I swear eternal gratitude--yes, gratitude, love, devotion, beyond eternity.

Hannibal. In all treaties we fix the time: I could hardly ask a longer. Go back to thy station. I would see what the surgeon is about, and hear what he thinks. The life of Marcellus! the triumph of Hannibal! what else has the world in it? Only Rome and Carthage: these follow.

Marcellus. I must die then? The gods be praised! The commander of a Roman army is no captive.

Hannibal. [*To the Surgeon.*] Could not he bear a sea voyage? Extract the arrow.

Surgeon. He expires that moment.

Marcellus. It pains me: extract it.

Hannibal. Marcellus, I see no expression of pain on your countenance, and never will I consent to hasten the death of an enemy in my power. Since your recovery is hopeless, you say truly you are no captive.

[*To the Surgeon.*] Is there nothing, man, that can assuage the mortal pain? for, suppress the signs of it as he may, he must feel it. Is there nothing to alleviate and allay it?

Marcellus. Hannibal, give me thy hand--thou hast found it and brought it me, compassion.

[*To the Surgeon.*] Go, friend; others want thy aid; several fell around me.

Hannibal. Recommend to your country, O Marcellus, while time permits it, reconciliation and peace with me, informing the Senate of my superiority in force, and the impossibility of resistance. The tablet is ready: let me take off this ring--try to write, to sign it, at least. Oh, what satisfaction I feel at seeing you able to rest upon the elbow, and even to smile!

Marcellus. Within an hour or less, with how severe a brow would Minos say to me, 'Marcellus, is this thy writing?'

Rome loses one man: she hath lost many such, and she still hath many left.

Hannibal. Afraid as you are of falsehood, say you this? I confess in shame the ferocity of my countrymen. Unfortunately, too, the nearer posts are occupied by Gauls, infinitely more cruel. The Numidians are so in revenge: the Gauls both in revenge and in sport. My presence is required at a distance, and I apprehend the barbarity of one or other, learning, as they must do, your refusal to execute my wishes for the common good, and feeling that by this refusal you deprive them of their country, after so long an absence.

Marcellus. Hannibal, thou art not dying.

Hannibal. What then? What mean you?

Marcellus. That thou mayest, and very justly, have many things yet to apprehend: I can have none. The barbarity of thy soldiers is nothing to me: mine would not dare be cruel. Hannibal is forced to be absent; and his authority goes away with his horse. On this turf lies defaced the semblance of a general; but Marcellus is yet the regulator of his army. Dost thou abdicate a power conferred on thee by thy nation? Or wouldst thou acknowledge it to have become, by thy own sole fault, less plenary than thy adversary's?

I have spoken too much: let me rest; this mantle oppresses me.

Hannibal. I placed my mantle on your head when the helmet was first removed, and while you were lying in the sun. Let me fold it under, and then replace the ring.

Marcellus. Take it, Hannibal. It was given me by a poor woman who flew to me at Syracuse, and who covered it with her hair, torn off in desperation that she had no other gift to offer. Little thought I that her gift and her words should be mine. How suddenly may the most powerful be in the situation of the most helpless! Let that ring and the mantle under my head be the exchange of guests at parting. The time may come, Hannibal, when thou (and the gods alone know whether as conqueror or conquered) mayest sit under the roof of my children, and in either case it shall serve thee. In thy adverse fortune, they will remember on whose pillow their father breathed his last; in thy prosperity (Heaven grant it may shine upon thee in some other country!) it will rejoice thee to protect them. We feel ourselves the most exempt from affliction when we relieve it, although we are then the most conscious that it may befall us.

There is one thing here which is not at the disposal of either.

Hannibal. What?

Marcellus. This body.

Hannibal. Whither would you be lifted? Men are ready.

Marcellus. I meant not so. My strength is failing. I seem to hear rather what is within than what is without. My sight and my other senses are in confusion. I would have said--this body, when a few bubbles of air shall have left it, is no more worthy of thy notice than of mine; but thy glory will not let thee refuse it to the piety of my family.

Hannibal. You would ask something else. I perceive an inquietude not visible till now.

Marcellus. Duty and Death make us think of home sometimes.

Hannibal. Thitherward the thoughts of the conqueror and of the conquered fly together.

Marcellus. Hast thou any prisoners from my escort?

Hannibal. A few dying lie about--and let them lie--they are Tuscans. The remainder I saw at a distance, flying, and but one brave man among them--he appeared a Roman--a youth who turned back, though wounded. They surrounded and dragged him away, spurring his horse with their swords. These Etrurians measure their courage carefully, and tack it well together before they put it on, but throw it off again with lordly ease.

Marcellus, why think about them? or does aught else disquiet your thoughts?

Marcellus. I have suppressed it long enough. My son--my beloved son!

Hannibal. Where is he? Can it be? Was he with you?

Marcellus. He would have shared my fate--and has not. Gods of my country! beneficent throughout life to me, in death surpassingly beneficent: I render you, for the last time, thanks.

QUEEN ELIZABETH AND CECIL

Elizabeth. I advise thee again, churlish Cecil, how that our Edmund Spenser, whom thou callest most uncourteously a whining whelp, hath good and solid reason for his complaint. God's blood! shall the lady that tieth my garter and shuffles the smock over my head, or the lord that steadieth my chair's back while I eat, or the other that looketh to my buck-hounds lest they be mangy, be holden by me in higher esteem and estate than he who hath placed me among the bravest of past times, and will as safely and surely set me down among the loveliest in the future?

Cecil. Your Highness must remember he carouseth fully for such deserts: fifty pounds a year of unclipped moneys, and a butt of canary wine; not to mention three thousand acres in Ireland, worth fairly another fifty and another butt, in seasonable and quiet years.

Elizabeth. The moneys are not enough to sustain a pair of grooms and a pair of palfreys, and more wine hath been drunken in my presence at a feast. The moneys are given to such men, that they may not incline nor be obligated to any vile or lowly occupation; and the canary, that they may entertain such promising wits as court their company and converse; and that in such manner there may be alway in our land a succession of these heirs unto fame. He hath written, not indeed with his wonted fancifulness, nor in learned and majestical language, but in homely and rustic wise, some verses which have moved me, and haply the more inasmuch as they demonstrate to me that his genius hath been dampened by his adversities. Read them.

Cecil.

> How much is lost when neither heart nor eye
>   Rosewinged Desire or fabling Hope deceives;
> When boyhood with quick throb hath ceased to spy
>   The dubious apple in the yellow leaves;
>
> When, rising from the turf where youth reposed,
>   We find but deserts in the far-sought shore;
> When the huge book of Faery-land lies closed,
>   And those strong brazen clasps will yield no more.

Elizabeth. The said Edmund hath also furnished unto the weaver at Arras, John Blanquieres, on my account, a description for some of his cunningest wenches to work at, supplied by mine own self, indeed, as far as the subject-matter goes, but set forth by him with figures and fancies, and daintily enough bedecked. I could have wished he had thereunto joined a fair comparison between Dian--no matter--he might perhaps have fared the better for it; but poets' wits--God help them!--when did they ever sit close about them? Read the poesy, not over-rich, and concluding very awkwardly and meanly.

Cecil.

> Where forms the lotus, with its level leaves
>   And solid blossoms, many floating isles,
> What heavenly radiance swift descending cleaves
>   The darksome wave! Unwonted beauty smiles
>
> On its pure bosom, on each bright-eyed flower,

   On every nymph, and twenty sate around,
Lo! 'twas Diana--from the sultry hour
   Hither she fled, nor fear'd she sight or sound.

Unhappy youth, whom thirst and quiver-reeds
   Drew to these haunts, whom awe forbade to fly!
Three faithful dogs before him rais'd their heads,
   And watched and wonder'd at that fixed eye.

Forth sprang his favourite--with her arrow-hand
   Too late the goddess hid what hand may hide,
Of every nymph and every reed complain'd,
   And dashed upon the bank the waters wide.

On the prone head and sandal'd feet they flew--
   Lo! slender hoofs and branching horns appear!
The last marr'd voice not e'en the favourite knew,
   But bay'd and fasten'd on the upbraiding deer.

Far be, chaste goddess, far from me and mine
   The stream that tempts thee in the summer noon!
Alas, that vengeance dwells with charms divine----

Elizabeth. Pshaw! give me the paper: I forewarned thee how it ended--pitifully, pitifully.

Cecil. I cannot think otherwise than that the undertaker of the aforecited poesy hath chosen your Highness; for I have seen painted--I know not where, but I think no farther off than Putney--the identically same Dian, with full as many nymphs, as he calls them, and more dogs. So small a matter as a page of poesy shall never stir my choler nor twitch my purse-string.

Elizabeth. I have read in Plinius and Mela of a runlet near Dodona, which kindled by approximation an unlighted torch, and extinguished a lighted one. Now, Cecil, I desire no such a jetty to be celebrated as the decoration of my court: in simpler words, which your gravity may more easily understand, I would not from the fountain of honour give lustre to the dull and ignorant, deadening and leaving in its tomb the lamp of literature and genius. I ardently wish my reign to be remembered: if my actions were different from what they are, I should as ardently wish it to be forgotten. Those are the worst of suicides, who voluntarily and propensely stab or suffocate their fame, when God hath commanded them to stand on high for an example. We call him parricide who destroys the author of his existence: tell me, what shall we call him who casts forth to the dogs and birds of prey its most faithful propagator and most firm support? Mark me, I do not speak of that existence which the proudest must close in a ditch--the narrowest, too, of ditches and the soonest filled and fouled, and whereunto a pinch of ratsbane or a poppy-head may bend him; but of that which reposes on our own good deeds, carefully picked up, skilfully put together, and decorously laid out for us by another's kind understanding: I speak of an existence such as no father is author of, or provides for. The parent gives us few days and sorrowful; the poet, many and glorious: the one (supposing him discreet and kindly) best reproves our faults; the other best remunerates our virtues.

A page of poesy is a little matter: be it so; but of a truth I do tell thee, Cecil, it shall master full many a bold heart that the Spaniard cannot trouble; it shall win to it full many a proud and flighty one that even chivalry and manly comeliness cannot touch. I may shake titles and dignities by the dozen from my breakfast-board; but I may not save those upon whose heads I shake them from rottenness and oblivion. This year they and their sovereign dwell together; next year, they and their beagle. Both have names, but names perishable.

The keeper of my privy seal is an earl: what then? the keeper of my poultry-yard is a Caesar. In honest truth, a name given to a man is no better than a skin given to him: what is not natively his own falls off and comes to nothing.

I desire in future to hear no contempt of penmen, unless a depraved use of the pen shall have so cramped them as to incapacitate them for the sword and for the council chamber. If Alexander was the Great, what was Aristoteles who made him so, and taught him every art and science he knew, except three--those of drinking, of blaspheming, and of murdering his bosom friends? Come along: I will bring thee back again nearer home. Thou mightest toss and tumble in thy bed many nights, and never eke out the substance of a stanza; but Edmund, if perchance I should call upon him for his counsel, would give me as wholesome and prudent as any of you. We should indemnify such men for the injustice we do unto them in not calling them about us, and for the mortification they must suffer at seeing their inferiors set before them. Edmund is grave and gentle: he complains of fortune, not of Elizabeth; of courts, not of Cecil. I am resolved--so help me, God!--he shall have no further cause for his repining. Go, convey unto him those twelve silver spoons, with the apostles on them, gloriously gilded; and deliver into his hand these twelve large golden pieces, sufficing for the yearly maintenance of another horse and groom. Beside which, set open before him with due reverence this Bible, wherein he may read the mercies of God toward those who waited in patience for His blessing; and this pair of crimson silk hose, which thou knowest I have worn only thirteen months, taking heed that the heel-piece be put into good and sufficient restoration, at my sole charges, by the Italian woman nigh the pollard elm at Charing Cross.

EPICTETUS AND SENECA

Seneca. Epictetus, I desired your master, Epaphroditus, to send you hither, having been much pleased with his report of your conduct, and much surprised at the ingenuity of your writings.

Epictetus. Then I am afraid, my friend----

Seneca. My friend! are these the expressions--Well, let it pass. Philosophers must bear bravely. The people expect it.

Epictetus. Are philosophers, then, only philosophers for the people; and, instead of instructing them, must they play tricks before them? Give me rather the gravity of dancing dogs. Their motions are for the rabble; their reverential eyes and pendant paws are under the pressure of awe at a master; but they are dogs, and not below their destinies.

Seneca. Epictetus! I will give you three talents to let me take that sentiment for my own.

Epictetus. I would give thee twenty, if I had them, to make it thine.

Seneca. You mean, by lending it the graces of my language?

Epictetus. I mean, by lending it to thy conduct. And now let me console and comfort thee, under the calamity I brought on thee by calling thee *my friend*. If thou art not my friend, why send for me? Enemy I can have none: being a slave, Fortune has now done with me.

Seneca. Continue, then, your former observations. What were you saying?

Epictetus. That which thou interruptedst.

Seneca. What was it?

Epictetus. I should have remarked that, if thou foundest ingenuity in my writings, thou must have discovered in them some deviation from the plain, homely truths of Zeno and Cleanthes.

Seneca. We all swerve a little from them.

Epictetus. In practice too?

Seneca. Yes, even in practice, I am afraid.

Epictetus. Often?

Seneca. Too often.

Epictetus. Strange! I have been attentive, and yet have remarked but one difference among you great personages at Rome.

Seneca. What difference fell under your observation?

Epictetus. Crates and Zeno and Cleanthes taught us that our desires were to be subdued by philosophy alone. In this city, their acute and inventive scholars take us aside, and show us that there is not only one way, but two.

Seneca. Two ways?

Epictetus. They whisper in our ear, 'These two ways are philosophy and enjoyment: the wiser man will take the readier, or, not finding it, the alternative.' Thou reddenest.

Seneca. Monstrous degeneracy.

Epictetus. What magnificent rings! I did not notice them until thou liftedst up thy hands to heaven, in detestation of such effeminacy and impudence.

Seneca. The rings are not amiss; my rank rivets them upon my fingers: I am forced to wear them. Our emperor gave me one, Epaphroditus another, Tigellinus the third. I cannot lay them aside a single day, for fear of offending the gods, and those whom they love the most worthily.

Epictetus. Although they make thee stretch out thy fingers, like the arms and legs of one of us slaves upon a cross.

Seneca. Oh, horrible! Find some other resemblance.

Epictetus. The extremities of a fig-leaf.

Seneca. Ignoble!

Epictetus. The claws of a toad, trodden on or stoned.

Seneca. You have great need, Epictetus, of an instructor in eloquence and rhetoric: you want topics, and tropes, and figures.

Epictetus. I have no room for them. They make such a buzz in the house, a man's own wife cannot understand what he says to her.

Seneca. Let us reason a little upon style. I would set you right, and remove from before you the prejudices of a somewhat rustic education. We may adorn the simplicity of the wisest.

Epictetus. Thou canst not adorn simplicity. What is naked or defective is susceptible of decoration: what is decorated is simplicity no longer. Thou mayest give another thing in exchange for it; but if thou wert master of it, thou wouldst preserve it inviolate. It is no wonder that we mortals, little able as we are to see truth, should be less able to express it.

Seneca. You have formed at present no idea of style.

Epictetus. I never think about it. First, I consider whether what I am about to say is true; then, whether I can say it with brevity, in such a manner as that others shall see it as clearly as I do in the light of truth; for, if they survey it as an ingenuity, my desire is ungratified, my duty unfulfilled. I go not with those who dance round the image of Truth, less out of honour to her than to display their agility and address.

Seneca. We must attract the attention of readers by novelty, and force, and grandeur of expression.

Epictetus. We must. Nothing is so grand as truth, nothing so forcible, nothing so novel.

Seneca. Sonorous sentences are wanted to awaken the lethargy of indolence.

Epictetus. Awaken it to what? Here lies the question; and a weighty one it is. If thou awakenest men where they can see nothing and do no work, it is better to let them rest: but will not they, thinkest thou, look up at a rainbow, unless they are called to it by a clap of thunder?

Seneca. Your early youth, Epictetus, has been, I will not say neglected, but cultivated with rude instruments and unskilful hands.

Epictetus. I thank God for it. Those rude instruments have left the turf lying yet toward the sun; and those unskilful hands have plucked out the docks.

Seneca. We hope and believe that we have attained a vein of eloquence, brighter and more varied than has been hitherto laid open to the world.

Epictetus. Than any in the Greek?

Seneca. We trust so.

Epictetus. Than your Cicero's?

Seneca. If the declaration may be made without an offence to modesty. Surely, you cannot estimate or value the eloquence of that noble pleader?

Epictetus. Imperfectly, not being born in Italy; and the noble pleader is a much less man with me than the noble philosopher. I regret that, having farms and villas, he would not keep his distance from the pumping up of foul words against thieves, cut-throats, and other rogues; and that he lied, sweated, and thumped his head and thighs, in behalf of those who were no better.

Seneca. Senators must have clients, and must protect them.

Epictetus. Innocent or guilty?

Seneca. Doubtless.

Epictetus. If I regret what is and might not be, I may regret more what both is and must be. However, it is an amiable thing, and no small merit in the wealthy, even to trifle and play at their leisure hours with philosophy. It cannot be expected that such a personage should espouse her, or should recommend her as an inseparable mate to his heir.

Seneca. I would.

Epictetus. Yes, Seneca, but thou hast no son to make the match for; and thy recommendation, I suspect, would be given him before he could consummate the marriage. Every man wishes his sons to be philosophers while they are young; but takes especial care, as they grow older, to teach them its insufficiency and unfitness for their intercourse with mankind. The paternal voice says: 'You must not be particular; you are about to have a profession to live by; follow those who have thriven the best in it.' Now, among these, whatever be the profession, canst thou point out to me one single philosopher?

Seneca. Not just now; nor, upon reflection, do I think it feasible.

Epictetus. Thou, indeed, mayest live much to thy ease and satisfaction with philosophy, having (they say) two thousand talents.

Seneca. And a trifle to spare--pressed upon me by that godlike youth, my pupil Nero.

Epictetus. Seneca! where God hath placed a mine, He hath placed the materials of an earthquake.

Seneca. A true philosopher is beyond the reach of Fortune.

Epictetus. The false one thinks himself so. Fortune cares little about philosophers; but she remembers where she hath set a rich man, and she laughs to see the Destinies at his door.

PETER THE GREAT AND ALEXIS

Peter. And so, after flying from thy father's house, thou hast returned again from Vienna. After this affront in the face of Europe, thou darest to appear before me?

Alexis. My emperor and father! I am brought before your Majesty, not at my own desire.

Peter. I believe it well.

Alexis. I would not anger you.

Peter. What hope hadst thou, rebel, in thy flight to Vienna?

Alexis. The hope of peace and privacy; the hope of security; and, above all things, of never more offending you.

Peter. That hope thou hast accomplished. Thou imaginedst, then, that my brother of Austria would maintain thee at his court--speak!

Alexis. No, sir! I imagined that he would have afforded me a place of refuge.

Peter. Didst thou, then, take money with thee?

Alexis. A few gold pieces.

Peter. How many?

Alexis. About sixty.

Peter. He would have given thee promises for half the money; but the double of it does not purchase a house, ignorant wretch!

Alexis. I knew as much as that: although my birth did not appear to destine me to purchase a house anywhere; and hitherto your liberality, my father, hath supplied my wants of every kind.

Peter. Not of wisdom, not of duty, not of spirit, not of courage, not of ambition. I have educated thee among my guards and horses, among my drums and trumpets, among my flags and masts. When thou wert a child, and couldst hardly walk, I have taken thee into the arsenal, though children should not enter according to regulations: I have there rolled cannon-balls before thee over iron plates; and I have shown thee bright new arms, bayonets and sabres; and I have pricked the back of my hands until the blood came out in many places; and I have made thee lick it; and I have then done the same to thine. Afterward, from thy tenth year, I have mixed gunpowder in thy grog; I have peppered thy peaches; I have poured bilge-water (with a little good wholesome tar in it) upon thy melons; I have brought out girls to mock thee and cocker thee, and talk like mariners, to make thee braver. Nothing would do. Nay, recollect thee! I have myself led thee forth to the window when fellows were hanged and shot; and I have shown thee every day the halves and quarters of bodies; and I have sent an orderly or chamberlain for the heads; and I have pulled the cap up from over the eyes; and I have made thee, in spite of thee, look steadfastly upon them, incorrigible coward!

And now another word with thee about thy scandalous flight from the palace, in time of quiet, too! To the point! Did my brother of Austria invite thee? Did he, or did he not?

Alexis. May I answer without doing an injury or disservice to his Imperial Majesty?

Peter. Thou mayest. What injury canst thou or any one do, by the tongue, to such as he is?

Alexis. At the moment, no; he did not. Nor indeed can I assert that he at any time invited me; but he said he pitied me.

Peter. About what? hold thy tongue; let that pass. Princes never pity but when they would make traitors: then their hearts grow tenderer than tripe. He pitied thee, kind soul, when he would throw thee at thy father's head; but finding thy father too strong for him, he now commiserates the parent, laments the son's rashness and disobedience, and would not make God angry for the world. At first, however, there must have been some overture on his part; otherwise thou are too shamefaced for intrusion. Come--thou hast never had wit enough to lie--tell me the truth, the whole truth.

Alexis. He said that if ever I wanted an asylum, his court was open to me.

Peter. Open! so is the tavern; but folks pay for what they get there. Open, truly! and didst thou find it so?

Alexis. He received me kindly.

Peter. I see he did.

Alexis. Derision, O my father! is not the fate I merit.

Peter. True, true! it was not intended.

Alexis. Kind father! punish me then as you will.

Peter. Villain! wouldst thou kiss my hand, too? Art thou ignorant that the Austrian threw thee away from him, with the same indifference as he would the outermost leaf of a sandy sunburnt lettuce?

Alexis. Alas! I am not ignorant of this.

Peter. He dismissed thee at my order. If I had demanded from him his daughter, to be the bedfellow of a Kalmuc, he would have given her, and praised God.

Alexis. O father! is his baseness my crime?

Peter. No; thine is greater. Thy intention, I know, is to subvert the institutions it has been the labour of my lifetime to establish. Thou hast never rejoiced at my victories.

Alexis. I have rejoiced at your happiness and your safety.

Peter. Liar! coward! traitor! when the Polanders and Swedes fell before me, didst thou from thy soul congratulate me? Didst thou get drunk at home or abroad, or praise the Lord of Hosts and Saint Nicholas? Wert thou not silent and civil and low-spirited?

Alexis. I lamented the irretrievable loss of human life; I lamented that the bravest and noblest were swept away the first; that the gentlest and most domestic were the earliest mourners; that frugality was supplanted by intemperance; that order was succeeded by confusion; and that your Majesty was destroying the glorious plans you alone were capable of devising.

Peter. I destroy them! how? Of what plans art thou speaking?

Alexis. Of civilizing the Muscovites. The Polanders in part were civilized: the Swedes, more than any other nation on the Continent; and so excellently versed were they in military science, and so courageous, that every man you killed cost you seven or eight.

Peter. Thou liest; nor six. And civilized, forsooth? Why, the robes of the metropolitan, him at Upsal, are not worth three ducats, between Jew and Livornese. I have no notion that Poland and Sweden shall be the only countries that produce great princes. What right have they to such as Gustavus and Sobieski? Europe ought to look to this before discontents become general, and the people do to us what we have the privilege of doing to the people. I am wasting my words: there is no arguing with positive fools like thee. So thou wouldst have desired me to let the Polanders and Swedes lie still and quiet! Two such powerful nations!

Alexis. For that reason and others I would have gladly seen them rest, until our own people had increased in numbers and prosperity.

Peter. And thus thou disputest my right, before my face, to the exercise of the supreme power.

Alexis. Sir! God forbid!

Peter. God forbid, indeed! What care such villains as thou art what God forbids! He forbids the son to be disobedient to the father; He forbids--He forbids--twenty things. I do not wish, and will not have, a successor who dreams of dead people.

Alexis. My father! I have dreamed of none such.

Peter. Thou hast, and hast talked about them--Scythians, I think, they call 'em. Now, who told thee, Mr. Professor, that the Scythians were a happier people than we are; that they were inoffensive; that they were free; that they wandered with their carts from pasture to pasture, from river to river; that they traded with good faith; that they fought with good courage; that they injured none, invaded none, and feared none? At this rate I have effected nothing. The great founder of Rome, I heard in Holland, slew his brother for despiting the weakness of his walls; and shall the founder of this better place spare a degenerate son, who prefers a vagabond life to a civilized one, a cart to a city, a Scythian to a Muscovite? Have I not shaved my people, and breeched them? Have I not formed them into regular armies, with bands of music and haversacks? Are bows better than cannon? shepherds than dragoons, mare's milk than brandy, raw steaks than broiled? Thine are tenets that strike at the root of politeness and sound government. Every prince in Europe is interested in rooting them out by fire and sword. There is no other way with false doctrines: breath against breath does little.

Alexis. Sire, I never have attempted to disseminate my opinions.

Peter. How couldst thou? the seed would fall only on granite. Those, however, who caught it brought it to me.

Alexis. Never have I undervalued civilization: on the contrary, I regretted whatever impeded it. In my opinion, the evils that have been attributed to it sprang from its imperfections and voids; and no nation has yet acquired it more than very scantily.

Peter. How so? give me thy reasons--thy fancies, rather; for reason thou hast none.

Alexis. When I find the first of men, in rank and genius, hating one another, and becoming slanderers and liars in order to lower and vilify an opponent; when I hear the God of mercy invoked to massacres, and thanked for furthering what He reprobates and condemns--I look back in vain on any barbarous people for worse barbarism. I have expressed my admiration of our forefathers, who, not being Christians, were yet more virtuous than those who are; more temperate, more just, more sincere, more chaste, more peaceable.

Peter. Malignant atheist!

Alexis. Indeed, my father, were I malignant I must be an atheist; for malignity is contrary to the command, and inconsistent with the belief, of God.

Peter. Am I Czar of Muscovy, and hear discourses on reason and religion? from my own son, too! No, by the Holy Trinity! thou art no son of mine. If thou touchest my knee again, I crack thy knuckles with this tobacco-stopper: I wish it were a sledge-hammer for thy sake. Off, sycophant! Off, runaway slave!

Alexis. Father! father! my heart is broken! If I have offended, forgive me!

Peter. The State requires thy signal punishment.

Alexis. If the State requires it, be it so; but let my father's anger cease!

Peter. The world shall judge between us. I will brand thee with infamy.

Alexis. Until now, O father! I never had a proper sense of glory. Hear me, O Czar! let not a thing so vile as I am stand between you and the world! Let none accuse you!

Peter. Accuse me, rebel! Accuse me, traitor!

Alexis. Let none speak ill of you, O my father! The public voice shakes the palace; the public voice penetrates the grave; it precedes the chariot of Almighty God, and is heard at the judgment-seat.

Peter. Let it go to the devil! I will have none of it here in Petersburg. Our church says nothing about it; our laws forbid it. As for thee, unnatural brute, I have no more to do with thee neither!

Ho, there! chancellor! What! come at last! Wert napping, or counting thy ducats?

Chancellor. Your Majesty's will and pleasure!

Peter. Is the Senate assembled in that room?

Chancellor. Every member, sire.

Peter. Conduct this youth with thee, and let them judge him; thou understandest me.

Chancellor. Your Majesty's commands are the breath of our nostrils.

Peter. If these rascals are amiss, I will try my new cargo of Livonian hemp upon 'em.

Chancellor. [*Returning.*] Sire, sire!

Peter. Speak, fellow! Surely they have not condemned him to death, without giving themselves time to read the accusation, that thou comest back so quickly.

Chancellor. No, sire! Nor has either been done.

Peter. Then thy head quits thy shoulders.

Chancellor. O sire!

Peter. Curse thy silly *sires*! what art thou about?

Chancellor. Alas! he fell.

Peter. Tie him up to thy chair, then. Cowardly beast! what made him fall?

Chancellor. The hand of Death; the name of father.

Peter. Thou puzzlest me; prithee speak plainlier.

Chancellor. We told him that his crime was proven and manifest; that his life was forfeited.

Peter. So far, well enough.

Chancellor. He smiled.

Peter. He did! did he? Impudence shall do him little good. Who could have expected it from that smock-face! Go on--what then?

Chancellor. He said calmly, but not without sighing twice or thrice, 'Lead me to the scaffold: I am weary of life; nobody loves me.' I condoled with him, and wept upon his hand, holding the paper against my bosom. He took the corner of it between his fingers, and said, 'Read me this paper; read my death-warrant. Your silence and tears have signified it; yet the law has its forms. Do not keep me in suspense. My father says, too truly, I am not courageous; but the death that leads me to my God shall never terrify me.'

Peter. I have seen these white-livered knaves die resolutely; I have seen them quietly fierce like white ferrets with their watery eyes and tiny teeth. You read it?

Chancellor. In part, sire! When he heard your Majesty's name accusing him of treason and attempts at rebellion and parricide, he fell speechless. We raised him up: he was motionless; he was dead!

Peter. Inconsiderate and barbarous varlet as thou art, dost thou recite this ill accident to a father! and to one who has not dined! Bring me a glass of brandy.

Chancellor. And it please your Majesty, might I call a--a----

Peter. Away and bring it: scamper! All equally and alike shall obey and serve me.

Hark ye! bring the bottle with it: I must cool myself--and--hark ye! a rasher of bacon on thy life! and some pickled sturgeon, and some krout and caviare, and good strong cheese.

HENRY VIII AND ANNE BOLEYN

Henry. Dost thou know me, Nanny, in this yeoman's dress? 'Sblood! does it require so long and vacant a stare to recollect a husband after a week or two? No tragedy-tricks with me! a scream, a sob, or thy kerchief a trifle the wetter, were enough. Why, verily the little fool faints in earnest. These whey faces, like their kinsfolk the ghosts, give us no warning. Hast had water enough upon thee? Take that, then: art thyself again?

Anne. Father of mercies! do I meet again my husband, as was my last prayer on earth? Do I behold my beloved lord--in peace--and pardoned, my partner in eternal bliss? it was his voice. I cannot see him: why cannot I? Oh, why do these pangs interrupt the transports of the blessed?

Henry. Thou openest thy arms: faith! I came for that. Nanny, thou art a sweet slut. Thou groanest, wench: art in labour? Faith! among the mistakes of the night, I am ready to think almost that thou hast been drinking, and that I have not.

Anne. God preserve your Highness: grant me your forgiveness for one slight offence. My eyes were heavy; I fell asleep while I was reading. I did not know of your presence at first; and, when I did, I could not speak. I strove for utterance: I wanted no respect for my liege and husband.

Henry. My pretty warm nestling, thou wilt then lie! Thou wert reading, and aloud too, with thy saintly cup of water by thee, and--what! thou art still girlishly fond of those dried cherries!

Anne. I had no other fruit to offer your Highness the first time I saw you, and you were then pleased to invent for me some reason why they should be acceptable. I did not dry these: may I present them, such as they are? We shall have fresh next month.

Henry. Thou art always driving away from the discourse. One moment it suits thee to know me, another not.

Anne. Remember, it is hardly three months since I miscarried. I am weak, and liable to swoons.

Henry. Thou hast, however, thy bridal cheeks, with lustre upon them when there is none elsewhere, and obstinate lips resisting all impression; but, now thou talkest about miscarrying, who is the father of that boy?

Anne. Yours and mine--He who hath taken him to his own home, before (like me) he could struggle or cry for it.

Henry. Pagan, or worse, to talk so! He did not come into the world alive: there was no baptism.

Anne. I thought only of our loss: my senses are confounded. I did not give him my milk, and yet I loved him tenderly; for I often fancied, had he lived, how contented and joyful he would have made you and England.

Henry. No subterfuges and escapes. I warrant, thou canst not say whether at my entrance thou wert waking or wandering.

Anne. Faintness and drowsiness came upon me suddenly.

Henry. Well, since thou really and truly sleepedst, what didst dream of?

Anne. I begin to doubt whether I did indeed sleep.

Henry. Ha! false one--never two sentences of truth together! But come, what didst think about, asleep or awake?

Anne. I thought that God had pardoned me my offences, and had received me unto Him.

Henry. And nothing more?

Anne. That my prayers had been heard and my wishes were accomplishing: the angels alone can enjoy more beatitude than this.

Henry. Vexatious little devil! She says nothing now about me, merely from perverseness. Hast thou never thought about me, nor about thy falsehood and adultery?

Anne. If I had committed any kind of falsehood, in regard to you or not, I should never have rested until I had thrown myself at your feet and obtained your pardon; but, if ever I had been guilty of that other crime, I know not whether I should have dared to implore it, even of God's mercy.

Henry. Thou hast heretofore cast some soft glances upon Smeaton; hast thou not?

Anne. He taught me to play on the virginals, as you know, when I was little, and thereby to please your Highness.

Henry. And Brereton and Norris--what have they taught thee?

Anne. They are your servants, and trusty ones.

Henry. Has not Weston told thee plainly that he loved thee?

Anne. Yes; and----

Henry. What didst thou?

Anne. I defied him.

Henry. Is that all?

Anne. I could have done no more if he had told me that he hated me. Then, indeed, I should have incurred more justly the reproaches of your Highness: I should have smiled.

Henry. We have proofs abundant: the fellows shall one and all confront thee. Aye, clap thy hands and kiss thy sleeve, harlot!

Anne. Oh that so great a favour is vouchsafed me! My honour is secure; my husband will be happy again; he will see my innocence.

Henry. Give me now an account of the moneys thou hast received from me within these nine months. I want them not back: they are letters of gold in record of thy guilt. Thou hast had no fewer than fifteen thousand pounds in that period, without even thy asking; what hast done with it, wanton?

Anne. I have regularly placed it out to interest.

Henry. Where? I demand of thee.

Anne. Among the needy and ailing. My Lord Archbishop has the account of it, sealed by him weekly. I also had a copy myself; those who took away my papers may easily find it; for there are few others, and they lie open.

Henry. Think on my munificence to thee; recollect who made thee. Dost sigh for what thou hast lost?

Anne. I do, indeed.

Henry. I never thought thee ambitious; but thy vices creep out one by one.

Anne. I do not regret that I have been a queen and am no longer one; nor that my innocence is called in question by those who never knew me; but I lament that the good people who loved me so cordially, hate and curse me; that those who pointed me out to their daughters for imitation check them when they speak about me; and that he whom next to God I have served with most devotion is my accuser.

Henry. Wast thou conning over something in that dingy book for thy defence? Come, tell me, what wast thou reading?

Anne. This ancient chronicle. I was looking for someone in my own condition, and must have missed the page. Surely in so many hundred years there shall have been other young maidens, first too happy for exaltation, and after too exalted for happiness--not, perchance, doomed to die upon a scaffold, by those they ever honoured and served faithfully; that, indeed, I did not look for nor think of; but my heart was bounding for any one I could love and pity. She would be unto me as a sister dead and gone; but hearing me, seeing me, consoling me, and being consoled. O my husband! it is so heavenly a thing----

Henry. To whine and whimper, no doubt, is vastly heavenly.

Anne. I said not so; but those, if there be any such, who never weep, have nothing in them of heavenly or of earthly. The plants, the trees, the very rocks and unsunned clouds, show us at least the semblances of weeping; and there is not an aspect of the globe we live on, nor of the waters and skies around it, without a reference and a similitude to our joys or sorrows.

Henry. I do not remember that notion anywhere. Take care no enemy rake out of it something of materialism. Guard well thy empty hot brain; it may hatch more evil. As for those odd words, I myself would fain see no great harm in them, knowing that grief and frenzy strike out many things which would else lie still, and neither spurt nor sparkle. I also know that thou hast never read anything but Bible and history--the two worst books in the world for young people, and the most certain to lead astray both prince and subject. For which reason I have interdicted and entirely put down the one, and will (by the blessing of the Virgin and of holy Paul) commit the other to a rigid censor. If it behoves us kings to enact what our people shall eat and drink--of which the most unruly and rebellious spirit can entertain no doubt--greatly more doth it behove us to examine what they read and think. The body is moved according to the mind and will; we must take care that the movement be a right one, on pain of God's anger in this life and the next.

Anne. O my dear husband! it must be a naughty thing, indeed, that makes Him angry beyond remission. Did you ever try how pleasant it is to forgive any one? There is nothing else wherein we can resemble God perfectly and easily.

Henry. Resemble God perfectly and easily! Do vile creatures talk thus of the Creator?

Anne. No, Henry, when His creatures talk thus of Him, they are no longer vile creatures! When they know that He is good, they love Him; and, when they love Him, they are good themselves. O Henry! my husband and king! the judgments of our Heavenly Father are righteous; on this, surely, we must think alike.

Henry. And what, then? Speak out; again I command thee, speak plainly! thy tongue was not so torpid but this moment. Art ready? Must I wait?

Anne. If any doubt remains upon your royal mind of your equity in this business: should it haply seem possible to you that passion or prejudice, in yourself or another, may have warped so strong an understanding--do but supplicate the Almighty to strengthen and enlighten it, and He will hear you.

Henry. What! thou wouldst fain change thy quarters, ay?

Anne. My spirit is detached and ready, and I shall change them shortly, whatever your Highness may determine.

Henry. Yet thou appearest hale and resolute, and (they tell me) smirkest and smilest to everybody.

Anne. The withered leaf catches the sun sometimes, little as it can profit by it; and I have heard stories of the breeze in other climates that sets in when daylight is about to close, and how constant it is, and how refreshing. My heart, indeed, is now sustained strangely; it became the more sensibly so from that time forward, when power and grandeur and all things terrestrial were sunk from sight. Every act of kindness in those about me gives me satisfaction and pleasure, such as I did not feel formerly. I was worse before God chastened me; yet I was never an ingrate. What pains have I taken to find out the village-girls who placed their posies in my chamber ere I arose in the morning! How gladly would I have recompensed the forester who lit up a brake on my birthnight, which else had warmed him half the winter! But these are times past: I was not Queen of England.

Henry. Nor adulterous, nor heretical.

Anne. God be praised!

Henry. Learned saint! thou knowest nothing of the lighter, but perhaps canst inform me about the graver, of them.

Anne. Which may it be, my liege?

Henry. Which may it be? Pestilence! I marvel that the walls of this tower do not crack around thee at such impiety.

Anne. I would be instructed by the wisest of theologians: such is your Highness.

Henry. Are the sins of the body, foul as they are, comparable to those of the soul?

Anne. When they are united, they must be worse.

Henry. Go on, go on: thou pushest thy own breast against the sword. God hath deprived thee of thy reason for thy punishment. I must hear more: proceed, I charge thee.

Anne. An aptitude to believe one thing rather than another, from ignorance or weakness, or from the more persuasive manner of the teacher, or from his purity of life, or from the strong impression of a particular text at a particular time, and various things beside, may influence and decide our opinion; and the hand of the Almighty, let us hope, will fall gently on human fallibility.

Henry. Opinion in matters of faith! rare wisdom! rare religion! Troth, Anne! thou hast well sobered me. I came rather warmly and lovingly; but these light ringlets, by the holy rood, shall not shade this shoulder much longer. Nay, do not start; I tap it for the last time, my sweetest. If the Church permitted it, thou shouldst set forth on thy long journey with the Eucharist between thy teeth, however loath.

Anne. Love your Elizabeth, my honoured lord, and God bless you! She will soon forget to call me. Do not chide her: think how young she is.

Could I, could I kiss her, but once again! it would comfort my heart--or break it.

JOSEPH SCALIGER AND MONTAIGNE

Montaigne. What could have brought you, M. de l'Escale, to visit the old man of the mountain, other than a good heart? Oh, how delighted and charmed I am to hear you speak such excellent Gascon. You rise early, I see: you must have risen with the sun, to be here at this hour; it is a stout half-hour's walk from the brook. I have capital white wine, and the best cheese in Auvergne. You saw the goats and the two cows before the castle.

Pierre, thou hast done well: set it upon the table, and tell Master Matthew to split a couple of chickens and broil them, and to pepper but one. Do you like pepper, M. de l'Escale?

Scaliger. Not much.

Montaigne. Hold hard! let the pepper alone: I hate it. Tell him to broil plenty of ham; only two slices at a time, upon his salvation.

Scaliger. This, I perceive, is the antechamber to your library: here are your everyday books.

Montaigne. Faith! I have no other. These are plenty, methinks; is not that your opinion?

Scaliger. You have great resources within yourself, and therefore can do with fewer.

Montaigne. Why, how many now do you think here may be?

Scaliger. I did not believe at first that there could be above fourscore.

Montaigne. Well! are fourscore few?--are we talking of peas and beans?

Scaliger. I and my father (put together) have written well-nigh as many.

Montaigne. Ah! to write them is quite another thing: but one reads books without a spur, or even a pat from our Lady Vanity. How do you like my wine?--it comes from the little knoll yonder: you cannot see the vines, those chestnut-trees are between.

Scaliger. The wine is excellent; light, odoriferous, with a smartness like a sharp child's prattle.

Montaigne. It never goes to the head, nor pulls the nerves, which many do as if they were guitar-strings. I drink a couple of bottles a day, winter and summer, and never am the worse for it. You gentlemen of the Agennois have better in your province, and indeed the very best under the sun. I do not wonder that the Parliament of Bordeaux should be jealous of their privileges, and call it Bordeaux. Now, if you prefer your own country wine, only say it: I have several bottles in my cellar, with corks as long as rapiers, and as polished. I do not know, M. de l'Escale, whether you are particular in these matters: not quite, I should imagine, so great a judge in them as in others?

Scaliger. I know three things: wine, poetry, and the world.

Montaigne. You know one too many, then. I hardly know whether I know anything about poetry; for I like Clem Marot better than Ronsard. Ronsard is so plaguily stiff and stately, where there is no occasion for it; I verily do think the man must have slept with his wife in a cuirass.

Scaliger. It pleases me greatly that you like Marot. His versions of the Psalms is lately set to music, and added to the New Testament of Geneva.

Montaigne. It is putting a slice of honeycomb into a barrel of vinegar, which will never grow the sweeter for it.

Scaliger. Surely, you do not think in this fashion of the New Testament!

Montaigne. Who supposes it? Whatever is mild and kindly is there. But Jack Calvin has thrown bird-lime and vitriol upon it, and whoever but touches the cover dirties his fingers or burns them.

Scaliger. Calvin is a very great man, I do assure you, M. de Montaigne.

Montaigne. I do not like your great men who beckon me to them, call me their begotten, their dear child, and their entrails; and, if I happen to say on any occasion, 'I beg leave, sir, to dissent a little from you,' stamp and cry, 'The devil you do!' and whistle to the executioner.

Scaliger. You exaggerate, my worthy friend!

Montaigne. Exaggerate do I, M. de l'Escale? What was it he did the other day to the poor devil there with an odd name?--Melancthon, I think it is.

Scaliger. I do not know: I have received no intelligence of late from Geneva.

Montaigne. It was but last night that our curate rode over from Lyons (he made two days of it, as you may suppose) and supped with me. He told me that Jack had got his old friend hanged and burned. I could not join him in the joke, for I find none such in the New Testament, on which he would have founded it; and, if it is one, it is not in my manner or to my taste.

Scaliger. I cannot well believe the report, my dear sir. He was rather urgent, indeed, on the combustion of the heretic Michael Servetus some years past.

Montaigne. A thousand to one, my spiritual guide mistook the name. He has heard of both, I warrant him, and thinks in his conscience that either is as good a roast as the other.

Scaliger. Theologians are proud and intolerant, and truly the farthest of all men from theology, if theology means the rational sense of religion, or indeed has anything to do with it in any way. Melancthon was the very best of the reformers; quiet, sedate, charitable, intrepid, firm in friendship, ardent in faith, acute in argument, and profound in learning.

Montaigne. Who cares about his argumentation or his learning, if he was the rest?

Scaliger. I hope you will suspend your judgment on this affair until you receive some more certain and positive information.

Montaigne. I can believe it of the Sieur Calvin.

Scaliger. I cannot. John Calvin is a grave man, orderly and reasonable.

Montaigne. In my opinion he has not the order nor the reason of my cook. Mat never took a man for a sucking-pig, cleaning and scraping and buttering and roasting him; nor ever twitched God by the sleeve and swore He should not have His own way.

Scaliger. M. de Montaigne, have you ever studied the doctrine of predestination?

Montaigne. I should not understand it, if I had; and I would not break through an old fence merely to get into a cavern. I would not give a fig or a fig-leaf to know the truth of it, as far as any man can teach it me. Would it make me honester or happier, or, in other things, wiser?

Scaliger. I do not know whether it would materially.

Montaigne. I should be an egregious fool then to care about it. Our disputes on controverted points have filled the country with missionaries and cut-throats. Both parties have shown a disposition to turn this comfortable old house of mine into a fortress. If I had inclined to either, the other would have done it. Come walk about it with me; after a ride, you can do nothing better to take off fatigue.

Scaliger. A most spacious kitchen!

Montaigne. Look up!

Scaliger. You have twenty or more flitches of bacon hanging there.

Montaigne. And if I had been a doctor or a captain, I should have had a cobweb and predestination in the place of them. Your soldiers of the ***religion*** on the one side, and of the ***good old faith*** on the other, would not have left unto me safe and sound even that good old woman there.

Scaliger. Oh, yes! they would, I hope.

Old Woman. Why dost giggle, Mat? What should he know about the business? He speaks mighty bad French, and is as spiteful as the devil. Praised be God, we have a kind master, who thinks about us, and feels for us.

Scaliger. Upon my word, M. de Montaigne, this gallery is an interesting one.

Montaigne. I can show you nothing but my house and my dairy. We have no chase in the month of May, you know--unless you would like to bait the badger in the stable. This is rare sport in rainy days.

Scaliger. Are you in earnest, M. de Montaigne?

Montaigne. No, no, no, I cannot afford to worry him outright: only a little for pastime--a morning's merriment for the dogs and wenches.

Scaliger. You really are then of so happy a temperament that, at your time of life, you can be amused by baiting a badger!

Montaigne. Why not? Your father, a wiser and graver and older man than I am, was amused by baiting a professor or critic. I have not a dog in the kennel that would treat the badger worse than brave Julius treated Cardan and Erasmus, and some dozens more. We are all childish, old as well as young; and our very last tooth would fain stick, M. de l'Escale, in some tender place of a neighbour. Boys laugh at a person who falls in the dirt; men laugh rather when they make him fall, and most when the dirt is of their own laying.

Is not the gallery rather cold, after the kitchen? We must go through it to get into the court where I keep my tame rabbits; the stable is hard by: come along, come along.

Scaliger. Permit me to look a little at those banners. Some of them are old indeed.

Montaigne. Upon my word, I blush to think I never took notice how they are tattered. I have no fewer than three women in the house, and in a summer's evening, only two hours long, the worst of these rags might have been darned across.

Scaliger. You would not have done it surely!

Montaigne. I am not over-thrifty; the women might have been better employed. It is as well as it is then; ay?

Scaliger. I think so.

Montaigne. So be it.

Scaliger. They remind me of my own family, we being descended from the great Cane della Scala, Prince of Verona, and from the House of Hapsburg, as you must have heard from my father.

Montaigne. What signifies it to the world whether the great Cane was tied to his grandmother or not? As for the House of Hapsburg, if you could put together as many such houses as would make up a city larger than Cairo, they would not be worth his study, or a sheet of paper on the table of it.

BOCCACCIO AND PETRARCA

Boccaccio. Remaining among us, I doubt not that you would soon receive the same distinctions in your native country as others have conferred upon you: indeed, in confidence I may promise it. For greatly are the Florentines ashamed that the most elegant of their writers and the most independent of their citizens lives in exile, by the injustice he had suffered in the detriment done to his property, through the intemperate administration of their laws.

Petrarca. Let them recall me soon and honourably: then perhaps I may assist them to remove their ignominy, which I carry about with me wherever I go, and which is pointed out by my exotic laurel.

Boccaccio. There is, and ever will be, in all countries and under all governments, an ostracism for their greatest men.

Petrarca. At present we will talk no more about it. To-morrow I pursue my journey towards Padua, where I am expected; where some few value and esteem me, honest and learned and ingenious men; although neither those Transpadane regions, nor whatever extends beyond them, have yet produced an equal to Boccaccio.

Boccaccio. Then, in the name of friendship, do not go thither!--form such rather from your fellow-citizens. I love my equals heartily; and shall love them the better when I see them raised up here, from our own mother earth, by you.

Petrarca. Let us continue our walk.

Boccaccio. If you have been delighted (and you say you have been) at seeing again, after so long an absence, the house and garden wherein I have placed the relaters of my stories, as reported in the ***Decameron***, come a little way farther up the ascent, and we will pass through the vineyard on the west of the villa. You will see presently another on the right, lying in its warm little garden close to the roadside, the scene lately of somewhat that would have looked well, as illustration, in the midst of your Latin reflections. It shows us that people the most serious and determined may act at last contrariwise to the line of conduct they have laid down.

Petrarca. Relate it to me, Messer Giovanni; for you are able to give reality the merits and charms of fiction, just as easily as you give fiction the semblance, the stature, and the movement of reality.

Boccaccio. I must here forgo such powers, if in good truth I possess them.

Petrarca. This long green alley, defended by box and cypresses, is very pleasant. The smell of box, although not sweet, is more agreeable to me than many that are: I cannot say from what resuscitation of early and tender feeling. The cypress, too, seems to strengthen the nerves of the brain. Indeed, I delight in the odour of most trees and plants.

Will not that dog hurt us?--he comes closer.

Boccaccio. Dog! thou hast the colours of a magpie and the tongue of one; prithee be quiet: art thou not ashamed?

Petrarca. Verily he trots off, comforting his angry belly with his plenteous tail, flattened and bestrewn under it. He looks back, going on, and puffs out his upper lip without a bark.

Boccaccio. These creatures are more accessible to temperate and just rebuke than the creatures of our species, usually angry with less reason, and from no sense, as dogs are, of duty. Look into that white arcade! Surely it was white the other day; and now I perceive it is still so: the setting sun tinges it with yellow.

Petrarca. The house has nothing of either the rustic or the magnificent about it; nothing quite regular, nothing much varied. If there is anything at all affecting, as I fear there is, in the story you are about to tell me, I could wish the edifice itself bore externally some little of the interesting that I might hereafter turn my mind toward it, looking out of the catastrophe, though not away from it. But I do not even find the peculiar and uncostly decoration of our Tuscan villas: the central turret, round which the kite perpetually circles in search of pigeons or smaller prey, borne onward, like the Flemish skater, by effortless will in motionless progression. The view of Fiesole must be lovely from that window; but I fancy to myself it loses the cascade under the single high arch of the Mugnone.

Boccaccio. I think so. In this villa--come rather farther off: the inhabitants of it may hear us, if they should happen to be in the arbour, as most people are at the present hour of day--in this villa, Messer Francesco, lives Monna Tita Monalda, who tenderly loved Amadeo degli Oricellari. She, however, was reserved and coy; and Father Pietro de' Pucci, an enemy to the family of Amadeo, told her nevermore to think of him, for that, just before he knew her, he had thrown his arm round the neck of Nunciata Righi, his mother's maid, calling her most immodestly a sweet creature, and of a whiteness that marble would split with envy at.

Monna Tita trembled and turned pale. 'Father, is the girl really so very fair?' said she anxiously.

'Madonna,' replied the father, 'after confession she is not much amiss: white she is, with a certain tint of pink not belonging to her, but coming over her as through the wing of an angel pleased at the holy function; and her breath is such, the very ear smells it: poor, innocent, sinful soul! Hei! The wretch, Amadeo, would have endangered her salvation.'

'She must be a wicked girl to let him,' said Monna Tita. 'A young man of good parentage and education would not dare to do such a thing of his own accord. I will see him no more, however. But it was before he knew me: and it may not be true. I cannot think any young woman would let a young man do so, even in the last hour before Lent. Now in what month was it supposed to be?'

'Supposed to be!' cried the father indignantly: 'in June; I say in June.'

'Oh! that now is quite impossible: for on the second of July, forty-one days from this, and at this very hour of it, he swore to me eternal love and constancy. I will inquire of him whether it is true: I will charge him with it.'

She did. Amadeo confessed his fault, and, thinking it a venial one, would have taken and kissed her hand as he asked forgiveness.

Petrarca. Children! children! I will go into the house, and if their relatives, as I suppose, have approved of the marriage, I will endeavour to persuade the young lady that a fault like this, on the repentance of her lover, is not unpardonable. But first, is Amadeo a young man of loose habits?

Boccaccio. Less than our others: in fact, I never heard of any deviation, excepting this.

Petrarca. Come, then, with me.

Boccaccio. Wait a little.

Petrarca. I hope the modest Tita, after a trial, will not be too severe with him.

Boccaccio. Severity is far from her nature; but, such is her purity and innocence, she shed many and bitter tears at his confession, and declared her unalterable determination of taking the veil among the nuns of Fiesole. Amadeo fell at her feet, and wept upon them. She pushed him from her gently, and told him she would still love him if he would follow her example, leave the world, and become a friar of San Marco. Amadeo was speechless; and, if he had not been so, he never would have made a promise he intended to violate. She retired from him. After a time he arose, less wounded than benumbed by the sharp uncovered stones in the garden-walk; and, as a man who fears to fall from a precipice goes farther from it than is necessary, so did Amadeo shun the quarter where the gate is, and, oppressed by his agony and despair, throw his arms across the sundial and rest his brow upon it, hot as it must have been on a cloudless day in August. When the evening was about to close, he was aroused by the cries of rooks overhead; they flew towards Florence, and beyond; he, too, went back into the city.

Tita fell sick from her inquietude. Every morning ere sunrise did Amadeo return; but could hear only from the labourers in the field that Monna Tita was ill, because she had promised to take the veil and had not taken it, knowing, as she must do, that the heavenly bridegroom is a bridegroom never to be trifled with, let the spouse be young and beautiful as she may be. Amadeo had often conversed with the peasant of the farm, who much pitied so worthy and loving a gentleman; and, finding him one evening fixing some thick and high stakes in the ground, offered to help him. After due thanks, 'It is time,' said the peasant, 'to rebuild the hovel and watch the grapes.'

'This is my house,' cried he. 'Could I never, in my stupidity, think about rebuilding it before? Bring me another mat or two: I will sleep here to-night, to-morrow night, every night, all autumn, all winter.'

He slept there, and was consoled at last by hearing that Monna Tita was out of danger, and recovering from her illness by spiritual means. His heart grew lighter day after day. Every evening did he observe the rooks, in the same order, pass along the same track in the heavens, just over San Marco; and it now occurred to him, after three weeks, indeed, that Monna Tita had perhaps some strange idea, in choosing his monastery, not unconnected with the passage of these birds. He grew calmer upon it, until he asked himself whether he might hope. In the midst of this half-meditation, half-dream, his whole frame was shaken by the voices, however low and gentle, of two monks, coming from the villa and approaching him. He would have concealed himself under this bank whereon we are standing; but they saw him, and called him by name. He now perceived that the younger of them was Guiberto Oddi, with whom he had been at school about six or seven years ago, and who admired him for his courage and frankness when he was almost a child.

'Do not let us mortify poor Amadeo,' said Guiberto to his companion. 'Return to the road: I will speak a few words to him, and engage him (I trust) to comply with reason and yield to necessity.' The elder monk, who saw he should have to climb the hill again, assented to the proposal, and went into the road. After the first embraces and few words, 'Amadeo! Amadeo!' said Guiberto, 'it was love that made me a friar; let anything else make you one.'

'Kind heart!' replied Amadeo. 'If death or religion, or hatred of me, deprives me of Tita Monalda, I will die, where she commanded me, in the cowl. It is you who prepare her, then, to throw away her life and mine!'

'Hold! Amadeo!' said Guiberto, 'I officiate together with good Father Fontesecco, who invariably falls asleep amid our holy function.'

Now, Messer Francesco, I must inform you that Father Fontesecco has the heart of a flower. It feels nothing, it wants nothing; it is pure and simple, and full of its own little light. Innocent as a child, as an angel, nothing ever troubled him but how to devise what he should confess. A confession costs him more trouble to invent than any Giornata in my **Decameron** cost me. He was once overheard to say on this occasion, 'God forgive me in His infinite mercy, for making it appear that I am a little worse than He has chosen I should be!' He is temperate; for he never drinks more than exactly half the wine and water set before him. In fact, he drinks the wine and leaves the water, saying: 'We have the same water up at San Domenico; we send it hither: it would be uncivil to take back our own gift, and still more to leave a suspicion that we thought other people's wine poor beverage.' Being afflicted by the gravel, the physician of his convent advised him, as he never was fond of wine, to leave it off entirely; on which he said, 'I know few things; but this I know well--in water there is often gravel, in wine never. It hath pleased God to afflict me, and even to go a little out of His way in order to do it, for the greater warning to other sinners. I will drink wine, brother Anselmini, and help His work.'

I have led you away from the younger monk.

'While Father Fontesecco is in the first stage of beatitude, chanting through his nose the **Benedicite**, I will attempt,' said Guiberto, 'to comfort Monna Tita.'

'Good, blessed Guiberto!' exclaimed Amadeo in a transport of gratitude, at which Guiberto smiled with his usual grace and suavity. 'O Guiberto! Guiberto! my heart is breaking. Why should she want you to comfort her?--but--comfort her then!' and he covered his face within his hands.

'Remember,' said Guiberto placidly, 'her uncle is bedridden; her aunt never leaves him; the servants are old and sullen, and will stir for nobody. Finding her resolved, as they believe, to become a nun, they are little assiduous in their services. Humour her, if none else does, Amadeo; let her fancy that you intend to be a friar; and, for the present, walk not on these grounds.'

'Are you true, or are you traitorous?' cried Amadeo, grasping his friend's hand most fiercely.

'Follow your own counsel, if you think mine insincere,' said the young friar, not withdrawing his hand, but placing the other on Amadeo's. 'Let me, however, advise you to conceal yourself; and I will direct Silvestrina to bring you such accounts of her mistress as may at least make you easy in regard to her health. Adieu.'

Amadeo was now rather tranquil; more than he had ever been, not only since the displeasure of Monna Tita, but since the first sight of her. Profuse at all times in his gratitude to Silvestrina, whenever she brought him good news, news better than usual, he pressed her to his bosom. Silvestrina Pioppi is about fifteen, slender, fresh, intelligent, lively, good-humoured, sensitive; and any one but Amadeo might call her very pretty.

Petrarca. Ah, Giovanni! here I find your heart obtaining the mastery over your vivid and volatile imagination. Well have you said, the maiden being really pretty, any one but Amadeo might think her so. On the banks of the Sorga there are beautiful maids; the woods and the rocks have a thousand times repeated it. I heard but one echo; I heard but one name: I would have fled from them for ever at another.

Boccaccio. Francesco, do not beat your breast just now: wait a little. Monna Tita would take the veil. The fatal certainty was announced to Amadeo by his true Guiberto, who had earnestly and repeatedly prayed her to consider the thing a few months longer.

'I will see her first! By all the saints of heaven I will see her!' cried the desperate Amadeo, and ran into the house, toward the still apartment of his beloved. Fortunately Guiberto was neither less active nor less strong than he, and overtaking him at the moment, drew him into the room opposite. 'If you will be quiet and reasonable, there is yet a possibility left you,' said Guiberto in his ear, although perhaps he did not think it. 'But if you utter a voice or are seen by any one, you ruin the fame of her you love, and obstruct your own prospects for ever. It being known that you have not slept in Florence these several nights, it will be suspected by the malicious that you have slept in the villa with the connivance of Monna Tita. Compose yourself; answer nothing; rest where you are: do not add a worse imprudence to a very bad one. I promise you my assistance, my speedy return, and best counsel: you shall be released at daybreak.' He ordered Silvestrina to supply the unfortunate youth with the cordials usually administered to the uncle, or with the rich old wine they were made of; and she performed the order with such promptitude and attention, that he was soon in some sort refreshed.

Petrarca. I pity him from my innermost heart, poor young man! Alas, we are none of us, by original sin, free from infirmities or from vices.

Boccaccio. If we could find a man exempt by nature from vices and infirmities, we should find one not worth knowing: he would also be void of tenderness and compassion. What allowances then could his best friends expect from him in their frailties? What help, consolation, and assistance in their misfortunes? We are in the midst of a workshop well stored with sharp instruments: we may do ill with many, unless we take heed; and good with all, if we will but learn how to employ them.

Petrarca. There is somewhat of reason in this. You strengthen me to proceed with you: I can bear the rest.

Boccaccio. Guiberto had taken leave of his friend, and had advanced a quarter of a mile, which (as you perceive) is nearly the whole way, on his return to the monastery, when he was overtaken by some peasants who were hastening homeward from Florence. The information he collected from them made him determine to retrace his steps. He entered the room again, and, from the intelligence he had just acquired, gave Amadeo the assurance that Monna Tita must delay her entrance into the convent; for that the abbess had that moment gone down the hill on her way toward Siena to venerate some holy relics, carrying with her three candles, each five feet long, to burn before them; which candles contained many particles of the myrrh presented at the Nativity of our Saviour by the Wise Men of the East. Amadeo breathed freely, and was persuaded by Guiberto to take another cup of old wine, and to eat with him some cold roast kid, which had been offered him for ***merenda***. After the agitation of his mind a heavy sleep fell upon the lover, coming almost before Guiberto departed: so heavy indeed that Silvestrina was alarmed. It was her apartment; and she performed the honours of it as well as any lady in Florence could have done.

Petrarca. I easily believe it: the poor are more attentive than the rich, and the young are more compassionate than the old.

Boccaccio. O Francesco! what inconsistent creatures are we!

Petrarca. True, indeed! I now foresee the end. He might have done worse.

Boccaccio. I think so.

Petrarca. He almost deserved it.

Boccaccio. I think that too.

Petrarca. Wretched mortals! our passions for ever lead us into this, or worse.

Boccaccio. Ay, truly; much worse generally.

Petrarca. The very twig on which the flowers grew lately scourges us to the bone in its maturity.

Boccaccio. Incredible will it be to you, and, by my faith, to me it was hardly credible. Certain, however, is it that Guiberto on his return by sunrise found Amadeo in the arms of sleep.

Petrarca. Not at all, not at all: the truest lover might suffer and act as he did.

Boccaccio. But, Francesco, there was another pair of arms about him, worth twenty such, divinity as he is. A loud burst of laughter from Guiberto did not arouse either of the parties; but Monna Tita heard it, and rushed into the room, tearing her hair, and invoking the saints of heaven against the perfidy of man. She seized Silvestrina by that arm which appeared the most offending: the girl opened her eyes, turned on her face, rolled out of bed, and threw herself at the feet of her mistress, shedding tears, and wiping them away with the only piece of linen about her. Monna Tita too shed tears. Amadeo still slept profoundly; a flush, almost of crimson, overspreading his cheeks. Monna Tita led away, after some pause, poor Silvestrina, and made her confess the whole. She then wept more and more, and made the girl confess it again, and explain her confession. 'I cannot believe such wickedness,' she cried: 'he could not be so hardened. O sinful Silvestrina! how will you ever tell Father Doni one half, one quarter? He never can absolve you.'

Petrarca. Giovanni, I am glad I did not enter the house; you were prudent in restraining me. I have no pity for the youth at all: never did one so deserve to lose a mistress.

Boccaccio. Say, rather, to gain a wife.

Petrarca. Absurdity! impossibility!

Boccaccio. He won her fairly; strangely, and on a strange table, as he played his game. Listen! that guitar is Monna Tita's. Listen! what a fine voice (do not you think it?) is Amadeo's.

Amadeo. [*Singing.*]

>   Oh, I have err'd!
> I laid my hand upon the nest
> (Tita, I sigh to sing the rest)

Of the wrong bird.

Petrarca. She laughs too at it! Ah! Monna Tita was made by nature to live on this side of Fiesole.

BOSSUET AND THE DUCHESS DE FONTANGES

Bossuet. Mademoiselle, it is the king's desire that I compliment you on the elevation you have attained.

Fontanges. O monseigneur, I know very well what you mean. His Majesty is kind and polite to everybody. The last thing he said to me was, 'Angelique! do not forget to compliment Monseigneur the bishop on the dignity I have conferred upon him, of almoner to the dauphiness. I desired the appointment for him only that he might be of rank sufficient to confess, now you are duchess. Let him be your confessor, my little girl.'

Bossuet. I dare not presume to ask you, mademoiselle, what was your gracious reply to the condescension of our royal master.

Fontanges. Oh, yes! you may. I told him I was almost sure I should be ashamed of confessing such naughty things to a person of high rank, who writes like an angel.

Bossuet. The observation was inspired, mademoiselle, by your goodness and modesty.

Fontanges. You are so agreeable a man, monseigneur, I will confess to you, directly, if you like.

Bossuet. Have you brought yourself to a proper frame of mind, young lady?

Fontanges. What is that?

Bossuet. Do you hate sin?

Fontanges. Very much.

Bossuet. Are you resolved to leave it off?

Fontanges. I have left it off entirely since the king began to love me. I have never said a spiteful word of anybody since.

Bossuet. In your opinion, mademoiselle, are there no other sins than malice?

Fontanges. I never stole anything; I never committed adultery; I never coveted my neighbour's wife; I never killed any person, though several have told me they should die for me.

Bossuet. Vain, idle talk! Did you listen to it?

Fontanges. Indeed I did, with both ears; it seemed so funny.

Bossuet. You have something to answer for, then.

Fontanges. No, indeed, I have not, monseigneur. I have asked many times after them, and found they were all alive, which mortified me.

Bossuet. So, then! you would really have them die for you?

Fontanges. Oh, no, no! but I wanted to see whether they were in earnest, or told me fibs; for, if they told me fibs, I would never trust them again.

Bossuet. Do you hate the world, mademoiselle?

Fontanges. A good deal of it: all Picardy, for example, and all Sologne; nothing is uglier--and, oh my life! what frightful men and women!

Bossuet. I would say, in plain language, do you hate the flesh and the devil?

Fontanges. Who does not hate the devil? If you will hold my hand the while, I will tell him so. I hate you, beast! There now. As for flesh, I never could bear a fat man. Such people can neither dance nor hunt, nor do anything that I know of.

Bossuet. Mademoiselle Marie-Angelique de Scoraille de Rousille, Duchess de Fontanges! do you hate titles and dignities and yourself?

Fontanges. Myself! does any one hate me? Why should I be the first? Hatred is the worst thing in the world: it makes one so very ugly.

Bossuet. To love God, we must hate ourselves. We must detest our bodies, if we would save our souls.

Fontanges. That is hard: how can I do it? I see nothing so detestable in mine. Do you? To love is easier. I love God whenever I think of Him, He has been so very good to me; but I cannot hate myself, if I would. As God hath not hated me, why should I? Beside, it was He who made the king to love me; for I heard you say in a sermon that the hearts of kings are in His rule and governance. As for titles and dignities, I do not care much about them while his Majesty loves me, and calls me his Angelique. They make people more civil about us; and therefore it must be a simpleton who hates or disregards them, and a hypocrite who pretends it. I am glad to be a duchess. Manon and Lisette have never tied my garter so as to hurt me since, nor has the mischievous old La Grange said anything cross or bold: on the contrary, she told me what a fine colour and what a plumpness it gave me. Would not you rather be a duchess than a waiting-maid or a nun, if the king gave you your choice?

Bossuet. Pardon me, mademoiselle, I am confounded at the levity of your question.

Fontanges. I am in earnest, as you see.

Bossuet. Flattery will come before you in other and more dangerous forms: you will be commended for excellences which do not belong to you; and this you will find as injurious to your repose as to your virtue. An ingenuous mind feels in unmerited praise the bitterest reproof. If you reject it, you are unhappy; if you accept it, you are undone. The compliments of a king are of themselves sufficient to pervert your intellect.

Fontanges. There you are mistaken twice over. It is not my person that pleases him so greatly: it is my spirit, my wit, my talents, my genius, and that very thing which you have mentioned--what was it? my intellect. He never complimented me the least upon my beauty. Others have said that I am the most beautiful young creature under heaven; a blossom of Paradise, a nymph, an angel; worth (let me whisper it in your ear--do I lean too hard?) a thousand Montespans. But his Majesty never said more on the occasion than that I was ***imparagonable!*** (what is that?) and that he adored me; holding my hand and sitting quite still, when he might have romped with me and kissed me.

Bossuet. I would aspire to the glory of converting you.

Fontanges. You may do anything with me but convert me: you must not do that; I am a Catholic born. M. de Turenne and Mademoiselle de Duras were heretics: you did right there. The king told the chancellor that he prepared them, that the business was arranged for you, and that you had nothing to do but get ready the arguments and responses, which you did gallantly--did not you? And yet Mademoiselle de Duras was very awkward for a long while afterwards in crossing herself, and was once remarked to beat her breast in the litany with the points of two fingers at a time, when every one is taught to use only the second, whether it has a ring upon it or not. I am sorry she did so; for people might think her insincere in her conversion, and pretend that she kept a finger for each religion.

Bossuet. It would be as uncharitable to doubt the conviction of Mademoiselle de Duras as that of M. le Marechal.

Fontanges. I have heard some fine verses, I can assure you, monseigneur, in which you are called the conqueror of Turenne. I should like to have been his conqueror myself, he was so great a man. I understand that you have lately done a much more difficult thing.

Bossuet. To what do you refer, mademoiselle?

Fontanges. That you have overcome quietism. Now, in the name of wonder, how could you manage that?

Bossuet. By the grace of God.

Fontanges. Yes, indeed; but never until now did God give any preacher so much of His grace as to subdue this pest.

Bossuet. It has appeared among us but lately.

Fontanges. Oh, dear me! I have always been subject to it dreadfully, from a child.

Bossuet. Really! I never heard so.

Fontanges. I checked myself as well as I could, although they constantly told me I looked well in it.

Bossuet. In what, mademoiselle?

Fontanges. In quietism; that is, when I fell asleep at sermon time. I am ashamed that such a learned and pious man as M. de Fenelon should incline to it,[1] as they say he does.

Bossuet. Mademoiselle, you quite mistake the matter.

Fontanges. Is not then M. de Fenelon thought a very pious and learned person?

Bossuet. And justly.

Fontanges. I have read a great way in a romance he has begun, about a knight-errant in search of a father. The king says there are many such about his court; but I never saw them nor heard of them before. The Marchioness de la Motte, his relative, brought it to me, written out in a charming hand, as much as the copy-book would hold; and I got through, I know not how far. If he had gone on with the nymphs in the grotto, I never should have been tired of him; but he quite forgot his own story, and left them at once; in a hurry (I suppose) to set out upon his mission to Saintonge in the ***pays de d'Aunis***, where the king has promised him a famous ***heretic hunt***. He is, I do assure you, a wonderful creature: he understands so much Latin and Greek, and knows all the tricks of the sorceresses. Yet you keep him under.

Bossuet. Mademoiselle, if you really have anything to confess, and if you desire that I should have the honour of absolving you, it would be better to proceed in it, than to oppress me with unmerited eulogies on my humble labours.

Fontanges. You must first direct me, monseigneur: I have nothing particular. The king assures me there is no harm whatever in his love toward me.

Bossuet. That depends on your thoughts at the moment. If you abstract the mind from the body, and turn your heart toward Heaven----

Fontanges. O monseigneur, I always did so--every time but once--you quite make me blush. Let us converse about something else, or I shall grow too serious, just as you made me the other day at the funeral sermon. And now let me tell you, my lord, you compose such pretty funeral sermons, I hope I shall have the pleasure of hearing you preach mine.

Bossuet. Rather let us hope, mademoiselle, that the hour is yet far distant when so melancholy a service will be performed for you. May he who is unborn be the sad announcer of your departure hence![2] May he indicate to those around him many virtues not perhaps yet full-blown in you, and point triumphantly to many faults and foibles checked by you in their early growth, and lying dead on the open road, you shall have left behind you! To me the painful duty will, I trust, be spared: I am advanced in age; you are a child.

Fontanges. Oh, no! I am seventeen.

Bossuet. I should have supposed you younger by two years at least. But do you collect nothing from your own reflection, which raises so many in my breast? You think it possible that I, aged as I am, may preach a sermon at your funeral. We say that our days are few; and saying it, we say too much. Marie-Angelique, we have but one: the past are not ours, and who can promise us the future? This in which we live is ours only while we live in it; the next moment may strike it off from us; the next sentence I would utter may be broken and fall between us.[3] The beauty that has made a thousand hearts to beat at one instant, at the succeeding has been without pulse and colour, without admirer, friend, companion, follower. She by whose eyes the march of victory shall have been directed, whose name shall have animated armies at the extremities of the earth, drops into one of its crevices and mingles with its dust. Duchess de Fontanges! think on this! Lady! so live as to think on it undisturbed!

Fontanges. O God! I am quite alarmed. Do not talk thus gravely. It is in vain that you speak to me in so sweet a voice. I am frightened even at the rattle of the beads about my neck: take them off, and let us talk on other things. What was it that dropped on the floor as you were speaking? It seemed to shake the room, though it sounded like a pin or button.

Bossuet. Leave it there!

Fontanges. Your ring fell from your hand, my lord bishop! How quick you are! Could not you have trusted me to pick it up?

Bossuet. Madame is too condescending: had this happened, I should have been overwhelmed with confusion. My hand is shrivelled: the ring has ceased to fit it. A mere accident may draw us into perdition; a mere accident may bestow on us the means of grace. A pebble has moved you more than my words.

Fontanges. It pleases me vastly: I admire rubies. I will ask the king for one exactly like it. This is the time he usually comes from the chase. I am sorry you cannot be present to hear how prettily I shall ask him: but that is impossible, you know; for I shall do it just when I am certain he would give me anything. He said so himself: he said but yesterday--

'Such a sweet creature is worth a world':

and no actor on the stage was more like a king than his Majesty was when he spoke it, if he had but kept his wig and robe on. And yet you know he is rather stiff and wrinkled for so great a monarch; and his eyes, I am afraid, are beginning to fail him, he looks so close at things.

Bossuet. Mademoiselle, such is the duty of a prince who desires to conciliate our regard and love.

Fontanges. Well, I think so, too, though I did not like it in him at first. I am sure he will order the ring for me, and I will confess to you with it upon my finger. But first I must be cautious and particular to know of him how much it is his royal will that I should say.

NOTES:

[1] The opinions of Molinos on Mysticism and Quietism had begun to spread abroad; but Fenelon, who had acquired already a very high celebrity for eloquence, had not yet written on the subject. We may well suppose that Bossuet was among the earliest assailants of a system which he afterward attacked so vehemently.

[2] Bossuet was in his fifty-fourth year; Mademoiselle de Fontanges died in child-bed the year following: he survived her twenty-three years.

[3] Though Bossuet was capable of uttering and even of feeling such a sentiment, his conduct towards Fenelon, the fairest apparition that Christianity ever presented, was ungenerous and unjust.

While the diocese of Cambray was ravaged by Louis, it was spared by Marlborough; who said to the archbishop that, if he was sorry he had not taken Cambray, it was chiefly because he lost for a time the pleasure of visiting so great a man. Peterborough, the next of our generals in glory, paid his respects to him some years afterward.

JOHN OF GAUNT AND JOANNA OF KENT

Joanna, called the Fair Maid of Kent, was cousin of the Black Prince, whom she married. John of Gaunt was suspected of aiming at the crown in the beginning of Richard's minority, which, increasing the hatred of the people against him for favouring the sect of Wickliffe, excited them to demolish his house and to demand his impeachment.

Joanna. How is this, my cousin, that you are besieged in your own house by the citizens of London? I thought you were their idol.

Gaunt. If their idol, madam, I am one which they may tread on as they list when down; but which, by my soul and knighthood! the ten best battle-axes among them shall find it hard work to unshrine.

Pardon me: I have no right, perhaps, to take or touch this hand; yet, my sister, bricks and stones and arrows are not presents fit for you. Let me conduct you some paces hence.

Joanna. I will speak to those below in the street. Quit my hand: they shall obey me.

Gaunt. If you intend to order my death, madam, your guards who have entered my court, and whose spurs and halberts I hear upon the staircase, may overpower my domestics; and, seeing no such escape as becomes my dignity, I submit to you. Behold my sword and gauntlet at your feet! Some formalities, I trust, will be used in the proceedings against me. Entitle me, in my attainder, not John of Gaunt, not Duke of Lancaster, not King of Castile; nor commemorate my father, the most glorious of princes, the vanquisher and pardoner of the most powerful; nor style me, what those who loved or who flattered me did when I was happier, cousin to the Fair Maid of Kent. Joanna, those days are over! But no enemy, no law, no eternity can take away from me, or move further off, my affinity in blood to the conqueror in the field of Crecy, of Poitiers, and Najera. Edward was my brother when he was but your cousin; and the edge of my shield has clinked on his in many a battle. Yes, we were ever near--if not in worth, in danger. She weeps.

Joanna. Attainder! God avert it! Duke of Lancaster, what dark thought--alas! that the Regency should have known it! I came hither, sir, for no such purpose as to ensnare or incriminate or alarm you.

These weeds might surely have protected me from the fresh tears you have drawn forth.

Gaunt. Sister, be comforted! this visor, too, has felt them.

Joanna. O my Edward! my own so lately! Thy memory--thy beloved image--which never hath abandoned me, makes me bold: I dare not say 'generous'; for in saying it I should cease to be so--and who could be called generous by the side of thee? I will rescue from perdition the enemy of my son.

Cousin, you loved your brother. Love, then, what was dearer to him than his life: protect what he, valiant as you have seen him, cannot! The father, who foiled so many, hath left no enemies; the innocent child, who can injure no one, finds them!

Why have you unlaced and laid aside your visor? Do not expose your body to those missiles. Hold your shield before yourself, and step aside. I need it not. I am resolved----

Gaunt. On what, my cousin? Speak, and, by the saints! it shall be done. This breast is your shield; this arm is mine.

Joanna. Heavens! who could have hurled those masses of stone from below? they stunned me. Did they descend all of them together; or did they split into fragments on hitting the pavement?

Gaunt. Truly, I was not looking that way: they came, I must believe, while you were speaking.

Joanna. Aside, aside! further back! disregard *me*! Look! that last arrow sticks half its head deep in the wainscot. It shook so violently I did not see the feather at first.

No, no, Lancaster! I will not permit it. Take your shield up again; and keep it all before you. Now step aside: I am resolved to prove whether the people will hear me.

Gaunt. Then, madam, by your leave----

Joanna. Hold!

Gaunt. Villains! take back to your kitchens those spits and skewers that you, forsooth, would fain call swords and arrows; and keep your bricks and stones for your graves!

Joanna. Imprudent man! who can save you? I shall be frightened: I must speak at once.

O good kind people! ye who so greatly loved me, when I am sure I had done nothing to deserve it, have I (unhappy me!) no merit with you now, when I would assuage your anger, protect your fair fame, and send you home contented with yourselves and me? Who is he, worthy citizens, whom ye would drag to slaughter?

True, indeed, he did revile someone. Neither I nor you can say whom--some feaster and rioter, it seems, who had little right (he thought) to carry sword or bow, and who, to show it, hath slunk away. And then another raised his anger: he was indignant that, under his roof, a woman should be exposed to stoning. Which of you would not be as choleric in a like affront? In the house of which among you should I not be protected as resolutely?

No, no: I never can believe those angry cries. Let none ever tell me again he is the enemy of my son, of his king, your darling child, Richard. Are your fears more lively than a poor weak female's? than a mother's? yours, whom he hath so often led to victory, and praised to his father, naming each--he, John of Gaunt, the defender of the helpless, the comforter of the desolate, the rallying signal of the desperately brave!

Retire, Duke of Lancaster! This is no time----

Gaunt. Madam, I obey; but not through terror of that puddle at the house door, which my handful of dust would dry up. Deign to command me!

Joanna. In the name of my son, then, retire!

Gaunt. Angelic goodness! I must fairly win it.

Joanna. I think I know his voice that crieth out: 'Who will answer for him?' An honest and loyal man's, one who would counsel and save me in any difficulty and danger. With what pleasure and satisfaction, with what perfect joy and confidence, do I answer our right-trusty and well-judging friend!

'Let Lancaster bring his sureties,' say you, 'and we separate.' A moment yet before we separate; if I might delay you so long, to receive your sanction of those securities: for, in such grave matters, it would ill become us to be over-hasty. I could bring fifty, I could bring a hundred, not from among soldiers, not from among courtiers; but selected from yourselves, were it equitable and fair to show such partialities, or decorous in the parent and guardian of a king to offer any other than herself.

Raised by the hand of the Almighty from amidst you, but still one of you, if the mother of a family is a part of it, here I stand surety for John of Gaunt, Duke of Lancaster, for his loyalty and allegiance.

Gaunt. [***Running back toward Joanna.***] Are the rioters, then, bursting into the chamber through the windows?

Joanna. The windows and doors of this solid edifice rattled and shook at the people's acclamation. My word is given for you: this was theirs in return. Lancaster! what a voice have the people when they speak out! It shakes me with astonishment, almost with consternation, while it establishes the throne: what must it be when it is lifted up in vengeance!

Gaunt. Wind; vapour----

Joanna. Which none can wield nor hold. Need I say this to my cousin of Lancaster?

Gaunt. Rather say, madam, that there is always one star above which can tranquillize and control them.

Joanna. Go, cousin! another time more sincerity!

Gaunt. You have this day saved my life from the people; for I now see my danger better, when it is no longer close before me. My Christ! if ever I forget----

Joanna. Swear not: every man in England hath sworn what you would swear. But if you abandon my Richard, my brave and beautiful child, may--Oh! I could never curse, nor wish an evil; but, if you desert him in the hour of need, you will think of those who have not deserted you, and your own great heart will lie heavy on you, Lancaster!

Am I graver than I ought to be, that you look dejected? Come, then, gentle cousin, lead me to my horse, and accompany me home. Richard will embrace us tenderly. Every one is dear to every other upon rising out fresh from peril; affectionately then will he look, sweet boy, upon his mother and his uncle! Never mind how many questions he may ask you, nor how strange ones. His only displeasure, if he has any, will be that he stood not against the rioters or among them.

Gaunt. Older than he have been as fond of mischief, and as fickle in the choice of a party.

I shall tell him that, coming to blows, the assailant is often in the right; that the assailed is always.

LEOFRIC AND GODIVA

Godiva. There is a dearth in the land, my sweet Leofric! Remember how many weeks of drought we have had, even in the deep pastures of Leicestershire; and how many Sundays we have heard the same prayers for rain, and supplications that it would please the Lord in His mercy to turn aside His anger from the poor, pining cattle. You, my dear husband, have imprisoned more than one malefactor for leaving his dead ox in the public way; and other hinds have fled before you out of the traces, in which they, and their sons and their daughters, and haply their old fathers and mothers, were dragging the abandoned wain homeward. Although we were accompanied by many brave spearmen and skilful archers, it was perilous to pass the creatures which the farmyard dogs, driven from the hearth by the poverty of their masters, were tearing and devouring; while others, bitten and lamed, filled the air either with long and deep howls or sharp and quick barkings, as they struggled with hunger and feebleness, or were exasperated by heat and pain. Nor could the thyme from the heath, nor the bruised branches of the fir-tree, extinguish or abate the foul odour.

Leofric. And now, Godiva, my darling, thou art afraid we should be eaten up before we enter the gates of Coventry; or perchance that in the gardens there are no roses to greet thee, no sweet herbs for thy mat and pillow.

Godiva. Leofric, I have no such fears. This is the month of roses: I find them everywhere since my blessed marriage. They, and all other sweet herbs, I know not why, seem to greet me wherever I look at them, as though they knew and expected me. Surely they cannot feel that I am fond of them.

Leofric. O light, laughing simpleton! But what wouldst thou? I came not hither to pray; and yet if praying would satisfy thee, or remove the drought, I would ride up straightway to Saint Michael's and pray until morning.

Godiva. I would do the same, O Leofric! but God hath turned away His ear from holier lips than mine. Would my own dear husband hear me, if I implored him for what is easier to accomplish--what he can do like God?

Leofric. How! what is it?

Godiva. I would not, in the first hurry of your wrath, appeal to you, my loving lord, on behalf of these unhappy men who have offended you.

Leofric. Unhappy! is that all?

Godiva. Unhappy they must surely be, to have offended you so grievously. What a soft air breathes over us! how quiet and serene and still an evening! how calm are the heavens and the earth! Shall none enjoy them; not even we, my Leofric? The sun is ready to set: let it never set, O Leofric, on your anger. These are not my words: they are better than mine. Should they lose their virtue from my unworthiness in uttering them?

Leofric. Godiva, wouldst thou plead to me for rebels?

Godiva. They have, then, drawn the sword against you? Indeed, I knew it not.

Leofric. They have omitted to send me my dues, established by my ancestors, well knowing of our nuptials, and of the charges and festivities they require, and that in a season of such scarcity my own lands are insufficient.

Godiva. If they were starving, as they said they were----

Leofric. Must I starve too? Is it not enough to lose my vassals?

Godiva. Enough! O God! too much! too much! May you never lose them! Give them life, peace, comfort, contentment. There are those among them who kissed me in my infancy, and who blessed me at the baptismal font. Leofric, Leofric! the first old man I meet I shall think is one of those; and I shall think on the blessing he gave, and (ah me!) on the blessing I bring back to him. My heart will bleed, will burst; and he will weep at it! he will weep, poor soul, for the wife of a cruel lord who denounces vengeance on him, who carries death into his family!

Leofric. We must hold solemn festivals.

Godiva. We must, indeed.

Leofric. Well, then?

Godiva. Is the clamorousness that succeeds the death of God's dumb creatures, are crowded halls, are slaughtered cattle festivals?--are maddening songs, and giddy dances, and hireling praises from parti-coloured coats? Can the voice of a minstrel tell us better things of ourselves than our own internal one might tell us; or can his breath make our breath softer in sleep? O my beloved! let everything be a joyance to us: it will, if we will. Sad is the day, and worse must follow, when we hear the blackbird in the garden, and do not throb with joy. But, Leofric, the high festival is strown by the servant of God upon the heart of man. It is gladness, it is thanksgiving; it is the orphan, the starveling, pressed to the bosom, and bidden as its first commandment to remember its benefactor. We will hold this festival; the guests are ready: we may keep it up for weeks, and months, and years together, and always be the happier and the richer for it. The beverage of this feast, O Leofric, is sweeter than bee or flower or vine can give us: it flows from heaven; and in heaven will it abundantly be poured out again to him who pours it out here abundantly.

Leofric. Thou art wild.

Godiva. I have, indeed, lost myself. Some Power, some good kind Power, melts me (body and soul and voice) into tenderness and love. O my husband, we must obey it. Look upon me! look upon me! lift your sweet eyes from the ground! I will not cease to supplicate; I dare not.

Leofric. We may think upon it.

Godiva. Oh, never say that! What! think upon goodness when you can be good? Let not the infants cry for sustenance! The Mother of Our Blessed Lord will hear them; us never, never afterward.

Leofric. Here comes the bishop: we are but one mile from the walls. Why dismountest thou? no bishop can expect this. Godiva! my honour and rank among men are humbled by this. Earl Godwin will hear of it. Up! up! the bishop hath seen it: he urgeth his horse onward. Dost thou not hear him now upon the solid turf behind thee?

Godiva. Never, no, never will I rise, O Leofric, until you remit this most impious task--this tax on hard labour, on hard life.

Leofric. Turn round: look how the fat nag canters, as to the tune of a sinner's psalm, slow and hard-breathing. What reason or right can the people have to complain, while their bishop's steed is so sleek and well caparisoned? Inclination to change, desire to abolish old usages. Up! up! for shame! They shall smart for it, idlers! Sir Bishop, I must blush for my young bride.

Godiva. My husband, my husband! will you pardon the city?

Leofric. Sir Bishop! I could think you would have seen her in this plight. Will I pardon? Yea, Godiva, by the holy rood, will I pardon the city, when thou ridest naked at noontide through the streets!

Godiva. O my dear, cruel Leofric, where is the heart you gave me? It was not so: can mine have hardened it?

Bishop. Earl, thou abashest thy spouse; she turneth pale, and weepeth. Lady Godiva, peace be with thee.

Godiva. Thanks, holy man! peace will be with me when peace is with your city. Did you hear my lord's cruel word?

Bishop. I did, lady.

Godiva. Will you remember it, and pray against it?

Bishop. Wilt *thou* forget it, daughter?

Godiva. I am not offended.

Bishop. Angel of peace and purity!

Godiva. But treasure it up in your heart: deem it an incense, good only when it is consumed and spent, ascending with prayer and sacrifice. And, now, what was it?

Bishop. Christ save us! that He will pardon the city when thou ridest naked through the streets at noon.

Godiva. Did he swear an oath?

Bishop. He sware by the holy rood.

Godiva. My Redeemer, Thou hast heard it! save the city!

Leofric. We are now upon the beginning of the pavement: these are the suburbs. Let us think of feasting: we may pray afterward; to-morrow we shall rest.

Godiva. No judgments, then, to-morrow, Leofric?

Leofric. None: we will carouse.

Godiva. The saints of heaven have given me strength and confidence; my prayers are heard; the heart of my beloved is now softened.

Leofric. Ay, ay.

Godiva. Say, dearest Leofric, is there indeed no other hope, no other mediation?

Leofric. I have sworn. Beside, thou hast made me redden and turn my face away from thee, and all the knaves have seen it: this adds to the city's crime.

Godiva. I have blushed, too, Leofric, and was not rash nor obdurate.

Leofric. But thou, my sweetest, art given to blushing: there is no conquering it in thee. I wish thou hadst not alighted so hastily and roughly: it hath shaken down a sheaf of thy hair. Take heed thou sit not upon it, lest it anguish thee. Well done! it mingleth now sweetly with the cloth of gold upon the saddle, running here and there, as if it had life and faculties and business, and were working thereupon some newer and cunninger device. O my beauteous Eve! there is a Paradise about thee! the world is refreshed as thou movest and breathest on it. I cannot see or think of evil where thou art. I could throw my arms even here about thee. No signs for me! no shaking of sunbeams! no reproof or frown of wonderment.--I ***will*** say it--now, then, for worse--I could close with my kisses thy half-open lips, ay, and those lovely and loving eyes, before the people.

Godiva. To-morrow you shall kiss me, and they shall bless you for it. I shall be very pale, for to-night I must fast and pray.

Leofric. I do not hear thee; the voices of the folk are so loud under this archway.

Godiva. [***To herself.***] God help them! good kind souls! I hope they will not crowd about me so to-morrow. O Leofric! could my name be forgotten, and yours alone remembered! But perhaps my innocence may save me from reproach; and how many as innocent are in fear and famine! No eye will open on me but fresh from tears. What a young mother for so large a family! Shall my youth harm me? Under God's hand it gives me courage. Ah! when will the morning come? Ah! when will the noon be over?

The story of Godiva, at one of whose festivals or fairs I was present in my boyhood, has always much interested me; and I wrote a poem on it, sitting, I remember, by the ***square pool*** at Rugby. When I showed it to the friend in whom I had most confidence, he began to scoff at the subject; and, on his reaching the last line, his laughter was loud and immoderate. This conversation has brought both laughter and stanza back to me, and the earnestness with which I entreated and implored my friend ***not to tell the lads***, so heart-strickenly and desperately was I ashamed. The verses are these, if any one else should wish another laugh at me:

'In every hour, in every mood,
O lady, it is sweet and good
  To bathe the soul in prayer;
And, at the close of such a day,
When we have ceased to bless and pray,
  To dream on thy long hair.'

May the peppermint be still growing on the bank in that place!

ESSEX AND SPENSER

Essex. Instantly on hearing of thy arrival from Ireland, I sent a message to thee, good Edmund, that I might learn, from one so judicious and dispassionate as thou art, the real state of things in that distracted country; it having pleased the queen's Majesty to think of appointing me her deputy, in order to bring the rebellious to submission.

Spenser. Wisely and well considered; but more worthily of her judgment than her affection. May your lordship overcome, as you have ever done, the difficulties and dangers you foresee.

Essex. We grow weak by striking at random; and knowing that I must strike, and strike heavily, I would fain see exactly where the stroke shall fall.

Now what tale have you for us?

Spenser. Interrogate me, my lord, that I may answer each question distinctly, my mind being in sad confusion at what I have seen and undergone.

Essex. Give me thy account and opinion of these very affairs as thou leftest them; for I would rather know one part well than all imperfectly; and the violences of which I have heard within the day surpass belief.

Why weepest thou, my gentle Spenser? Have the rebels sacked thy house?

Spenser. They have plundered and utterly destroyed it.

Essex. I grieve for thee, and will see thee righted.

Spenser. In this they have little harmed me.

Essex. How! I have heard it reported that thy grounds are fertile, and thy mansion large and pleasant.

Spenser. If river and lake and meadow-ground and mountain could render any place the abode of pleasantness, pleasant was mine, indeed!

On the lovely banks of Mulla I found deep contentment. Under the dark alders did I muse and meditate. Innocent hopes were my gravest cares, and my playfullest fancy was with kindly wishes. Ah! surely of all cruelties the worst is to extinguish our kindness. Mine is gone: I love the people and the land no longer. My lord, ask me not about them: I may speak injuriously.

Essex. Think rather, then, of thy happier hours and busier occupations; these likewise may instruct me.

Spenser. The first seeds I sowed in the garden, ere the old castle was made habitable for my lovely bride, were acorns from Penshurst. I planted a little oak before my mansion at the birth of each child. My sons, I said to myself, shall often play in the shade of them when I am gone; and every year shall they take the measure of their growth, as fondly as I take theirs.

Essex. Well, well; but let not this thought make thee weep so bitterly.

Spenser. Poison may ooze from beautiful plants; deadly grief from dearest reminiscences. I **must** grieve, I **must** weep: it seems the law of God, and the only one that men are not disposed to contravene. In the performance of this alone do they effectually aid one another.

Essex. Spenser! I wish I had at hand any arguments or persuasions of force sufficient to remove thy sorrow; but, really, I am not in the habit of seeing men grieve at anything except the loss of favour at court, or of a hawk, or of a buck-hound. And were I to swear out condolences to a man of thy discernment, in the same round, roll-call phrases we employ with one another upon these occasions, I should be guilty, not of insincerity, but of insolence. True grief hath ever something sacred in it; and, when it visiteth a wise man and a brave one, is most holy.

Nay, kiss not my hand: he whom God smiteth hath God with him. In His presence what am I?

Spenser. Never so great, my lord, as at this hour, when you see aright who is greater. May He guide your counsels, and preserve your life and glory!

Essex. Where are thy friends? Are they with thee?

Spenser. Ah, where, indeed! Generous, true-hearted Philip! where art thou, whose presence was unto me peace and safety; whose smile was contentment, and whose praise renown? My lord! I cannot but think of him among still heavier losses: he was my earliest friend, and would have taught me wisdom.

Essex. Pastoral poetry, my dear Spenser, doth not require tears and lamentations. Dry thine eyes; rebuild thine house: the queen and council, I venture to promise thee, will make ample amends for every evil thou hast sustained. What! does that enforce thee to wail still louder?

Spenser. Pardon me, bear with me, most noble heart! I have lost what no council, no queen, no Essex, can restore.

Essex. We will see that. There are other swords, and other arms to yield them, beside a Leicester's and a Raleigh's. Others can crush their enemies, and serve their friends.

Spenser. O my sweet child! And of many so powerful, many so wise and so beneficent, was there none to save thee? None, none!

Essex. I now perceive that thou lamentest what almost every father is destined to lament. Happiness must be bought, although the payment may be delayed. Consider: the same calamity might have befallen thee here in London. Neither the houses of ambassadors, nor the palaces of kings, nor the altars of God Himself, are asylums against death. How do I know but under this very roof there may sleep some latent calamity, that in an instant shall cover with gloom every inmate of the house, and every far dependent?

Spenser. God avert it!

Essex. Every day, every hour of the year, do hundreds mourn what thou mournest.

Spenser. Oh, no, no, no! Calamities there are around us; calamities there are all over the earth; calamities there are in all seasons: but none in any season, none in any place, like mine.

Essex. So say all fathers, so say all husbands. Look at any old mansion-house, and let the sun shine as gloriously as it may on the golden vanes, or the arms recently quartered over the gateway or the embayed window, and on the happy pair that haply is toying at it: nevertheless, thou mayest say that of a certainty the same fabric hath seen much sorrow within its chambers, and heard many wailings; and each time this was the heaviest stroke of all. Funerals have passed along through the stout-hearted knights upon the wainscot, and amid the laughing nymphs upon the arras. Old servants have shaken their heads, as if somebody had deceived them, when they found that beauty and nobility could perish.

Edmund! the things that are too true pass by us as if they were not true at all; and when they have singled us out, then only do they strike us. Thou and I must go too. Perhaps the next year may blow us away with its fallen leaves.

Spenser. For you, my lord, many years (I trust) are waiting: I never shall see those fallen leaves. No leaf, no bud, will spring upon the earth before I sink into her breast for ever.

Essex. Thou, who art wiser than most men, shouldst bear with patience, equanimity, and courage what is common to all.

Spenser. Enough, enough, enough! Have all men seen their infant burnt to ashes before their eyes?

Essex. Gracious God! Merciful Father! what is this?

Spenser. Burnt alive! burnt to ashes! burnt to ashes! The flames dart their serpent tongues through the nursery window. I cannot quit thee, my Elizabeth! I cannot lay down our Edmund! Oh, these flames! They persecute, they enthral me; they curl round my temples; they hiss upon my brain; they taunt me with their fierce, foul voices; they carp at me, they wither me, they consume me, throwing back to me a little of life to roll and suffer in, with their fangs upon me. Ask me, my lord, the things you wish to know from me: I may answer them; I am now composed again. Command me, my gracious lord! I would yet serve you: soon I shall be unable. You have stooped to raise me up; you have borne with me; you have pitied me, even like one not powerful. You have brought comfort, and will leave it with me, for gratitude is comfort.

Oh! my memory stands all a-tiptoe on one burning point: when it drops from it, then it perishes. Spare me: ask me nothing; let me weep before you in peace--the kindest act of greatness.

Essex. I should rather have dared to mount into the midst of the conflagration than I now dare entreat thee not to weep. The tears that overflow thy heart, my Spenser, will staunch and heal it in their sacred stream; but not without hope in God.

Spenser. My hope in God is that I may soon see again what He has taken from me. Amid the myriads of angels, there is not one so beautiful; and even he (if there be any) who is appointed my guardian could never love me so. Ah! these are idle thoughts, vain wanderings, distempered dreams. If there ever were guardian angels, he who so wanted one--my helpless boy--would not have left these arms upon my knees.

Essex. God help and sustain thee, too gentle Spenser! I never will desert thee. But what am I? Great they have called me! Alas, how powerless, then, and infantile is greatness in the presence of calamity!

Come, give me thy hand: let us walk up and down the gallery. Bravely done! I will envy no more a Sidney or a Raleigh.

LORD BACON AND RICHARD HOOKER

Bacon. Hearing much of your worthiness and wisdom, Master Richard Hooker, I have besought your comfort and consolation in this my too heavy affliction: for we often do stand in need of hearing what we know full well, and our own balsams must be poured into our breasts by another's hand. As the air at our doors is sometimes more expeditious in removing pain and heaviness from the body than the most far-fetched remedies would be, so the voice alone of a neighbourly and friendly visitant may be more effectual in assuaging our sorrows, than whatever is most forcible in rhetoric and most recondite in wisdom. On these occasions we cannot put ourselves in a posture to receive the latter, and still less are we at leisure to look into the corners of our store-room, and to uncurl the leaves of our references. As for Memory, who, you may tell me, would save us the trouble, she is footsore enough in all conscience with me, without going farther back. Withdrawn as you live from court and courtly men, and having ears occupied by better reports than such as are flying about me, yet haply so hard a case as mine, befalling a man heretofore not averse from the studies in which you take delight, may have touched you with some concern.

Hooker. I do think, my Lord of Verulam, that, unhappy as you appear, God in sooth has forgone to chasten you, and that the day which in His wisdom He appointed for your trial, was the very day on which the king's Majesty gave unto your ward and custody the great seal of his

English realm. And yet perhaps it may be--let me utter it without offence--that your features and stature were from that day forward no longer what they were before. Such an effect do power and rank and office produce even on prudent and religious men.

A hound's whelp howleth, if you pluck him up above where he stood: man, in much greater peril from falling, doth rejoice. You, my lord, as befitted you, are smitten and contrite, and do appear in deep wretchedness and tribulation to your servants and those about you; but I know that there is always a balm which lies uppermost in these afflictions, and that no heart rightly softened can be very sore.

Bacon. And yet, Master Richard, it is surely no small matter to lose the respect of those who looked up to us for countenance; and the favour of a right learned king; and, O Master Hooker, such a power of money! But money is mere dross. I should always hold it so, if it possessed not two qualities: that of making men treat us reverently, and that of enabling us to help the needy.

Hooker. The respect, I think, of those who respect us for what a fool can give and a rogue can take away, may easily be dispensed with; but it is indeed a high prerogative to help the needy; and when it pleases the Almighty to deprive us of it, let us believe that He foreknoweth our inclination to negligence in the charge entrusted to us, and that in His mercy He hath removed from us a most fearful responsibility.

Bacon. I know a number of poor gentlemen to whom I could have rendered aid.

Hooker. Have you examined and sifted their worthiness?

Bacon. Well and deeply.

Hooker. Then must you have known them long before your adversity, and while the means of succouring them were in your hands.

Bacon. You have circumvented and entrapped me, Master Hooker. Faith! I am mortified: you the schoolman, I the schoolboy!

Hooker. Say not so, my lord. Your years, indeed, are fewer than mine, by seven or thereabout; but your knowledge is far higher, your experience richer. Our wits are not always in blossom upon us. When the roses are overcharged and languid, up springs a spike of rue. Mortified on such an occasion? God forfend it! But again to the business. I should never be over-penitent for my neglect of needy gentlemen who have neglected themselves much worse. They have chosen their profession with its chances and contingencies. If they had protected their country by their courage or adorned it by their studies, they would have merited, and under a king of such learning and such equity would have received in some sort, their reward. I look upon them as so many old cabinets of ivory and tortoise-shell, scratched, flawed, splintered, rotten, defective both within and without, hard to unlock, insecure to lock up again, unfit to use.

Bacon. Methinks it beginneth to rain, Master Richard. What if we comfort our bodies with a small cup of wine, against the ill-temper of the air. Wherefore, in God's name, are you affrightened?

Hooker. Not so, my lord; not so.

Bacon. What then affects you?

Hooker. Why, indeed, since your lordship interrogates me--I looked, idly and imprudently, into that rich buffet; and I saw, unless the haze of the weather has come into the parlour, or my sight is the worse for last night's reading, no fewer than six silver pints.

Surely, six tables for company are laid only at coronations.

Bacon. There are many men so squeamish that forsooth they would keep a cup to themselves, and never communicate it to their nearest and best friend; a fashion which seems to me offensive in an honest house, where no disease of ill repute ought to be feared. We have lately, Master Richard, adopted strange fashions; we have run into the wildest luxuries. The Lord Leicester, I heard it from my father--God forfend it should ever be recorded in our history!--when he entertained Queen Elizabeth at Kenilworth Castle, laid before her Majesty a fork of pure silver. I the more easily credit it, as Master Thomas Coriatt doth vouch for having seen the same monstrous sign of voluptuousness at Venice. We are surely the especial favourites of Providence, when such wantonness hath not melted us quite away. After this portent, it would otherwise have appeared incredible that we should have broken the Spanish Armada.

Pledge me: hither comes our wine.

[*To the Servant.*] Dolt! villain! is not this the beverage I reserve for myself?

The blockhead must imagine that Malmsey runs in a stream under the ocean, like the Alpheus. Bear with me, good Master Hooker, but verily I have little of this wine, and I keep it as a medicine for my many and growing infirmities. You are healthy at present: God in His infinite mercy long maintain you so! Weaker drink is more wholesome for you. The lighter ones of France are best accommodated by Nature to our constitutions, and therefore she has placed them so within our reach that we have only to stretch out our necks, in a manner, and drink them from the vat. But this Malmsey, this Malmsey, flies from centre to circumference, and makes youthful blood boil.

Hooker. Of a truth, my knowledge in such matters is but spare. My Lord of Canterbury once ordered part of a goblet, containing some strong Spanish wine, to be taken to me from his table when I dined by sufferance with his chaplains, and, although a most discreet, prudent man as befitteth his high station, was not so chary of my health as your lordship. Wine is little to be trifled with, physic less. The Cretans, the brewers of this Malmsey, have many aromatic and powerful herbs among them. On their mountains, and notably on Ida, grows that dittany which works such marvels, and which perhaps may give activity to this hot medicinal drink of theirs. I would not touch it, knowingly: an unregarded leaf, dropped into it above the ordinary, might add such puissance to the concoction as almost to break the buckles in my shoes; since we have good and valid authority that the wounded hart, on eating thereof, casts the arrow out of his haunch or entrails, although it stuck a palm deep.[4]

Bacon. When I read of such things I doubt them. Religion and politics belong to God, and to God's vicegerent the king; we must not touch upon them unadvisedly: but if I could procure a plant of dittany on easy terms, I would persuade my apothecary and my gamekeeper to make some experiments.

Hooker. I dare not distrust what grave writers have declared in matters beyond my knowledge.

Bacon. Good Master Hooker, I have read many of your reasonings, and they are admirably well sustained: added to which, your genius has given such a strong current to your language as can come only from a mighty elevation and a most abundant plenteousness. Yet forgive me, in God's name, my worthy master, if you descried in me some expression of wonder at your simplicity. We are all weak and vulnerable somewhere: common men in the higher parts; heroes, as was feigned of Achilles, in the lower. You would define to a hair's-breadth the qualities, states, and dependencies of principalities, dominations, and powers; you would be unerring about the apostles and the churches; and 'tis marvellous how you wander about a pot-herb!

Hooker. I know my poor weak intellects, most noble lord, and how scantily they have profited by my hard painstaking. Comprehending few things, and those imperfectly, I say only what others have said before, wise men and holy; and if, by passing through my heart into the wide world around me, it pleaseth God that this little treasure shall have lost nothing of its weight and pureness, my exultation is then the exultation of humility. Wisdom consisteth not in knowing many things, nor even in knowing them thoroughly; but in choosing and in following what conduces the most certainly to our lasting happiness and true glory. And this wisdom, my Lord of Verulam, cometh from above.

Bacon. I have observed among the well-informed and the ill-informed nearly the same quantity of infirmities and follies: those who are rather the wiser keep them separate, and those who are wisest of all keep them better out of sight. Now, examine the sayings and writings of the prime philosophers, and you will often find them, Master Richard, to be untruths made to resemble truths. The business with them is to approximate as nearly as possible, and not to touch it: the goal of the charioteer is ***evitata fervidis rotis***, as some poet saith. But we who care nothing for chants and cadences, and have no time to catch at applauses, push forward over stones and sands straightway to our object. I have persuaded men, and shall persuade them for ages, that I possess a wide range of thought unexplored by others, and first thrown open by me, with many fair enclosures of choice and abstruse knowledge. I have incited and instructed them to examine all subjects of useful and rational inquiry; few that occurred to me have I myself left untouched or untried: one, however, hath almost escaped me, and surely one worth the trouble.

Hooker. Pray, my lord, if I am guilty of no indiscretion, what may it be?

Bacon. Francis Bacon.

NOTE:

[4] Lest it be thought that authority is wanting for the strong expression of Hooker on the effects of dittany, the reader is referred to the curious treatise of Plutarch on the reasoning faculty of animals, in which (near the end) he asks: 'Who instructed deer wounded by the Cretan arrow to seek for dittany? on the tasting of which herb the bolts fall immediately from their bodies.'

OLIVER CROMWELL AND WALTER NOBLE

Cromwell. What brings thee back from Staffordshire, friend Walter?

Noble. I hope, General Cromwell, to persuade you that the death of Charles will be considered by all Europe as a most atrocious action.

Cromwell. Thou hast already persuaded me: what then?

Noble. Surely, then, you will prevent it, for your authority is great. Even those who upon their consciences found him guilty would remit the penalty of blood, some from policy, some from mercy. I have conversed with Hutchinson, with Ludlow,[5] your friend and mine, with Henry Nevile, and Walter Long: you will oblige these worthy friends, and unite in your favour the suffrages of the truest and trustiest men living. There are many others, with whom I am in no habits of intercourse, who are known to entertain the same sentiments; and these also are among the country gentlemen, to whom our parliament owes the better part of its reputation.

Cromwell. You country gentlemen bring with you into the People's House a freshness and sweet savour which our citizens lack mightily. I would fain merit your esteem, heedless of those pursy fellows from hulks and warehouses, with one ear lappeted by the pen behind it, and the other an heirloom, as Charles would have had it, in Laud's Star-chamber. Oh, they are proud and bloody men! My heart melts; but, alas! my authority is null: I am the servant of the Commonwealth. I will not, dare not, betray it. If Charles Stuart had threatened my death only, in the letter we ripped out of the saddle, I would have reproved him manfully and turned him adrift: but others are concerned; lives more precious than mine, worn as it is with fastings, prayers, long services, and preyed upon by a pouncing disease. The Lord hath led him into the toils laid for the innocent. Foolish man! he never could eschew evil counsel.

Noble. In comparison with you, he is but as a pinnacle to a buttress. I acknowledge his weaknesses, and cannot wink upon his crimes: but that which you visit as the heaviest of them perhaps was not so, although the most disastrous to both parties--the bearing of arms against his people. He fought for what he considered his hereditary property; we do the same: should we be hanged for losing a lawsuit?

Cromwell. No, unless it is the second. Thou talkest finely and foolishly, Wat, for a man of thy calm discernment. If a rogue holds a pistol to my breast, do I ask him who he is? Do I care whether his doublet be of cat-skin or of dog-skin? Fie upon such wicked sophisms! Marvellous, how the devil works upon good men's minds!

Noble. Charles was always more to be dreaded by his friends than by his enemies, and now by neither.

Cromwell. God forbid that Englishmen should be feared by Englishmen! but to be daunted by the weakest, to bend before the worst--I tell thee, Walter Noble, if Moses and the prophets commanded me to this villainy, I would draw back and mount my horse.

Noble. I wish that our history, already too dark with blood, should contain, as far as we are concerned in it, some unpolluted pages.

Cromwell. 'Twere better, much better. Never shall I be called, I promise thee, an unnecessary shedder of blood. Remember, my good, prudent friend, of what materials our sectaries are composed: what hostility against all eminence, what rancour against all glory. Not only kingly power offends them, but every other; and they talk of ***putting to the sword***, as if it were the quietest, gentlest, and most ordinary thing in the world. The knaves even dictate from their stools and benches to men in armour, bruised and bleeding for them; and with school-dames' scourges in their fists do they give counsel to those who protect them from the cart and halter. In the name of the Lord, I must spit outright (or worse) upon these crackling bouncing firebrands, before I can make them tractable.

Noble. I lament their blindness; but follies wear out the faster by being hard run upon. This fermenting sourness will presently turn vapid, and people will cast it out. I am not surprised that you are discontented and angry at what thwarts your better nature. But come, Cromwell, overlook them, despise them, and erect to yourself a glorious name by sparing a mortal enemy.

Cromwell. A glorious name, by God's blessing, I will erect; and all our fellow-labourers shall rejoice at it: but I see better than they do the blow descending on them, and my arm better than theirs can ward it off. Noble, thy heart overflows with kindness for Charles Stuart: if he were at liberty to-morrow by thy intercession, he would sign thy death-warrant the day after, for serving the Commonwealth. A generation of vipers! there is nothing upright nor grateful in them: never was there a drop of even Scotch blood in their veins. Indeed, we have a clue to their bedchamber still hanging on the door, and I suspect that an Italian fiddler or French valet has more than once crossed the current.

Noble. That may be: nor indeed is it credible that any royal or courtly family has gone on for three generations without a spur from interloper. Look at France! some stout Parisian saint performed the last miracle there.

Cromwell. Now thou talkest gravely and sensibly: I could hear thee discourse thus for hours together.

Noble. Hear me, Cromwell, with equal patience on matters more important. We all have our sufferings: why increase one another's wantonly? Be the blood Scotch or English, French or Italian, a drummer's or a buffoon's, it carries a soul upon its stream; and every soul has many places to touch at, and much business to perform, before it reaches its ultimate destination. Abolish the power of Charles; extinguish not his virtues. Whatever is worthy to be loved for anything is worthy to be preserved. A wise and dispassionate legislator, if any such should arise among men, will not condemn to death him who has done, or is likely to do, more service than injury to society. Blocks and gibbets are the nearest objects to ours, and their business is never with virtues or with hopes.

Cromwell. Walter! Walter! we laugh at speculators.

Noble. Many indeed are ready enough to laugh at speculators, because many profit, or expect to profit, by established and widening abuses. Speculations toward evil lose their name by adoption; speculations towards good are for ever speculations, and he who hath proposed them is a chimerical and silly creature. Among the matters under this denomination I never find a cruel project, I never find an oppressive or unjust one: how happens it?

Cromwell. Proportions should exist in all things. Sovereigns are paid higher than others for their office; they should therefore be punished more severely for abusing it, even if the consequences of this abuse were in nothing more grievous or extensive. We cannot clap them in the stocks conveniently, nor whip them at the market-place. Where there is a crown there must be an axe: I would keep it there only.

Noble. Lop off the rotten, press out the poisonous, preserve the rest; let it suffice to have given this memorable example of national power and justice.

Cromwell. Justice is perfect; an attribute of God: we must not trifle with it.

Noble. Should we be less merciful to our fellow-creatures than to our domestic animals? Before we deliver them to be killed, we weigh their services against their inconveniences. On the foundation of policy, when we have no better, let us erect the trophies of humanity: let us consider that, educated in the same manner and situated in the same position, we ourselves might have acted as reprovably. Abolish that for ever which must else for ever generate abuses; and attribute the faults of the man to the office, not the faults of the office to the man.

Cromwell. I have no bowels for hypocrisy, and I abominate and detest kingship.

Noble. I abominate and detest hangmanship; but in certain stages of society both are necessary. Let them go together; we want neither now.

Cromwell. Men, like nails, lose their usefulness when they lose their direction and begin to bend: such nails are then thrown into the dust or into the furnace. I must do my duty; I must accomplish what is commanded me; I must not be turned aside. I am loath to be cast into the furnace or the dust; but God's will be done! Prithee, Wat, since thou readest, as I see, the books of philosophers, didst thou ever hear of Digby's remedies by sympathy?

Noble. Yes, formerly.

Cromwell. Well, now, I protest, I do believe there is something in them. To cure my headache, I must breathe a vein in the neck of Charles.

Noble. Oliver, Oliver! others are wittiest over wine, thou over blood: cold-hearted, cruel man.

Cromwell. Why, dost thou verily think me so, Walter? Perhaps thou art right in the main: but He alone who fashioned me in my mother's womb, and who sees things deeper than we do, knows that.

NOTE:

[5] Ludlow, a most humane and temperate man, signed the death-warrant of Charles, for violating the constitution he had sworn to defend, for depriving the subject of property, liberty, limbs, and life unlawfully. In equity he could do no otherwise; and to equity was the only appeal, since the laws of the land had been erased by the king himself.

LORD BROOKE AND SIR PHILIP SIDNEY

Lord Brooke is less known than the personage with whom he converses, and upon whose friendship he had the virtue and good sense to found his chief distinction. On his monument at Warwick, written by himself, we read that he was servant of Queen Elizabeth, counsellor of King James and friend of Sir Philip Sidney. His style is stiff, but his sentiments are sound and manly.

Brooke. I come again unto the woods and unto the wilds of Penshurst, whither my heart and the friend of my heart have long invited me.

Sidney. Welcome, welcome! And now, Greville, seat yourself under this oak; since if you had hungered or thirsted from your journey, you would have renewed the alacrity of your old servants in the hall.

Brooke. In truth I did; for no otherwise the good household would have it. The birds met me first, affrightened by the tossing up of caps; and by these harbingers I knew who were coming. When my palfrey eyed them askance for their clamorousness, and shrank somewhat back, they quarrelled with him almost before they saluted me, and asked him many pert questions. What a pleasant spot, Sidney, have you chosen here for meditation! A solitude is the audience-chamber of God. Few days in our year are like this; there is a fresh pleasure in every fresh posture of the limbs, in every turn the eye takes.

> Youth! credulous of happiness, throw down
> Upon this turf thy wallet--stored and swoln
> With morrow-morns, bird-eggs, and bladders burst--
> That tires thee with its wagging to and fro:
> Thou too wouldst breathe more freely for it, Age!
> Who lackest heart to laugh at life's deceit.

It sometimes requires a stout push, and sometimes a sudden resistance, in the wisest men, not to become for a moment the most foolish. What have I done? I have fairly challenged you, so much my master.

Sidney. You have warmed me: I must cool a little and watch my opportunity. So now, Greville, return you to your invitations, and I will clear the ground for the company; for Youth, for Age, and whatever comes between, with kindred and dependencies. Verily we need no taunts like those in your verses: here we have few vices, and consequently few repinings. I take especial care that my young labourers and farmers shall never be idle, and I supply them with bows and arrows, with bowls and ninepins, for their Sunday evening,[6] lest they drink and quarrel. In church they are taught to love God; after church they are practised to love their neighbour: for business on workdays keeps them apart and scattered, and on market-days they are prone to a rivalry bordering on malice, as competitors for custom. Goodness does not more certainly make men happy than happiness makes them good. We must distinguish between felicity and prosperity; for prosperity leads often to ambition, and ambition to disappointment: the course is then over; the wheel turns round but once; while the reaction of goodness and happiness is perpetual.

Brooke. You reason justly and you act rightly. Piety--warm, soft, and passive as the ether round the throne of Grace--is made callous and inactive by kneeling too much: her vitality faints under rigorous and wearisome observances. A forced match between a man and his religion sours his temper, and leaves a barren bed.

Sidney. Desire of lucre, the worst and most general country vice, arises here from the necessity of looking to small gains; it is, however, but the tartar that encrusts economy.

Brooke. Oh that anything so monstrous should exist in this profusion and prodigality of blessings! The herbs, elastic with health, seem to partake of sensitive and animated life, and to feel under my hand the benediction I would bestow on them. What a hum of satisfaction in God's creatures! How is it, Sidney, the smallest do seem the happiest?

Sidney. Compensation for their weaknesses and their fears; compensation for the shortness of their existence. Their spirits mount upon the sunbeam above the eagle; and they have more enjoyment in their one summer than the elephant in his century.

Brooke. Are not also the little and lowly in our species the most happy?

Sidney. I would not willingly try nor over-curiously examine it. We, Greville, are happy in these parks and forests: we were happy in my close winter-walk of box and laurustine. In our earlier days did we not emboss our bosoms with the daffodils, and shake them almost unto shedding with our transport? Ay, my friend, there is a greater difference, both in the stages of life and in the seasons of the year, than in the conditions of men: yet the healthy pass through the seasons, from the clement to the inclement, not only unreluctantly but rejoicingly, knowing that the worst will soon finish, and the best begin anew; and we are desirous of pushing forward into every stage of life, excepting that alone which ought reasonably to allure us most, as opening to us the ***Via Sacra***, along which we move in triumph to our eternal country. We may in some measure frame our minds for the reception of happiness, for more or for less; we should, however, well consider to what port we are steering in search of it, and that even in the richest its quantity is but too exhaustible. There is a sickliness in the firmest of us, which induceth us to change our side, though reposing ever so softly: yet, wittingly or unwittingly, we turn again soon into our old position.

God hath granted unto both of us hearts easily contented, hearts fitted for every station, because fitted for every duty. What appears the dullest may contribute most to our genius; what is most gloomy may soften the seeds and relax the fibres of gaiety. We enjoy the solemnity of the spreading oak above us: perhaps we owe to it in part the mood of our minds at this instant; perhaps an inanimate thing supplies me, while I am speaking, with whatever I possess of animation. Do you imagine that any contest of shepherds can afford them the same pleasure as I receive from the description of it; or that even in their loves, however innocent and faithful, they are so free from anxiety as I am while I celebrate them? The exertion of intellectual power, of fancy and imagination, keeps from us greatly more than their wretchedness, and affords us greatly more than their enjoyment. We are motes in the midst of generations: we have our sunbeams to circuit and climb. Look at the summits of the trees around us, how they move, and the loftiest the most: nothing is at rest within the compass of our view, except the grey moss on the park-pales. Let it eat away the dead oak, but let it not be compared with the living one.

Poets are in general prone to melancholy; yet the most plaintive ditty hath imparted a fuller joy, and of longer duration, to its composer, than the conquest of Persia to the Macedonian. A bottle of wine bringeth as much pleasure as the acquisition of a kingdom, and not unlike it in kind: the senses in both cases are confused and perverted.

Brooke. Merciful Heaven! and for the fruition of an hour's drunkenness, from which they must awaken with heaviness, pain, and terror, men consume a whole crop of their kind at one harvest home. Shame upon those light ones who carol at the feast of blood! and worse upon those graver ones who nail upon their escutcheon the name of great! Ambition is but Avarice on stilts and masked. God sometimes sends a famine, sometimes a pestilence, and sometimes a hero, for the chastisement of mankind; none of them surely for our admiration. Only some cause like unto that which is now scattering the mental fog of the Netherlands, and is preparing them for the fruits of freedom, can justify us in drawing the sword abroad.

Sidney. And only the accomplishment of our purpose can permit us again to sheathe it; for the aggrandizement of our neighbour is nought of detriment to us: on the contrary, if we are honest and industrious, his wealth is ours. We have nothing to dread while our laws are equitable and our impositions light: but children fly from mothers who strip and scourge them.

Brooke. We are come to an age when we ought to read and speak plainly what our discretion tells us is fit: we are not to be set in a corner for mockery and derision, with our hands hanging down motionless and our pockets turned inside out.

*   *   *   *   *

But away, away with politics: let not this city-stench infect our fresh country air!

NOTE:

[6] Censurable as that practice may appear, it belonged to the age of Sidney. Amusements were permitted the English on the seventh day, nor were they restricted until the Puritans gained the ascendancy.

SOUTHEY AND PORSON

Porson. I suspect, Mr. Southey, you are angry with me for the freedom with which I have spoken of your poetry and Wordsworth's.

Southey. What could have induced you to imagine it, Mr. Professor? You have indeed bent your eyes upon me, since we have been together, with somewhat of fierceness and defiance: I presume you fancied me to be a commentator. You wrong me in your belief that any opinion on my poetical works hath molested me; but you afford me more than compensation in supposing me acutely sensible of injustice done to Wordsworth. If we must converse on these topics, we will converse on him. What man ever existed who spent a more inoffensive life, or adorned it with nobler studies?

Porson. I believe so; and they who attack him with virulence are men of as little morality as reflection. I have demonstrated that one of them, he who wrote the ***Pursuits of Literature***, could not construe a Greek sentence or scan a verse; and I have fallen on the very ***Index*** from which he drew out his forlorn hope on the parade. This is incomparably the most impudent fellow I have met with in the course of my reading, which has lain, you know, in a province where impudence is no rarity.

* * * * *

I had visited a friend in **King's Road** when he entered.

'Have you seen the **Review**?' cried he. 'Worse than ever! I am resolved to insert a paragraph in the papers, declaring that I had no concern in the last number.'

'Is it so very bad?' said I, quietly.

'Infamous! detestable!' exclaimed he.

'Sit down, then: nobody will believe you,' was my answer.

Since that morning he has discovered that I drink harder than usual, that my faculties are wearing fast away, that once, indeed, I had some Greek in my head, but--he then claps the forefinger to the side of his nose, turns his eye slowly upward, and looks compassionately and calmly.

Southey. Come, Mr. Porson, grant him his merits: no critic is better contrived to make any work a monthly one, no writer more dexterous in giving a finishing touch.

Porson. The plagiary has a greater latitude of choice than we; and if he brings home a parsnip or turnip-top, when he could as easily have pocketed a nectarine or a pineapple, he must be a blockhead. I never heard the name of the **Pursuer of Literature**, who has little more merit in having stolen than he would have had if he had never stolen at all; and I have forgotten that other man's, who evinced his fitness to be the censor of our age, by a translation of the most naked and impure satires of antiquity--those of Juvenal, which owe their preservation to the partiality of the friars. I shall entertain an unfavourable opinion of him if he has translated them well: pray, has he?

Southey. Indeed, I do not know. I read poets for their poetry, and to extract that nutriment of the intellect and of the heart which poetry should contain. I never listen to the swans of the cesspool, and must declare that nothing is heavier to me than rottenness and corruption.

Porson. You are right, sir, perfectly right. A translator of Juvenal would open a public drain to look for a needle, and may miss it. My nose is not easily offended; but I must have something to fill my belly. Come, we will lay aside the scrip of the transpositor and the pouch of the pursuer, in reserve for the days of unleavened bread; and again, if you please, to the lakes and mountains. Now we are both in better humour, I must bring you to a confession that in your friend Wordsworth there is occasionally a little trash.

Southey. A haunch of venison would be trash to a Brahmin, a bottle of Burgundy to the xerif of Mecca. We are guided by precept, by habit, by taste, by constitution. Hitherto our sentiments on poetry have been delivered down to us from authority; and if it can be demonstrated, as I think it may be, that the authority is inadequate, and that the dictates are often inapplicable and often misinterpreted, you will allow me to remove the cause out of court. Every man can see what is very bad in a poem; almost every one can see what is very good: but you, Mr. Porson, who have turned over all the volumes of all the commentators, will inform me whether I am right or wrong in asserting that no critic hath yet appeared who hath been able to fix or to discern the exact degrees of excellence above a certain point.

Porson. None.

Southey. The reason is, because the eyes of no one have been upon a level with it. Supposing, for the sake of argument, the contest of Hesiod and Homer to have taken place: the judges who decided in favour of the worse, and he, indeed, in poetry has little merit, may have been elegant, wise, and conscientious men. Their decision was in favour of that to the species of which they had been the most accustomed. Corinna was preferred to Pindar no fewer than five times, and the best judges in Greece gave her the preference; yet whatever were her powers, and beyond a question they were extraordinary, we may assure ourselves that she stood many degrees below Pindar. Nothing is more absurd than the report that the judges were prepossessed by her beauty. Plutarch tells us that she was much older than her competitor, who consulted her judgment in his earlier odes. Now, granting their first competition to have been when Pindar was twenty years old, and that the others were in the years succeeding, her beauty must have been somewhat on the decline; for in Greece there are few women who retain the graces, none who retain the bloom of youth, beyond the twenty-third year. Her countenance, I doubt not, was expressive: but expression, although it gives beauty to men, makes women pay dearly for its stamp, and pay soon. Nature seems, in protection to their loveliness, to have ordered that they who are our superiors in quickness and sensibility should be little disposed to laborious thought, or to long excursions in the labyrinths of fancy. We may be convinced that the verdict of the judges was biased by nothing else than the habitudes of thinking; we may be convinced, too, that living in an age when poetry was cultivated highly, and selected from the most acute and the most dispassionate, they were subject to no greater errors of opinion than are the learned messmates of our English colleges.

Porson. You are more liberal in your largesses to the fair Greeks than a friend of mine was, who resided in Athens to acquire the language. He assured me that beauty there was in bud at thirteen, in full blossom at fifteen, losing a leaf or two every day at seventeen, trembling on the thorn at nineteen, and under the tree at twenty.

Southey. Mr. Porson, it does not appear to me that anything more is necessary, in the first instance, than to interrogate our hearts in what manner they have been affected. If the ear is satisfied; if at one moment a tumult is aroused in the breast, and tranquillized at another, with a perfect consciousness of equal power exerted in both cases; if we rise up from the perusal of the work with a strong excitement to thought, to imagination, to sensibility; above all, if we sat down with some propensities toward evil, and walk away with much stronger toward good, in the midst of a world which we never had entered and of which we never had dreamed before--shall we perversely put on again the ***old man*** of criticism, and dissemble that we have been conducted by a most beneficent and most potent genius? Nothing proves to me so manifestly in what a pestiferous condition are its lazarettos, as when I observe how little hath been objected against those who have substituted words for things, and how much against those who have reinstated things for words.

Let Wordsworth prove to the world that there may be animation without blood and broken bones, and tenderness remote from the stews. Some will doubt it; for even things the most evident are often but little perceived and strangely estimated. Swift ridiculed the music of Handel and the generalship of Marlborough; Pope the perspicacity and the scholarship of Bentley; Gray the abilities of Shaftesbury and the eloquence of Rousseau. Shakespeare hardly found those who would collect his tragedies; Milton was read from godliness; Virgil was antiquated and rustic; Cicero, Asiatic. What a rabble has persecuted my friend! An elephant is born to be consumed by ants in the midst of his unapproachable solitudes: Wordsworth is the prey of Jeffrey. Why repine? Let us rather amuse ourselves with allegories, and recollect that God in the creation left His noblest creature at the mercy of a serpent.

* * * * *

Porson. Wordsworth goes out of his way to be attacked; he picks up a piece of dirt, throws it on the carpet in the midst of the company, and cries, *This is a better man than any of you!* He does indeed mould the base material into what form he chooses; but why not rather invite us to contemplate it than challenge us to condemn it? Here surely is false taste.

Southey. The principal and the most general accusation against him is, that the vehicle of his thoughts is unequal to them. Now did ever the judges at the Olympic games say: 'We would have awarded to you the meed of victory, if your chariot had been equal to your horses: it is true they have won; but the people are displeased at a car neither new nor richly gilt, and without a gryphon or sphinx engraved on the axle'? You admire simplicity in Euripides; you censure it in Wordsworth: believe me, sir, it arises in neither from penury of thought--which seldom has produced it--but from the strength of temperance, and at the suggestion of principle.

Take up a poem of Wordsworth's and read it--I would rather say, read them all; and, knowing that a mind like yours must grasp closely what comes within it, I will then appeal to you whether any poet of our country, since Milton, hath exerted greater powers with less of strain and less of ostentation. I would, however, by his permission, lay before you for this purpose a poem which is yet unpublished and incomplete.

Porson. Pity, with such abilities, he does not imitate the ancients somewhat more.

Southey. Whom did they imitate? If his genius is equal to theirs he has no need of a guide. He also will be an ancient; and the very counterparts of those who now decry him will extol him a thousand years hence in malignity to the moderns.

THE ABBE DELILLE AND WALTER LANDOR

The Abbe Delille was the happiest of creatures, when he could weep over the charms of innocence and the country in some crowded and fashionable circle at Paris. We embraced most pathetically on our first meeting there, as if the one were condemned to quit the earth, the other to live upon it.

Delille. You are reported to have said that descriptive poetry has all the merits of a handkerchief that smells of roses?

Landor. This, if I said it, is among the things which are neither false enough nor true enough to be displeasing. But the Abbe Delille has merits of his own. To translate Milton well is more laudable than originality in trifling matters; just as to transport an obelisk from Egypt, and to erect it in one of the squares, must be considered a greater labour than to build a new chandler's shop.

Delille. Milton is indeed extremely difficult to translate; for, however noble and majestic, he is sometimes heavy, and often rough and unequal.

Landor. Dear Abbe, porphyry is heavy, gold is heavier; Ossa and Olympus are rough and unequal; the steppes of Tartary, though high, are of uniform elevation: there is not a rock, nor a birch, nor a cytisus, nor an arbutus upon them great enough to shelter a new-dropped lamb. Level the Alps one with another, and where is their sublimity? Raise up the vale of Tempe to the downs above, and where are those sylvan creeks and harbours in which the imagination watches while the soul reposes; those recesses in which the gods partook the weaknesses of mortals, and mortals the enjoyments of the gods?

You have treated our poet with courtesy and distinction; in your trimmed and measured dress, he might be taken for a Frenchman. Do not think me flattering. You have conducted Eve from Paradise to Paris, and she really looks prettier and smarter than before she tripped. With what elegance she rises from a most awful dream! You represent her (I repeat your expression) as springing up *en sursaut*, as if you had caught her asleep and tickled the young creature on that sofa.

Homer and Virgil have been excelled in sublimity by Shakespeare and Milton, as the Caucasus and Atlas of the old world by the Andes and Teneriffe of the new; but you would embellish them all.

Delille. I owe to Voltaire my first sentiment of admiration for Milton and Shakespeare.

Landor. He stuck to them as a woodpecker to an old forest-tree, only for the purpose of picking out what was rotten: he has made the holes deeper than he found them, and, after all his cries and chatter, has brought home but scanty sustenance to his starveling nest.

Delille. You must acknowledge that there are fine verses in his tragedies.

Landor. Whenever such is the first observation, be assured, M. l'Abbe, that the poem, if heroic or dramatic, is bad. Should a work of this kind be excellent, we say, 'How admirably the characters are sustained! What delicacy of discrimination! There is nothing to be taken away or altered without an injury to the part or to the whole.'

We may afterward descend on the versification. In poetry, there is a greater difference between the good and the excellent than there is between the bad and the good. Poetry has no golden mean; mediocrity here is of another metal, which Voltaire, however, had skill enough to encrust and polish. In the least wretched of his tragedies, whatever is tolerable is Shakespeare's; but, gracious Heaven! how deteriorated! When he pretends to extol a poet he chooses some defective part, and renders it more so whenever he translates it. I will repeat a few verses from Metastasio in support of my assertion. Metastasio was both a better critic and a better poet, although of the second order in each quality; his tyrants are less philosophical, and his chambermaids less dogmatic. Voltaire was, however, a man of abilities, and author of many passable epigrams, beside those which are contained in his tragedies and heroics; yet it must be confessed that, like your Parisian lackeys, they are usually the smartest when out of place.

Delille. What you call epigram gives life and spirit to grave works, and seems principally wanted to relieve a long poem. I do not see why what pleases us in a star should not please us in a constellation.

DIOGENES AND PLATO

Diogenes. Stop! stop! come hither! Why lookest thou so scornfully and askance upon me?

Plato. Let me go! loose me! I am resolved to pass.

Diogenes. Nay, then, by Jupiter and this tub! thou leavest three good ells of Milesian cloth behind thee. Whither wouldst thou amble?

Plato. I am not obliged in courtesy to tell you.

Diogenes. Upon whose errand? Answer me directly.

Plato. Upon my own.

Diogenes. Oh, then, I will hold thee yet awhile. If it were upon another's, it might be a hardship to a good citizen, though not to a good philosopher.

Plato. That can be no impediment to my release: you do not think me one.

Diogenes. No, by my Father Jove!

Plato. Your father!

Diogenes. Why not? Thou shouldst be the last man to doubt it. Hast not thou declared it irrational to refuse our belief to those who assert that they are begotten by the gods, though the assertion (these are thy words) be unfounded on reason or probability? In me there is a chance of it: whereas in the generation of such people as thou art fondest of frequenting, who claim it loudly, there are always too many competitors to leave it probable.

Plato. Those who speak against the great do not usually speak from morality, but from envy.

Diogenes. Thou hast a glimpse of the truth in this place, but as thou hast already shown thy ignorance in attempting to prove to me what a ***man*** is, ill can I expect to learn from thee what is a great man.

Plato. No doubt your experience and intercourse will afford me the information.

Diogenes. Attend, and take it. The great man is he who hath nothing to fear and nothing to hope from another. It is he who, while he demonstrates the iniquity of the laws, and is able to correct them, obeys them peaceably. It is he who looks on the ambitious both as weak and fraudulent. It is he who hath no disposition or occasion for any kind of deceit, no reason for being or for appearing different from what he is. It is he who can call together the most select company when it pleases him.

Plato. Excuse my interruption. In the beginning of your definition I fancied that you were designating your own person, as most people do in describing what is admirable; now I find that you have some other in contemplation.

Diogenes. I thank thee for allowing me what perhaps I ***do*** possess, but what I was not then thinking of; as is often the case with rich possessors: in fact, the latter part of the description suits me as well as any portion of the former.

Plato. You may call together the best company, by using your hands in the call, as you did with me; otherwise I am not sure that you would succeed in it.

Diogenes. My thoughts are my company; I can bring them together, select them, detain them, dismiss them. Imbecile and vicious men cannot do any of these things. Their thoughts are scattered, vague, uncertain, cumbersome: and the worst stick to them the longest; many indeed by choice, the greater part by necessity, and accompanied, some by weak wishes, others by vain remorse.

Plato. Is there nothing of greatness, O Diogenes! in exhibiting how cities and communities may be governed best, how morals may be kept the purest, and power become the most stable?

Diogenes. Something of greatness does not constitute the great man. Let me, however, see him who hath done what thou sayest: he must be the most universal and the most indefatigable traveller, he must also be the oldest creature, upon earth.

Plato. How so?

Diogenes. Because he must know perfectly the climate, the soil, the situation, the peculiarities, of the races, of their allies, of their enemies; he must have sounded their harbours, he must have measured the quantity of their arable land and pasture, of their woods and mountains; he must have ascertained whether there are fisheries on their coasts, and even what winds are prevalent. On these causes, with some others, depend the bodily strength, the numbers, the wealth, the wants, the capacities of the people.

Plato. Such are low thoughts.

Diogenes. The bird of wisdom flies low, and seeks her food under hedges: the eagle himself would be starved if he always soared aloft and against the sun. The sweetest fruit grows near the ground, and the plants that bear it require ventilation and lopping. Were this not to be done in thy garden, every walk and alley, every plot and border, would be covered with runners and roots, with boughs and suckers. We want no poets or logicians or metaphysicians to govern us: we want practical men, honest men, continent men, unambitious men, fearful to solicit a trust, slow to accept, and resolute never to betray one. Experimentalists may be the best philosophers: they are always the worst politicians. Teach people their duties, and they will know their interests. Change as little as possible, and correct as much.

Philosophers are absurd from many causes, but principally from laying out unthriftily their distinctions. They set up four virtues: fortitude, prudence, temperance, and justice. Now a man may be a very bad one, and yet possess three out of the four. Every cut-throat must, if he has been a cut-throat on many occasions, have more fortitude and more prudence than the greater part of those whom we consider as the best men. And what cruel wretches, both executioners and judges, have been strictly just! how little have they cared what gentleness, what generosity, what genius, their sentence hath removed from the earth! Temperance and beneficence contain all other virtues. Take them home, Plato; split them, expound them; do what thou wilt with them, if thou but use them.

Before I gave thee this lesson, which is a better than thou ever gavest any one, and easier to remember, thou wert accusing me of invidiousness and malice against those whom thou callest the great, meaning to say the powerful. Thy imagination, I am well aware, had taken its flight toward Sicily, where thou seekest thy great man, as earnestly and undoubtingly as Ceres sought her Persephone. Faith! honest Plato, I have no reason to envy thy worthy friend Dionysius. Look at my nose! A lad seven or eight years old threw an apple at me yesterday, while I was gazing at the clouds, and gave me nose enough for two moderate men. Instead of such a godsend, what should I have thought of my fortune, if, after living all my lifetime among golden vases, rougher than my hand with their emeralds and rubies, their engravings and embossments; among Parian caryatides and porphyry sphinxes; among philosophers with rings upon their fingers and linen next their skin; and among singing-boys and dancing-girls, to whom alone thou speakest intelligibly--I ask thee again, what should I in reason have thought of my fortune, if, after these facilities and superfluities, I had at last been pelted out of my house, not by one young rogue, but by thousands of all ages, and not with an apple (I wish I could say a rotten one), but with pebbles and broken pots; and, to crown my deserts, had been compelled to become the teacher of so promising a generation? Great men, forsooth! thou knowest at last who they are.

Plato. There are great men of various kinds.

Diogenes. No, by my beard, are there not!

Plato. What! are there not great captains, great geometricians, great dialectitians?

Diogenes. Who denied it? A great man was the postulate. Try thy hand now at the powerful one.

Plato. On seeing the exercise of power, a child cannot doubt who is powerful, more or less; for power is relative. All men are weak, not only if compared to the Demiurgos, but if compared to the sea or the earth, or certain things upon each of them, such as elephants and whales. So placid and tranquil is the scene around us, we can hardly bring to mind the images of strength and force, the precipices, the abysses----

Diogenes. Prithee hold thy loose tongue, twinkling and glittering like a serpent's in the midst of luxuriance and rankness! Did never this reflection of thine warn thee that, in human life, the precipices and abysses would be much farther from our admiration if we were less inconsiderate, selfish, and vile? I will not however stop thee long, for thou wert going on quite consistently. As thy great men are fighters and wranglers, so thy mighty things upon the earth and sea are troublesome and intractable encumbrances. Thou perceivedst not what was greater in the former case, neither art thou aware what is greater in this. Didst thou feel the gentle air that passed us?

Plato. I did not, just then.

Diogenes. That air, so gentle, so imperceptible to thee, is more powerful not only than all the creatures that breathe and live by it; not only than all the oaks of the forest, which it rears in an age and shatters in a moment; not only than all the monsters of the sea, but than the sea itself, which it tosses up into foam, and breaks against every rock in its vast circumference; for it carries in its bosom, with perfect calm and composure, the incontrollable ocean and the peopled earth, like an atom of a feather.

To the world's turmoils and pageantries is attracted, not only the admiration of the populace, but the zeal of the orator, the enthusiasm of the poet, the investigation of the historian, and the contemplation of the philosopher: yet how silent and invisible are they in the depths of air! Do I say in those depths and deserts? No; I say in the distance of a swallow's flight--at the distance she rises above us, ere a sentence brief as this could be uttered.

What are its mines and mountains? Fragments welded up and dislocated by the expansion of water from below; the most part reduced to mud, the rest to splinters. Afterwards sprang up fire in many places, and again tore and mangled the mutilated carcass, and still growls over it.

What are its cities and ramparts, and moles and monuments? Segments of a fragment, which one man puts together and another throws down. Here we stumble upon thy great ones at their work. Show me now, if thou canst, in history, three great warriors, or three great statesmen, who have acted otherwise than spiteful children.

Plato. I will begin to look for them in history when I have discovered the same number in the philosophers or the poets. A prudent man searches in his own garden after the plant he wants, before he casts his eyes over the stalls in Kenkrea or Keramicos.

Returning to your observation on the potency of the air, I am not ignorant or unmindful of it. May I venture to express my opinion to you, Diogenes, that the earlier discoverers and distributors of wisdom (which wisdom lies among us in ruins and remnants, partly distorted and partly concealed by theological allegory) meant by Jupiter the air in its agitated state; by Juno the air in its quiescent. These are the great agents, and therefore called the king and queen of the gods. Jupiter is denominated by Homer the ***compeller of clouds***: Juno receives them, and remits them in showers to plants and animals.

I may trust you, I hope, O Diogenes?

Diogenes. Thou mayest lower the gods in my presence, as safely as men in the presence of Timon.

Plato. I would not lower them: I would exalt them.

Diogenes. More foolish and presumptuous still!

Plato. Fair words, O Sinopean! I protest to you my aim is truth.

Diogenes. I cannot lead thee where of a certainty thou mayest always find it; but I will tell thee what it is. Truth is a point; the subtilest and finest; harder than adamant; never to be broken, worn away, or blunted. Its only bad quality is, that it is sure to hurt those who touch it; and likely to draw blood, perhaps the life-blood, of those who press earnestly upon it. Let us away from this narrow lane skirted with hemlock, and pursue our road again through the wind and dust toward the ***great*** man and the ***powerful***. Him I would call the powerful one who controls the storms of his mind, and turns to good account the worst accidents of his fortune. The great man, I was going on to demonstrate, is somewhat more. He must be able to do this, and he must have an intellect which puts into motion the intellect of others.

Plato. Socrates, then, was your great man.

Diogenes. He was indeed; nor can all thou hast attributed to him ever make me think the contrary. I wish he could have kept a little more at home, and have thought it as well worth his while to converse with his own children as with others.

Plato. He knew himself born for the benefit of the human race.

Diogenes. Those who are born for the benefit of the human race go but little into it: those who are born for its curse are crowded.

Plato. It was requisite to dispel the mists of ignorance and error.

Diogenes. Has he done it? What doubt has he elucidated, or what fact has he established? Although I was but twelve years old and resident in another city when he died, I have taken some pains in my inquiries about him from persons of less vanity and less perverseness than his disciples. He did not leave behind him any true philosopher among them; any who followed his mode of argumentation, his subjects of disquisition, or his course of life; any who would subdue the malignant passions or coerce the looser; any who would abstain from calumny or from cavil; any who would devote his days to the glory of his country, or, what is easier and perhaps wiser, to his own well-founded contentment and well-merited repose. Xenophon, the best of them, offered up sacrifices, believed in oracles, consulted soothsayers, turned pale at a jay, and was dysenteric at a magpie.

Plato. He had courage at least.

Diogenes. His courage was of so strange a quality, that he was ready, if jay or magpie did not cross him, to fight for Spartan or Persian. Plato, whom thou esteemest much, and knowest somewhat less, careth as little for portent and omen as doth Diogenes. What he would have done for a Persian I cannot say; certain I am that he would have no more fought for a Spartan than he would for his own father: yet he mortally hates the man who hath a kinder muse or a better milliner, or a seat nearer the minion of a king. So much for the two disciples of Socrates who have acquired the greatest celebrity!

* * * * *

Plato. Diogenes! if you must argue or discourse with me, I will endure your asperity for the sake of your acuteness; but it appears to me a more philosophical thing to avoid what is insulting and vexatious, than to breast and brave it.

Diogenes. Thou hast spoken well.

Plato. It belongs to the vulgar, not to us, to fly from a man's opinions to his actions, and to stab him in his own house for having received no wound in the school. One merit you will allow me: I always keep my temper; which you seldom do.

Diogenes. Is mine a good or a bad one?

Plato. Now, must I speak sincerely?

Diogenes. Dost thou, a philosopher, ask such a question of me, a philosopher? Ay, sincerely or not at all.

Plato. Sincerely as you could wish, I must declare, then, your temper is the worst in the world.

Diogenes. I am much in the right, therefore, not to keep it. Embrace me: I have spoken now in thy own manner. Because thou sayest the most malicious things the most placidly, thou thinkest or pretendest thou art sincere.

Plato. Certainly those who are most the masters of their resentments are likely to speak less erroneously than the passionate and morose.

Diogenes. If they would, they might; but the moderate are not usually the most sincere, for the same circumspection which makes them moderate makes them likewise retentive of what could give offence: they are also timid in regard to fortune and favour, and hazard little. There is no mass of sincerity in any place. What there is must be picked up patiently, a grain or two at a time; and the season for it is after a storm, after the overflowing of banks, and bursting of mounds, and sweeping away of landmarks. Men will always hold something back; they must be shaken and loosened a little, to make them let go what is deepest in them, and weightiest and purest.

Plato. Shaking and loosening as much about you as was requisite for the occasion, it became you to demonstrate where and in what manner I had made Socrates appear less sagacious and less eloquent than he was; it became you likewise to consider the great difficulty of finding new thoughts and new expressions for those who had more of them than any other men, and to represent them in all the brilliancy of their wit and in all the majesty of their genius. I do not assert that I have done it; but if I have not, what man has? what man has come so nigh to it? He who could bring Socrates, or Solon, or Diogenes through a dialogue, without disparagement, is much nearer in his intellectual powers to them, than any other is near to him.

Diogenes. Let Diogenes alone, and Socrates, and Solon. None of the three ever occupied his hours in tingeing and curling the tarnished plumes of prostitute Philosophy, or deemed anything worth his attention, care, or notice, that did not make men brave and independent. As thou callest on me to show thee where and in what manner thou hast misrepresented thy teacher, and as thou seemest to set an equal value on eloquence and on reasoning, I shall attend to thee awhile on each of these matters, first inquiring of thee whether the axiom is Socratic, that it is never becoming to get drunk, ***unless*** in the solemnities of Bacchus?

Plato. This god was the discoverer of the vine and of its uses.

Diogenes. Is drunkenness one of its uses, or the discovery of a god? If Pallas or Jupiter hath given us reason, we should sacrifice our reason with more propriety to Jupiter or Pallas. To Bacchus is due a libation of wine; the same being his gift, as thou preachest.

Another and a graver question.

Did Socrates teach thee that 'slaves are to be scourged, and by no means admonished as though they were the children of the master'?

Plato. He did not argue upon government.

Diogenes. He argued upon humanity, whereon all government is founded: whatever is beside it is usurpation.

Plato. Are slaves then never to be scourged, whatever be their transgressions and enormities?

Diogenes. Whatever they be, they are less than his who reduced them to this condition.

Plato. What! though they murder his whole family?

Diogenes. Ay, and poison the public fountain of the city.

What am I saying? and to whom? Horrible as is this crime, and next in atrocity to parricide, thou deemest it a lighter one than stealing a fig or grape. The stealer of these is scourged by thee; the sentence on the poisoner is to cleanse out the receptacle. There is, however, a kind of poisoning which, to do thee justice, comes before thee with all its horrors, and which thou wouldst punish capitally, even in such a sacred personage as an aruspex or diviner: I mean the poisoning by incantation. I, and my whole family, my whole race, my whole city, may bite the dust in agony from a truss of henbane in the well; and little harm done forsooth! Let an idle fool set an image of me in wax before the fire, and whistle and caper to it, and purr and pray, and chant a hymn to Hecate while it melts, entreating and imploring her that I may melt as easily--and thou wouldst, in thy equity and holiness, strangle him at the first stave of his psalmody.

Plato. If this is an absurdity, can you find another?

Diogenes. Truly, in reading thy book, I doubted at first, and for a long continuance, whether thou couldst have been serious; and whether it were not rather a satire on those busy-bodies who are incessantly intermeddling in other people's affairs. It was only on the protestation of thy intimate friends that I believed thee to have written it in earnest. As for thy question, it is idle to stoop and pick out absurdities from a mass of inconsistency and injustice; but another and another I could throw in, and another and another afterward, from any page in the volume. Two bare, staring falsehoods lift their beaks one upon the other, like spring frogs. Thou sayest that no punishment decreed by the laws tendeth to evil. What! not if immoderate? not if partial? Why then repeal any penal statute while the subject of its animadversion exists? In prisons the less criminal are placed among the more criminal, the inexperienced in vice together with the hardened in it. This is part of the punishment, though it precedes the sentence; nay, it is often inflicted on those whom the judges acquit: the law, by allowing it, does it.

The next is, that he who is punished by the laws is the better for it, however the less depraved. What! if anteriorly to the sentence he lives and converses with worse men, some of whom console him by deadening the sense of shame, others by removing the apprehension of punishment? Many laws as certainly make men bad, as bad men make many laws; yet under thy regimen they take us from the bosom of the nurse, turn the meat about upon the platter, pull the bed-clothes off, make us sleep when we would wake, and wake when we would sleep, and never cease to rummage and twitch us, until they see us safe landed at the grave. We can do nothing (but be poisoned) with impunity. What is worst of all, we must marry certain relatives and connexions, be they distorted, blear-eyed, toothless, carbuncled, with hair (if any) eclipsing the reddest torch of Hymen, and with a hide outrivalling in colour and plaits his trimmest saffron robe. At the mention of this indeed, friend Plato, even thou, although resolved to stand out of harm's way, beginnest to make a wry mouth, and findest it difficult to pucker and purse it up again, without an astringent store of moral sentences. Hymen is truly no acquaintance of thine. We know the delicacies of love which thou wouldst reserve for the gluttony of heroes and the fastidiousness of philosophers. Heroes, like gods, must have their own way; but against thee and thy confraternity of elders I would turn the closet-key, and your mouths might water over, but your tongues should never enter those little pots of comfiture. Seriously, you who wear embroidered slippers ought to be very cautious of treading in the mire. Philosophers should not only live the simplest lives, but should also use the plainest language. Poets, in employing magnificent and sonorous words, teach philosophy the better by thus disarming suspicion that the finest poetry contains and conveys the finest philosophy. You will never let any man hold his right station: you would rank Solon with Homer for poetry. This is absurd. The only resemblance is in both being eminently wise. Pindar, too, makes even the cadences of his dithyrambics keep time to the flute of Reason. My tub, which holds fifty-fold thy wisdom, would crack at the reverberation of thy voice.

Plato. Farewell.

* * * * *

Diogenes. I mean that every one of thy whimsies hath been picked up somewhere by thee in thy travels; and each of them hath been rendered more weak and puny by its place of concealment in thy closet. What thou hast written on the immortality of the soul goes rather to prove the immortality of the body; and applies as well to the body of a weasel or an eel as to the fairer one of Agathon or of Aster. Why not at once introduce a new religion, since religions keep and are relished in proportion as they are salted with absurdity, inside and out? and all of them must have one great crystal of it for the centre; but Philosophy pines and dies unless she drinks limpid water. When Pherecydes and Pythagoras felt in themselves the majesty of contemplation, they spurned the idea that flesh and bones and arteries should confer it: and that what comprehends the past and the future should sink in a moment and be annihilated for ever. 'No,' cried they, 'the power of thinking is no more in the brain than in the hair, although the brain may be the instrument on which it plays. It is not corporeal, it is not of this world; its existence is eternity, its residence is infinity.' I forbear to discuss the rationality of their belief, and pass on straightway to thine; if, indeed, I am to consider as one, belief and doctrine.

Plato. As you will.

Diogenes. I should rather, then, regard these things as mere ornaments; just as many decorate their apartments with lyres and harps, which they themselves look at from the couch, supinely complacent, and leave for visitors to admire and play on.

Plato. I foresee not how you can disprove my argument on the immortality of the soul, which, being contained in the best of my dialogues, and being often asked for among my friends, I carry with me.

Diogenes. At this time?

Plato. Even so.

Diogenes. Give me then a certain part of it for my perusal.

Plato. Willingly.

Diogenes. Hermes and Pallas! I wanted but a cubit of it, or at most a fathom, and thou art pulling it out by the plethron.

Plato. This is the place in question.

Diogenes. Read it.

Plato. [*Reads.*] 'Sayest thou not that death is the opposite of life, and that they spring the one from the other?' '*Yes.*' 'What springs then from the living?' '*The dead.*' 'And what from the dead?' '*The living.*' 'Then all things alive spring from the dead.'

Diogenes. Why the repetition? but go on.

Plato. [*Reads.*] 'Souls therefore exist after death in the infernal regions.'

Diogenes. Where is the *therefore*? where is it even as to *existence*? As to the *infernal regions*, there is nothing that points toward a proof, or promises an indication. Death neither springs from life, nor life from death. Although death is the inevitable consequence of life, if the observation and experience of ages go for anything, yet nothing shows us, or ever hath signified, that life comes from death. Thou mightest as well say that a barley-corn dies before the germ of another barley-corn grows up from it, than which nothing is more untrue; for it is only the protecting part of the germ that perishes, when its protection is no longer necessary. The consequence, that souls exist after death, cannot be drawn from the corruption of the body, even if it were demonstrable that out of this corruption a live one could rise up. Thou hast not said that the soul is among those dead things which living things must spring from; thou hast not said that a living soul produces a dead soul, or that a dead soul produces a living one.

Plato. No, indeed.

Diogenes. On my faith, thou hast said, however, things no less inconsiderate, no less inconsequent, no less unwise; and this very thing must be said and proved, to make thy argument of any value. Do dead men beget children?

Plato. I have not said it.

Diogenes. Thy argument implies it.

Plato. These are high mysteries, and to be approached with reverence.

Diogenes. Whatever we cannot account for is in the same predicament. We may be gainers by being ignorant if we can be thought mysterious. It is better to shake our heads and to let nothing out of them, than to be plain and explicit in matters of difficulty. I do not mean in confessing our ignorance or our imperfect knowledge of them, but in clearing them up perspicuously: for, if we answer with ease, we may haply be thought good-natured, quick, communicative; never deep, never sagacious; not very defective possibly in our intellectual faculties, yet unequal and chinky, and liable to the probation of every clown's knuckle.

Plato. The brightest of stars appear the most unsteady and tremulous in their light; not from any quality inherent in themselves, but from the vapours that float below, and from the imperfection of vision in the surveyor.

Diogenes. Draw thy robe round thee; let the folds fall gracefully, and look majestic. That sentence is an admirable one; but not for me. I want sense, not stars. What then? Do no vapours float below the others? and is there no imperfection in the vision of those who look at *them*, if they are the same men, and look the next moment? We must move on: I shall follow the dead bodies, and the benighted driver of their fantastic bier, close and keen as any hyena.

Plato. Certainly, O Diogenes, you excel me in elucidations and similes: mine was less obvious.

*   *   *   *   *

Diogenes. I know the respect thou bearest to the dogly character, and can attribute to nothing else the complacency with which thou hast listened to me since I released thy cloak. If ever the Athenians, in their inconstancy, should issue a decree to deprive me of the appellation they have conferred on me, rise up, I pray thee, in my defence, and protest that I have not merited so severe a mulct. Something I do deserve at thy hands; having supplied thee, first with a store of patience, when thou wert going without any about thee, although it is the readiest viaticum and the heartiest sustenance of human life; and then with weapons from this tub, wherewith to drive the importunate cock before thee out of doors again.

ALFIERI AND SALOMON THE FLORENTINE JEW

Alfieri. Let us walk to the window, Signor Salomon. And now, instead of the silly, simpering compliments repeated at introductions, let me assure you that you are the only man in Florence with whom I would willingly exchange a salutation.

Salomon. I must think myself highly flattered, Signor Conte, having always heard that you are not only the greatest democrat, but also the greatest aristocrat, in Europe.

Alfieri. These two things, however opposite, which your smile would indicate, are not so irreconcilable as you imagine. Let us first understand the words, and then talk about them. The democrat is he who wishes the people to have a due share in the government, and this share if you please shall be the principal one. The aristocrat of our days is contented with no actual share in it; but if a man of family is conscious of his dignity, and resentful that another has invaded it, he may be, and is universally, called an aristocrat. The principal difference is, that one carries outward what the other carries inward. I am thought an aristocrat by the Florentines for conversing with few people, and for changing my shirt and shaving my beard on other days than festivals; which the most aristocratical of them never do, considering it, no doubt, as an excess. I am, however, from my soul a republican, if prudence and modesty will authorize any man to call himself so; and this, I trust, I have demonstrated in the most valuable of my works, the ***Treatise on Tyranny*** and the ***Dialogue*** with my friends at Siena. The aristocratical part of me, if part of me it must be called, hangs loose and keeps off insects. I see no aristocracy in the children of sharpers from behind the counter, nor, placing the matter in the most favourable point of view, in the descendants of free citizens who accepted from any vile enslaver--French, Spanish, German, or priest, or monk (represented with a piece of buffoonery, like a beehive on his head and a picklock key at his girdle)--the titles of counts and marquises. In Piedmont the matter is different: we must either have been the rabble or the lords; we were military, and we retain over the populace the same rank and spirit as our ancestors held over the soldiery.

Salomon. Signor Conte, I have heard of levellers, but I have never seen one: all are disposed to level down, but nobody to level up. As for nobility, there is none in Europe beside the Venetian. Nobility must be self-constituted and independent: the free alone are noble; slavery, like death, levels all. The English come nearest to the Venetian: they are independent, but want the main characteristic, the ***self-constituted***. You have been in England, Signor Conte, and can judge of them better than I can.

* * * * *

Alfieri. It is among those who stand between the peerage and the people that there exists a greater mass of virtue and of wisdom than in the rest of Europe. Much of their dignified simplicity may be attributed to the plainness of their religion, and, what will always be imitated, to the decorous life of their king: for whatever may be the defects of either, if we compare them with others round us, they are excellent.

Salomon. A young religion jumps upon the shoulders of an older one, and soon becomes like her, by mockery of her tricks, her cant, and her decrepitude. Meanwhile the old one shakes with indignation, and swears there is neither relationship nor likeness. Was there ever a religion in the world that was not the true religion, or was there ever a king that was not the best of kings?

Alfieri. In the latter case we must have arrived nigh perfection; since it is evident from the authority of the gravest men--theologians, presidents, judges, corporations, universities, senates--that every prince is better than his father, 'of blessed memory, now with God'. If they continue to rise thus transcendently, earth in a little time will be incapable of holding them, and higher heavens must be raised upon the highest heavens for their reception. The lumber of our Italian courts, the most crazy part of which is that which rests upon a red cushion in a gilt chair, with stars and sheep and crosses dangling from it, must be approached as Artaxerxes and Domitian. These automatons, we are told nevertheless, are very condescending. Poor fools who tell us it! ignorant that where on one side is condescension, on the other side must be baseness. The rascals have ruined my physiognomy. I wear an habitual sneer upon my face, God confound them for it! even when I whisper a word of love in the prone ear of my donna.

Salomon. This temper or constitution of mind I am afraid may do injury to your works.

Alfieri. Surely not to all: my satire at least must be the better for it.

Salomon. I think differently. No satire can be excellent where displeasure is expressed with acrimony and vehemence. When satire ceases to smile, it should be momentarily, and for the purpose of inculcating a moral. Juvenal is hardly more a satirist than Lucan: he is indeed a vigorous and bold declaimer, but he stamps too often, and splashes up too much filth. We Italians have no delicacy in wit: we have indeed no conception of it; we fancy we must be weak if we are not offensive. The scream of Pulcinello is imitated more easily than the masterly strokes of Plautus, or the sly insinuations of Catullus and of Flaccus.

Alfieri. We are the least witty of men because we are the most trifling.

Salomon. You would persuade me then that to be witty one must be grave: this is surely a contradiction.

Alfieri. I would persuade you only that banter, pun, and quibble are the properties of light men and shallow capacities; that genuine humour and true wit require a sound and capacious mind, which is always a grave one. Contemptuousness is not incompatible with them: worthless is that man who feels no contempt for the worthless, and weak who treats their emptiness as a thing of weight. At first it may seem a paradox, but it is perfectly true, that the gravest nations have been the wittiest; and in those nations some of the gravest men. In England, Swift and Addison; in Spain, Cervantes. Rabelais and La Fontaine are recorded by their countrymen to have been ***reveurs***. Few men have been graver than Pascal; few have been wittier.

* * * * *

That Shakespeare was gay and pleasurable in conversation I can easily admit; for there never was a mind at once so plastic and so pliant: but without much gravity, could there have been that potency and comprehensiveness of thought, that depth of feeling, that creation of imperishable ideas, that sojourn in the souls of other men? He was amused in his workshop: such was society. But when he left it, he meditated intensely upon those limbs and muscles on which he was about to bestow new action, grace, and majesty; and so great an intensity of meditation must have strongly impressed his whole character.

* * * * *

Salomon. Certainly no race of men upon earth ever was so unwarlike, so indifferent to national dignity and to personal honour, as the Florentines are now: yet in former days a certain pride, arising from a resemblance in their government to that of Athens, excited a vivifying desire of approximation where no danger or loss accompanied it; and Genius was no less confident of his security than of his power. Look from the window. That cottage on the declivity was Dante's: that square and large mansion, with a circular garden before it elevated artificially, was the first scene of Boccaccio's *Decameron*. A boy might stand at an equal distance between them, and break the windows of each with his sling. What idle fabricators of crazy systems will tell me that climate is the creator of genius? The climate of Austria is more regular and more temperate than ours, which I am inclined to believe is the most variable in the whole universe, subject, as you have perceived, to heavy fogs for two months in winter, and to a stifling heat, concentrated within the hills, for five more. Yet a single man of genius hath never appeared in the whole extent of Austria, an extent of several thousand times greater than our city; and this very street has given birth to fifty.

Alfieri. Since the destruction of the republic, Florence has produced only one great man, Galileo, and abandoned him to every indignity that fanaticism and despotism could invent. Extraordinary men, like the stones that are formed in the higher regions of the air, fall upon the earth only to be broken and cast into the furnace. The precursor of Newton lived in the deserts of the moral world, drank water, and ate locusts and wild honey. It was fortunate that his head also was not lopped off: had a singer asked it, instead of a dancer, it would have been.

Salomon. In fact it was; for the fruits of it were shaken down and thrown away: he was forbidden to publish the most important of his discoveries, and the better part of his manuscripts was burned after his death.

Alfieri. Yes, Signor Salomon, those things may rather be called our heads than this knob above the shoulder, of which (as matters stand) we are rather the porters than the proprietors, and which is really the joint concern of barber and dentist.

Salomon. Our thoughts, if they may not rest at home, may wander freely. Delighting in the remoter glories of my native city, I forget at times its humiliation and ignominy. A town so little that the voice of a cabbage-girl in the midst of it may be heard at the extremities, reared within three centuries a greater number of citizens illustrious for their genius than all the remainder of the Continent (excepting her sister Athens) in six thousand years. My ignorance of the Greek forbids me to compare our Dante with Homer. The propriety and force of language and the harmony of verse in the glorious Grecian are quite lost to me. Dante had not only to compose a poem, but in great part a language. Fantastical as the plan of his poem is, and, I will add, uninteresting and uninviting; unimportant, mean, contemptible, as are nine-tenths of his characters and his details, and wearisome as is the scheme of his versification--there are more thoughts highly poetical, there is more reflection, and the nobler properties of mind and intellect are brought into more intense action, not only than in the whole course of French poetry, but also in the whole of continental; nor do I think (I must here also speak with hesitation) that any one drama of Shakespeare contains so many. Smile as you will, Signor

Conte, what must I think of a city where Michel Angelo, Frate Bartolomeo, Ghiberti (who formed them), Guicciardini, and Machiavelli were secondary men? And certainly such were they, if we compare them with Galileo and Boccaccio and Dante.

Alfieri. I smiled from pure delight, which I rarely do; for I take an interest deep and vital in such men, and in those who appreciate them rightly and praise them unreservedly. These are my fellow-citizens: I acknowledge no other; we are of the same tribe, of the same household; I bow to them as being older than myself, and I love them as being better.

Salomon. Let us hope that our Italy is not yet effete. Filangieri died but lately: what think you of him?

Alfieri. If it were possible that I could ever see his statue in a square at Constantinople, though I should be scourged for an idolater, I would kiss the pedestal. As this, however, is less likely than that I should suffer for writing satirically, and as criticism is less likely to mislead me than speculation, I will revert to our former subject.

Indignation and contempt may be expressed in other poems than such as are usually called satires. Filicaia, in his celebrated address to Italy, steers a middle course.

* * * * *

A perfect piece of criticism must exhibit **where** a work is good or bad; **why** it is good or bad; in what degree it is good or bad; must also demonstrate in what manner, and to what extent, the same ideas or reflections have come to others, and, if they be clothed in poetry, why by an apparently slight variation, what in one author is mediocrity, in another is excellence. I have never seen a critic of Florence, or Pisa, or Milan, or Bologna, who did not commend and admire the sonnet of Cassiani on the rape of Proserpine, without a suspicion of its manifold and grave defects.

* * * * *

Does not this describe the devils of our carnival, rather than the majestic brother of Jupiter, at whose side upon asphodel and amaranth the sweet Persephone sits pensively contented, in that deep motionless quiet which mortals pity and which the gods enjoy; rather than him who, under the umbrage of Elysium, gazes at once upon all the beauties that on earth were separated--Helena and Eriphyle, Polyxena and Hermione, Deidamia and Deianira, Leda and Omphale, Atalanta and Cydippe, Laodamia, with her arm round the neck of a fond youth whom she still seems afraid of losing, and, apart, the daughters of Niobe clinging to their parent?

Salomon. These images are better than satires; but continue, in preference to other thoughts or pursuits, the noble career you have entered. Be contented, Signor Conte, with the glory of our first great dramatist, and neglect altogether any inferior one. Why vex and torment yourself about the French? They buzz and are troublesome while they are swarming; but the master will soon hive them. Is the whole nation worth the worst of your tragedies? All the present race of them, all the creatures in the world which excite your indignation, will lie in the grave, while young and old are clapping their hands or beating their bosoms at your **Bruto Primo**. Consider also that kings and emperors should in your estimation be but as grasshoppers and beetles: let them consume a few blades of your clover without molesting them, without bringing them to crawl on you and claw you. The difference between them and men of genius is almost as great as between men of genius and those higher intelligences who act in immediate subordination to the Almighty. Yes, I assert it, without flattery and without fear, the angels are not higher above mortals than you are above the proudest that trample on them.

Alfieri. I believe, sir, you were the first in commending my tragedies.

Salomon. He who first praises a good book becomingly is next in merit to the author.

Alfieri. As a writer and as a man I know my station: if I found in the world five equal to myself, I would walk out of it, not to be jostled.

I must now, Signor Salomon, take my leave of you; for his Eminence my coachman and their Excellencies my horses are waiting.

ROUSSEAU AND MALESHERBES

Rousseau. I am ashamed, sir, of my countrymen: let my humiliation expiate their offence. I wish it had not been a minister of the Gospel who received you with such inhospitality.

Malesherbes. Nothing can be more ardent and more cordial than the expressions with which you greet me, M. Rousseau, on my return from your lakes and mountains.

Rousseau. If the pastor took you for a courtier, I reverence him for his contemptuousness.

Malesherbes. Why so? Indeed you are in the wrong, my friend. No person has a right to treat another with contemptuousness unless he knows him to deserve it. When a courtier enters the house of a pastor in preference to the next, the pastor should partake in the sentiment that induced him, or at least not to be offended to be preferred. A courtier is such at court: in the house of a clergyman he is not a courtier, but a guest. If to be a courtier is offensive, remember that we punish offences where they are committed, where they can be examined, where pleadings can be heard for and against the accused, and where nothing is admitted extraneous from the indictment, excepting what may be adduced in his behalf by witnesses to the general tenor of his character.

Rousseau. Is it really true that the man told you to mount the hayloft if you wished a night's lodging?

Malesherbes. He did: a certain proof that he no more took me to be a courtier than I took him to be. I accepted his offer, and never slept so soundly. Moderate fatigue, the Alpine air, the blaze of a good fire (for I was admitted to it some moments), and a profusion of odoriferous hay, below which a cow was sleeping, subdued my senses, and protracted my slumbers beyond the usual hour.

Rousseau. You have no right, sir, to be the patron and remunerator of inhospitality. Three or four such men as you would corrupt all Switzerland, and prepare it for the fangs of France and Austria. Kings, like hyenas, will always fall upon dead carcasses, although their bellies are full, and although they are conscious that in the end they will tear one another to pieces over them. Why should you prepare their prey? Were your fire and effulgence given you for this? Why, in short, did you thank this churl? Why did you recommend him to his superiors for preferment on the next vacancy?

Malesherbes. I must adopt your opinion of his behaviour in order to answer you satisfactorily. You suppose him inhospitable: what milder or more effectual mode of reproving him, than to make every dish at his table admonish him? If he did evil, have I no authority before me which commands me to render him good for it? Believe me, M. Rousseau, the execution of this command is always accompanied by the heart's applause, and opportunities of obedience are more frequent here than anywhere. Would not you exchange resentment for the contrary feeling, even if religion or duty said nothing about the matter? I am afraid the most philosophical of us are sometimes a little perverse, and will not be so happy as they might be, because the path is pointed out to them, and because he who points it out is wise and powerful. Obstinacy and jealousy, the worst parts of childhood and of manhood, have range enough for their ill humours without the heavens.

Rousseau. Sir, I perceive you are among my enemies. I did not think it; for, whatever may be my faults, I am totally free from suspicion.

Malesherbes. And do not think it now, I entreat you, my good friend.

Rousseau. Courts and society have corrupted the best heart in France, and have perverted the best intellect.

Malesherbes. They have done much evil then.

Rousseau. Answer me, and your own conscience: how could you choose to live among the perfidies of Paris and Versailles?

Malesherbes. Lawyers, and advocates in particular, must live there; philosophers need not. If every honest man thought it requisite to leave those cities, would the inhabitants be the better?

Rousseau. You have entered into intimacies with the members of various administrations, opposite in plans and sentiments, but alike hostile to you, and all of whom, if they could have kept your talents down, would have done it. Finding the thing impossible, they ceased to persecute, and would gladly tempt you under the semblance of friendship and esteem to supplicate for some office, that they might indicate to the world your unworthiness by refusing you: a proof, as you know, quite sufficient and self-evident.

Malesherbes. They will never tempt me to supplicate for anything but justice, and that in behalf of others. I know nothing of parties. If I am acquainted with two persons of opposite sides in politics, I consider them as you consider a watchmaker and a cabinet-maker: one desires to rise by one way, the other by another. Administrations and systems of government would be quite indifferent to those very functionaries and their opponents, who appear the most zealous partisans, if their fortunes and consequence were not affixed to them. Several of these men seem consistent, and indeed are; the reason is, versatility would loosen and detach from them the public esteem and confidence----

Rousseau. By which their girandoles are lighted, their dinners served, their lackeys liveried, and their opera-girls vie in benefit-nights. There is no State in Europe where the least wise have not governed the most wise. We find the light and foolish keeping up with the machinery of government easily and leisurely, just as we see butterflies keep up with carriages at full speed. This is owing in both cases to their levity and their position: the stronger and the more active are left behind. I am resolved to prove that farmers-general are the main causes of the defects in our music.

Malesherbes. Prove it, or anything else, provided that the discussion does not irritate and torment you.

Rousseau. Truth is the object of philosophy.

Malesherbes. Not of philosophers: the display of ingenuity, for the most part, is and always has been it. I must here offer you an opinion of my own, which, if you think well of me, you will pardon, though you should disbelieve its solidity. My opinion then is, that truth is not reasonably the main and ultimate object of philosophy; but that philosophy should seek truth merely as the means of acquiring and of propagating happiness. Truths are simple; wisdom, which is formed by their apposition and application, is concrete: out of this, in its vast varieties, open to our wants and wishes, comes happiness. But the knowledge of all the truths ever yet discovered does not lead immediately to it, nor indeed will ever reach it, unless you make the more important of them bear upon your heart and intellect, and form, as it were, the blood that moves and nurtures them.

Rousseau. I never until now entertained a doubt that truth is the ultimate aim and object of philosophy: no writer has denied it, I think.

Malesherbes. Designedly none may: but when it is agreed that happiness is the chief good, it must also be agreed that the chief wisdom will pursue it; and I have already said, what your own experience cannot but have pointed out to you, that no truth, or series of truths, hypothetically, can communicate or attain it. Come, M. Rousseau, tell me candidly, do you derive no pleasure from a sense of superiority in genius and independence?

Rousseau. The highest, sir, from a consciousness of independence.

Malesherbes. Ingenuous is the epithet we affix to modesty, but modesty often makes men act otherwise than ingenuously: you, for example, now. You are angry at the servility of people, and disgusted at their obtuseness and indifference, on matters of most import to their welfare. If they were equal to you, this anger would cease; but the fire would break out somewhere else, on ground which appears at present sound and level. Voltaire, for instance, is less eloquent than you: but Voltaire is wittier than any man living. This quality----

Rousseau. Is the quality of a buffoon and a courtier. But the buffoon should have most of it, to support his higher dignity.

Malesherbes. Voltaire's is Attic.

Rousseau. If malignity is Attic. Petulance is not wit, although a few grains of wit may be found in petulance: quartz is not gold, although a few grains of gold may be found in quartz. Voltaire is a monkey in mischief, and a spaniel in obsequiousness. He declaims against the cruel and tyrannical; and he kisses the hands of adulteresses who murder their husbands, and of robbers who decimate their gang.

Malesherbes. I will not discuss with you the character of the man, and only that part of the author's on which I spoke. There may be malignity in wit, there cannot be violence. You may irritate and disquiet with it; but it must be by means of a flower or a feather. Wit and humour stand on one side, irony and sarcasm on the other.

Rousseau. They are in near neighbourhood.

Malesherbes. So are the Elysian fields and Tartarus.

Rousseau. Pray, go on: teach me to stand quiet in my stall, while my masters and managers pass by.

Malesherbes. Well then--Pascal argues as closely and methodically; Bossuet is as scientific in the structure of his sentences; Demosthenes, many think, has equal fire, vigour, dexterity: equal selection of topics and equal temperance in treating them, immeasurably as he falls short of you in appeals to the sensibility, and in everything which by way of excellence we usually call genius.

Rousseau. Sir, I see no resemblance between a pleader at the bar, or a haranguer of the populace, and me.

Malesherbes. Certainly his questions are occasional: but one great question hangs in the centre, and high above the rest; and this is, whether the Mother of liberty and civilization shall exist, or whether she shall be extinguished in the bosom of her family. As we often apply to Eloquence and her parts the terms we apply to Architecture and hers, let me do it also, and remark that nothing can be more simple, solid, and symmetrical, nothing more frugal in decoration or more appropriate in distribution, than the apartments of Demosthenes. Yours excel them in space and altitude; your ornaments are equally chaste and beautiful, with more variety and invention, more airiness and light. But why, among the Loves and Graces, does Apollo flay Marsyas?--and why may not the tiara still cover the ears of Midas? Cannot you, who detest kings and courtiers, keep away from them? If I must be with them, let me be in good humour and good spirits. If I will tread upon a Persian carpet, let it at least be in clean shoes.

As the raciest wine makes the sharpest vinegar, so the richest fancies turn the most readily to acrimony. Keep yours, my dear M. Rousseau, from the exposure and heats that generate it. Be contented; enjoy your fine imagination; and do not throw your salad out of window, nor shove your cat off your knee, on hearing it said that Shakespeare has a finer, or that a minister is of opinion that you know more of music than of state. My friend! the quarrels of ingenious men are generally far less reasonable and just, less placable and moderate, than those of the stupid and ignorant. We ought to blush at this: and we should blush yet more deeply if we bring them in as parties to our differences. Let us conquer by kindness; which we cannot do easily or well without communication.

Rousseau. The minister would expel me from his antechamber, and order his valets to buffet me, if I offered him any proposal for the advantage of mankind.

Malesherbes. Call to him, then, from this room, where the valets are civiler. Nature has given you a speaking-trumpet, which neither storm can drown nor enemy can silence. If you esteem him, instruct him; if you despise him, do the same. Surely, you who have much benevolence would not despise any one willingly or unnecessarily. Contempt is for the incorrigible: now, where upon earth is he whom your genius, if rightly and temperately exerted, would not influence and correct?

I never was more flattered or honoured than by your patience in listening to me. Consider me as an old woman who sits by the bedside in your infirmity, who brings you no savoury viand, no exotic fruit, but a basin of whey or a basket of strawberries from your native hills; assures you that what oppressed you was a dream, occasioned by the wrong position in which you lay; opens the window, gives you fresh air, and entreats you to recollect the features of Nature, and to observe (which no man ever did so accurately) their beauty. In your politics you cut down a forest to make a toothpick, and cannot make even that out of it! Do not let us in jurisprudence be like critics in the classics, and change whatever can be changed, right or wrong. No statesman will take your advice. Supposing that any one is liberal in his sentiments and clear-sighted in his views, nevertheless love of power is jealous, and he would rejoice to see you fleeing from persecution or turning to meet it. The very men whom you would benefit will treat you worse. As the ministers of kings wish their masters to possess absolute power that the exercise of it may be delegated to them, which it naturally is from the violence and sloth alternate with despots as with wild beasts, and that they may apprehend no check or control from those who discover their misdemeanours, in like manner the people places more trust in favour than in fortune, and hopes to obtain by subserviency what it never might by election or by chance. Else in free governments, so some are called (for names once given are the last things lost), all minor offices and employments would be assigned by ballot. Each province or canton would present a list annually of such persons in it as are worthy to occupy the local administrations.

To avoid any allusion to the country in which we live, let us take England for example. Is it not absurd, iniquitous, and revolting, that the minister of a church in Yorkshire should be appointed by a lawyer in London, who never knew him, never saw him, never heard from a single one of the parishioners a recommendation of any kind? Is it not more reasonable that a justice of the peace should be chosen by those who have always been witnesses of his integrity?

Rousseau. The king should appoint his ministers, and should invest them with power and splendour; but those ministers should not appoint to any civil or religious place of trust or profit which the community could manifestly fill better. The greater part of offices and dignities should be conferred for a short and stated time, that all might hope to attain and strive to deserve them. Embassies in particular should never exceed one year in Europe, nor consulates two. To the latter office I assign this duration as the more difficult to fulfil properly, from requiring a knowledge of trade, although a slight one, and because those who possess any such knowledge are inclined for the greater part to turn it to their own account, which a consul ought by no means to do. Frequent election of representatives and of civil officers in the subordinate employments would remove most causes of discontent in the people, and of instability in kingly power. Here is a lottery in which every one is sure of a prize, if not for himself, at least for somebody in his family or among his friends; and the ticket would be fairly paid for out of the taxes.

Malesherbes. So it appears to me. What other system can present so obviously to the great mass of the people the two principal piers and buttresses of government, tangible interest and reasonable hope? No danger of any kind can arise from it, no antipathies, no divisions, no imposture of demagogues, no caprice of despots. On the contrary, many and great advantages in places which at the first survey do not appear to border on it. At present, the best of the English juridical institutions, that of justices of the peace, is viewed with diffidence and distrust. Elected as they would be, and increased in number, the whole judicature, civil and criminal, might be confided to them, and their labours be not only not aggravated but diminished. Suppose them in four divisions to meet at four places in every county once in twenty days, and to possess the power of imposing a fine not exceeding two hundred francs on every cause implying oppression, and one not exceeding fifty on such as they should unanimously declare frivolous.

Rousseau. Few would become attorneys, and those from among the indigent.

Malesherbes. Almost the greatest evil that exists in the world, moral or physical, would be removed. A second appeal might be made in the following session; a third could only come before Parliament, and this alone by means of attorneys, the number of whom altogether would not exceed the number of coroners; for in England there are as many who cut their own throats as who would cut their own purses.

Rousseau. The famous **trial by jury** would cease: this would disgust the English.

Malesherbes. The number of justices would be much augmented: nearly all those who now are jurymen would enjoy this rank and dignity, and would be flattered by sitting on the same bench with the first gentlemen of the land.

Rousseau. What number would sit?

Malesherbes. Three or five in the first instance; five or seven in the second--as the number of causes should permit.

Rousseau. The laws of England are extremely intricate and perplexed:

such men would be puzzled.

Malesherbes. Such men having no interest in the perplexity, but on the contrary an interest in unravelling it, would see such laws corrected. Intricate as they are, questions on those which are the most so are usually referred by the judges themselves to private arbitration; of which my plan, I conceive, has all the advantages, united to those of open and free discussion among men of unperverted sense, and unbiased by professional hopes and interests. The different courts of law in England cost about seventy millions of francs annually. On my system, the justices or judges would receive five-and-twenty francs daily; as the **special jurymen** do now, without any sense of shame or impropriety, however rich they may be: such being the established practice.

Rousseau. Seventy millions! seventy millions!

Malesherbes. There are attorneys and conveyancers in London who gain one hundred thousand francs a year, and advocates more. The chancellor----

Rousseau. The Celeno of these harpies----

Malesherbes. Nets above one million, and is greatly more than an archbishop in the Church, scattering preferment in Cumberland and Cornwall from his bench at Westminster.

Rousseau. Absurdities and enormities are great in proportion to custom or insuetude. If we had lived from childhood with a boa constrictor, we should think it no more a monster than a canary-bird. The sum you mentioned, of seventy millions, is incredible.

Malesherbes. In this estimate the expense of letters by the post, and of journeys made by the parties, is not and cannot be included.

Rousseau. The whole machine of government, civil and religious, ought never to bear upon the people with a weight so oppressive. I do not add the national defence, which being principally naval is more costly, nor institutions for the promotion of the arts, which in a country like England ought to be liberal. But such an expenditure should nearly suffice for these also, in time of peace. Religion and law indeed should cost nothing: at present the one hangs property, the other quarters it. I am confounded at the profusion. I doubt whether the Romans expended so much in that year's war which dissolved the Carthaginian empire, and left them masters of the universe. What is certain, and what is better, it did not cost a tenth of it to colonize Pennsylvania, in whose forests the cradle of freedom is suspended, and where the eye of philanthropy, tired with tears and vigils, may wander and may rest. Your system, or rather your arrangement of one already established, pleases me. Ministers would only lose thereby that portion of their possessions which they give away to needy relatives, unworthy dependants, or the requisite supporters of their authority and power.

Malesherbes. On this plan, no such supporters would be necessary, no such dependants could exist, and no such relatives could be disappointed. Beside, the conflicts of their opponents must be periodical, weak, and irregular.

Rousseau. The craving for the rich carrion would be less keen; the zeal of opposition, as usual, would be measured by the stomach, whereon hope and overlooking have always a strong influence.

Malesherbes. My excellent friend, do not be offended with me for an ingenuous and frank confession: promise me your pardon.

Rousseau. You need none.

Malesherbes. Promise it, nevertheless.

Rousseau. You have said nothing, done nothing, which could in any way displease me.

Malesherbes. You grant me, then, a bill of indemnity for what I may have undertaken with a good intention since we have been together?

Rousseau. Willingly.

Malesherbes. I fell into your views, I walked along with you side by side, merely to occupy your mind, which I perceived was agitated.

In compliance with your humour, to engage your fancy, to divert it awhile from Switzerland, by which you appear and partly on my account to be offended, I began with reflections upon England: I raised up another cloud in the region of them, light enough to be fantastic and diaphanous, and to catch some little irradiation from its western sun. Do not run after it farther; it has vanished already. Consider: the three great nations----

Rousseau. Pray, which are those?

Malesherbes. I cannot in conscience give the palm to the Hottentots, the Greenlanders, or the Hurons: I meant to designate those who united to empire the most social virtue and civil freedom. Athens, Rome, and England have received on the subject of government elaborate treatises from their greatest men. You have reasoned more dispassionately and profoundly on it than Plato has done, or probably than Cicero, led away as he often is by the authority of those who are inferior to himself: but do you excel Aristoteles in calm and patient investigation? Or, think you, are your reading and range of thought more extensive than Harrington's and Milton's? Yet what effect have the political works of these marvellous men produced upon the world?--what effect upon any one state, any one city, any one hamlet? A clerk in office, an accountant, a gauger of small beer, a songwriter for a tavern dinner, produces more. He thrusts his rags into the hole whence the wind comes, and sleeps soundly. While you and I are talking about elevations and proportions, pillars and pilasters, architraves and friezes, the buildings we should repair are falling to the earth, and the materials for their restoration are in the quarry.

Rousseau. I could answer you: but my mind has certain moments of repose, or rather of oscillation, which I would not for the world disturb. Music, eloquence, friendship, bring and prolong them.

Malesherbes. Enjoy them, my dear friend, and convert them if possible to months and years. It is as much at your arbitration on what theme you shall meditate, as in what meadow you shall botanize; and you have as much at your option the choice of your thoughts, as of the keys in your harpsichord.

Rousseau. If this were true, who could be unhappy?

Malesherbes. Those of whom it is not true. Those who from want of practice cannot manage their thoughts, who have few to select from, and who, because of their sloth or of their weakness, do not roll away the heaviest from before them.

LUCULLUS AND CAESAR

Caesar. Lucius Lucullus, I come to you privately and unattended for reasons which you will know; confiding, I dare not say in your friendship, since no service of mine toward you hath deserved it, but in your generous and disinterested love of peace. Hear me on. Cneius Pompeius, according to the report of my connexions in the city, had, on the instant of my leaving it for the province, begun to solicit his dependants to strip me ignominiously of authority. Neither vows nor affinity can bind him. He would degrade the father of his wife; he would humiliate his own children, the unoffending, the unborn; he would poison his own nascent love--at the suggestion of Ambition. Matters are now brought so far, that either he or I must submit to a reverse of fortune; since no concession can assuage his malice, divert his envy, or gratify his cupidity. No sooner could I raise myself up, from the consternation and stupefaction into which the certainty of these reports had thrown me, than I began to consider in what manner my own private afflictions might become the least noxious to the republic. Into whose arms, then, could I throw myself more naturally and more securely, to whose bosom could I commit and consign more sacredly the hopes and destinies of our beloved country, than his who laid down power in the midst of its enjoyments, in the vigour of youth, in the pride of triumph, when Dignity solicited, when Friendship urged, entreated, supplicated, and when Liberty herself invited and beckoned to him from the senatorial order and from the curule chair? Betrayed and abandoned by those we had confided in, our next friendship, if ever our hearts receive any, or if any will venture in those places of desolation, flies forward instinctively to what is most contrary and dissimilar. Caesar is hence the visitant of Lucullus.

Lucullus. I had always thought Pompeius more moderate and more reserved than you represent him, Caius Julius; and yet I am considered in general, and surely you also will consider me, but little liable to be prepossessed by him.

Caesar. Unless he may have ingratiated himself with you recently, by the administration of that worthy whom last winter his partisans dragged before the Senate, and forced to assert publicly that you and Cato had instigated a party to circumvent and murder him; and whose carcass, a few days afterward, when it had been announced that he had died by a natural death, was found covered with bruises, stabs, and dislocations.

Lucullus. You bring much to my memory which had quite slipped out of it, and I wonder that it could make such an impression on yours. A proof to me that the interest you take in my behalf began earlier than your delicacy will permit you to acknowledge. You are fatigued, which I ought to have perceived before.

Caesar. Not at all; the fresh air has given me life and alertness: I feel it upon my cheek even in the room.

Lucullus. After our dinner and sleep, we will spend the remainder of the day on the subject of your visit.

Caesar. Those Ethiopian slaves of yours shiver with cold upon the mountain here; and truly I myself was not insensible to the change of climate, in the way from Mutina.

What white bread! I never found such even at Naples or Capua. This Formian wine (which I prefer to the Chian), how exquisite!

Lucullus. Such is the urbanity of Caesar, even while he bites his lip with displeasure. How! surely it bleeds! Permit me to examine the cup.

Caesar. I believe a jewel has fallen out of the rim in the carriage: the gold is rough there.

Lucullus. Marcipor, let me never see that cup again! No answer, I desire. My guest pardons heavier faults. Mind that dinner be prepared for us shortly.

Caesar. In the meantime, Lucullus, if your health permits it, shall we walk a few paces round the villa? for I have not seen anything of the kind before.

Lucullus. The walls are double; the space between them two feet: the materials for the most part earth and straw. Two hundred slaves, and about as many mules and oxen, brought the beams and rafters up the mountain; my architects fixed them at once in their places: every part was ready, even the wooden nails. The roof is thatched, you see.

Caesar. Is there no danger that so light a material should be carried off by the winds, on such an eminence?

Lucullus. None resists them equally well.

Caesar. On this immensely high mountain, I should be apprehensive of the lightning, which the poets, and I think the philosophers too, have told us strikes the highest.

Lucullus. The poets are right; for whatever is received as truth is truth in poetry; and a fable may illustrate like a fact. But the philosophers are wrong, as they generally are, even in the commonest things; because they seldom look beyond their own tenets, unless through captiousness, and because they argue more than they meditate, and display more than they examine. Archimedes and Euclid are, in my opinion, after our Epicurus, the worthiest of the name, having kept apart to the demonstrable, the practical, and the useful. Many of the rest are good writers and good disputants; but unfaithful suitors of simple science, boasters of their acquaintance with gods and goddesses, plagiarists and impostors. I had forgotten my roof, although it is composed of much the same materials as the philosophers'. Let the lightning fall: one handful of silver, or less, repairs the damage.

Caesar. Impossible! nor indeed one thousand, nor twenty, if those tapestries and pictures are consumed.

Lucullus. True; but only the thatch would burn. For, before the baths were tessellated, I filled the area with alum and water, and soaked the timbers and laths for many months, and covered them afterward with alum in powder, by means of liquid glue. Mithridates taught me this. Having in vain attacked with combustibles a wooden tower, I took it by stratagem, and found within it a mass of alum, which, if a great hurry had not been observed by us among the enemy in the attempt to conceal it, would have escaped our notice. I never scrupled to extort the truth from my prisoners; but my instruments were purple robes and plate, and the only wheel in my armoury destined to such purposes was the wheel of Fortune.

Caesar. I wish, in my campaigns, I could have equalled your clemency and humanity; but the Gauls are more uncertain, fierce, and perfidious than the wildest tribes of Caucasus; and our policy cannot be carried with us, it must be formed upon the spot. They love you, not for abstaining from hurting them, but for ceasing; and they embrace you only at two seasons--when stripes are fresh, or when stripes are imminent. Elsewhere, I hope to become the rival of Lucullus in this admirable part of virtue.

I shall never build villas, because--but what are your proportions? Surely the edifice is extremely low.

Lucullus. There is only one floor; the height of the apartments is twenty feet to the cornice, five above it; the breadth is twenty-five, the length forty. The building, as you perceive, is quadrangular: three sides contain four rooms each; the other has many partitions and two stories, for domestics and offices. Here is my salt-bath.

Caesar. A bath, indeed, for all the Nereids named by Hesiod, with room enough for the Tritons and their herds and horses.

Lucullus. Here stand my two cows. Their milk is brought to me with its warmth and froth; for it loses its salubrity both by repose and by motion. Pardon me, Caesar: I shall appear to you to have forgotten that I am not conducting Marcus Varro.

Caesar. You would convert him into Cacus: he would drive them off. What beautiful beasts! how sleek and white and cleanly! I never saw any like them, excepting when we sacrifice to Jupiter the stately leader from the pastures of the Clitumnus.

Lucullus. Often do I make a visit to these quiet creatures, and with no less pleasure than in former days to my horses. Nor indeed can I much wonder that whole nations have been consentaneous in treating them as objects of devotion: the only thing wonderful is that gratitude seems to have acted as powerfully and extensively as fear;

indeed, more extensively, for no object of worship whatever has attracted so many worshippers. Where Jupiter has one, the cow has ten: she was venerated before he was born, and will be when even the carvers have forgotten him.

Caesar. Unwillingly should I see it; for the character of our gods hath formed the character of our nation. Serapis and Isis have stolen in among them within our memory, and others will follow, until at last Saturn will not be the only one emasculated by his successor. What can be more august than our rites? The first dignitaries of the republic are emulous to administer them: nothing of low or venal has any place in them; nothing pusillanimous, nothing unsocial and austere. I speak of them as they were; before Superstition woke up again from her slumber, and caught to her bosom with maternal love the alluvial monsters of the Nile. Philosophy, never fit for the people, had entered the best houses, and the image of Epicurus had taken the place of the Lemures. But men cannot bear to be deprived long together of anything they are used to, not even of their fears; and, by a reaction of the mind appertaining to our nature, new stimulants were looked for, not on the side of pleasure, where nothing new could be expected or imagined, but on the opposite. Irreligion is followed by fanaticism, and fanaticism by irreligion, alternately and perpetually.

Lucullus. The religion of our country, as you observe, is well adapted to its inhabitants. Our progenitor, Mars, hath Venus recumbent on his breast and looking up to him, teaching us that pleasure is to be sought in the bosom of valour and by the means of war. No great alteration, I think, will ever be made in our rites and ceremonies--the best and most imposing that could be collected from all nations, and uniting them to us by our complacence in adopting them. The gods themselves may change names, to flatter new power: and, indeed, as we degenerate, Religion will accommodate herself to our propensities and desires. Our heaven is now popular: it will become monarchal; not without a crowded court, as befits it, of apparitors and satellites and minions of both sexes, paid and caressed for carrying to their stern, dark-bearded master prayers and supplications. Altars must be strown with broken minds, and incense rise amid abject aspirations. Gods will be found unfit for their places; and it is not impossible that, in the ruin imminent from our contentions for power, and in the necessary extinction both of ancient families and of generous sentiments, our consular fasces may become the water-sprinklers of some upstart priesthood, and that my son may apply for lustration to the son of my groom. The interest of such men requires that the spirit of arms and of arts be extinguished. They will predicate peace, that the people may be tractable to them; but a religion altogether pacific is the fomenter of wars and the nurse of crimes, alluring Sloth from within and Violence from afar. If ever it should prevail among the Romans, it must prevail alone: for nations more vigorous and energetic will invade them, close upon them, trample them under foot; and the name of Roman, which is now the most glorious, will become the most opprobrious upon earth.

Caesar. The time, I hope, may be distant; for next to my own name I hold my country's.

Lucullus. Mine, not coming from Troy or Ida, is lower in my estimation: I place my country's first.

You are surveying the little lake beside us. It contains no fish, birds never alight on it, the water is extremely pure and cold; the walk round is pleasant, not only because there is always a gentle breeze from it, but because the turf is fine and the surface of the mountain on this summit is perfectly on a level to a great extent in length--not a trifling advantage to me, who walk often and am weak. I have no alley, no garden, no enclosure; the park is in the vale below, where a brook supplies the ponds, and where my servants are lodged;

for here I have only twelve in attendance.

Caesar. What is that so white, towards the Adriatic?

Lucullus. The Adriatic itself. Turn round and you may descry the Tuscan Sea. Our situation is reported to be among the highest of the Apennines. Marcipor has made the sign to me that dinner is ready. Pass this way.

Caesar. What a library is here! Ah, Marcus Tullius! I salute thy image. Why frownest thou upon me--collecting the consular robe and uplifting the right arm, as when Rome stood firm again, and Catiline fled before thee?

Lucullus. Just so; such was the action the statuary chose, as adding a new endearment to the memory of my absent friend.

Caesar. Sylla, who honoured you above all men, is not here.

Lucullus. I have his *Commentaries*: he inscribed them, as you know, to me. Something even of our benefactors may be forgotten, and gratitude be unreproved.

Caesar. The impression on that couch, and the two fresh honeysuckles in the leaves of those two books, would show, even to a stranger, that this room is peculiarly the master's. Are they sacred?

Lucullus. To me and Caesar.

Caesar. I would have asked permission----

Lucullus. Caius Julius, you have nothing to ask of Polybius and

Thucydides; nor of Xenophon, the next to them on the table.

Caesar. Thucydides! the most generous, the most unprejudiced, the most sagacious, of historians. Now, Lucullus, you whose judgment in style is more accurate than any other Roman's, do tell me whether a commander, desirous of writing his **Commentaries**, could take to himself a more perfect model than Thucydides?

Lucullus. Nothing is more perfect, nor ever will be: the scholar of Pericles, the master of Demosthenes, the equal of the one in military science, and of the other not the inferior in civil and forensic; the calm dispassionate judge of the general by whom he was defeated, his defender, his encomiast. To talk of such men is conducive not only to virtue but to health.

* * * * *

This other is my dining-room. You expect the dishes.

Caesar. I misunderstood--I fancied----

Lucullus. Repose yourself, and touch with the ebony wand, beside you, the sphinx on either of those obelisks, right or left.

Caesar. Let me look at them first.

Lucullus. The contrivance was intended for one person, or two at most, desirous of privacy and quiet. The blocks of jasper in my pair, and of porphyry in yours, easily yield in their grooves, each forming one partition. There are four, containing four platforms. The lower holds four dishes, such as sucking forest-boars, venison, hares, tunnies, sturgeons, which you will find within; the upper three, eight each, but diminutive. The confectionery is brought separately, for the steam would spoil it, if any should escape. The melons are in the snow, thirty feet under us: they came early this morning from a place in the vicinity of Luni, travelling by night.

Caesar. I wonder not at anything of refined elegance in Lucullus; but really here Antiochia and Alexandria seem to have cooked for us, and magicians to be our attendants.

Lucullus. The absence of slaves from our repast is the luxury, for Marcipor alone enters, and he only when I press a spring with my foot or wand. When you desire his appearance, touch that chalcedony just before you.

Caesar. I eat quick and rather plentifully; yet the valetudinarian (excuse my rusticity, for I rejoice at seeing it) appears to equal the traveller in appetite, and to be contented with one dish.

Lucullus. It is milk: such, with strawberries, which ripen on the Apennines many months in continuance, and some other berries of sharp and grateful flavour, has been my only diet since my first residence here. The state of my health requires it; and the habitude of nearly three months renders this food not only more commodious to my studies and more conducive to my sleep, but also more agreeable to my palate than any other.

Caesar. Returning to Rome or Baiae, you must domesticate and tame them. The cherries you introduced from Pontus are now growing in Cisalpine and Transalpine Gaul; and the largest and best in the world, perhaps, are upon the more sterile side of Lake Larius.

Lucullus. There are some fruits, and some virtues, which require a harsh soil and bleak exposure for their perfection.

Caesar. In such a profusion of viands, and so savoury, I perceive no odour.

Lucullus. A flue conducts heat through the compartments of the obelisks; and, if you look up, you may observe that those gilt roses, between the astragals in the cornice, are prominent from it half a span. Here is an aperture in the wall, between which and the outer is a perpetual current of air. We are now in the dog-days; and I have never felt in the whole summer more heat than at Rome in many days of March.

Caesar. Usually you are attended by troops of domestics and of dinner-friends, not to mention the learned and scientific, nor your own family, your attachment to which, from youth upward, is one of the higher graces in your character. Your brother was seldom absent from you.

Lucullus. Marcus was coming; but the vehement heats along the Arno, in which valley he has a property he never saw before, inflamed his blood, and he now is resting for a few days at Faesulae, a little town destroyed by Sylla within our memory, who left it only air and water, the best in Tuscany. The health of Marcus, like mine, has been declining for several months: we are running our last race against each other, and never was I, in youth along the Tiber, so anxious of first reaching the goal. I would not outlive him: I should reflect too painfully on earlier days, and look forward too despondently on future. As for friends, lampreys and turbots beget them, and they spawn not amid the solitude of the Apennines. To dine in company with more than two is a Gaulish and German thing. I can hardly bring myself to believe that I have eaten in concert with twenty; so barbarous and herdlike a practice does not now appeal to me--such an incentive to drink much and talk loosely; not to add, such a necessity to speak loud, which is clownish and odious in the extreme. On this mountain summit I hear no noises, no voices, not even of salutation; we have no flies about us, and scarcely an insect or reptile.

Caesar. Your amiable son is probably with his uncle: is he well?

Lucullus. Perfectly. He was indeed with my brother in his intended visit to me; but Marcus, unable to accompany him hither, or superintend his studies in the present state of his health, sent him directly to his Uncle Cato at Tusculum--a man fitter than either of us to direct his education, and preferable to any, excepting yourself and Marcus Tullius, in eloquence and urbanity.

Caesar. Cato is so great, that whoever is greater must be the happiest and first of men.

Lucullus. That any such be still existing, O Julius, ought to excite no groan from the breast of a Roman citizen. But perhaps I wrong you; perhaps your mind was forced reluctantly back again, on your past animosities and contests in the Senate.

Caesar. I revere him, but cannot love him.

Lucullus. Then, Caius Julius, you groaned with reason; and I would pity rather than reprove you.

On the ceiling at which you are looking, there is no gilding, and little painting--a mere trellis of vines bearing grapes, and the heads, shoulders, and arms rising from the cornice only, of boys and girls climbing up to steal them, and scrambling for them: nothing overhead; no giants tumbling down, no Jupiter thundering, no Mars and Venus caught at mid-day, no river-gods pouring out their urns upon us; for, as I think nothing so insipid as a flat ceiling, I think nothing so absurd as a storied one. Before I was aware, and without my participation, the painter had adorned that of my bedchamber with a golden shower, bursting from varied and irradiated clouds. On my expostulation, his excuse was that he knew the Danae of Scopas, in a recumbent posture, was to occupy the centre of the room. The walls, behind the tapestry and pictures, are quite rough. In forty-three days the whole fabric was put together and habitable.

The wine has probably lost its freshness: will you try some other?

Caesar. Its temperature is exact; its flavour exquisite. Latterly I have never sat long after dinner, and am curious to pass through the other apartments, if you will trust me.

Lucullus. I attend you.

Caesar. Lucullus, who is here? What figure is that on the poop of the vessel? Can it be----

Lucullus. The subject was dictated by myself; you gave it.

Caesar. Oh, how beautifully is the water painted! How vividly the sun strikes against the snows on Taurus! The grey temples and pierhead of Tarsus catch it differently, and the monumental mound on the left is half in shade. In the countenance of those pirates I did not observe such diversity, nor that any boy pulled his father back: I did not indeed mark them or notice them at all.

Lucullus. The painter in this fresco, the last work finished, had dissatisfied me in one particular. 'That beautiful young face,' said I, 'appears not to threaten death.'

'Lucius,' he replied, 'if one muscle were moved it were not Caesar's: beside, he said it jokingly, though resolved.'

'I am contented with your apology, Antipho; but what are you doing now? for you never lay down or suspend your pencil, let who will talk and argue. The lines of that smaller face in the distance are the same.'

'Not the same,' replied he, 'nor very different: it smiles, as surely the goddess must have done at the first heroic act of her descendant.'

Caesar. In her exultation and impatience to press forward she seems to forget that she is standing at the extremity of the shell, which rises up behind out of the water; and she takes no notice of the terror on the countenance of this Cupid who would detain her, nor of this who is flying off and looking back. The reflection of the shell has given a warmer hue below the knee; a long streak of yellow light in the horizon is on the level of her bosom, some of her hair is almost lost in it; above her head on every side is the pure azure of the heavens.

Oh! and you would not have shown me this? You, among whose primary studies is the most perfect satisfaction of your guests!

Lucullus. In the next apartment are seven or eight other pictures from our history.

There are no more: what do you look for?

Caesar. I find not among the rest any descriptive of your own exploits. Ah, Lucullus! there is no surer way of making them remembered.

This, I presume by the harps in the two corners, is the music-room.

Lucullus. No, indeed; nor can I be said to have one here; for I love best the music of a single instrument, and listen to it willingly at all times, but most willingly while I am reading. At such seasons a voice or even a whisper disturbs me; but music refreshes my brain when I have read long, and strengthen it from the beginning. I find also that if I write anything in poetry (a youthful propensity still remaining), it gives rapidity and variety and brightness to my ideas. On ceasing, I command a fresh measure and instrument, or another voice; which is to the mind like a change of posture, or of air to the body. My heal this benefited by the gentle play thus opened to the most delicate of the fibres.

Caesar. Let me augur that a disorder so tractable may be soon removed. What is it thought to be?

Lucullus. I am inclined to think, and my physician did not long attempt to persuade me of the contrary, that the ancient realms of Aeaetes have supplied me with some other plants than the cherry, and such as I should be sorry to see domesticated here in Italy.

Caesar. The gods forbid! Anticipate better things! The reason of Lucullus is stronger than the medicaments of Mithridates; but why not use them too? Let nothing be neglected. You may reasonably hope for many years of life: your mother still enjoys it.

Lucullus. To stand upon one's guard against Death exasperates her malice and protracts our sufferings.

Caesar. Rightly and gravely said: but your country at this time cannot do well without you.

Lucullus. The bowl of milk, which to-day is presented to me, will shortly be presented to my Manes.

Caesar. Do you suspect the hand?

Lucullus. I will not suspect a Roman: let us converse no more about it.

Caesar. It is the only subject on which I am resolved never to think, as relates to myself. Life may concern us, death not; for in death we neither can act nor reason, we neither can persuade nor command; and our statues are worth more than we are, let them be but wax.

* * * * *

Lucullus. From being for ever in action, for ever in contention, and from excelling in them all other mortals, what advantage derive we? I would not ask what satisfaction, what glory? The insects have more activity than ourselves, the beasts more strength, even inert matter more firmness and stability; the gods alone more goodness. To the exercise of this every country lies open; and neither I eastward nor you westward have found any exhausted by contests for it.

Must we give men blows because they will not look at us? or chain them to make them hold the balance evener?

Do not expect to be acknowledged for what you are, much less for what you would be; since no one can well measure a great man but upon the bier. There was a time when the most ardent friend to Alexander of Macedon would have embraced the partisan for his enthusiasm, who should have compared him with Alexander of Pherae. It must have been at a splendid feast, and late at it, when Scipio should have been raised to an equality with Romulus, or Cato with Curius. It has been whispered in my ear, after a speech of Cicero, 'If he goes on so, he will tread down the sandal of Marcus Antonius in the long run, and perhaps leave Hortensius behind.' Officers of mine, speaking about you, have exclaimed with admiration: 'He fights like Cinna.' Think, Caius Julius (for you have been instructed to think both as a poet and as a philosopher), that among the hundred hands of Ambition, to whom we may attribute them more properly than to Briareus, there is not one which holds anything firmly. In the precipitancy of her course, what appears great is small, and what appears small is great. Our estimate of men is apt to be as inaccurate and inexact as that of things, or more. Wishing to have all on our side, we often leave those we should keep by us, run after those we should avoid, and call importunately on others who sit quiet and will not come. We cannot at once catch the applause of the vulgar and expect the approbation of the wise. What are parties? Do men really great ever enter into them? Are they not ball-courts, where ragged adventurers strip and strive, and where dissolute youths abuse one another, and challenge and game and wager? If you and I cannot quite divest ourselves of infirmities and passions, let us think, however, that there is enough in us to be divided into two portions, and let us keep the upper undisturbed and pure. A part of Olympus itself lies in dreariness and in clouds, variable and stormy; but it is not the highest: there the gods govern. Your soul is large enough to embrace your country: all other affection is for less objects, and less men are capable of it. Abandon, O Caesar! such thoughts and wishes as now agitate and propel you: leave them to mere men of the marsh, to fat hearts and miry intellects. Fortunate may we call ourselves to have been born in an age so productive of eloquence, so rich in erudition. Neither of us would be excluded, or hooted at, on canvassing for these honours. He who can think dispassionately and deeply as I do, is great as I am; none other. But his opinions are at freedom to diverge from mine, as mine are from his; and indeed, on recollection, I never loved those most who thought with me, but those rather who deemed my sentiments worth discussion, and who corrected me with frankness and affability.

Caesar. Lucullus, you perhaps have taken the wiser and better part, certainly the pleasanter. I cannot argue with you: I would gladly hear one who could, but you again more gladly. I should think unworthily of you if I thought you capable of yielding or receding. I do not even ask you to keep our conversation long a secret, so greatly does it preponderate in your favour; so much more of gentleness, of eloquence, and of argument. I came hither with one soldier, avoiding the cities, and sleeping at the villa of a confidential friend. To-night I sleep in yours, and, if your dinner does not disturb me, shall sleep soundly. You go early to rest I know.

Lucullus. Not, however, by daylight. Be assured, Caius Julius, that greatly as your discourse afflicts me, no part of it shall escape my lips. If you approach the city with arms, with arms I meet you; then your denouncer and enemy, at present your host and confidant.

Caesar. I shall conquer you.

Lucullus. That smile would cease upon it: you sigh already.

Caesar. Yes, Lucullus, if I am oppressed I shall overcome my oppressor: I know my army and myself. A sigh escaped me, and many more will follow; but one transport will rise amid them, when, vanquisher of my enemies and avenger of my dignity, I press again the hand of Lucullus, mindful of this day.

EPICURUS, LEONTION, AND TERNISSA

Ternissa. The broad and billowy summits of yon monstrous trees, one would imagine, were made for the storms to rest upon when they are tired of raving. And what bark! It occurs to me, Epicurus, that I have rarely seen climbing plants attach themselves to these trees, as they do to the oak, the maple, the beech, and others.

Leontion. If your remark be true, perhaps the resinous are not embraced by them so frequently because they dislike the odour of the resin, or some other property of the juices; for they, too, have their affections and antipathies no less than countries and their climes.

Ternissa. For shame! what would you with me?

Epicurus. I would not interrupt you while you were speaking, nor while Leontion was replying; this is against my rules and practice. Having now ended, kiss me, Ternissa!

Ternissa. Impudent man! in the name of Pallas, why should I kiss you?

Epicurus. Because you expressed hatred.

Ternissa. Do we kiss when we hate?

Epicurus. There is no better end of hating. The sentiment should not exist one moment; and if the hater gives a kiss on being ordered to do it, even to a tree or a stone, that tree or stone becomes the monument of a fault extinct.

Ternissa. I promise you I never will hate a tree again.

Epicurus. I told you so.

Leontion. Nevertheless, I suspect, my Ternissa, you will often be surprised into it. I was very near saying, 'I hate these rude square stones!' Why did you leave them here, Epicurus?

Epicurus. It is true, they are the greater part square, and seem to have been cut out in ancient times for plinths and columns; they are also rude. Removing the smaller, that I might plant violets and cyclamens and convolvuluses and strawberries, and such other herbs as grow willingly in dry places, I left a few of these for seats, a few for tables and for couches.

Leontion. Delectable couches!

Epicurus. Laugh as you may, they will become so when they are covered with moss and ivy, and those other two sweet plants whose names I do not remember to have found in any ancient treatise, but which I fancy I have heard Theophrastus call 'Leontion' and 'Ternissa'.

Ternissa. The bold, insidious, false creature!

Epicurus. What is that volume, may I venture to ask, Leontion? Why do you blush?

Leontion. I do not blush about it.

Epicurus. You are offended, then, my dear girl.

Leontion. No, nor offended. I will tell you presently what it contains. Account to me first for your choice of so strange a place to walk in: a broad ridge, the summit and one side barren, the other a wood of rose-laurels impossible to penetrate. The worst of all is, we can see nothing of the city or the Parthenon, unless from the very top.

Epicurus. The place commands, in my opinion, a most perfect view.

Leontion. Of what, pray?

Epicurus. Of itself; seeming to indicate that we, Leontion, who philosophize, should do the same.

Leontion. Go on, go on! say what you please: I will not hate anything yet. Why have you torn up by the root all these little mountain ash-trees? This is the season of their beauty: come, Ternissa, let us make ourselves necklaces and armlets, such as may captivate old Sylvanus and Pan; you shall have your choice. But why have you torn them up?

Epicurus. On the contrary, they were brought hither this morning. Sosimenes is spending large sums of money on an olive-ground, and has uprooted some hundreds of them, of all ages and sizes. I shall cover the rougher part of the hill with them, setting the clematis and vine and honeysuckle against them, to unite them.

Ternissa. Oh, what a pleasant thing it is to walk in the green light of the vine trees, and to breathe the sweet odour of their invisible flowers!

Epicurus. The scent of them is so delicate that it requires a sigh to inhale it; and this, being accompanied and followed by enjoyment, renders the fragrance so exquisite. Ternissa, it is this, my sweet friend, that made you remember the green light of the foliage, and think of the invisible flowers as you would of some blessing from heaven.

Ternissa. I see feathers flying at certain distances just above the middle of the promontory: what can they mean?

Epicurus. Cannot you imagine them to be the feathers from the wings of Zethes and Calaeis, who came hither out of Thrace to behold the favourite haunts of their mother Oreithyia? From the precipice that hangs over the sea a few paces from the pinasters she is reported to have been carried off by Boreas; and these remains of the primeval forest have always been held sacred on that belief.

Leontion. The story is an idle one.

Ternissa. Oh no, Leontion! the story is very true.

Leontion. Indeed!

Ternissa. I have heard not only odes, but sacred and most ancient hymns upon it; and the voice of Boreas is often audible here, and the screams of Oreithyia.

Leontion. The feathers, then, really may belong to Calaeis and Zethes.

Ternissa. I don't believe it; the winds would have carried them away.

Leontion. The gods, to manifest their power, as they often do by miracles, could as easily fix a feather eternally on the most tempestuous promontory, as the mark of their feet upon the flint.

Ternissa. They could indeed; but we know the one to a certainty, and have no such authority for the other. I have seen these pinasters from the extremity of the Piraeus, and have heard mention of the altar raised to Boreas: where is it?

Epicurus. As it stands in the centre of the platform, we cannot see it from hence; there is the only piece of level ground in the place.

Leontion. Ternissa intends the altar to prove the truth of the story.

Epicurus. Ternissa is slow to admit that even the young can deceive, much less the old; the gay, much less the serious.

Leontion. It is as wise to moderate our belief as our desires.

Epicurus. Some minds require much belief, some thrive on little. Rather an exuberance of it is feminine and beautiful. It acts differently on different hearts; it troubles some, it consoles others; in the generous it is the nurse of tenderness and kindness, of heroism and self-devotion; in the ungenerous it fosters pride, impatience of contradiction and appeal, and, like some waters, what it finds a dry stick or hollow straw, it leaves a stone.

Ternissa. We want it chiefly to make the way of death an easy one.

Epicurus. There is no easy path leading out of life, and few are the easy ones that lie within it. I would adorn and smoothen the declivity, and make my residence as commodious as its situation and dimensions may allow; but principally I would cast under-foot the empty fear of death.

Ternissa. Oh, how can you?

Epicurus. By many arguments already laid down: then by thinking that some perhaps, in almost every age, have been timid and delicate as Ternissa; and yet have slept soundly, have felt no parent's or friend's tear upon their faces, no throb against their breasts: in short, have been in the calmest of all possible conditions, while those around were in the most deplorable and desperate.

Ternissa. It would pain me to die, if it were only at the idea that any one I love would grieve too much for me.

Epicurus. Let the loss of our friends be our only grief, and the apprehension of displeasing them our only fear.

Leontion. No apostrophes! no interjections! Your argument was unsound; your means futile.

Epicurus. Tell me, then, whether the horse of a rider on the road should not be spurred forward if he started at a shadow.

Leontion. Yes.

Epicurus. I thought so: it would, however, be better to guide him quietly up to it, and to show him that it was one. Death is less than a shadow: it represents nothing, even imperfectly.

Leontion. Then at the best what is it? why care about it, think about it, or remind us that it must befall us? Would you take the same trouble, when you see my hair entwined with ivy, to make me remember that, although the leaves are green and pliable, the stem is fragile and rough, and that before I go to bed I shall have many knots and entanglements to extricate? Let me have them; but let me not hear of them until the time is come.

Epicurus. I would never think of death as an embarrassment, but as a blessing.

Ternissa. How? a blessing?

Epicurus. What, if it makes our enemies cease to hate us? what, if it makes our friends love us the more?

Leontion. Us? According to your doctrine we shall not exist at all.

Epicurus. I spoke of that which is consolatory while we are here, and of that which in plain reason ought to render us contented to stay no longer. You, Leontion, would make others better; and better they certainly will be, when their hostilities languish in an empty field, and their rancour is tired with treading upon dust. The generous affections stir about us at the dreary hour of death, as the blossoms of the Median apple swell and diffuse their fragrance in the cold.

Ternissa. I cannot bear to think of passing the Styx, lest Charon should touch me; he is so old and wilful, so cross and ugly.

Epicurus. Ternissa! Ternissa! I would accompany you thither, and stand between. Would you not too, Leontion?

Leontion. I don't know.

Ternissa. Oh, that we could go together!

Leontion. Indeed!

Ternissa. All three, I mean--I said--or was going to say it. How ill-natured you are, Leontion, to misinterpret me; I could almost cry.

Leontion. Do not, do not, Ternissa! Should that tear drop from your eyelash you would look less beautiful.

Epicurus. If it is well to conquer a world, it is better to conquer two.

Ternissa. That is what Alexander of Macedon wept because he could not accomplish.

Epicurus. Ternissa! we three can accomplish it; or any one of us.

Ternissa. How? pray!

Epicurus. We can conquer this world and the next; for you will have another, and nothing should be refused you.

Ternissa. The next by piety: but this, in what manner?

Epicurus. By indifference to all who are indifferent to us; by taking joyfully the benefit that comes spontaneously; by wishing no more intensely for what is a hair's-breadth beyond our reach than for a draught of water from the Ganges; and by fearing nothing in another life.

Ternissa. This, O Epicurus! is the grand impossibility.

Epicurus. Do you believe the gods to be as benevolent and good as you are? or do you not?

Ternissa. Much kinder, much better in every way.

Epicurus. Would you kill or hurt the sparrow that you keep in your little dressing-room with a string around the leg, because he hath flown where you did not wish him to fly?

Ternissa. No! it would be cruel; the string about the leg of so little and weak a creature is enough.

Epicurus. You think so; I think so; God thinks so. This I may say confidently; for whenever there is a sentiment in which strict justice and pure benevolence unite, it must be His.

Ternissa. O Epicurus! when you speak thus--

Leontion. Well, Ternissa, what then?

Ternissa. When Epicurus teaches us such sentiments as these, I am grieved that he has not so great an authority with the Athenians as some others have.

Leontion. You will grieve more, I suspect, my Ternissa, when he possesses that authority.

Ternissa. What will he do?

Leontion. Why turn pale? I am not about to answer that he will forget or leave you. No; but the voice comes deepest from the sepulchre, and a great name hath its root in the dead body. If you invited a company to a feast, you might as well place round the table live sheep and oxen and vases of fish and cages of quails, as you would invite a company of friendly hearers to the philosopher who is yet living. One would imagine that the iris of our intellectual eye were lessened by the glory of his presence, and that, like eastern kings, he could be looked at near only when his limbs are stiff, by waxlight, in close curtains.

Epicurus. One of whom we know little leaves us a ring or other token of remembrance, and we express a sense of pleasure and of gratitude; one of whom we know nothing writes a book, the contents of which might (if we would let them) have done us more good and might have given us more pleasure, and we revile him for it. The book may do what the legacy cannot; it may be pleasurable and serviceable to others as well as ourselves: we would hinder this too. In fact, all other love is extinguished by self-love: beneficence, humanity, justice, philosophy, sink under it. While we insist that we are looking for Truth, we commit a falsehood. It never was the first object with any one, and with few the second.

Feed unto replenishment your quieter fancies, my sweetest little Ternissa! and let the gods, both youthful and aged, both gentle and boisterous, administer to them hourly on these sunny downs: what can they do better?

Leontion. But those feathers, Ternissa, what god's may they be? since you will not pick them up, nor restore them to Calaeis nor to Zethes.

Ternissa. I do not think they belong to any god whatever; and shall never be persuaded of it unless Epicurus says it is so.

Leontion. O unbelieving creature! do you reason against the immortals?

Ternissa. It was yourself who doubted, or appeared to doubt, the flight of Oreithyia. By admitting too much we endanger our religion. Beside, I think I discern some upright stakes at equal distances, and am pretty sure the feathers are tied to them by long strings.

Epicurus. You have guessed the truth.

Ternissa. Of what use are they there?

Epicurus. If you have ever seen the foot of a statue broken off just below the ankle, you have then, Leontion and Ternissa, seen the form of the ground about us. The lower extremities of it are divided into small ridges, as you will perceive if you look around; and these are covered with corn, olives, and vines. At the upper part, where cultivation ceases, and where those sheep and goats are grazing, begins my purchase. The ground rises gradually unto near the summit, where it grows somewhat steep, and terminates in a precipice. Across the middle I have traced a line, denoted by those feathers, from one dingle to the other; the two terminations of my intended garden. The distance is nearly a thousand paces, and the path, perfectly on a level, will be two paces broad, so that I may walk between you; but another could not join us conveniently. From this there will be several circuitous and spiral, leading by the easiest ascent to the summit; and several more, to the road along the cultivation underneath: here will, however, be but one entrance. Among the projecting fragments and the massive stones yet standing of the boundary-wall, which old pomegranates imperfectly defend, and which my neighbour has guarded more effectively against invasion, there are hillocks of crumbling mould, covered in some places with a variety of moss; in others are elevated tufts, or dim labyrinths of eglantine.

Ternissa. Where will you place the statues? for undoubtedly you must have some.

Epicurus. I will have some models for statues. Pygmalion prayed the gods to give life to the image he adored: I will not pray them to give marble to mine. Never may I lay my wet cheek upon the foot under which is inscribed the name of Leontion or Ternissa!

Leontion. Do not make us melancholy; never let us think that the time can come when we shall lose our friends. Glory, literature, philosophy have this advantage over friendship: remove one object from them, and others fill the void; remove one from friendship, one only, and not the earth nor the universality of worlds, no, nor the intellect that soars above and comprehends them, can replace it!

Epicurus. Dear Leontion! always amiable, always graceful! How lovely do you now appear to me! what beauteous action accompanied your words!

Leontion. I used none whatever.

Epicurus. That white arm was then, as it is now, over the shoulder of Ternissa; and her breath imparted a fresh bloom to your cheek, a new music to your voice. No friendship is so cordial or so delicious as that of girl for girl; no hatred so intense and immovable as that of woman for woman. In youth you love one above the others of your sex; in riper age you hate all, more or less, in proportion to similarity of accomplishments and pursuits--which sometimes (I wish it were oftener) are bonds of union to man. In us you more easily pardon faults than excellences in each other. *Your* tempers are such, my beloved scholars, that even this truth does not ruffle them; and such is your affection, that I look with confidence to its unabated ardour at twenty.

Leontion. Oh, then I am to love Ternissa almost fifteen months!

Ternissa. And I am destined to survive the loss of it three months above four years!

Epicurus. Incomparable creatures! may it be eternal! In loving ye shall follow no example; ye shall step securely over the iron rule laid down for others by the Destinies, and ***you*** for ever be Leontion, and ***you*** Ternissa.

Leontion. Then indeed we should not want statues.

Ternissa. But men, who are vainer creatures, would be good for nothing without them: they must be flattered even by the stones.

Epicurus. Very true. Neither the higher arts nor the civic virtues can flourish extensively without the statues of illustrious men. But gardens are not the places for them. Sparrows, wooing on the general's truncheon (unless he be such a general as one of ours in the last war), and snails besliming the emblems of the poet, do not remind us worthily of their characters. Porticos are their proper situations, and those the most frequented. Even there they may lose all honour and distinction, whether from the thoughtlessness of magistrates or from the malignity of rivals. Our own city, the least exposed of any to the effects of either, presents us a disheartening example. When the Thebans in their jealousy condemned Pindar to the payment of a fine for having praised the Athenians too highly, our citizens erected a statue of bronze to him.

Leontion. Jealousy of Athens made the Thebans fine him; and jealousy of Thebes made the Athenians thus record it.

Epicurus. And jealousy of Pindar, I suspect, made some poet persuade the archons to render the distinction a vile and worthless one, by placing his effigy near a king's--one Evagoras of Cyprus.

Ternissa. Evagoras, I think I remember to have read in the inscription, was rewarded in this manner for his reception of Conon, defeated by the Lacedemonians.

Epicurus. Gratitude was due to him, and some such memorial to record it. External reverence should be paid unsparingly to the higher magistrates of every country who perform their offices exemplarily; yet they are not on this account to be placed in the same degree with men of primary genius. They never exalt the human race, and rarely benefit it; and their benefits are local and transitory, while those of a great writer are universal and eternal.

If the gods did indeed bestow on us a portion of their fire, they seem to have lighted it in sport and left it; the harder task and the nobler is performed by that genius who raises it clear and glowing from its embers, and makes it applicable to the purposes that dignify or delight our nature. I have ever said, 'Reverence the rulers.' Let, then, his image stand; but stand apart from Pindar's. Pallas and Jove! defend me from being carried down the stream of time among a shoal of royalets, and the rootless weeds they are hatched on!

Ternissa. So much piety would deserve the exemption, even though your writings did not hold out the decree.

Leontion. Child, the compliment is ill turned: if you are ironical, as you must be on the piety of Epicurus, Atticism requires that you should continue to be so, at least to the end of the sentence.

Ternissa. Irony is my abhorrence. Epicurus may appear less pious than some others, but I am certain he is more; otherwise the gods would never have given him----

Leontion. What? what? let us hear!

Ternissa. Leontion!

Leontion. Silly girl! Were there any hibiscus or broom growing near at hand, I would send him away and whip you.

Epicurus. There is fern, which is better.

Leontion. I was not speaking to you: but now you shall have something to answer for yourself. Although you admit no statues in the country, you might at least, methinks, have discovered a retirement with a fountain in it: here I see not even a spring.

Epicurus. Fountain I can hardly say there is; but on the left there is a long crevice or chasm, which we have never yet visited, and which we cannot discern until we reach it. This is full of soft mould, very moist, and many high reeds and canes are growing there; and the rock itself too drips with humidity along it, and is covered with more tufted moss and more variegated lichens. This crevice, with its windings and sinuosities, is about four hundred paces long, and in many parts eleven, twelve, thirteen feet wide, but generally six or seven. I shall plant it wholly with lilies of the valley, leaving the irises which occupy the sides as well as the clefts, and also those other flowers of paler purple, from the autumnal cups of which we collect the saffron; and forming a narrow path of such turf as I can find there, or rather following it as it creeps among the bays and hazels and sweet-brier, which had fallen at different times from the summit and are now grown old, with an infinity of primroses at the roots. There are nowhere twenty steps without a projection and a turn, nor in any ten together is the chasm of the same width or figure. Hence the ascent in its windings is easy and imperceptible quite to the termination, where the rocks are somewhat high and precipitous; at the entrance they lose themselves in privet and elder, and you must make your way between them through the canes. Do not you remember where I carried you both across the muddy hollow in the footpath?

Ternissa. Leontion does.

Epicurus. That place is always wet; not only in this month of Puanepsion,[7] which we are beginning to-day, but in midsummer. The water that causes it comes out a little way above it, but originates from the crevice, which I will cover at top with rose-laurel and mountain-ash, with clematis and vine; and I will intercept the little rill in its wandering, draw it from its concealment, and place it like Bacchus under the protection of the nymphs, who will smile upon it in its marble cradle, which at present I keep at home.

Ternissa. Leontion, why do you turn away your face? have the nymphs smiled upon you in it?

Leontion. I bathed in it once, if you must know, Ternissa! Why now, Ternissa, why do you turn away yours? have the nymphs frowned upon you for invading their secrets?

Ternissa. Epicurus, you are in the right to bring it away from Athens, from under the eye of Pallas: she might be angry.

Epicurus. You approve of its removal then, my lovely friend?

Ternissa. Mightily. [*Aside.*] I wish it may break in pieces on the road.

Epicurus. What did you say?

Ternissa. I wish it were now on the road, that I might try whether it would hold me--I mean with my clothes on.

Epicurus. It would hold you, and one a span longer. I have another in the house; but it is not decorated with fauns and satyrs and foliage, like this.

Leontion. I remember putting my hand upon the frightful satyr's head, to leap in: it seems made for the purpose. But the sculptor needed not to place the naiad quite so near--he must have been a very impudent man; it is impossible to look for a moment at such a piece of workmanship.

Ternissa. For shame! Leontion!--why, what was it? I do not desire to know.

Epicurus. I don't remember it.

Leontion. Nor I neither; only the head.

Epicurus. I shall place the satyr toward the rock, that you may never see him, Ternissa.

Ternissa. Very right; he cannot turn round.

Leontion. The poor naiad had done it, in vain.

Ternissa. All these labourers will soon finish the plantation, if you superintend them, and are not appointed to some magistrature.

Epicurus. Those who govern us are pleased at seeing a philosopher out of the city, and more still at finding in a season of scarcity forty poor citizens, who might become seditious, made happy and quiet by such employment.

Two evils, of almost equal weight, may befall the man of erudition:

never to be listened to, and to be listened to always. Aware of these, I devote a large portion of my time and labours to the cultivation of such minds as flourish best in cities, where my garden at the gate, although smaller than this, we find sufficiently capacious. There I secure my listeners; here my thoughts and imaginations have their free natural current, and tarry or wander as the will invites: may it ever be among those dearest to me!--those whose hearts possess the rarest and divinest faculty, of retaining or forgetting at option what ought to be forgotten or retained.

Leontion. The whole ground then will be covered with trees and shrubs?

Epicurus. There are some protuberances in various parts of the eminence, which you do not perceive till you are upon them or above them. They are almost level at the top, and overgrown with fine grass; for they catch the better soil brought down in small quantities by the rains. These are to be left unplanted: so is the platform under the pinasters, whence there is a prospect of the city, the harbour, the isle of Salamis, and the territory of Megara. 'What then!' cried Sosimenes, 'you would hide from your view my young olives, and the whole length of the new wall I have been building at my own expense between us! and, when you might see at once the whole of Attica, you will hardly see more of it than I could buy.'

Leontion. I do not perceive the new wall, for which Sosimenes, no doubt, thinks himself another Pericles.

Epicurus. Those old junipers quite conceal it.

Ternissa. They look warm and sheltering; but I like the rose-laurels much better: and what a thicket of them here is!

Epicurus. Leaving all the larger, I shall remove many thousands of them; enough to border the greater part of the walk, intermixed with roses.

There is an infinity of other plants and flowers, or weeds as Sosimenes calls them, of which he has cleared his oliveyard, and which I shall adopt. Twenty of his slaves came in yesterday, laden with hyacinths and narcissi, anemones and jonquils. 'The curses of our vineyards,' cried he, 'and good neither for man nor beast. I have another estate infested with lilies of the valley: I should not wonder if you accepted these too.'

'And with thanks,' answered I.

The whole of his remark I could not collect: he turned aside, and (I believe) prayed. I only heard 'Pallas'--'Father'--'sound mind'--'inoffensive man'--'good neighbour'. As we walked together I perceived him looking grave, and I could not resist my inclination to smile as I turned my eyes toward him. He observed it, at first with unconcern, but by degrees some doubts arose within him, and he said, 'Epicurus, you have been throwing away no less than half a talent on this sorry piece of mountain, and I fear you are about to waste as much in labour: for nothing was ever so terrible as the price we are obliged to pay the workman, since the conquest of Persia and the increase of luxury in our city. Under three obols none will do his day's work. But what, in the name of all the deities, could induce you to plant those roots, which other people dig up and throw away?'

'I have been doing,' said I, 'the same thing my whole life through, Sosimenes!'

'How!' cried he; 'I never knew that.'

'Those very doctrines,' added I, 'which others hate and extirpate, I inculcate and cherish. They bring no riches, and therefore are thought to bring no advantage; to me, they appear the more advantageous for that reason. They give us immediately what we solicit through the means of wealth. We toil for the wealth first; and then it remains to be proved whether we can purchase with it what we look for. Now, to carry our money to the market, and not to find in the market our money's worth, is great vexation; yet much greater has already preceded, in running up and down for it among so many competitors, and through so many thieves.'

After a while he rejoined, 'You really, then, have not overreached me?'

'In what, my friend?' said I.

'These roots,' he answered, 'may perhaps be good and saleable for some purpose. Shall you send them into Persia? or whither?'

'Sosimenes, I shall make love-potions of the flowers.'

Leontion. O Epicurus! should it ever be known in Athens that they are good for this, you will not have, with all your fences of prunes and pomegranates, and precipices with brier upon them, a single root left under ground after the month of Elaphebolion.[8]

Epicurus. It is not every one that knows the preparation.

Leontion. Everybody will try it.

Epicurus. And you, too, Ternissa?

Ternissa. Will you teach me?

Epicurus. This, and anything else I know. We must walk together when they are in flower.

Ternissa. And can you teach me, then?

Epicurus. I teach by degrees.

Leontion. By very slow ones, Epicurus! I have no patience with you; tell us directly.

Epicurus. It is very material what kind of recipient you bring with you. Enchantresses use a brazen one; silver and gold are employed in other arts.

Leontion. I will bring any.

Ternissa. My mother has a fine golden one. She will lend it me; she allows me everything.

Epicurus. Leontion and Ternissa, those eyes of yours brighten at inquiry, as if they carried a light within them for a guidance.

Leontion. No flattery!

Ternissa. No flattery! Come, teach us!

Epicurus. Will you hear me through in silence?

Leontion. We promise.

Epicurus. Sweet girls! the calm pleasures, such as I hope you will ever find in your walks among these gardens, will improve your beauty, animate your discourse, and correct the little that may hereafter rise up for correction in your dispositions. The smiling ideas left in our bosoms from our infancy, that many plants are the favourites of the gods, and that others were even the objects of their love--having once been invested with the human form, beautiful and lively and happy as yourselves--give them an interest beyond the vision; yes, and a station--let me say it--on the vestibule of our affections. Resign your ingenuous hearts to simple pleasures; and there is none in man, where men are Attic, that will not follow and outstrip their movements.

Ternissa. O Epicurus!

Epicurus. What said Ternissa?

Leontion. Some of those anemones, I do think, must be still in blossom. Ternissa's golden cup is at home; but she has brought with her a little vase for the filter--and has filled it to the brim. Do not hide your head behind my shoulder, Ternissa; no, nor in my lap.

Epicurus. Yes, there let it lie--the lovelier for that tendril of sunny brown hair upon it. How it falls and rises! Which is the hair? which the shadow?

Leontion. Let the hair rest.

Epicurus. I must not, perhaps, clasp the shadow!

Leontion. You philosophers are fond of such unsubstantial things. Oh, you have taken my volume! This is deceit.

You live so little in public, and entertain such a contempt for opinion, as to be both indifferent and ignorant what it is that people blame you for.

Epicurus. I know what it is I should blame myself for, if I attended to them. Prove them to be wiser and more disinterested in their wisdom than I am, and I will then go down to them and listen to them. When I have well considered a thing, I deliver it--regardless of what those think who neither take the time nor possess the faculty of considering anything well, and who have always lived far remote from the scope of our speculations.

Leontion. In the volume you snatched away from me so slyly, I have defended a position of yours which many philosophers turn into ridicule--namely, that politeness is among the virtues. I wish you yourself had spoken more at large upon the subject.

Epicurus. It is one upon which a lady is likely to display more ingenuity and discernment. If philosophers have ridiculed my sentiment, the reason is, it is among those virtues which in general they find most difficult to assume or counterfeit.

Leontion. Surely life runs on the smoother for this equability and polish; and the gratification it affords is more extensive than is afforded even by the highest virtue. Courage, on nearly all occasions, inflicts as much of evil as it imparts of good. It may be exerted in defence of our country, in defence of those who love us, in defence of the harmless and the helpless; but those against whom it is thus exerted may possess an equal share of it. If they succeed, then manifestly the ill it produces is greater than the benefit; if they succumb, it is nearly as great. For many of their adversaries are first killed and maimed, and many of their own kindred are left to lament the consequences of the aggression.

Epicurus. You have spoken first of courage, as that virtue which attracts your sex principally.

Ternissa. Not me; I am always afraid of it. I love those best who can tell me the most things I never knew before, and who have patience with me, and look kindly while they teach me, and almost as if they were waiting for fresh questions. Now let me hear directly what you were about to say to Leontion.

Epicurus. I was proceeding to remark that temperance comes next; and temperance has then its highest merit when it is the support of civility and politeness. So that I think I am right and equitable in attributing to politeness a distinguished rank, not among the ornaments of life, but among the virtues. And you, Leontion and Ternissa, will have leaned the more propensely toward this opinion, if you considered, as I am sure you did, that the peace and concord of families, friends, and cities are preserved by it; in other terms, the harmony of the world.

Ternissa. Leontion spoke of courage, you of temperance; the next great virtue, in the division made by the philosophers, is justice.

Epicurus. Temperance includes it; for temperance is imperfect if it is only an abstinence from too much food, too much wine, too much conviviality or other luxury. It indicates every kind of forbearance. Justice is forbearance from what belongs to another. Giving to this one rightly what that one would hold wrongfully in magistrature not in the abstract, and is only a part of its office. The perfectly temperate man is also the perfectly just man; but the perfectly just man (as philosophers now define him) may not be the perfectly temperate one. I include the less in the greater.

Leontion. We hear of judges, and upright ones too, being immoderate eaters and drinkers.

Epicurus. The Lacedemonians are temperate in food and courageous in battle; but men like these, if they existed in sufficient numbers, would devastate the universe. We alone, we Athenians, with less military skill perhaps, and certainly less rigid abstinence from voluptuousness and luxury, have set before it the only grand example of social government and of polished life. From us the seed is scattered; from us flow the streams that irrigate it; and ours are the hands, O Leontion, that collect it, cleanse it, deposit it, and convey and distribute it sound and weighty through every race and age. Exhausted as we are by war, we can do nothing better than lie down and doze while the weather is fine overhead, and dream (if we can) that we are affluent and free.

O sweet sea air! how bland art thou and refreshing! Breathe upon Leontion! breathe upon Ternissa! bring them health and spirits and serenity, many springs and many summers, and when the vine-leaves have reddened and rustle under their feet!

These, my beloved girls, are the children of Eternity: they played around Theseus and the beauteous Amazon; they gave to Pallas the bloom of Venus, and to Venus the animation of Pallas. Is it not better to enjoy by the hour their soft, salubrious influence, than to catch by fits the rancid breath of demagogues; than to swell and move under it without or against our will; than to acquire the semblance of eloquence by the bitterness of passion, the tone of philosophy by disappointment, or the credit of prudence by distrust? Can fortune, can industry, can desert itself, bestow on us anything we have not here?

Leontion. And when shall those three meet? The gods have never united them, knowing that men would put them asunder at the first appearance.

Epicurus. I am glad to leave the city as often as possible, full as it is of high and glorious reminiscences, and am inclined much rather to indulge in quieter scenes, whither the Graces and Friendship lead me. I would not contend even with men able to contend with me. You, Leontion, I see, think differently, and have composed at last your long-meditated work against the philosophy of Theophrastus.

Leontion. Why not? he has been praised above his merits.

Epicurus. My Leontion! you have inadvertently given me the reason and origin of all controversial writings. They flow not from a love of truth or a regard for science, but from envy and ill-will. Setting aside the evil of malignity--always hurtful to ourselves, not always to others--there is weakness in the argument you have adduced. When a writer is praised above his merits in his own times, he is certain of being estimated below them in the times succeeding. Paradox is dear to most people: it bears the appearance of originality, but is usually the talent of the superficial, the perverse, and the obstinate.

Nothing is more gratifying than the attention you are bestowing on me, which you always apportion to the seriousness of my observations.

Leontion. I dislike Theophrastus for his affected contempt of your doctrines.

Epicurus. Unreasonably, for the contempt of them; reasonably, if affected. Good men may differ widely from me, and wiser ones misunderstand me; for, their wisdom having raised up to them schools of their own, they have not found leisure to converse with me; and from others they have received a partial and inexact report. My opinion is, that certain things are indifferent and unworthy of pursuit or attention, as lying beyond our research and almost our conjecture; which things the generality of philosophers (for the generality are speculative) deem of the first importance. Questions relating to them I answer evasively, or altogether decline. Again, there are modes of living which are suitable to some and unsuitable to others. What I myself follow and embrace, what I recommend to the studious, to the irritable, to the weak in health, would ill agree with the commonality of citizens. Yet my adversaries cry out: 'Such is the opinion and practice of Epicurus!' For instance, I have never taken a wife, and never will take one; but he from among the mass, who should avow his imitation of my example, would act as wisely and more religiously in saying that he chose celibacy because Pallas had done the same.

Leontion. If Pallas had many such votaries she would soon have few citizens to supply them.

Epicurus. And extremely bad ones, if all followed me in retiring from the offices of magistracy and of war. Having seen that the most sensible men are the most unhappy, I could not but examine the causes of it; and, finding that the same sensibility to which they are indebted for the activity of their intellect is also the restless mover of their jealousy and ambition, I would lead them aside from whatever operates upon these, and throw under their feet the terrors their imagination has created. My philosophy is not for the populace nor for the proud: the ferocious will never attain it; the gentle will embrace it, but will not call it mine. I do not desire that they should: let them rest their heads upon that part of the pillow which they find the softest, and enjoy their own dreams unbroken.

Leontion. The old are all against you, Epicurus, the name of pleasure is an affront to them: they know no other kind of it than that which has flowered and seeded, and of which the withered stems have indeed a rueful look.

Epicurus. Unhappily the aged are retentive of long-acquired maxims, and insensible to new impressions, whether from fancy or from truth: in fact, their eyes blend the two together. Well might the poet tell us:

> Fewer the gifts that gnarled Age presents
> To elegantly-handed Infancy,
> Than elegantly-handed Infancy
> Presents to gnarled Age. From both they drop;
> The middle course of life receives them all,
> Save the light few that laughing Youth runs off with,
> Unvalued as a mistress or a flower.

Leontion. Since, in obedience to your institutions, O Epicurus, I must not say I am angry, I am offended at least with Theophrastus for having so misrepresented your opinions, on the necessity of keeping the mind composed and tranquil, and remote from every object and every sentiment by which a painful sympathy may be excited. In order to display his elegance of language, he runs wherever he can lay a censure on you, whether he believes in its equity or not.

Epicurus. This is the case with all eloquent men, and all disputants. Truth neither warms nor elevates them, neither obtains for them profit nor applause.

Ternissa. I have heard wise remarks very often and very warmly praised.

Epicurus. Not for the truth in them, but for the grace, or because they touched the spring of some preconception or some passion. Man is a hater of truth, a lover of fiction.

Theophrastus is a writer of many acquirements and some shrewdness, usually judicious, often somewhat witty, always elegant; his thoughts are never confused, his sentences are never incomprehensible. If Aristoteles thought more highly of him than his due, surely you ought not to censure Theophrastus with severity on the supposition of his rating me below mine; unless you argue that a slight error in a short sum is less pardonable than in a longer. Had Aristoteles been living, and had he given the same opinion of me, your friendship and perhaps my self-love might have been wounded; for, if on one occasion he spoke too favourably, he never spoke unfavourably but with justice. This is among the indications of orderly and elevated minds; and here stands the barrier that separates them from the common and the waste. Is a man to be angry because an infant is fretful? Is a philosopher to unpack and throw away his philosophy, because an idiot has tried to overturn it on the road, and has pursued it with gibes and ribaldry?

Leontion. Theophrastus would persuade us that, according to your system, we not only should decline the succour of the wretched, but avoid the sympathies that poets and historians would awaken in us. Probably for the sake of introducing some idle verses, written by a friend of his, he says that, following the guidance of Epicurus, we should altogether shun the theatre; and not only when Prometheus and Oedipus and Philoctetes are introduced, but even when generous and kindly sentiments are predominant, if they partake of that tenderness which belongs to pity. I know not what Thracian lord recovers his daughter from her ravisher; such are among the words they exchange:

Father.

> Insects that dwell in rotten reeds, inert
> Upon the surface of a stream or pool,
> Then rush into the air on meshy vans,
> Are not so different in their varying lives
> As we are.--Oh! what father on this earth,

Holding his child's cool cheek within his palms
And kissing his fair front, would wish him man?--
Inheritor of wants and jealousies,
Of labour, of ambition, of distress,
And, cruellest of all the passions, lust.
Who that behold me, persecuted, scorned,
A wanderer, e'er could think what friends were mine,
How numerous, how devoted? with what glee
Smiled my old house, with what acclaim my courts
Rang from without whene'er my war-horse neighed?

Daughter.

Thy fortieth birthday is not shouted yet
By the young peasantry, with rural gifts
And nightly fires along the pointed hills,
Yet do thy temples glitter with grey hair
Scattered not thinly: ah, what sudden change!
Only thy voice and heart remain the same:
No! that voice trembles, and that heart (I feel),
While it would comfort and console me, breaks.

Epicurus. I would never close my bosom against the feelings of humanity; but I would calmly and well consider by what conduct of life they may enter it with the least importunity and violence. A consciousness that we have promoted the happiness of others, to the uttermost of our power, is certain not only to meet them at the threshold, but to bring them along with us, and to render them accurate and faithful prompters, when we bend perplexedly over the problem of evil figured by the tragedians. If there were more of pain than of pleasure in the exhibitions of the dramatist, no man in his senses would attend them twice. All the imitative arts have delight for the principal object: the first of these is poetry; the highest of poetry is tragic.

Leontion. The epic has been called so.

Epicurus. Improperly; for the epic has much more in it of what is prosaic. Its magnitude is no argument. An Egyptian pyramid contains more materials than an Ionic temple, but requires less contrivance, and exhibits less beauty of design. My simile is yet a defective one; for a tragedy must be carried on with an unbroken interest, and, undecorated by loose foliage or fantastic branches, it must rise, like the palm-tree, with a lofty unity. On these matters I am unable to argue at large, or perhaps correctly; on those, however, which I have studied and treated, my terms are so explicit and clear, that Theophrastus can never have misunderstood them. Let me recall to your attention but two axioms.

Abstinence from low pleasures is the only means of meriting or of obtaining the higher.

Kindness in ourselves is the honey that blunts the sting of unkindness in another.

Leontion. Explain to me, then, O Epicurus, why we suffer so much from ingratitude.

Epicurus. We fancy we suffer from ingratitude, while in reality we suffer from self-love. Passion weeps while she says, 'I did not deserve this from him'; Reason, while she says it, smoothens her brow at the clear fountain of the heart. Permit me also, like Theophrastus, to borrow a few words from a poet.

Ternissa. Borrow as many such as any one will entrust to you, and may Hermes prosper your commerce! Leontion may go to the theatre then;

for she loves it.

Epicurus. Girls! be the bosom friends of Antigone and Ismene; and you shall enter the wood of the Eumenides without shuddering, and leave it without the trace of a tear. Never did you appear so graceful to me, O Ternissa--no, not even after this walk do you--as when I saw you blow a fly from the forehead of Philoctetes in the propylea. The wing, with which Sophocles and the statuary represent him, to drive away the summer insects in his agony, had wearied his flaccid arm, hanging down beside him.

Ternissa. Do you imagine, then, I thought him a living man?

Epicurus. The sentiment was both more delicate and more august from being indistinct. You would have done it, even if he ***had*** been a living man; even if he could have clasped you in his arms, imploring the deities to resemble you in gentleness, you would have done it.

Ternissa. He looked so abandoned by all, and so heroic, yet so feeble and so helpless! I did not think of turning around to see if any one was near me; or else, perhaps----

Epicurus. If you could have thought of looking around, you would no longer have been Ternissa. The gods would have transformed you for it into some tree.

Leontion. And Epicurus had been walking under it this day, perhaps.

Epicurus. With Leontion, the partner of his sentiments. But the walk would have been earlier or later than the present hour; since the middle of the day, like the middle of certain fruits, is good for nothing.

Leontion. For dinner, surely?

Epicurus. Dinner is a less gratification to me than to many: I dine alone.

Ternissa. Why?

Epicurus. To avoid the noise, the heat, and the intermixture both of odours and of occupations. I cannot bear the indecency of speaking with a mouth in which there is food. I careen my body (since it is always in want of repair) in as unobstructed a space as I can, and I lie down and sleep awhile when the work is over.

Leontion. Epicurus! although it would be very interesting, no doubt, to hear more of what you do after dinner--[*Aside to him.*] now don't smile: I shall never forgive you if you say a single word--yet I would rather hear a little about the theatre, and whether you think at last that women should frequent it; for you have often said the contrary.

Epicurus. I think they should visit it rarely; not because it excites their affections, but because it deadens them. To me nothing is so odious as to be at once among the rabble and among the heroes, and, while I am receiving into my heart the most exquisite of human sensations, to feel upon my shoulder the hand of some inattentive and insensible young officer.

Leontion. Oh, very bad indeed! horrible!

Ternissa. You quite fire at the idea.

Leontion. Not I: I don't care about it.

Ternissa. Not about what is very bad indeed? quite horrible?

Leontion. I seldom go thither.

Epicurus. The theatre is delightful when we erect it in our own house or arbour, and when there is but one spectator.

Leontion. You must lose the illusion in great part, if you only read the tragedy, which I fancy to be your meaning.

Epicurus. I lose the less of it. Do not imagine that the illusion is, or can be, or ought to be, complete. If it were possible, no Phalaris or Perillus could devise a crueller torture. Here are two imitations: first, the poet's of the sufferer; secondly, the actor's of both: poetry is superinduced. No man in pain ever uttered the better part of the language used by Sophocles. We admit it, and willingly, and are at least as much illuded by it as by anything else we hear or see upon the stage. Poets and statuaries and painters give us an adorned imitation of the object, so skilfully treated that we receive it for a correct one. This is the only illusion they aim at: this is the perfection of their arts.

Leontion. Do you derive no pleasure from the representation of a consummate actor?

Epicurus. High pleasure; but liable to be overturned in an instant: pleasure at the mercy of any one who sits beside me.

* * * * *

Leontion. In my treatise I have only defended your tenets against Theophrastus.

Epicurus. I am certain you have done it with spirit and eloquence, dear Leontion; and there are but two words in it I would wish you to erase.

Leontion. Which are they?

Epicurus. Theophrastus and Epicurus. If you love me, you will do nothing that may make you uneasy when you grow older; nothing that may allow my adversary to say, 'Leontion soon forgot her Epicurus.' My maxim is, never to defend my systems or paradoxes; if you undertake it, the Athenians will insist that I impelled you secretly, or that my philosophy and my friendship were ineffectual on you.

Leontion. They shall never say that.

Epicurus. I am not unmoved by the kindness of your intentions. Most people, and philosophers, too, among the rest, when their own conduct or opinions are questioned, are admirably prompt and dexterous in the science of defence; but when another's are assailed, they parry with as ill a grace and faltering a hand as if they never had taken a lesson in it at home. Seldom will they see what they profess to look for; and, finding it, they pick up with it a thorn under the nail. They canter over the solid turf, and complain that there is no corn upon it; they canter over the corn, and curse the ridges and furrows. All schools of philosophy, and almost all authors, are rather to be frequented for exercise than for freight; but this exercise ought to acquire us health and strength, spirits and good-humour. There is none of them that does not supply some truth useful to every man, and some untruth equally so to the few that are able to wrestle with it. If there were no falsehood in the world, there would be no doubt; if there were no doubt, there would be no inquiry; if no inquiry, no wisdom, no knowledge, no genius: and Fancy herself would lie muffled up in her robe, inactive, pale, and bloated. I wish we could demonstrate the existence of utility in some other evils as easily as in this.

Leontion. My remarks on the conduct and on the style of Theophrastus are not confined to him solely. I have taken at last a general view of our literature, and traced as far as I am able its deviation and decline. In ancient works we sometimes see the mark of the chisel; in modern we might almost suppose that no chisel was employed at all, and that everything was done by grinding and rubbing. There is an ordinariness, an indistinctness, a generalization, not even to be found in a flock of sheep. As most reduce what is sand into dust, the few that avoid it run to a contrary extreme, and would force us to believe that what is original must be unpolished and uncouth.

Epicurus. There have been in all ages, and in all there will be, sharp and slender heads made purposely and peculiarly for creeping into the crevices of our nature. While we contemplate the magnificence of the universe, and mensurate the fitness and adaptation of one part to another, the small philosopher hangs upon a hair or creeps within a wrinkle, and cries out shrilly from his elevation that we are blind and superficial. He discovers a wart, he pries into a pore; and he calls it knowledge of man. Poetry and criticism, and all the fine arts, have generated such living things, which not only will be co-existent with them but will (I fear) survive them. Hence history takes alternately the form of reproval and of panegyric; and science in its pulverized state, in its shapeless and colourless atoms, assumes the name of metaphysics. We find no longer the rich succulence of Herodotus, no longer the strong filament of Thucydides, but thoughts fit only for the slave, and language for the rustic and the robber. These writings can never reach posterity, nor serve better authors near us; for who would receive as documents the perversions of venality and party? Alexander we know was intemperate, and Philip both intemperate and perfidious: we require not a volume of dissertation on the thread of history, to demonstrate that one or other left a tailor's bill unpaid, and the immorality of doing so; nor a supplement to ascertain on the best authorities which of the two it was. History should explain to us how nations rose and fell, what nurtured them in their growth, what sustained them in their maturity; not which orator ran swiftest through the crowd from the right hand to the left, which assassin was too strong for manacles, or which felon too opulent for crucifixion.

Leontion. It is better, I own it, that such writers should amuse our idleness than excite our spleen.

Ternissa. What is spleen?

Epicurus. Do not ask her; she cannot tell you. The spleen, Ternissa, is to the heart what Arimanes is to Oromazes.

Ternissa. I am little the wiser yet. Does he ever use such hard words with you?

Leontion. He means the evil Genius and the good Genius, in the theogony of the Persians: and would perhaps tell you, as he hath told me, that the heart in itself is free from evil, but very capable of receiving and too tenacious of holding it.

Epicurus. In our moral system, the spleen hangs about the heart and renders it sad and sorrowful, unless we continually keep it in exercise by kind offices, or in its proper place by serious investigation and solitary questionings. Otherwise, it is apt to adhere and to accumulate, until it deadens the principles of sound action, and obscures the sight.

Ternissa. It must make us very ugly when we grow old.

Leontion. In youth it makes us uglier, as not appertaining to it: a little more or less ugliness in decrepitude is hardly worth considering, there being quite enough of it from other quarters: I would stop it here, however.

Ternissa. Oh, what a thing is age!

Leontion. Death without death's quiet.

Ternissa. Leontion said that even bad writers may amuse our idle hours: alas! even good ones do not much amuse mine, unless they record an action of love or generosity. As for the graver, why cannot they come among us and teach us, just as you do?

Epicurus. Would you wish it?

Ternissa. No, no! I do not want them: only I was imagining how pleasant it is to converse as we are doing, and how sorry I should be to pore over a book instead of it. Books always make me sigh, and think about other things. Why do you laugh, Leontion?

Epicurus. She was mistaken in saying bad authors may amuse our idleness. Leontion knows not then how sweet and sacred idleness is.

Leontion. To render it sweet and sacred, the heart must have a little garden of its own, with its umbrage and fountains and perennial flowers--a careless company! Sleep is called sacred as well as sweet by Homer; and idleness is but a step from it. The idleness of the wise and virtuous should be both, it being the repose and refreshment necessary for past exertions and for future; it punishes the bad man, it rewards the good; the deities enjoy it, and Epicurus praises it. I was indeed wrong in my remark; for we should never seek amusement in the foibles of another, never in coarse language, never in low thoughts. When the mind loses its feeling for elegance, it grows corrupt and grovelling, and seeks in the crowd what ought to be found at home.

Epicurus. Aspasia believed so, and bequeathed to Leontion, with every other gift that Nature had bestowed upon her, the power of delivering her oracles from diviner lips.

Leontion. Fie! Epicurus! It is well you hide my face for me with your hand. Now take it away; we cannot walk in this manner.

Epicurus. No word could ever fall from you without its weight; no breath from you ought to lose itself in the common air.

Leontion. For shame! What would you have?

Ternissa. He knows not what he would have nor what he would say. I must sit down again. I declare I scarcely understand a single syllable. Well, he is very good, to tease you no longer. Epicurus has an excellent heart; he would give pain to no one; least of all to you.

Leontion, I have pained him by this foolish book, and he would only assure me that he does not for a moment bear me malice. Take the volume; take it, Epicurus! tear it in pieces.

Epicurus. No, Leontion! I shall often look with pleasure on this trophy of brave humanity; let me kiss the hand that raises it!

Ternissa. I am tired of sitting: I am quite stiff: when shall we walk homeward?

Epicurus. Take my arm, Ternissa!

Ternissa. Oh! I had forgotten that I proposed to myself a trip as far up as the pinasters, to look at the precipice of Oreithyia. Come along! come along! how alert does the sea air make us! I seem to feel growing at my feet and shoulders the wings of Zethes or Calaeis.

Epicurus. Leontion walks the nimblest to-day.

Ternissa. To display her activity and strength, she runs before us. Sweet Leontion, how good she is! but she should have stayed for us: it would be in vain to try to overtake her.

No, Epicurus! Mind! take care! you are crushing these little oleanders--and now the strawberry plants--the whole heap. Not I, indeed. What would my mother say, if she knew it? And Leontion! she will certainly look back.

Epicurus. The fairest of the Eudaimones never look back: such are the Hours and Love, Opportunity and Leontion.

Ternissa. How could you dare to treat me in this manner? I did not say again I hated anything.

Epicurus. Forgive me!

Ternissa. Violent creature!

Epicurus. If tenderness is violence. Forgive me; and say you love me.

Ternissa. All at once? could you endure such boldness?

Epicurus. Pronounce it! whisper it.

Ternissa. Go, go. Would it be proper?

Epicurus. Is that sweet voice asking its heart or me? let the worthier give the answer.

Ternissa. O Epicurus! you are very, very dear to me; and are the last in the world that would ever tell you were called so.

NOTES:

[7] The Attic month of Puanepsion had its commencement in the latter days of October; its name is derived from +puana+, the legumes which were offered in sacrifice to Apollo at that season.

[8] The thirteenth of Elaphebolion was the tenth of April.

DANTE AND BEATRICE

Dante. When you saw me profoundly pierced with love, and reddening and trembling, did it become you, did it become you, you whom I have always called ***the most gentle Bice***, to join in the heartless laughter of those girls around you? Answer me. Reply unhesitatingly. Requires it so long a space for dissimulation and duplicity? Pardon! pardon! pardon! My senses have left me; my heart being gone, they follow.

Beatrice. Childish man! pursuing the impossible.

Dante. And was it this you laughed at? We cannot touch the hem of God's garment; yet we fall at His feet and weep.

Beatrice. But weep not, gentle Dante! fall not before the weakest of His creatures, willing to comfort, unable to relieve you. Consider a little. Is laughter at all times the signal or the precursor of derision? I smiled, let me avow it, from the pride I felt in your preference of me; and if I laughed, it was to conceal my sentiments. Did you never cover sweet fruit with worthless leaves? Come, do not drop again so soon so faint a smile. I will not have you grave, nor very serious. I pity you; I must not love you: if I might, I would.

Dante. Yet how much love is due to me, O Bice, who have loved you, as you well remember, even from your tenth year. But it is reported, and your words confirm it, that you are going to be married.

Beatrice. If so, and if I could have laughed at that, and if my laughter could have estranged you from me, would you blame me?

Dante. Tell me the truth.

Beatrice. The report is general.

Dante. The truth! the truth! Tell me, Bice.

Beatrice. Marriages, it is said, are made in heaven.

Dante. Is heaven then under the paternal roof?

Beatrice. It has been to me hitherto.

Dante. And now you seek it elsewhere.

Beatrice. I seek it not. The wiser choose for the weaker. Nay, do not sigh so. What would you have, my grave pensive Dante? What can I do?

Dante. Love me.

Beatrice. I always did.

Dante. Love me? O bliss of heaven!

Beatrice. No, no, no! Forbear! Men's kisses are always mischievous and hurtful; everybody says it. If you truly loved me, you would never think of doing so.

Dante. Nor even this!

Beatrice. You forget that you are no longer a boy; and that it is not thought proper at your time of life to continue the arm at all about the waist. Beside, I think you would better not put your head against my bosom; it beats too much to be pleasant to you. Why do you wish it? why fancy it can do you any good? It grows no cooler; it seems to grow even hotter. Oh, how it burns! Go, go; it hurts me too: it struggles, it aches, it sobs. Thank you, my gentle friend, for removing your brow away; your hair is very thick and long; and it began to heat me more than you can imagine. While it was there, I could not see your face so well, nor talk with you so quietly.

Dante. Oh, when shall we talk quietly in future?

Beatrice. When I am married. I shall often come to visit my father. He has always been solitary since my mother's death, which happened in my infancy, long before you knew me.

Dante. How can he endure the solitude of his house when you have left it?

Beatrice. The very question I asked him.

Dante. You did not then wish to ... to ... go away?

Beatrice. Ah no! It is sad to be an outcast at fifteen.

Dante. An outcast?

Beatrice. Forced to leave a home.

Dante. For another?

Beatrice. Childhood can never have a second.

Dante. But childhood is now over.

Beatrice. I wonder who was so malicious as to tell my father that? He wanted me to be married a whole year ago.

Dante. And, Bice, you hesitated?

Beatrice. No; I only wept. He is a dear good father. I never disobeyed him but in those wicked tears; and they ran the faster the more he reprehended them.

Dante. Say, who is the happy youth?

Beatrice. I know not who ought to be happy if you are not.

Dante. I?

Beatrice. Surely you deserve all happiness.

Dante. Happiness! any happiness is denied me. Ah, hours of childhood! bright hours! what fragrant blossoms ye unfold! what bitter fruits to ripen!

Beatrice. Now cannot you continue to sit under that old fig-tree at the corner of the garden? It is always delightful to me to think of it.

Dante. Again you smile: I wish I could smile too.

Beatrice. You were usually more grave than I, although very often, two years ago, you told me I was the graver. Perhaps I *was* then indeed; and perhaps I ought to be now: but really I must smile at the recollection, and make you smile with me.

Dante. Recollection of what in particular?

Beatrice. Of your ignorance that a fig-tree is the brittlest of trees, especially when it is in leaf; and moreover of your tumble, when your head was just above the wall, and your hand (with the verses in it) on the very coping-stone. Nobody suspected that I went every day to the bottom of our garden, to hear you repeat your poetry on the other side; nobody but yourself; you soon found me out. But on that occasion I thought you might have been hurt; and I clambered up our high peach-tree in the grass plot nearest the place; and thence I saw Messer Dante, with his white sleeve reddened by the fig-juice, and the seeds sticking to it pertinaciously, and Messer blushing, and trying to conceal his calamity, and still holding the verses. They were all about me.

Dante. Never shall any verse of mine be uttered from my lips, or from the lips of others, without the memorial of Bice.

Beatrice. Sweet Dante! in the purity of your soul shall Bice live; as (we are told by the goatherds and foresters) poor creatures have been found preserved in the serene and lofty regions of the Alps, many years after the breath of life had left them. Already you rival Guido Cavalcante and Cino da Pistoja: you must attempt, nor perhaps shall it be vainly, to surpass them in celebrity.

Dante. If ever I am above them ... and I must be ... I know already what angel's hand will have helped me up the ladder. Beatrice, I vow to heaven, shall stand higher than Selvaggia, high and glorious and immortal as that name will be. You have given me joy and sorrow; for the worst of these (I will not say the least) I will confer on you all the generations of our Italy, all the ages of our world. But first (alas, from me you must not have it!) may happiness, long happiness, attend you!

Beatrice. Ah, those words rend your bosom! why should they?

Dante. I could go away contented, or almost contented, were I sure of it. Hope is nearly as strong as despair, and greatly more pertinacious and enduring. You have made me see clearly that you never can be mine in this world: but at the same time, O Beatrice, you have made me see quite as clearly that you may and must be mine in another! I am older than you: precedency is given to age, and not to worthiness; I will pray for you when I am nearer to God, and purified from the stains of earth and mortality. He will permit me to behold you, lovely as when I left you. Angels in vain should call me onward.

Beatrice. Hush, sweetest Dante! hush!

Dante. It is there where I shall have caught the first glimpse of you again, that I wish all my portion of Paradise to be assigned me; and there, if far below you, yet within the sight of you, to establish my perdurable abode.

Beatrice. Is this piety? Is this wisdom? O Dante! And may not I be called away first?

Dante. Alas, alas, how many small feet have swept off the early dew of life, leaving the path black behind them! But to think that you should go before me! It almost sends me forward on my way, to receive and welcome you. If indeed, O Beatrice, such should be God's immutable will, sometimes look down on me when the song to Him is suspended. Oh! look often on me with prayer and pity; for there all prayers are accepted, and all pity is devoid of pain! Why are you silent?

Beatrice. It is very sinful not to love all creatures in the world. But it is true, O Dante! that we always love those the most who make us the most unhappy?

Dante. The remark, I fear, is just.

Beatrice. Then, unless the Virgin be pleased to change my inclinations, I shall begin at last to love my betrothed; for already the very idea of him renders me sad, wearisome, and comfortless. Yesterday he sent me a bunch of violets. When I took them up, delighted as I felt at that sweetest of odours, which you and I once inhaled together....

Dante. And only once.

Beatrice. You know why. Be quiet now, and hear me. I dropped the posy; for around it, hidden by various kinds of foliage, was twined the bridal necklace of pearls. O Dante, how worthless are the finest of them (and there are many fine ones) in comparison with those little pebbles, some of which (for perhaps I may not have gathered up all) may be still lying under the peach-tree, and some (do I blush to say it?) under the fig! Tell me not who threw these, nor for what. But you know you were always thoughtful, and sometimes reading, sometimes writing, and sometimes forgetting me, while I waited to see the crimson cap, and the two bay-leaves I fastened in it, rise above the garden-wall. How silently you are listening, if you do listen!

Dante. Oh, could my thoughts incessantly and eternally dwell among these recollections, undisturbed by any other voice ... undistracted by any other presence! Soon must they abide with me alone, and be repeated by none but me ... repeated in the accents of anguish and despair! Why could you not have held in the sad home of your heart that necklace and those violets?

Beatrice. My Dante! we must all obey ... I my father, you your God. He will never abandon you.

Dante. I have ever sung, and will for ever sing, the most glorious of His works: and yet, O Bice! He abandons me, He casts me off; and He uses your hand for this infliction.

Beatrice. Men travel far and wide, and see many on whom to fix or transfer their affections; but we maidens have neither the power nor the will. Casting our eyes on the ground, we walk along the straight and narrow road prescribed for us; and, doing this, we avoid in great measure the thorns and entanglements of life. We know we are performing our duty; and the fruit of this knowledge is contentment. Season after season, day after day, you have made me serious, pensive, meditative, and almost wise. Being so little a girl, I was proud that you, so much taller, should lean on my shoulder to overlook my work. And greatly more proud was I when in time you taught me several Latin words, and then whole sentences, both in prose and verse, pasting a strip of paper over, or obscuring with impenetrable ink, those passages in the poets which were beyond my comprehension, and might perplex me. But proudest of all was I when you began to reason with me. What will now be my pride if you are convinced by the first arguments I ever have opposed to you; or if you only take them up and try if they are applicable. Certainly do I know (indeed, indeed I do) that even the patience to consider them will make you happier. Will it not then make me so? I entertain no other wish. Is not this true love?

Dante. Ah, yes! the truest, the purest, the least perishable, but not the sweetest. Here are the rue and hyssop; but where the rose?

Beatrice. Wicked must be whatever torments you: and will you let love do it? Love is the gentlest and kindest breath of God. Are you willing that the tempter should intercept it, and respire it polluted into your ear? Do not make me hesitate to pray to the Virgin for you, nor tremble lest she look down on you with a reproachful pity. To her alone, O Dante, dare I confide all my thoughts! Lessen not my confidence in my only refuge.

Dante. God annihilate a power so criminal! Oh, could my love flow into your breast with hers! It should flow with equal purity.

Beatrice. You have stored my little mind with many thoughts; dear because they are yours, and because they are virtuous. May I not, O my Dante! bring some of them back again to your bosom; as the **contadina** lets down the string from the cottage-beam in winter, and culls a few bunches of the soundest for the master of the vineyard? You have not given me glory that the world should shudder at its eclipse. To prove that I am worthy of the smallest part of it, I must obey God; and, under God, my father. Surely the voice of Heaven comes to us audibly from a parent's lips. You will be great, and, what is above, all greatness, good.

Dante. Rightly and wisely, my sweet Beatrice, have you spoken in this estimate. Greatness is to goodness what gravel is to porphyry: the one is a movable accumulation, swept along the surface of the earth; the other stands fixed and solid and alone, above the violence of war and of the tempest; above all that is residuous of a wasted world. Little men build up great ones; but the snow colossus soon melts: the good stand under the eye of God; and therefore stand.

Beatrice. Now you are calm and reasonable, listen to me, Bice. You must marry.

Dante. Marry?

Beatrice. Unless you do, how can we meet again unreservedly? Worse, worse than ever! I cannot bear to see those large heavy tears following one another, heavy and slow as nuns at the funeral of a sister. Come, I will kiss off one, if you will promise me faithfully to shed no more. Be tranquil, be tranquil; only hear reason. There are many who know you; and all who know you must love you. Don't you hear me? Why turn aside? and why go farther off? I will have that hand. It twists about as if it hated its confinement. Perverse and peevish creature! you have no more reason to be sorry than I have; and you have many to the contrary which I have not. Being a man, you are at liberty to admire a variety, and to make a choice. Is that no comfort to you?

Dante.

> Bid this bosom cease to grieve?
>   Bid these eyes fresh objects see?
> Where's the comfort to believe
>   None might once have rivall'd me?
> What! my freedom to receive?
>   Broken hearts, are they the free?
> For another can I live
>   When I may not live for thee?

Beatrice. I will never be fond of you again if you are so violent. We have been together too long, and we may be noticed.

Dante. Is this our last meeting? If it is ... and that it is, my heart has told me ... you will not, surely you will not refuse....

Beatrice. Dante! Dante! they make the heart sad after: do not wish it. But prayers ... oh, how much better are they, how much quieter and lighter they render it! They carry it up to heaven with them; and those we love are left behind no longer.

FRA FILIPPO LIPPI AND POPE EUGENIUS THE FOURTH

Eugenius. Filippo! I am informed by my son Cosimo de' Medici of many things relating to thy life and actions, and among the rest, of thy throwing off the habit of a friar. Speak to me as to a friend. Was that well done?

Filippo. Holy Father! it was done most unadvisedly.

Eugenius. Continue to treat me with the same confidence and ingenuousness; and, beside the remuneration I intend to bestow on thee for the paintings wherewith thou hast adorned my palace, I will remove with my own hand the heavy accumulation of thy sins, and ward off the peril of fresh ones, placing within thy reach every worldly solace and contentment.

Filippo. Infinite thanks, Holy Father! from the innermost heart of your unworthy servant, whose duty and wishes bind him alike and equally to a strict compliance with your paternal commands.

Eugenius. Was it a love of the world and its vanities that induced thee to throw aside the frock?

Filippo. It was indeed, Holy Father! I never had the courage to mention it in confession among my manifold offences.

Eugenius. Bad! bad! Repentance is of little use to the sinner, unless he pour it from a full and overflowing heart into the capacious ear of the confessor. Ye must not go straightforward and bluntly up to your Maker, startling Him with the horrors of your guilty conscience. Order, decency, time, place, opportunity, must be observed.

Filippo. I have observed the greater part of them: time, place, and opportunity.

Eugenius. That is much. In consideration of it, I hereby absolve thee.

Filippo. I feel quite easy, quite new-born.

Eugenius. I am desirous of hearing what sort of feelings thou experiencest, when thou givest loose to thy intractable and unruly wishes. Now, this love of the world, what can it mean? A love of music, of dancing, of riding? What in short is it in thee?

Filippo. Holy Father! I was ever of a hot and amorous constitution.

Eugenius. Well, well! I can guess, within a trifle, what that leads unto. I very much disapprove of it, whatever it may be. And then? and then? Prithee go on: I am inflamed with a miraculous zeal to cleanse thee.

Filippo. I have committed many follies, and some sins.

Eugenius. Let me hear the sins; I do not trouble my head about the follies; the Church has no business with them. The State is founded on follies, the Church on sins. Come then, unsack them.

Filippo. Concupiscence is both a folly and a sin. I felt more and more of it when I ceased to be a monk, not having (for a time) so ready means of allaying it.

Eugenius. No doubt. Thou shouldst have thought again and again before thou strippedst off the cowl.

Filippo. Ah! Holy Father! I am sore at heart. I thought indeed how often it had held two heads together under it, and that stripping it off was double decapitation. But compensation and contentment came, and we were warm enough without it.

Eugenius. I am minded to reprove thee gravely. No wonder it pleased the Virgin, and the saints about her, to permit that the enemy of our faith should lead thee captive into Barbary.

Filippo. The pleasure was all on their side.

Eugenius. I have heard a great many stories both of males and females who were taken by Tunisians and Algerines: and although there is a sameness in certain parts of them, my especial benevolence toward thee, worthy Filippo, would induce me to lend a vacant ear to thy report. And now, good Filippo, I could sip a small glass of Muscatel or Orvieto, and turn over a few bleached almonds, or essay a smart dried apricot at intervals, and listen while thou relatest to me the manners and customs of that country, and particularly as touching thy own adversities. First, how wast thou taken?

Filippo. I was visiting at Pesaro my worshipful friend the canonico Andrea Paccone, who delighted in the guitar, played it skilfully, and was always fond of hearing it well accompanied by the voice. My own instrument I had brought with me, together with many gay Florentine songs, some of which were of such a turn and tendency, that the canonico thought they would sound better on water, and rather far from shore, than within the walls of the canonicate. He proposed then, one evening when there was little wind stirring, to exercise three young abbates[9] on their several parts, a little way out of hearing from the water's edge.

Eugenius. I disapprove of exercising young abbates in that manner.

Filippo. Inadvertently, O Holy Father! I have made the affair seem worse than it really was. In fact, there were only two genuine abbates; the third was Donna Lisetta, the good canonico's pretty niece, who looks so archly at your Holiness when you bend your knees before her at bedtime.

Eugenius. How? Where?

Filippo. She is the angel on the right-hand side of the Holy Family, with a tip of amethyst-coloured wing over a basket of figs and pomegranates. I painted her from memory: she was then only fifteen, and worthy to be the niece of an archbishop. Alas! she never will be: she plays and sings among the infidels, and perhaps would eat a landrail on a Friday as unreluctantly as she would a roach.

Eugenius. Poor soul! So this is the angel with the amethyst-coloured wing? I thought she looked wanton: we must pray for her release ... from the bondage of sin. What followed in your excursion?

Filippo. Singing, playing, fresh air, and plashing water, stimulated our appetites. We had brought no eatable with us but fruit and thin *marzopane*, of which the sugar and rose-water were inadequate to ward off hunger; and the sight of a fishing-vessel between us and Ancona, raised our host immoderately. 'Yonder smack,' said he, 'is sailing at this moment just over the best sole-bank in the Adriatic. If she continues her course and we run toward her, we may be supplied, I trust in God, with the finest fish in Christendom. Methinks I see already the bellies of those magnificent sole bestar the deck, and emulate the glories of the orient sky.' He gave his orders with such a majestic air, that he looked rather like an admiral than a priest.

Eugenius. How now, rogue! Why should not the churchman look majestically and courageously? I myself have found occasion for it, and exerted it.

Filippo. The world knows the prowess of your Holiness.

Eugenius. Not mine, not mine, Filippo! but His who gave me the sword and the keys, and the will and the discretion to use them. I trust the canonico did not misapply his station and power, by taking the fish at any unreasonably low price; and that he gave his blessing to the remainder, and to the poor fishermen and to their nets.

Filippo. He was angry at observing that the vessel, while he thought it was within hail, stood out again to sea.

Eugenius. He ought to have borne more manfully so slight a vexation.

Filippo. On the contrary, he swore bitterly he would have the master's ear between his thumb and forefinger in another half-hour, and regretted that he had cut his nails in the morning lest they should grate on his guitar. 'They may fish well,' cried he, 'but they can neither sail nor row; and, when I am in the middle of that tub of theirs, I will teach them more than they look for.' Sure enough he was in the middle of it at the time he fixed: but it was by aid of a rope about his arms and the end of another laid lustily on his back and shoulders. 'Mount, lazy long-chined turnspit, as thou valuest thy life,' cried Abdul the corsair, 'and away for Tunis.' If silence is consent, he had it. The captain, in the Sicilian dialect, told us we might talk freely, for he had taken his siesta. 'Whose guitars are those?' said he. As the canonico raised his eyes to heaven and answered nothing, I replied, 'Sir, one is mine: the other is my worthy friend's there.' Next he asked the canonico to what market he was taking those young slaves, pointing to the abbates. The canonico sobbed and could not utter one word. I related the whole story; at which he laughed. He then took up the music, and commanded my reverend guest to sing an air peculiarly tender, invoking the compassion of a nymph, and calling her cold as ice. Never did so many or such profound sighs accompany it. When it ended, he sang one himself in his own language, on a lady whose eyes were exactly like the scimitars of Damascus, and whose eyebrows met in the middle like the cudgels of prize-fighters. On the whole she resembled both sun and moon, with the simple difference that she never allowed herself to be seen, lest all the nations of the earth should go to war for her, and not a man to be left to breathe out his soul before her. This poem had obtained the prize at the University of Fez, had been translated into the Arabic, the Persian, and the Turkish languages, and was the favourite lay of the corsair. He invited me lastly to try my talent. I played the same air on the guitar, and apologized for omitting the words, from my utter ignorance of the Moorish. Abdul was much pleased, and took the trouble to convince me that the poetry they conveyed, which he translated literally, was incomparably better than ours. 'Cold as ice!' he repeated, scoffing: 'anybody might say that who had seen Atlas: but a genuine poet would rather say, "Cold as a lizard or a lobster."' There is no controverting a critic who has twenty stout rowers, and twenty well-knotted rope-ends. Added to which, he seemed to know as much of the matter as the generality of those who talked about it. He was gratified by my attention and edification, and thus continued: 'I have remarked in the songs I have heard, that these wild woodland creatures of the west, these nymphs, are a strange fantastical race. But are your poets not ashamed to complain of their inconstancy? whose fault is that? If ever it should be my fortune to take one, I would try whether I could not bring her down to the level of her sex; and if her inconstancy caused any complaints, by Allah! they should be louder and shriller than ever rose from the throat of Abdul.' I still thought it better to be a disciple than a commentator.

Eugenius. If we could convert this barbarian and detain him awhile at Rome, he would learn that women and nymphs (and inconstancy also) are one and the same. These cruel men have no lenity, no suavity. They who do not as they would be done by, are done by very much as they do. Women will glide away from them like water; they can better bear two masters than half one; and a new metal must be discovered before any bars are strong enough to confine them. But proceed with your narrative.

Filippo. Night had now closed upon us. Abdul placed the younger of the company apart, and after giving them some boiled rice, sent them down into his own cabin. The sailors, observing the consideration and distinction with which their master had treated me, were civil and obliging. Permission was granted me, at my request, to sleep on deck.

Eugenius. What became of your canonico?

Filippo. The crew called him a conger, a priest, and a porpoise.

Eugenius. Foul-mouthed knaves! could not one of these terms content them? On thy leaving Barbary was he left behind?

Filippo. Your Holiness consecrated him, the other day, Bishop of Macerata.

Eugenius. True, true; I remember the name, Saccone. How did he contrive to get off?

Filippo. He was worth little at any work; and such men are the quickest both to get off and to get on. Abdul told me he had received three thousand crowns for his ransom.

Eugenius. He was worth more to him than to me. I received but two first-fruits, and such other things as of right belong to me by inheritance. The bishopric is passably rich: he may serve thee.

Filippo. While he was a canonico he was a jolly fellow; not very generous; for jolly fellows are seldom that; but he would give a friend a dinner, a flask of wine or two in preference, and a piece of advice as readily as either. I waited on monsignor at Macerata, soon after his elevation.

Eugenius. He must have been heartily glad to embrace his companion in captivity, and the more especially as he himself was the cause of so grievous a misfortune.

Filippo. He sent me word he was so unwell he could not see me. 'What!' said I to his valet, 'is monsignor's complaint in his eyes?' The fellow shrugged up his shoulders and walked away. Not believing that the message was a refusal to admit me, I went straight upstairs, and finding the door of an antechamber half open, and a chaplain milling an egg-posset over the fire, I accosted him. The air of familiarity and satisfaction he observed in me left no doubt in his mind that I had been invited by his patron. 'Will the man never come?' cried his lordship. 'Yes, monsignor!' exclaimed I, running in and embracing him; 'behold him here!' He started back, and then I first discovered the wide difference between an old friend and an egg-posset.

Eugenius. Son Filippo! thou hast seen but little of the world, and art but just come from Barbary. Go on.

Filippo. 'Fra Filippo!' said he gravely, 'I am glad to see you. I did not expect you just at present: I am not very well: I had ordered a medicine and was impatient to take it. If you will favour me with the name of your inn, I will send for you when I am in a condition to receive you; perhaps within a day or two.' 'Monsignor!' said I, 'a change of residence often gives a man a cold, and oftener a change of fortune. Whether you caught yours upon deck (where we last saw each other), from being more exposed than usual, or whether the mitre holds wind, is no question for me, and no concern of mine.'

Eugenius. A just reproof, if an archbishop had made it. On uttering it, I hope thou kneeledst and kissedst his hand.

Filippo. I did not indeed.

Eugenius. Oh, there wert thou greatly in the wrong! Having, it is reported, a good thousand crowns yearly of patrimony, and a canonicate worth six hundred more, he might have attempted to relieve thee from slavery, by assisting thy relatives in thy redemption.

Filippo. The three thousand crowns were the uttermost he could raise, he declared to Abdul, and he asserted that a part of the money was contributed by the inhabitants of Pesaro. 'Do they act out of pure mercy?' said he. 'Ay, they must, for what else could move them in behalf of such a lazy, unserviceable street-fed cur?' In the morning, at sunrise, he was sent aboard. And now, the vessel being under weigh, 'I have a letter from my lord Abdul,' said the master, 'which, being in thy language, two fellow slaves shall read unto thee publicly.' They came forward and began the reading. 'Yesterday I purchased these two slaves from a cruel, unrelenting master, under whose lash they have laboured for nearly thirty years. I hereby give orders that five ounces of my own gold be weighed out to them.' Here one of the slaves fell on his face; the other lifted up his hands, praised God, and blessed his benefactor.

Eugenius. The pirate? the unconverted pirate?

Filippo. Even so. 'Here is another slip of paper for thyself to read immediately in my presence,' said the master. The words it contained were, 'Do thou the same, or there enters thy lips neither food nor water until thou landest in Italy. I permit thee to carry away more than double the sum: I am no sutler: I do not contract for thy sustenance.' The canonico asked of the master whether he knew the contents of the letter; he replied no. 'Tell your master, lord Abdul, that I shall take them into consideration.' 'My lord expected a much plainer answer, and commanded me, in case of any such as thou hast delivered, to break this seal.' He pressed it to his forehead and then broke it. Having perused the characters reverentially, 'Christian! dost thou consent?' The canonico fell on his knees, and overthrew the two poor wretches who, saying their prayers, had remained in the same posture before him quite unnoticed. 'Open thy trunk and take out thy money-bag, or I will make room for it in thy bladder.' The canonico was prompt in the execution of the command. The master drew out his scales, and desired the canonico to weigh with his own hand five ounces. He groaned and trembled: the balance was unsteady. 'Throw in another piece: it will not vitiate the agreement,' cried the master. It was done. Fear and grief are among the thirsty passions, but add little to the appetite. It seemed, however, as if every sigh had left a vacancy in the stomach of the canonico. At dinner the cook brought him a salted bonito, half an ell in length; and in five minutes his reverence was drawing his middle finger along the white backbone, out of sheer idleness, until were placed before him some as fine dried locusts as ever provisioned the tents of Africa, together with olives the size of eggs and colour of bruises, shining in oil and brine. He found them savoury and pulpy, and, as the last love supersedes the foregoing, he gave them the preference, even over the delicate locusts. When he had finished them, he modestly requested a can of water. A sailor brought a large flask, and poured forth a plentiful supply. The canonico engulfed the whole, and instantly threw himself back in convulsive agony. 'How is this?' cried the sailor. The master ran up and, smelling the water, began to buffet him, exclaiming, as he turned round to all the crew, 'How came this flask here?' All were innocent. It appeared, however, that it was a flask of mineral water, strongly sulphureous, taken out of a Neapolitan vessel, laden with a great abundance of it for some hospital in the Levant. It had taken the captor by surprise in the same manner as the canonico. He himself brought out instantly a capacious stone jar covered with dew, and invited the sufferer into the cabin. Here he drew forth two richly-cut wineglasses, and, on filling one of them, the outside of it turned suddenly pale, with a myriad of indivisible drops, and the senses were refreshed with the most delicious fragrance. He held up the glass between himself and his guest, and looking at it attentively, said, 'Here is no appearance of wine; all I can see is water. Nothing is wickeder than too much curiosity: we must take what Allah sends us, and render thanks for it, although it fall far short of our expectations. Besides, our Prophet would rather we should even drink wine than poison.' The canonico had not tasted wine for two months: a longer abstinence than ever canonico endured before. He drooped: but the master looked still more disconsolate. 'I would give whatever I possess on earth rather than die of thirst,' cried the canonico. 'Who would not?' rejoined the captain, sighing and clasping his fingers. 'If it were not contrary to my commands, I could touch at some cove or inlet.' 'Do, for the love of Christ!' exclaimed the canonico. 'Or even sail back,' continued the captain. 'O Santa Vergine!' cried in anguish the canonico. 'Despondency,' said the captain, with calm solemnity, 'has left many a man to be thrown overboard: it even renders the plague, and many other disorders, more fatal. Thirst too has a powerful effect in exasperating them. Overcome such weaknesses, or I must do my duty. The health of the ship's company is placed under my care; and our lord Abdul, if he suspected the pest, would throw a Jew, or a Christian, or even a bale of silk, into the sea: such is the disinterestedness and magnanimity of my lord Abdul.' 'He believes in fate; does he not?' said the canonico. 'Doubtless: but he says it is as much fated that he should throw into the sea a fellow who is infected, as that the fellow should have ever been so.' 'Save me, oh, save me!' cried the canonico, moist as if the spray had pelted him. 'Willingly, if possible,' answered calmly the master. 'At present I can discover no certain symptoms; for sweat, unless followed by general prostration, both of muscular strength and animal spirits, may be cured without a hook at the heel.' 'Giesu-Maria!' ejaculated the canonico.

Eugenius. And the monster could withstand that appeal?

Filippo. It seems so. The renegade who related to me, on my return, these events as they happened, was very circumstantial. He is a Corsican, and had killed many men in battle, and more out; but is (he gave me his word for it) on the whole an honest man.

Eugenius. How so? honest? and a renegade?

Filippo. He declared to me that, although the Mahomedan is the best religion to live in, the Christian is the best to die in; and that, when he has made his fortune, he will make his confession, and lie snugly in the bosom of the Church.

Eugenius. See here the triumphs of our holy faith! The lost sheep will be found again.

Filippo. Having played the butcher first.

Eugenius. Return we to that bad man, the master or captain, who evinced no such dispositions.

Filippo. He added, 'The other captives, though older men, have stouter hearts than mine.' 'Alas! they are longer used to hardships,' answered he. 'Dost thou believe, in thy conscience,' said the captain, 'that the water we have aboard would be harmless to them? for we have no other; and wine is costly; and our quantity might be insufficient for those who can afford to pay for it.' 'I will answer for their lives,' replied the canonico. 'With thy own?' interrogated sharply the Tunisian. 'I must not tempt God,' said, in tears, the religious man. 'Let us be plain,' said the master. 'Thou knowest thy money is safe; I myself counted it before thee when I brought it from the scrivener's; thou hast sixty broad gold pieces; wilt thou be answerable, to the whole amount of them, for the lives of thy two countrymen if they drink this water?' 'O sir!' said the canonico, 'I will give it, if, only for these few days of voyage, you vouchsafe me one bottle daily of that restorative wine of Bordeaux. The other two are less liable to the plague: they do not sorrow and sweat as I do. They are spare men. There is enough of me to infect a fleet with it; and I cannot bear to think of being in any wise the cause of evil to my fellow-creatures.' 'The wine is my patron's,' cried the Tunisian; 'he leaves everything at my discretion: should I deceive him?' 'If he leaves everything at your discretion,' observed the logician of Pesaro, 'there is no deceit in disposing of it.' The master appeared to be satisfied with the argument. 'Thou shalt not find me exacting,' said he; 'give me the sixty pieces, and the wine shall be thine.' At a signal, when the contract was agreed to, the two slaves entered, bringing a hamper of jars. 'Read the contract before thou signest,' cried the master. He read. 'How is this? how is this? Sixty golden ducats to the brothers Antonio and Bernabo Panini, for wine received from them?' The aged men tottered under the stroke of joy; and Bernabo, who would have embraced his brother, fainted.

On the morrow there was a calm, and the weather was extremely sultry. The canonico sat in his shirt on deck, and was surprised to see, I forget which of the brothers, drink from a goblet a prodigious draught of water. 'Hold!' cried he angrily; 'you may eat instead; but putrid or sulphureous water, you have heard, may produce the plague, and honest men be the sufferers by your folly and intemperance.' They assured him the water was tasteless, and very excellent, and had been kept cool in the same kind of earthern jars as the wine. He tasted it, and lost his patience. It was better, he protested, than any wine in the world. They begged his acceptance of the jar containing it. But the master, who had witnessed at a distance the whole proceeding, now advanced, and, placing his hand against it, said sternly, 'Let him have his own.' Usually, when he had emptied the second bottle, a desire of converting the Mohammedans came over him: and they showed themselves much less obstinate and refractory than they are generally thought. He selected those for edification who swore the oftenest and the loudest by the Prophet; and he boasted in his heart of having overcome, by precept and example, the stiffest tenet of their abominable creed. Certainly they drank wine, and somewhat freely. The canonico clapped his hands, and declared that even some of the apostles had been more pertinacious recusants of the faith.

Eugenius. Did he so? Cappari! I would not have made him a bishop for twice the money if I had known it earlier. Could not he have left them alone? Suppose one or other of them did doubt and persecute, was he the man to blab it out among the heathen?

Filippo. A judgment, it appears, fell on him for so doing. A very quiet sailor, who had always declined his invitations, and had always heard his arguments at a distance and in silence, being pressed and urged by him, and reproved somewhat arrogantly and loudly, as less docile than his messmates, at last lifted up his leg behind him, pulled off his right slipper, and counted deliberately and distinctly thirty-nine sound strokes of the same, on the canonico's broadest tablet, which (please your Holiness) might be called, not inaptly, from that day the tablet of memory. In vain he cried out. Some of the mariners made their moves at chess and waved their left hands as if desirous of no interruption; others went backward and forward about their business, and took no more notice than if their messmate was occupied in caulking a seam or notching a flint. The master himself, who saw the operation, heard the complaint in the evening, and lifted up his shoulders and eyebrows, as if the whole were quite unknown to him. Then, acting as judge-advocate, he called the young man before him and repeated the accusation. To this the defence was purely interrogative. 'Why would he convert me? I never converted him.' Turning to his spiritual guide, he said, 'I quite forgive thee: nay, I am ready to appear in thy favour, and to declare that, in general, thou hast been more decorous than people of thy faith and profession usually are, and hast not scattered on deck that inflammatory language which I, habited in the dress of a Greek, heard last Easter. I went into three churches; and the preachers in all three denounced the curse of Allah on every soul that differed from them a tittle. They were children of perdition, children of darkness, children of the devil, one and all. It seemed a matter of wonder to me, that, in such numerous families and of such indifferent parentage, so many slippers were kept under the heel. Mine, in an evil hour, escaped me: but I quite forgive thee. After this free pardon I will indulge thee with a short specimen of my preaching. I will call none of you a generation of vipers, as ye call one another; for vipers neither bite nor eat during many months of the year: I will call none of you wolves in sheep's clothing; for if ye are, it must be acknowledged that the clothing is very clumsily put on. You priests, however, take people's souls aboard whether they will or not, just as we do your bodies: and you make them pay much more for keeping these in slavery than we make you pay for setting you free body and soul together. You declare that the precious souls, to the especial care of which Allah has called and appointed you, frequently grow corrupt, and stink in His nostrils. Now, I invoke thy own testimony to the fact that thy soul, gross as I imagine it to be from the greasy wallet that holds it, had no carnal thoughts whatsoever, and that thy carcass did not even receive a fly-blow, while it was under my custody. Thy guardian angel (I speak it in humility) could not ventilate thee better. Nevertheless, I should scorn to demand a single maravedi for my labour and skill, or for the wear and tear of my pantoufle. My reward will be in Paradise, where a houri is standing in the shade, above a vase of gold and silver fish, with a kiss on her lip, and an unbroken pair of green slippers in her hand for me.' Saying which, he took off his foot again, the one he had been using, and showed the sole of it, first to the master, then to all the crew, and declared it had become (as they might see) so smooth and oily by the application, that it was dangerous to walk on deck in it.

Eugenius. See! what notions these creatures have, both of their fool's paradise and of our holy faith! The seven Sacraments, I warrant you, go for nothing! Purgatory, purgatory itself, goes for nothing!

Filippo. Holy Father! we must stop thee. *That* does not go for nothing, however.

Eugenius. Filippo! God forbid I should suspect thee of any heretical taint; but this smells very like it. If thou hast it now, tell me honestly. I mean, hold thy tongue. Florentines are rather lax. Even Son Cosimo might be stricter: so they say: perhaps his enemies. The great always have them abundantly, beside those by whom they are served, and those also whom they serve. Now would I give a silver rose with my benediction on it, to know of a certainty what became of those poor creatures the abbates. The initiatory rite of Mohammedanism is most diabolically malicious. According to the canons of our Catholic Church, it disqualifies the neophyte for holy orders, without going so far as adapting him to the choir of the pontifical chapel. They limp; they halt.

Filippo. Beatitude! which of them?

Eugenius. The unbelievers: they surely are found wanting.

Filippo. The unbelievers too?

Eugenius. Ay, ay, thou half renegade! Couldst not thou go over with a purse of silver, and try whether the souls of these captives be recoverable? Even if they should have submitted to such unholy rites, I venture to say they have repented.

Filippo. The devil is in them if they have not.

Eugenius. They may become again as good Christians as before.

Filippo. Easily, methinks.

Eugenius. Not so easily; but by aid of Holy Church in the administration of indulgences.

Filippo. They never wanted those, whatever they want.

Eugenius. The corsair then is not one of those ferocious creatures which appear to connect our species with the lion and panther.

Filippo. By no means, Holy Father! He is an honest man; so are many of his countrymen, bating the Sacrament.

Eugenius. Bating! poor beguiled Filippo! Being unbaptized, they are only as the beasts that perish: nay worse: for the soul being imperishable, it must stick to their bodies at the last day, whether they will or no, and must sink with it into the fire and brimstone.

Filippo. Unbaptized! why, they baptize every morning.

Eugenius. Worse and worse! I thought they only missed the stirrup; I find they overleap the saddle. Obstinate blind reprobates! of whom it is written ... of whom it is written ... of whom, I say, it is written ... as shall be manifest before men and angels in the day of wrath.

Filippo. More is the pity! for they are hospitable, frank, and courteous. It is delightful to see their gardens, when one has not the weeding and irrigation of them. What fruit! what foliage! what trellises! what alcoves! what a contest of rose and jessamine for supremacy in odour! of lute and nightingale for victory in song! And how the little bright ripples of the docile brooks, the fresher for their races, leap up against one another, to look on! and how they chirrup and applaud, as if they too had a voice of some importance in these parties of pleasure that are loath to separate.

Eugenius. Parties of pleasure! birds, fruits, shallow-running waters, lute-players, and wantons! Parties of pleasure! and composed of these! Tell me now, Filippo, tell me truly, what complexion in general have the discreeter females of that hapless country.

Filippo. The colour of an orange-flower, on which an overladen bee has left a slight suffusion of her purest honey.

Eugenius. We must open their eyes.

Filippo. Knowing what excellent hides the slippers of this people are made of, I never once ventured on their less perfect theology, fearing to find it written that I should be abed on my face the next fortnight. My master had expressed his astonishment that a religion so admirable as ours was represented should be the only one in the world the precepts of which are disregarded by all conditions of men. 'Our Prophet,' said he, 'our Prophet ordered us to go forth and conquer; we did it: yours ordered you to sit quiet and forbear; and, after spitting in His face, you threw the order back into it, and fought like devils.'

Eugenius. The barbarians talk of our Holy Scriptures as if they understood them perfectly. The impostor they follow has nothing but fustian and rodomontade in his impudent lying book from beginning to end. I know it, Filippo, from those who have contrasted it, page by page, paragraph by paragraph, and have given the knave his due.

Filippo. Abdul is by no means deficient in a good opinion of his own capacity and his Prophet's all-sufficiency, but he never took me to task about my faith or his own.

Eugenius. How wert thou mainly occupied?

Filippo. I will give your Holiness a sample both of my employments and of his character. He was going one evening to a country-house, about fifteen miles from Tunis; and he ordered me to accompany him. I found there a spacious garden, overrun with wild flowers and most luxuriant grass, in irregular tufts, according to the dryness or the humidity of the spot. The clematis overtopped the lemon and orange-trees; and the perennial pea sent forth here a pink blossom, here a purple, here a white one, and after holding (as it were) a short conversation with the humbler plants, sprang up about an old cypress, played among its branches, and mitigated its gloom. White pigeons, and others in colour like the dawn of day, looked down on us and ceased to coo, until some of their companions, in whom they had more confidence, encouraged them loudly from remoter boughs, or alighted on the shoulders of Abdul, at whose side I was standing. A few of them examined me in every position their inquisitive eyes could take; displaying all the advantages of their versatile necks, and pretending querulous fear in the midst of petulant approaches.

Eugenius. Is it of pigeons thou art talking, O Filippo? I hope it may be.

Filippo. Of Abdul's pigeons. He was fond of taming all creatures; men, horses, pigeons, equally: but he tamed them all by kindness. In this wilderness is an edifice not unlike our Italian chapter-houses built by the Lombards, with long narrow windows, high above the ground. The centre is now a bath, the waters of which, in another part of the enclosure, had supplied a fountain, at present in ruins, and covered by tufted canes, and by every variety of aquatic plants. The structure has no remains of roof: and, of six windows, one alone is unconcealed by ivy. This had been walled up long ago, and the cement in the inside of it was hard and polished. 'Lippi!' said Abdul to me, after I had long admired the place in silence, 'I leave to thy superintendence this bath and garden. Be sparing of the leaves and branches: make paths only wide enough for me. Let me see no mark of hatchet or pruning-hook, and tell the labourers that whoever takes a nest or an egg shall be impaled.'

Eugenius. Monster! so then he would really have impaled a poor wretch for eating a bird's egg? How disproportionate is the punishment to the offence!

Filippo. He efficiently checked in his slaves the desire of transgressing his command. To spare them as much as possible, I ordered them merely to open a few spaces, and to remove the weaker trees from the stronger. Meanwhile I drew on the smooth blank window the figure of Abdul and of a beautiful girl.

Eugenius. Rather say handmaiden: choicer expression; more decorous.

Filippo. Holy Father! I have been lately so much out of practice, I take the first that comes in my way. Handmaiden I will use in preference for the future.

Eugenius. On then! and God speed thee!

Filippo. I drew Abdul with a blooming handmaiden. One of his feet is resting on her lap, and she is drying the ankle with a saffron robe, of which the greater part is fallen in doing it. That she is a bondmaid is discernible, not only by her occupation, but by her humility and patience, by her loose and flowing brown hair, and by her eyes expressing the timidity at once of servitude and of fondness. The countenance was taken from fancy, and was the loveliest I could imagine: of the figure I had some idea, having seen it to advantage in Tunis. After seven days Abdul returned. He was delighted with the improvement made in the garden. I requested him to visit the bath. 'We can do nothing to that,' answered he impatiently. 'There is no sudatory, no dormitory, no dressing-room, no couch. Sometimes I sit an hour there in the summer, because I never found a fly in it--the principal curse of hot countries, and against which plague there is neither prayer nor amulet, nor indeed any human defence.' He went away into the house. At dinner he sent me from his table some quails and ortolans, and tomatoes and honey and rice, beside a basket of fruit covered with moss and bay-leaves, under which I found a verdino fig, deliciously ripe, and bearing the impression of several small teeth, but certainly no reptile's.

Eugenius. There might have been poison in them, for all that.

Filippo. About two hours had passed, when I heard a whir and a crash in the windows of the bath (where I had dined and was about to sleep), occasioned by the settling and again the flight of some pheasants. Abdul entered. 'Beard of the Prophet! what hast thou been doing? That is myself! No, no, Lippi! thou never canst have seen her: the face proves it: but those limbs! thou hast divined them aright: thou hast had sweet dreams then! Dreams are large possessions: in them the possessor may cease to possess his own. To the slave, O Allah! to the slave is permitted what is not his!... I burn with anguish to think how much ... yea, at that very hour. I would not another should, even in a dream.... But, Lippi! thou never canst have seen above the sandal?' To which I answered, 'I never have allowed my eyes to look even on that. But if any one of my lord Abdul's fair slaves resembles, as they surely must all do, in duty and docility, the figure I have represented, let it express to him my congratulation on his happiness.' 'I believe,' said he, 'such representations are forbidden by the Koran; but as I do not remember it, I do not sin. There it shall stay, unless the angel Gabriel comes to forbid it.' He smiled in saying so.

Eugenius. There is hope of this Abdul. His faith hangs about him more like oil than pitch.

Filippo. He inquired of me whether I often thought of those I loved in Italy, and whether I could bring them before my eyes at will. To remove all suspicion from him, I declared I always could, and that one beautiful object occupied all the cells of my brain by night and day. He paused and pondered, and then said, 'Thou dost not love deeply.' I thought I had given the true signs. 'No, Lippi! we who love ardently, we, with all our wishes, all the efforts of our souls, cannot bring before us the features which, while they were present, we thought it impossible we ever could forget. Alas! when we most love the absent, when we most desire to see her, we try in vain to bring her image back to us. The troubled heart shakes and confounds it, even as ruffled waters do with shadows. Hateful things are more hateful when they haunt our sleep: the lovely flee away, or are changed into less lovely.'

Eugenius. What figures now have these unbelievers?

Filippo. Various in their combinations as the letters or the numerals; but they all, like these, signify something. Almeida (did I not inform your Holiness?) has large hazel eyes....

Eugenius. Has she? thou never toldest me that. Well, well! and what else has she? Mind! be cautious! use decent terms.

Filippo. Somewhat pouting lips.

Eugenius. Ha! ha! What did they pout at?

Filippo. And she is rather plump than otherwise.

Eugenius. No harm in that.

Filippo. And moreover is cool, smooth, and firm as a nectarine gathered before sunrise.

Eugenius. Ha! ha! do not remind me of nectarines. I am very fond of them; and this is not the season! Such females as thou describest are said to be among the likeliest to give reasonable cause for suspicion. I would not judge harshly, I would not think uncharitably; but, unhappily, being at so great a distance from spiritual aid, peradventure a desire, a suggestion, an inkling ... ay? If she, the lost Almeida, came before thee when her master was absent ... which I trust she never did.... But those flowers and shrubs and odours and alleys and long grass and alcoves, might strangely hold, perplex, and entangle, two incautious young persons ... ay?

Filippo. I confessed all I had to confess in this matter the evening I landed.

Eugenius. Ho! I am no candidate for a seat at the rehearsal of confessions: but perhaps my absolution might be somewhat more pleasing and unconditional. Well! well! since I am unworthy of such confidence, go about thy business ... paint! paint!

Filippo. Am I so unfortunate as to have offended your Beatitude?

Eugenius. Offend *me*, man! who offends *me*? I took an interest in thy adventures, and was concerned lest thou mightest have sinned; for by my soul! Filippo! those are the women that the devil hath set his mark on.

Filippo. It would do your Holiness's heart good to rub it out again, wherever he may have had the cunning to make it.

Eugenius. Deep! deep!

Filippo. Yet it may be got at; she being a Biscayan by birth, as she told me, and not only baptized, but going by sea along the coast for confirmation, when she was captured.

Eugenius. Alas! to what an imposition of hands was this tender young thing devoted! Poor soul!

Filippo. I sigh for her myself when I think of her.

Eugenius. Beware lest the sigh be mundane, and lest the thought recur too often. I wish it were presently in my power to examine her myself on her condition. What thinkest thou? Speak.

Filippo. Holy Father! she would laugh in your face.

Eugenius. So lost!

Filippo. She declared to me she thought she should have died, from the instant she was captured until she was comforted by Abdul: but that she was quite sure she should if she were ransomed.

Eugenius. Has the wretch then shaken her faith?

Filippo. The very last thing he would think of doing. Never did I see the virtue of resignation in higher perfection than in the laughing, light-hearted Almeida.

Eugenius. Lamentable! Poor lost creature! lost in this world and in the next.

Filippo. What could she do? how could she help herself?

Eugenius. She might have torn his eyes out, and have died a martyr.

Filippo. Or have been bastinadoed, whipped, and given up to the cooks and scullions for it.

Eugenius. Martyrdom is the more glorious the greater the indignities it endures.

Filippo. Almeida seems unambitious. There are many in our Tuscany who would jump at the crown over those sloughs and briers, rather than perish without them: she never sighs after the like.

Eugenius. Nevertheless, what must she witness! what abominations! what superstitions!

Filippo. Abdul neither practises nor exacts any other superstition than ablutions.

Eugenius. Detestable rites! without our authority. I venture to affirm that, in the whole of Italy and Spain, no convent of monks or nuns contains a bath; and that the worst inmate of either would shudder at the idea of observing such a practice in common with the unbeliever. For the washing of the feet indeed we have the authority of the earlier Christians; and it may be done; but solemnly and sparingly. Thy residence among the Mahomedans, I am afraid, hath rendered thee more favourable to them than beseems a Catholic, and thy mind, I do suspect, sometimes goes back into Barbary unreluctantly.

Filippo. While I continued in that country, although I was well treated, I often wished myself away, thinking of my friends in Florence, of music, of painting, of our villeggiatura at the vintage-time; whether in the green and narrow glades of Pratolino, with lofty trees above us, and little rills unseen, and little bells about the necks of sheep and goats, tinkling together ambiguously; or amid the grey quarries, or under the majestic walls of modern Fiesole; or down in the woods of the Doccia, where the cypresses are of such a girth that, when a youth stands against one of them, and a maiden stands opposite, and they clasp it, their hands at the time do little more than meet. Beautiful scenes, on which heaven smiles eternally, how often has my heart ached for you! He who hath lived in this country can enjoy no distant one. He breathes here another air; he lives more life; a brighter sun invigorates his studies, and serener stars influence his repose. Barbary hath also the blessing of climate; and although I do not desire to be there again, I feel sometimes a kind of regret at leaving it. A bell warbles the more mellifluously in the air when the sound of the stroke is over, and when another swims out from underneath it, and pants upon the element that gave it birth. In like manner the recollection of a thing is frequently more pleasing than the actuality; what is harsh is dropped in the space between. There is in Abdul a nobility of soul on which I often have reflected with admiration. I have seen many of the highest rank and distinction, in whom I could find nothing of the great man, excepting a fondness for low company, and an aptitude to shy and start at every spark of genius or virtue that sprang up above or before them. Abdul was solitary, but affable: he was proud, but patient and complacent. I ventured once to ask him how the master of so rich a house in the city, of so many slaves, of so many horses and mules, of such cornfields, of such pastures, of such gardens, woods, and fountains, should experience any delight or satisfaction in infesting the open sea, the high-road of nations. Instead of answering my question, he asked me in return whether I would not respect any relative of mine who avenged his country, enriched himself by his bravery, and endeared to him his friends and relatives by his bounty. On my reply in the affirmative, he said that his family had been deprived of possessions in Spain much more valuable than all the ships and cargoes he could ever hope to capture, and that the remains of his nation were threatened with ruin and expulsion. 'I do not fight,' said he, 'whenever it suits the convenience, or gratifies the malignity, or the caprice of two silly, quarrelsome princes, drawing my sword in perfectly good humour, and sheathing it again at word of command, just when I begin to get into a passion. No; I fight on my own account; not as a hired assassin, or still baser journeyman.'

Eugenius. It appears then really that the Infidels have some semblances of magnanimity and generosity?

Filippo. I thought so when I turned over the many changes of fine linen; and I was little short of conviction when I found at the bottom of my chest two hundred Venetian zecchins.

Eugenius. Corpo di Bacco! Better things, far better things, I would fain do for thee, not exactly of this description; it would excite many heart-burnings. Information has been laid before me, Filippo, that thou art attached to a certain young person, by name Lucrezia, daughter of Francesco Buti, a citizen of Prato.

Filippo. I acknowledge my attachment: it continues.

Eugenius. Furthermore, that thou hast offspring by her.

Filippo. Alas! 'tis undeniable.

Eugenius. I will not only legitimatize the said offspring by *motu proprio* and rescript to consistory and chancery....

Filippo. Holy Father! Holy Father! For the love of the Virgin, not a word to consistory or chancery of the two hundred zecchins. As I hope for salvation, I have but forty left, and thirty-nine would not serve them.

Eugenius. Fear nothing. Not only will I perform what I have promised, not only will I give the strictest order that no money be demanded by any officer of my courts, but, under the seal of Saint Peter, I will declare thee and Lucrezia Buti man and wife.

Filippo. Man and wife!

Eugenius. Moderate thy transport.

Filippo. O Holy Father! may I speak?

Eugenius. Surely she is not the wife of another?

Filippo. No, indeed.

Eugenius. Nor within the degrees of consanguinity and affinity?

Filippo. No, no, no. But ... man and wife! Consistory and chancery are nothing to this fulmination.

Eugenius. How so?

Filippo. It is man and wife the first fortnight, but wife and man ever after. The two figures change places: the unit is the decimal and the decimal is the unit.

Eugenius. What, then, can I do for thee?

Filippo. I love Lucrezia; let me love her; let her love me. I can make her at any time what she is not; I could never make her again what she is.

Eugenius. The only thing I can do then is to promise I will forget that I have heard anything about the matter. But, to forget it, I must hear it first.

Filippo. In the beautiful little town of Prato, reposing in its idleness against the hill that protects it from the north, and looking over fertile meadows, southward to Poggio Cajano, westward to Pistoja, there is the convent of Santa Margarita. I was invited by the sisters to paint an altar-piece for the chapel. A novice of fifteen, my own sweet Lucrezia, came one day alone to see me work at my Madonna. Her blessed countenance had already looked down on every beholder lower by the knees. I myself who made her could almost have worshipped her.

Eugenius. Not while incomplete; no half-virgin will do.

Filippo. But there knelt Lucrezia! there she knelt! first looking with devotion at the Madonna, then with admiring wonder and grateful delight at the artist. Could so little a heart be divided? 'Twere a pity! There was enough for me; there is never enough for the Madonna. Resolving on a sudden that the object of my love should be the object of adoration to thousands, born and unborn, I swept my brush across the maternal face, and left a blank in heaven. The little girl screamed; I pressed her to my bosom.

Eugenius. In the chapel?

Filippo. I knew not where I was; I thought I was in Paradise.

Eugenius. If it was not in the chapel, the sin is venial. But a brush against a Madonna's mouth is worse than a beard against her votary's.

Filippo. I thought so too, Holy Father!

Eugenius. Thou sayest thou hast forty zecchins; I will try in due season to add forty more. The fisherman must not venture to measure forces with the pirate. Farewell! I pray God my son Filippo, to have thee alway in His holy keeping.

NOTE:

[9] Little boys, wearing clerical habits, are often called *__abbati__*.

TASSO AND CORNELIA

Tasso. She is dead, Cornelia! she is dead!

Cornelia. Torquato! my Torquato! after so many years of separation do I bend once more your beloved head to my embrace?

Tasso. She is dead!

Cornelia. Tenderest of brothers! bravest and best and most unfortunate of men! What, in the name of heaven, so bewilders you?

Tasso. Sister! sister! sister! I could not save her.

Cornelia. Certainly it was a sad event; and they who are out of spirits may be ready to take it for an evil omen. At this season of the year the vintagers are joyous and negligent.

Tasso. How! What is this?

Cornelia. The little girl was crushed, they say, by a wheel of the car laden with grapes, as she held out a handful of vine-leaves to one of the oxen. And did you happen to be there at the moment?

Tasso. So then the little too can suffer! the ignorant, the indigent, the unaspiring! Poor child! She was kind-hearted, else never would calamity have befallen her.

Cornelia. I wish you had not seen the accident.

Tasso. I see it? I? I saw it not. No other is crushed where I am. The little girl died for her kindness! Natural death!

Cornelia. Be calm, be composed, my brother!

Tasso. You would not require me to be composed or calm if you comprehended a thousandth part of my sufferings.

Cornelia. Peace! peace! we know them all.

Tasso. Who has dared to name them? Imprisonment, derision, madness.

Cornelia. Hush! sweet Torquato! If ever these existed, they are past.

Tasso. You do think they are sufferings? ay?

Cornelia. Too surely.

Tasso. No, not too surely: I will not have that answer. They would have been; but Leonora was then living. Unmanly as I am! did I complain of them? and while she was left me?

Cornelia. My own Torquato! is there no comfort in a sister's love? Is there no happiness but under the passions? Think, O my brother, how many courts there are in Italy: are the princes more fortunate than you? Which among them all loves truly, deeply, and virtuously? Among them all is there any one, for his genius, for his generosity, for his gentleness, ay, for his mere humanity, worthy to be beloved?

Tasso. Princes! talk to me of princes! How much cross-grained wood a little gypsum covers! a little carmine quite beautifies! Wet your forefinger with your spittle; stick a broken gold-leaf on the sinciput; clip off a beggar's beard to make it tresses; kiss it; fall down before it; worship it. Are you not irradiated by the light of its countenance? Princes! princes! Italian princes! Estes! What matters that costly carrion? Who thinks about it? [**After a pause.**] She is dead! She is dead!

Cornelia. We have not heard it here.

Tasso. At Sorrento you hear nothing but the light surges of the sea, and the sweet sprinkles of the guitar.

Cornelia. Suppose the worst to be true.

Tasso. Always, always.

Cornelia. If she ceases, as then perhaps she must, to love and to lament you, think gratefully, contentedly, devoutly, that her arms had clasped your neck before they were crossed upon her bosom, in that long sleep which you have rendered placid, and from which your harmonious voice shall once more awaken her. Yes, Torquato! her bosom had throbbed to yours, often and often, before the organ peal shook the fringes round the catafalque. Is not this much, from one so high, so beautiful?

Tasso. Much? yes; for abject me. But I did so love her! so love her!

Cornelia. Ah! let the tears flow: she sends you that balm from heaven.

Tasso. So love her did poor Tasso! Else, O Cornelia, it had indeed been much. I thought, in the simplicity of my heart, that God was as great as an emperor, and could bestow and had bestowed on me as much as the German had conferred or could confer on his vassal. No part of my insanity was ever held in such ridicule as this. And yet the idea cleaves to me strangely, and is liable to stick to my shroud.

Cornelia. Woe betide the woman who bids you to forget that woman who has loved you: she sins against her sex. Leonora was unblameable. Never think ill of her for what you have suffered.

Tasso. Think ill of her? I? I? I? No; those we love, we love for everything; even for the pain they have given us. But she gave me none; it was where she was not that pain was.

Cornelia. Surely, if love and sorrow are destined for companionship, there is no reason why the last comer of the two should supersede the first.

Tasso. Argue with me, and you drive me into darkness. I am easily persuaded and led on while no reasons are thrown before me. With these you have made my temples throb again. Just heaven! dost thou grant us fairer fields, and wider, for the whirlwind to lay waste? Dost thou build us up habitations above the street, above the palace, above the citadel, for the plague to enter and carouse in? Has not my youth paid its dues, paid its penalties? Cannot our griefs come first, while we have strength to bear them? The fool! the fool! who thinks it a misfortune that his love is unrequited. Happier young man! look at the violets until thou drop asleep on them. Ah! but thou must awake!

Cornelia. O heavens! what must you have suffered! for a man's heart is sensitive in proportion to its greatness.

Tasso. And a woman's?

Cornelia. Alas! I know not; but I think it can be no other. Comfort thee, comfort thee, dear Torquato!

Tasso. Then do not rest thy face upon my arm; it so reminds me of her. And thy tears too! they melt me into her grave.

Cornelia. Hear you not her voice as it appeals to you, saying to you, as the priests around have been saying to *her*, Blessed soul! rest in peace?

Tasso. I heard it not; and yet I am sure she said it. A thousand times has she repeated it, laying her head on my heart to quiet it, simple girl! She told it to rest in peace ... and she went from me! Insatiable love! ever self-torturer, never self-destroyer! the world, with all its weight of miseries, cannot crush thee, cannot keep thee down. Generally men's tears, like the droppings of certain springs, only harden and petrify what they fall on; but mine sank deep into a tender heart, and were its very blood. Never will I believe she has left me utterly. Oftentimes, and long before her departure, I fancied we were in heaven together. I fancied it in the fields, in the gardens, in the palace, in the prison. I fancied it in the broad daylight, when my eyes were open, when blessed spirits drew around me that golden circle which one only of earth's inhabitants could enter. Oftentimes in my sleep also I fancied it; and sometimes in the intermediate state, in that serenity which breathes about the transported soul, enjoying its pure and perfect rest, a span below the feet of the Immortal.

Cornelia. She has not left you; do not disturb her peace by these repinings.

Tasso. She will bear with them. Thou knowest not what she was, Cornelia; for I wrote to thee about her while she seemed but human. In my hours of sadness, not only her beautiful form, but her very voice bent over me. How girlish in the gracefulness of her lofty form! how pliable in her majesty! what composure at my petulance and reproaches! what pity in her reproofs! Like the air that angels breathe in the metropolitan temple of the Christian world, her soul at every season preserved one temperature. But it was when she could and did love me! Unchanged must ever be the blessed one who has leaned in fond security on the unchangeable. The purifying flame shoots upward, and is the glory that encircles their brows when they meet above.

Cornelia. Indulge in these delightful thoughts, my Torquato! and believe that your love is and ought to be imperishable as your glory. Generations of men move forward in endless procession to consecrate and commemorate both. Colour-grinders and gilders, year after year, are bargained with to refresh the crumbling monuments and tarnished decorations of rude, unregarded royalty, and to fasten the nails that cramp the crown upon its head. Meanwhile, in the laurels of my Torquato there will always be one leaf above man's reach, above time's wrath and injury, inscribed with the name of Leonora.

Tasso. O Jerusalem! I have not then sung in vain the Holy Sepulchre.

Cornelia. After such devotion of your genius, you have undergone too many misfortunes.

Tasso. Congratulate the man who has had many, and may have more. I have had, I have, I can have, one only.

Cornelia. Life runs not smoothly at all seasons, even with the happiest; but after a long course, the rocks subside, the views widen, and it flows on more equably at the end.

Tasso. Have the stars smooth surfaces? No, no; but how they shine!

Cornelia. Capable of thoughts so exalted, so far above the earth we dwell on, why suffer any to depress and anguish you?

Tasso. Cornelia, Cornelia! the mind has within its temples and porticoes and palaces and towers: the mind has under it, ready for the course, steeds brighter than the sun and stronger than the storm; and beside them stand winged chariots, more in number than the Psalmist hath attributed to the Almighty. The mind, I tell thee again, hath its hundred gates, compared whereto the Theban are but willow wickets; and all those hundred gates can genius throw open. But there are some that groan heavily on their hinges, and the hand of God alone can close them.

Cornelia. Torquato has thrown open those of His holy temple; Torquato hath stood, another angel, at His tomb; and am I the sister of Torquato? Kiss me, my brother, and let my tears run only from my pride and joy! Princes have bestowed knighthood on the worthy and unworthy; thou hast called forth those princes from their ranks, pushing back the arrogant and presumptuous of them like intrusive varlets, and conferring on the bettermost crowns and robes, imperishable and unfading.

Tasso. I seem to live back into those days. I feel the helmet on my head; I wave the standard over it: brave men smile upon me; beautiful maidens pull them gently back by the scarf, and will not let them break my slumber, nor undraw the curtain. Corneliolina!...

Cornelia. Well, my dear brother! why do you stop so suddenly in the midst of them? They are the pleasantest and best company, and they make you look quite happy and joyous.

Tasso. Corneliolina, dost thou remember Bergamo? What city was ever so celebrated for honest and valiant men, in all classes, or for beautiful girls! There is but one class of those: Beauty is above all ranks; the true Madonna, the patroness and bestower of felicity, the queen of heaven.

Cornelia. Hush, Torquato, hush! talk not so.

Tasso. What rivers, how sunshiny and revelling, are the Brembo and the Serio! What a country the Valtellina! I went back to our father's house, thinking to find thee again, my little sister; thinking to kick away thy ball of yellow silk as thou wast stooping for it, to make thee run after me and beat me. I woke early in the morning; thou wert grown up and gone. Away to Sorrento: I knew the road: a few strides brought me back: here I am. To-morrow, my Cornelia, we will walk together, as we used to do, into the cool and quiet caves on the shore; and we will catch the little breezes as they come in and go out again on the backs of the jocund waves.

Cornelia. We will indeed to-morrow; but before we set out we must take a few hours' rest, that we may enjoy our ramble the better.

Tasso. Our Sorrentines, I see, are grown rich and avaricious. They have uprooted the old pomegranate hedges, and have built high walls to prohibit the wayfarer from their vineyards.

Cornelia. I have a basket of grapes for you in the book-room that overlooks our garden.

Tasso. Does the old twisted sage-tree grow still against the window?

Cornelia. It harboured too many insects at last, and there was always a nest of scorpions in the crevice.

Tasso. Oh! what a prince of a sage-tree! And the well, too, with its bucket of shining metal, large enough for the largest cocomero to cool in it for dinner.

Cornelia. The well, I assure you, is as cool as ever.

Tasso. Delicious! delicious! And the stone-work round it, bearing no other marks of waste than my pruning-hook and dagger left behind?

Cornelia. None whatever.

Tasso. White in that place no longer; there has been time enough for it to become all of one colour: grey, mossy, half-decayed.

Cornelia. No, no; not even the rope has wanted repair.

Tasso. Who sings yonder?

Cornelia. Enchanter! No sooner did you say the word cocomero than here comes a boy carrying one upon his head.

Tasso. Listen! listen! I have read in some book or other those verses long ago. They are not unlike my ***Aminta***. The very words!

Cornelia. Purifier of love, and humanizer of ferocity, how many, my Torquato, will your gentle thoughts make happy!

Tasso. At this moment I almost think I am one among them.[10]

Cornelia. Be quite persuaded of it. Come, brother, come with me. You shall bathe your heated brow and weary limbs in the chamber of your childhood. It is there we are always the most certain of repose. The boy shall sing to you those sweet verses; and we will reward him with a slice of his own fruit.

Tasso. He deserves it; cut it thick.

Cornelia. Come then, my truant! Come along, my sweet smiling Torquato!

Tasso. The passage is darker than ever. Is this the way to the little court? Surely those are not the steps that lead down toward the bath? Oh yes! we are right; I smell the lemon-blossoms. Beware of the old wilding that bears them; it may catch your veil; it may scratch your fingers! Pray, take care: it has many thorns about it. And now, Leonora! you shall hear my last verses! Lean your ear a little toward me; for I must repeat them softly under this low archway, else others may hear them too. Ah! you press my hand once more. Drop it, drop it! or the verses will sink into my breast again, and lie there silent! Good girl!

> Many, well I know, there are
> Ready in your joys to share,
> And (I never blame it) you
> Are almost as ready too.
> But when comes the darker day,
> And those friends have dropt away,
> Which is there among them all
> You should, if you could, recall?
> One who wisely loves and well
> Hears and shares the griefs you tell;
> Him you ever call apart
> When the springs o'erflow the heart;
> For you know that he alone
> Wishes they were **but** his own.
> Give, while these he may divide,

Smiles to all the world beside.

Cornelia. We are now in the full light of the chamber; cannot you remember it, having looked so intently all around?

Tasso. O sister! I could have slept another hour. You thought I wanted rest: why did you waken me so early? I could have slept another hour or longer. What a dream! But I am calm and happy.

Cornelia. May you never more be otherwise! Indeed, he cannot be whose last verses are such as those.

Tasso. Have you written any since that morning?

Cornelia. What morning?

Tasso. When you caught the swallow in my curtains, and trod upon my knees in catching it, luckily with naked feet. The little girl of thirteen laughed at the outcry of her brother Torquatino, and sang without a blush her earliest lay.

Cornelia. I do not recollect it.

Tasso. I do.

> Rondinello! rondinello!
> Tu sei nero, ma sei bello.
> Cosa fa se tu sei nero?
> Rondinello! sei il primiero
> De' volanti, palpitanti,
> (E vi sono quanti quanti!)
> Mai tenuto a questo petto,
> E percio sei il mio diletto.[11]

Cornelia. Here is the cocomero; it cannot be more insipid. Try it.

Tasso. Where is the boy who brought it? where is the boy who sang my ***Aminta***? Serve him first; give him largely. Cut deeper; the knife is too short: deeper; mia brava Corneliolina! quite through all the red, and into the middle of the seeds. Well done!

NOTES:

[10] The miseries of Tasso arose not only from the imagination and the heart. In the metropolis of the Christian world, with many admirers and many patrons, bishops, cardinals, princes, he was left destitute, and almost famished. These are his own words: '***Appena*** in questo stato ho comprato ***due meloni***: e benche io sia stato quasi sempre infermo, molte volte mi sono contentato del manzo: e la ministra di latte o di zucca, ***quando ho potuto averne***, mi e stata in vece di delizie.' In another part he says that he was unable to pay the carriage of a parcel. No wonder; if he had not wherewithal to buy enough of zucca for a meal. Even had he been in health and appetite, he might have satisfied his hunger with it for about five farthings, and have left half for supper. And now a word on his insanity. Having been so imprudent not only as to make it too evident in his poetry that he was the lover of Leonora, but also to signify (not very obscurely) that his love was returned, he much perplexed the Duke of Ferrara, who, with great discretion, suggested to him the necessity of feigning madness. The lady's honour required it from a brother; and a true lover, to convince the world, would embrace the project with alacrity. But there was no reason why the seclusion should be in a dungeon, or why exercise and air should be interdicted. This cruelty, and perhaps his uncertainty of Leonora's compassion, may well be imagined to have produced at last the malady he had feigned. But did Leonora love Tasso as a man would be loved? If we wish to do her

honour, let us hope it: for what greater glory can there be, than to have estimated at the full value so exalted a genius, so affectionate and so generous a heart!

[11] The author wrote the verses first in English, but he found it easy to write them better in Italian: they stood in the text as below: they only do for a girl of thirteen:

> 'Swallow! swallow! though so jetty
> Are your pinions, you are pretty:
> And what matter were it though
> You were blacker than a crow?
> Of the many birds that fly
> (And how many pass me by!)
> You 're the first I ever prest,
> Of the many, to my breast:
> Therefore it is very right
> You should be my own delight.'

LA FONTAINE AND DE LA ROCHEFOUCAULT

La Fontaine. I am truly sensible of the honour I receive, M. de la Rochefoucault, in a visit from a personage so distinguished by his birth and by his genius. Pardon my ambition, if I confess to you that I have long and ardently wished for the good fortune, which I never could promise myself, of knowing you personally.

Rochefoucault. My dear M. de la Fontaine!

La Fontaine. Not '*de* la', not '*de* la'. I am *La* Fontaine, purely and simply.

Rochefoucault. The whole; not derivative. You appear, in the midst of your purity, to have been educated at court, in the lap of the ladies. What was the last day (pardon!) I had the misfortune to miss you there?

La Fontaine. I never go to court. They say one cannot go without silk stockings; and I have only thread: plenty of them indeed, thank God! Yet, would you believe it? Nanon, in putting a *solette* to the bottom of one, last week, sewed it so carelessly, she made a kind of cord across: and I verily believe it will lame me for life; for I walked the whole morning upon it.

Rochefoucault. She ought to be whipped.

La Fontaine. I thought so too, and grew the warmer at being unable to find a wisp of osier or a roll of packthread in the house. Barely had I begun with my garter, when in came the Bishop of Grasse, my old friend Godeau, and another lord, whose name he mentioned, and they both interceded for her so long and so touchingly, that at last I was fain to let her rise up and go. I never saw men look down on the erring and afflicted more compassionately. The bishop was quite concerned for me also. But the other, although he professed to feel even more, and said that it must surely be the pain of purgatory to me, took a pinch of snuff, opened his waistcoat, drew down his ruffles, and seemed rather more indifferent.

Rochefoucault. Providentially, in such moving scenes, the worst is soon over. But Godeau's friend was not too sensitive.

La Fontaine. Sensitive! no more than if he had been educated at the butcher's or the Sorbonne.

Rochefoucault. I am afraid there are as many hard hearts under satin waistcoats as there are ugly visages under the same material in miniature cases.

La Fontaine. My lord, I could show you a miniature case which contains your humble servant, in which the painter has done what no tailor in his senses would do; he has given me credit for a coat of violet silk, with silver frogs as large as tortoises. But I am loath to get up for it while the generous heart of this dog (if I mentioned his name he would jump up) places such confidence on my knee.

Rochefoucault. Pray do not move on any account; above all, lest you should disturb that amiable grey cat, fast asleep in his innocence on your shoulder.

La Fontaine. Ah, rogue! art thou there? Why! thou hast not licked my face this half-hour.

Rochefoucault. And more, too, I should imagine. I do not judge from his somnolency, which, if he were President of the Parliament, could not be graver, but from his natural sagacity. Cats weigh practicabilities. What sort of tongue has he?

La Fontaine. He has the roughest tongue and the tenderest heart of any cat in Paris. If you observe the colour of his coat, it is rather blue than grey; a certain indication of goodness in these contemplative creatures.

Rochefoucault. We were talking of his tongue alone; by which cats, like men, are flatterers.

La Fontaine. Ah! you gentlemen of the court are much mistaken in thinking that vices have so extensive a range. There are some of our vices, like some of our diseases, from which the quadrupeds are exempt; and those, both diseases and vices, are the most discreditable.

Rochefoucault. I do not bear patiently any evil spoken of the court: for it must be acknowledged, by the most malicious, that the court is the purifier of the whole nation.

La Fontaine. I know little of the court, and less of the whole nation; but how can this be?

Rochefoucault. It collects all ramblers and gamblers; all the market-men and market-women who deal in articles which God has thrown into their baskets, without any trouble on their part; all the seducers and all who wish to be seduced; all the duellists who erase their crimes with their swords, and sweat out their cowardice with daily practice; all the nobles whose patents of nobility lie in gold snuff-boxes, or have worn Mechlin ruffles, or are deposited within the archives of knee-deep waistcoats; all stock-jobbers and church-jobbers, the black-legged and the red-legged game, the flower of the *justaucorps*, the *robe*, and the *soutane*. If these were spread over the surface of France, instead of close compressure in the court or cabinet, they would corrupt the whole country in two years. As matters now stand, it will require a quarter of a century to effect it.

La Fontaine. Am I not right then in preferring my beasts to yours? But if yours were loose, mine (as you prove to me) would be the last to suffer by it, poor dear creatures! Speaking of cats, I would have avoided all personality that might be offensive to them: I would not exactly have said, in so many words, that, by their tongues, they are flatterers, like men. Language may take a turn advantageously in favour of our friends. True, we resemble all animals in something. I am quite ashamed and mortified that your lordship, or anybody, should have had the start of me in this reflection. When a cat flatters with his tongue he is not insincere: you may safely take it for a real kindness. He is loyal, M. de la Rochefoucault! my word for him, he is loyal. Observe too, if you please, no cat ever licks you when he wants anything from you; so that there is nothing of baseness in such an act of adulation, if we must call it so. For my part, I am slow to designate by so foul a name, that (be it what it may) which is subsequent to a kindness. Cats ask plainly for what they want.

Rochefoucault. And, if they cannot get it by protocols they get it by invasion and assault.

La Fontaine. No! no! usually they go elsewhere, and fondle those from whom they obtain it. In this I see no resemblance to invaders and conquerors. I draw no parallels: I would excite no heart-burnings between us and them. Let all have their due.

I do not like to lift this creature off, for it would waken him, else I could find out, by some subsequent action, the reason why he has not been on the alert to lick my cheek for so long a time.

Rochefoucault. Cats are wary and provident. He would not enter into any contest with you, however friendly. He only licks your face, I presume, while your beard is but a match for his tongue.

La Fontaine. Ha! you remind me. Indeed I did begin to think my beard was rather of the roughest; for yesterday Madame de Rambouillet sent me a plate of strawberries, the first of the season, and raised (would you believe it?) under glass. One of these strawberries was dropping from my lips, and I attempted to stop it. When I thought it had fallen to the ground, 'Look for it, Nanon; pick it up and eat it,' said I.

'Master!' cried the wench, 'your beard has skewered and spitted it.' 'Honest girl,' I answered, 'come, cull it from the bed of its adoption.'

I had resolved to shave myself this morning: but our wisest and best resolutions too often come to nothing, poor mortals!

Rochefoucault. We often do very well everything but the only thing we hope to do best of all; and our projects often drop from us by their weight. A little while ago your friend Moliere exhibited a remarkable proof of it.

La Fontaine. Ah, poor Moliere! the best man in the world; but flighty, negligent, thoughtless. He throws himself into other men, and does not remember where. The sight of an eagle, M. de la

Rochefoucault, but the memory of a fly.

Rochefoucault. I will give you an example: but perhaps it is already known to you.

La Fontaine. Likely enough. We have each so many friends, neither of us can trip but the other is invited to the laugh. Well; I am sure he has no malice, and I hope I have none: but who can see his own faults?

Rochefoucault. He had brought out a new edition of his comedies.

La Fontaine. There will be fifty; there will be a hundred: nothing in our language, or in any, is so delightful, so graceful; I will add, so clear at once and so profound.

Rochefoucault. You are among the few who, seeing well his other qualities, see that Moliere is also profound. In order to present the new edition to the dauphin, he had put on a sky-blue velvet coat, powdered with fleurs-de-lis. He laid the volume on his library table; and, resolving that none of the courtiers should have an opportunity of ridiculing him for anything like absence of mind, he returned to his bedroom, which, as may often be the case in the economy of poets, is also his dressing-room. Here he surveyed himself in his mirror, as well as the creeks and lagoons in it would permit.

La Fontaine. I do assure you, from my own observation, M. de la Rochefoucault, that his mirror is a splendid one. I should take it to be nearly three feet high, reckoning the frame, with the Cupid above and the elephant under. I suspected it was the present of some great lady; and indeed I have since heard as much.

Rochefoucault. Perhaps then the whole story may be quite as fabulous as the part of it which I have been relating.

La Fontaine. In that case, I may be able to set you right again.

Rochefoucault. He found his peruke a model of perfection; tight, yet easy; not an inch more on one side than on the other. The black patch on the forehead....

La Fontaine. Black patch too! I would have given a fifteen-sous piece to have caught him with that black patch.

Rochefoucault. He found it lovely, marvellous, irresistible. Those on each cheek....

La Fontaine. Do you tell me he had one on each cheek?

Rochefoucault. Symmetrically. The cravat was of its proper descent, and with its appropriate charge of the best Strasburg snuff upon it. The waistcoat, for a moment, puzzled and perplexed him. He was not quite sure whether the right number of buttons were in their holes; nor how many above, nor how many below, it was the fashion of the week to leave without occupation. Such a piece of ignorance is enough to disgrace any courtier on earth. He was in the act of striking his forehead with desperation; but he thought of the patch, fell on his knees, and thanked Heaven for the intervention.

La Fontaine. Just like him! just like him! good soul!

Rochefoucault. The breeches ... ah! those require attention: all proper: everything in its place. Magnificent. The stockings rolled up, neither too loosely nor too negligently. A picture! The buckles in the shoes ... all but one ... soon set to rights ... well thought of! And now the sword ... ah, that cursed sword! it will bring at least one man to the ground if it has its own way much longer ... up with it! up with it higher.... **Allons!** we are out of danger.

La Fontaine. Delightful! I have him before my eyes. What simplicity! aye, what simplicity!

Rochefoucault. Now for hat. Feather in? Five at least. Bravo!

He took up hat and plumage, extended his arm to the full length, raised it a foot above his head, lowered it thereon, opened his fingers, and let them fall again at his side.

La Fontaine. Something of the comedian in that; aye, M. de la Rochefoucault? But, on the stage or off, all is natural in Moliere.

Rochefoucault. Away he went: he reached the palace, stood before the dauphin.... O consternation! O despair! 'Morbleu! bete que je suis,' exclaimed the hapless man, 'le livre, ou donc est-il?' You are forcibly struck, I perceive, by this adventure of your friend.

La Fontaine. Strange coincidence! quite unaccountable! There are agents at work in our dreams, M. de la Rochefoucault, which we shall never see out of them, on this side the grave. [**To himself.**]
Sky-blue? no. Fleurs-de-lis? bah! bah! Patches? I never wore one in my life.

Rochefoucault. It well becomes your character for generosity, M. La Fontaine, to look grave, and ponder, and ejaculate, on a friend's untoward accident, instead of laughing, as those who little know you, might expect. I beg your pardon for relating the occurrence.

La Fontaine. Right or wrong, I cannot help laughing any longer. Comical, by my faith! above the tiptop of comedy. Excuse my flashes and dashes and rushes of merriment. Incontrollable! incontrollable! Indeed the laughter is immoderate. And you all the while are sitting as grave as a judge; I mean a criminal one; who has nothing to do but to keep up his popularity by sending his rogues to the gallows. The civil indeed have much weighty matter on their minds: they must displease one party: and sometimes a doubt arises whether the fairer hand or the fuller shall turn the balance.

Rochefoucault. I congratulate you on the return of your gravity and composure.

La Fontaine. Seriously now: all my lifetime I have been the plaything of dreams. Sometimes they have taken such possession of me, that nobody could persuade me afterward they were other than real events. Some are very oppressive, very painful, M. de la Rochefoucault! I have never been able, altogether, to disembarrass my head of the most wonderful vision that ever took possession of any man's. There are some truly important differences, but in many respects this laughable adventure of my innocent, honest friend Moliere seemed to have befallen myself. I can only account for it by having heard the tale when I was half asleep.

Rochefoucault. Nothing more probable.

La Fontaine. You absolutely have relieved me from an incubus.

Rochefoucault. I do not yet see how.

La Fontaine. No longer ago than when you entered this chamber, I would have sworn that I myself had gone to the Louvre, that I myself had been commanded to attend the dauphin, that I myself had come into his presence, had fallen on my knee, and cried, 'Peste! ou est donc le livre?' Ah, M. de la Rochefoucault, permit me to embrace you: this is really to find a friend at court.

Rochefoucault. My visit is even more auspicious than I could have ventured to expect: it was chiefly for the purpose of asking your permission to make another at my return to Paris.... I am forced to go into the country on some family affairs: but hearing that you have spoken favourably of my *Maxims*, I presume to express my satisfaction and delight at your good opinion.

La Fontaine. Pray, M. de la Rochefoucault, do me the favour to continue here a few minutes. I would gladly reason with you on some of your doctrines.

Rochefoucault. For the pleasure of hearing your sentiments on the topics I have treated, I will, although it is late, steal a few minutes from the court, of which I must take my leave on parting for the province.

La Fontaine. Are you quite certain that all your *Maxims* are true, or, what is of greater consequence, that they are all original? I have lately read a treatise written by an Englishman, Mr. Hobbes; so loyal a man that, while others tell you kings are appointed by God, he tells you God is appointed by kings.

Rochefoucault. Ah! such are precisely the men we want. If he establishes this verity, the rest will follow.

La Fontaine. He does not seem to care so much about the rest. In his treatise I find the ground-plan of your chief positions.

Rochefoucault. I have indeed looked over his publication; and we agree on the natural depravity of man.

La Fontaine. Reconsider your expression. It appears to me that what is natural is not depraved: that depravity is deflection from nature. Let it pass: I cannot, however, concede to you that the generality of men are bad. Badness is accidental, like disease. We find more tempers good than bad, where proper care is taken in proper time.

Rochefoucault. Care is not nature.

La Fontaine. Nature is soon inoperative without it; so soon indeed as to allow no opportunity for experiment or hypothesis. Life itself requires care, and more continually than tempers and morals do. The strongest body ceases to be a body in a few days without a supply of food. When we speak of men being naturally bad or good, we mean susceptible and retentive and communicative of them. In this case (and there can be no other true or ostensible one) I believe that the more are good; and nearly in the same proportion as there are animals and plants produced healthy and vigorous than wayward and weakly. Strange is the opinion of Mr. Hobbes, that, when God hath poured so abundantly His benefits on other creatures, the only one capable of great good should be uniformly disposed to greater evil.

Rochefoucault. Yet Holy Writ, to which Hobbes would reluctantly appeal, countenances the supposition.

La Fontaine. The Jews, above all nations, were morose and splenetic. Nothing is holy to me that lessens in my view the beneficence of my Creator. If you could show Him ungentle and unkind in a single instance, you would render myriads of men so, throughout the whole course of their lives, and those too among the most religious. The less that people talk about God the better. He has left us a design to fill up: He has placed the canvas, the colours, and the pencils, within reach; His directing hand is over ours incessantly; it is our business to follow it, and neither to turn round and argue with our Master, nor to kiss and fondle Him. We must mind our lesson, and not neglect our time: for the room is closed early, and the lights are suspended in another, where no one works. If every man would do all the good he might within an hour's walk from his house, he would live the happier and the longer: for nothing is so conducive to longevity as the union of activity and content. But, like children, we deviate from the road, however well we know it, and run into mire and puddles in despite of frown and ferule.

Rochefoucault. Go on, M. La Fontaine! pray go on. We are walking in the same labyrinth, always within call, always within sight of each other. We set out at its two extremities, and shall meet at last.

La Fontaine. I doubt it. From deficiency of care proceed many vices, both in men and children, and more still from care taken improperly. Mr. Hobbes attributes not only the order and peace of society, but equity and moderation and every other virtue, to the coercion and restriction of the laws. The laws, as now constituted, do a great deal of good; they also do a great deal of mischief. They transfer more property from the right owner in six months than all the thieves of the kingdom do in twelve. What the thieves take they soon disseminate abroad again; what the laws take they hoard. The thief takes a part of your property: he who prosecutes the thief for you takes another part: he who condemns the thief goes to the tax-gatherer and takes the third. Power has been hitherto occupied in no employment but in keeping down Wisdom. Perhaps the time may come when Wisdom shall exert her energy in repressing the sallies of Power.

Rochefoucault. I think it more probable that they will agree; that they will call together their servants of all liveries, to collect what they can lay their hands upon; and that meanwhile they will sit together like good housewives, making nets from our purses to cover the coop for us. If you would be plump and in feather, pick up your millet and be quiet in your darkness. Speculate on nothing here below, and I promise you a nosegay in Paradise.

La Fontaine. Believe me, I shall be most happy to receive it there at your hands, my lord duke.

The greater number of men, I am inclined to think, with all the defects of education, all the frauds committed on their credulity, all the advantages taken of their ignorance and supineness, are disposed, on most occasions, rather to virtue than to vice, rather to the kindly affections than the unkindly, rather to the social than the selfish.

Rochefoucault. Here we differ: and were my opinion the same as yours, my book would be little read and less commended.

La Fontaine. Why think so?

Rochefoucault. For this reason. Every man likes to hear evil of all men: every man is delighted to take the air of the common, though not a soul will consent to stand within his own allotment. No enclosure act! no finger-posts! You may call every creature under heaven fool and rogue, and your auditor will join with you heartily: hint to him the slightest of his own defects or foibles, and he draws the rapier. You and he are the judges of the world, but not its denizens.

La Fontaine. Mr. Hobbes has taken advantage of these weaknesses. In his dissertation he betrays the timidity and malice of his character. It must be granted he reasons well, according to the view he has taken of things; but he has given no proof whatever that his view is a correct one. I will believe that it is, when I am persuaded that sickness is the natural state of the body, and health the unnatural. If you call him a sound philosopher, you may call a mummy a sound man. Its darkness, its hardness, its forced uprightness, and the place in which you find it, may commend it to you; give me rather some weakness and peccability, with vital warmth and human sympathies. A shrewd reasoner in one thing, a sound philosopher is another. I admire your power and precision. Monks will admonish us how little the author of the ***Maxims*** knows of the world; and heads of colleges will cry out 'a libel on human nature!' but when they hear your titles, and, above all, your credit at court, they will cast back cowl, and peruke, and lick your boots. You start with great advantages. Throwing off from a dukedom, you are sure of enjoying, if not the tongue of these puzzlers, the full cry of the more animating, and will certainly be as long-lived as the imperfection of our language will allow. I consider your ***Maxims*** as a broken ridge of hills, on the shady side of which you are fondest of taking your exercise: but the same ridge hath also a sunny one. You attribute (let me say it again) all actions to self-interest. Now, a sentiment of interest must be preceded by calculation, long or brief, right or erroneous. Tell me then in what region lies the origin of that pleasure which a family in the country feels on the arrival of an unexpected friend. I say a family in the country; because the sweetest souls, like the sweetest flowers, soon canker in cities, and no purity is rarer there than the purity of delight. If I may judge from the few examples I have been in a position to see, no earthly one can be greater. There are pleasures which lie near the surface, and which are blocked up by artificial ones, or are diverted by some mechanical scheme, or are confined by some stiff evergreen vista of low advantage. But these pleasures do occasionally burst forth in all their brightness; and, if ever you shall by chance find one of them, you will sit by it, I hope, complacently and cheerfully, and turn toward it the kindliest aspect of your meditations.

Rochefoucault. Many, indeed most people, will differ from me. Nothing is quite the same to the intellect of any two men, much less of all. When one says to another, 'I am entirely of your opinion,' he uses in general an easy and indifferent phrase, believing in its accuracy, without examination, without thought. The nearest resemblance in opinions, if we could trace every line of it, would be found greatly more divergent than the nearest in the human form or countenance, and in the same proportion as the varieties of mental qualities are more numerous and fine than of the bodily. Hence I do not expect nor wish that my opinions should in all cases be similar to those of others: but in many I shall be gratified if, by just degrees and after a long survey, those of others approximate to mine. Nor does this my sentiment spring from a love of power, as in many good men quite unconsciously, when they would make proselytes, since I shall see few and converse with fewer of them, and profit in no way by their adherence and favour; but it springs from a natural and a cultivated love of all truths whatever, and from a certainty that these delivered by me are conducive to the happiness and dignity of man. You shake your head.

La Fontaine. Make it out.

Rochefoucault. I have pointed out to him at what passes he hath deviated from his true interest, and where he hath mistaken selfishness for generosity, coldness for judgment, contraction of heart for policy, rank for merit, pomp for dignity; of all mistakes, the commonest and the greatest. I am accused of paradox and distortion. On paradox I shall only say, that every new moral truth has been called so. Inexperienced and negligent observers see no difference in the operations of ravelling and unravelling: they never come close enough: they despise plain work.

La Fontaine. The more we simplify things, the better we descry their substances and qualities. A good writer will not coil them up and press them into the narrowest possible space, nor macerate them into such particles that nothing shall be remaining of their natural contexture. You are accused of this too, by such as have forgotten your title-page, and who look for treatises where maxims only have been promised. Some of them perhaps are spinning out sermons and dissertations from the poorest paragraph in the volume.

Rochefoucault. Let them copy and write as they please; against or for, modestly or impudently. I have hitherto had no assailant who is not of too slender a make to be detained an hour in the stocks he had unwarily put his foot into. If you hear of any, do not tell of them. On the subjects of my remarks, had others thought as I do, my labour would have been spared me. I am ready to point out the road where I know it, to whosoever wants it; but I walk side by side with few or none.

La Fontaine. We usually like those roads which show us the fronts of our friends' houses and the pleasure-grounds about them, and the smooth garden-walks, and the trim espaliers, and look at them with more satisfaction than at the docks and nettles that are thrown in heaps behind. The ***Offices*** of Cicero are imperfect; yet who would not rather guide his children by them than by the line and compass of harder-handed guides; such as Hobbes for instance?

Rochefoucault. Imperfect as some gentlemen in hoods may call the ***Offices***, no founder of a philosophical or of a religious sect has been able to add to them anything important.

La Fontaine. Pity! that Cicero carried with him no better authorities than reason and humanity. He neither could work miracles, nor damn you for disbelieving them. Had he lived fourscore years later, who knows but he might have been another Simon Peter, and have talked Hebrew as fluently as Latin, all at once! Who knows but we might have heard of his patrimony! who knows but our venerable popes might have claimed dominion from him, as descendant from the kings of Rome!

Rochefoucault. The hint, some centuries ago, would have made your fortune, and that saintly cat there would have kittened in a mitre.

La Fontaine. Alas! the hint could have done nothing: Cicero could not have lived later.

Rochefoucault. I warrant him. Nothing is easier to correct than chronology. There is not a lady in Paris, nor a jockey in Normandy, that is not eligible to a professor's chair in it. I have seen a man's ancestor, whom nobody ever saw before, spring back over twenty generations. Our Vatican Jupiters have as little respect for old Chronos as the Cretan had: they mutilate him when and where they think necessary, limp as he may by the operation.

La Fontaine. When I think, as you make me do, how ambitious men are, even those whose teeth are too loose (one would fancy) for a bite at so hard an apple as the devil of ambition offers them, I am inclined to believe that we are actuated not so much by selfishness as you represent it, but under another form, the love of power. Not to speak of territorial dominion or political office, and such other things as we usually class under its appurtenances, do we not desire an exclusive control over what is beautiful and lovely? the possession of pleasant fields, of well-situated houses, of cabinets, of images, of pictures, and indeed of many things pleasant to see but useless to possess; even of rocks, of streams, and of fountains? These things, you will tell me, have their utility. True, but not to the wisher, nor does the idea of it enter his mind. Do not we wish that the object of our love should be devoted to us only; and that our children should love us better than their brothers and sisters, or even than the mother who bore them? Love would be arrayed in the purple robe of sovereignty, mildly as he may resolve to exercise his power.

Rochefoucault. Many things which appear to be incontrovertible are such for their age only, and must yield to others which, in their age, are equally so. There are only a few points that are always above the waves. Plain truths, like plain dishes, are commended by everybody, and everybody leaves them whole. If it were not even more impertinent and presumptuous to praise a great writer in his presence than to censure him in his absence, I would venture to say that your prose, from the few specimens you have given of it, is equal to your verse. Yet, even were I the possessor of such a style as yours, I would never employ it to support my *Maxims*. You would think a writer very impudent and self-sufficient who should quote his own works: to defend them is doing more. We are the worst auxiliaries in the world to the opinions we have brought into the field. Our business is, to measure the ground, and to calculate the forces; then let them try their strength. If the weak assails me, he thinks me weak; if the strong, he thinks me strong. He is more likely to compute ill his own vigour than mine. At all events, I love inquiry, even when I myself sit down. And I am not offended in my walks if my visitor asks me whither does that alley lead. It proves that he is ready to go on with me; that he sees some space before him; and that he believes there may be something worth looking after.

La Fontaine. You have been standing a long time, my lord duke: I must entreat you to be seated.

Rochefoucault. Excuse me, my dear M. la Fontaine; I would much rather stand.

La Fontaine. Mercy on us! have you been upon your legs ever since you rose to leave me?

Rochefoucault. A change of position is agreeable: a friend always permits it.

La Fontaine. Sad doings! sad oversight! The other two chairs were sent yesterday evening to be scoured and mended. But that dog is the best tempered dog! an angel of a dog, I do assure you; he would have gone down in a moment, at a word. I am quite ashamed of myself for such inattention. With your sentiments of friendship for me, why could you not have taken the liberty to shove him gently off, rather than give me this uneasiness?

Rochefoucault. My true and kind friend! we authors are too sedentary; we are heartily glad of standing to converse, whenever we can do it without any restraint on our acquaintance.

La Fontaine. I must reprove that animal when he uncurls his body. He seems to be dreaming of Paradise and houris. Ay, twitch thy ear, my child! I wish at my heart there were as troublesome a fly about the other: God forgive me! The rogue covers all my clean linen! shirt and cravat! what cares he!

Rochefoucault. Dogs are not very modest.

La Fontaine. Never say that, M. de la Rochefoucault! The most modest people upon earth! Look at a dog's eyes, and he half closes them, or gently turns them away, with a motion of the lips, which he licks languidly, and of the tail, which he stirs tremulously, begging your forbearance. I am neither blind nor indifferent to the defects of these good and generous creatures. They are subject to many such as men are subject to: among the rest, they disturb the neighbourhood in the discussion of their private causes; they quarrel and fight on small motives, such as a little bad food, or a little vainglory, or the sex. But it must be something present or near that excites them; and they calculate not the extent of evil they may do or suffer.

Rochefoucault. Certainly not: how should dogs calculate?

La Fontaine. I know nothing of the process. I am unable to inform you how they leap over hedges and brooks, with exertion just sufficient, and no more. In regard to honour and a sense of dignity, let me tell you, a dog accepts the subsidies of his friends, but never claims them: a dog would not take the field to obtain power for a son, but would leave the son to obtain it by his own activity and prowess. He conducts his visitor or inmate out a-hunting, and makes a present of the game to him as freely as an emperor to an elector. Fond as he is of slumber, which is indeed one of the pleasantest and best things in the universe, particularly after dinner, he shakes it off as willingly as he would a gadfly, in order to defend his master from theft or violence. Let the robber or assailant speak as courteously as he may, he waives your diplomatical terms, gives his reasons in plain language, and makes war. I could say many other things to his advantage; but I never was malicious, and would rather let both parties plead for themselves; give me the dog, however.

Rochefoucault. Faith! I will give you both, and never boast of my largess in so doing.

La Fontaine. I trust I have removed from you the suspicion of selfishness in my client, and I feel it quite as easy to make a properer disposal of another ill attribute, namely cruelty, which we vainly try to shuffle off our own shoulders upon others, by employing the offensive and most unjust term, brutality. But to convince you of my impartiality, now I have defended the dog from the first obloquy, I will defend the man from the last, hoping to make you think better of each. What you attribute to cruelty, both while we are children and afterward, may be assigned, for the greater part, to curiosity. Cruelty tends to the extinction of life, the dissolution of matter, the imprisonment and sepulture of truth; and if it were our ruling and chief propensity, the human race would have been extinguished in a few centuries after its appearance. Curiosity, in its primary sense, implies care and consideration.

Rochefoucault. Words often deflect from their primary sense. We find the most curious men the most idle and silly, the least observant and conservative.

La Fontaine. So we think; because we see every hour the idly curious, and not the strenuously; we see only the persons of the one set, and only the works of the other.

More is heard of cruelty than of curiosity, because while curiosity is silent both in itself and about its object, cruelty on most occasions is like the wind, boisterous in itself, and exciting a murmur and bustle in all the things it moves among. Added to which, many of the higher topics whereto our curiosity would turn, are intercepted from it by the policy of our guides and rulers; while the principal ones on which cruelty is most active, are pointed to by the sceptre and the truncheon, and wealth and dignity are the rewards of their attainment. What perversion! He who brings a bullock into a city for its sustenance is called a butcher, and nobody has the civility to take off the hat to him, although knowing him as perfectly as I know Matthieu le Mince, who served me with those fine kidneys you must have remarked in passing through the kitchen: on the contrary, he who reduces the same city to famine is styled M. le General or M. le Marechal, and gentlemen like you, unprejudiced (as one would think) and upright, make room for him in the antechamber.

Rochefoucault. He obeys orders without the degrading influence of any passion.

La Fontaine. Then he commits a baseness the more, a cruelty the greater. He goes off at another man's setting, as ingloriously as a rat-trap: he produces the worst effects of fury, and feels none: a

Cain unirritated by a brother's incense.

Rochefoucault. I would hide from you this little rapier, which, like the barber's pole, I have often thought too obtrusive in the streets.

La Fontaine. Never shall I think my countrymen half civilized while on the dress of a courtier is hung the instrument of a cut-throat. How deplorably feeble must be that honour which requires defending at every hour of the day!

Rochefoucault. Ingenious as you are, M. La Fontaine, I do not believe that, on this subject, you could add anything to what you have spoken already; but really, I do think one of the most instructive things in the world would be a dissertation on dress by you.

La Fontaine. Nothing can be devised more commodious than the dress in fashion. Perukes have fallen among us by the peculiar dispensation of Providence. As in all the regions of the globe the indigenous have given way to stronger creatures, so have they (partly at least) on the human head. At present the wren and the squirrel are dominant there. Whenever I have a mind for a filbert, I have only to shake my foretop. Improvement does not end in that quarter. I might forget to take my pinch of snuff when it would do me good, unless I saw a store of it on another's cravat. Furthermore, the slit in the coat behind tells in a moment what it was made for: a thing of which, in regard to ourselves, the best preachers have to remind us all our lives: then the central part of our habiliment has either its loop-hole or its portcullis in the opposite direction, still more demonstrative. All these are for very mundane purposes: but Religion and Humanity have whispered some later utilities. We pray the more commodiously, and of course the more frequently, for rolling up a royal ell of stocking round about our knees: and our high-heeled shoes must surely have been worn by some angel, to save those insects which the flat-footed would have crushed to death.

Rochefoucault. Ah! the good dog has awakened: he saw me and my rapier, and ran away. Of what breed is he? for I know nothing of dogs.

La Fontaine. And write so well!

Rochefoucault. Is he a truffler?

La Fontaine. No, not he; but quite as innocent.

Rochefoucault. Something of the shepherd-dog, I suspect.

La Fontaine. Nor that neither; although he fain would make you believe it. Indeed he is very like one: pointed nose, pointed ears, apparently stiff, but readily yielding; long hair, particularly about the neck; noble tail over his back, three curls deep, exceedingly pleasant to stroke down again; straw-colour all above, white all below. He might take it ill if you looked for it; but so it is, upon my word: an ermeline might envy it.

Rochefoucault. What are his pursuits?

La Fontaine. As to pursuit and occupation, he is good for nothing. In fact, I like those dogs best ... and those men too.

Rochefoucault. Send Nanon then for a pair of silk stockings, and mount my carriage with me: it stops at the Louvre.

LUCIAN AND TIMOTHEUS

Timotheus. I am delighted, my Cousin Lucian, to observe how popular are become your ***Dialogues of the Dead***. Nothing can be so gratifying and satisfactory to a rightly disposed mind, as the subversion of imposture by the force of ridicule. It hath scattered the crowd of heathen gods as if a thunderbolt had fallen in the midst of them. Now, I am confident you never would have assailed the false religion, unless you were prepared for the reception of the true. For it hath always been an indication of rashness and precipitancy, to throw down an edifice before you have collected materials for reconstruction.

Lucian. Of all metaphors and remarks, I believe this of yours, my good cousin Timotheus, is the most trite, and pardon me if I add, the most untrue. Surely we ought to remove an error the instant we detect it, although it may be out of our competence to state and establish what is right. A lie should be exposed as soon as born: we are not to wait until a healthier child is begotten. Whatever is evil in any way should be abolished. The husbandman never hesitates to eradicate weeds, or to burn them up, because he may not happen at the time to carry a sack on his shoulder with wheat or barley in it. Even if no wheat or barley is to be sown in future, the weeding and burning are in themselves beneficial, and something better will spring up.

Timotheus. That is not so certain.

Lucian. Doubt it as you may, at least you will allow that the temporary absence of evil is an advantage.

Timotheus. I think, O Lucian, you would reason much better if you would come over to our belief.

Lucian. I was unaware that belief is an encourager and guide to reason.

Timotheus. Depend upon it, there can be no stability of truth, no elevation of genius, without an unwavering faith in our holy mysteries. Babes and sucklings who are blest with it, stand higher, intellectually as well as morally, than stiff unbelievers and proud sceptics.

Lucian. I do not wonder that so many are firm holders of this novel doctrine. It is pleasant to grow wise and virtuous at so small an expenditure of thought or time. This saying of yours is exactly what I heard spoken with angry gravity not long ago.

Timotheus. Angry! no wonder! for it is impossible to keep our patience when truths so incontrovertible are assailed. What was your answer?

Lucian. My answer was: If you talk in this manner, my honest friend, you will excite a spirit of ridicule in the gravest and most saturnine of men, who never had let a laugh out of their breasts before. Lie to *me*, and welcome; but beware lest your own heart take you to task for it, reminding you that both anger and falsehood are reprehended by all religions, yours included.

Timotheus. Lucian! Lucian! you have always been called profane.

Lucian. For what? for having turned into ridicule the gods whom you have turned out of house and home, and are reducing to dust?

Timotheus. Well; but you are equally ready to turn into ridicule the true and holy.

Lucian. In other words, to turn myself into a fool. He who brings ridicule to bear against Truth, finds in his hand a blade without a hilt. The most sparkling and pointed flame of wit flickers and expires against the incombustible walls of her sanctuary.

Timotheus. Fine talking! Do you know, you have really been called an atheist?

Lucian. Yes, yes; I know it well. But, in fact, I believe there are almost as few atheists in the world as there are Christians.

Timotheus. How! as few? Most of Europe, most of Asia, most of Africa, is Christian.

Lucian. Show me five men in each who obey the commands of Christ, and I will show you five hundred in this very city who observe the dictates of Pythagoras. Every Pythagorean obeys his defunct philosopher; and almost every Christian disobeys his living God. Where is there one who practises the most important and the easiest of His commands, to abstain from strife? Men easily and perpetually find something new to quarrel about; but the objects of affection are limited in number, and grow up scantily and slowly. Even a small house is often too spacious for them, and there is a vacant seat at the table. Religious men themselves, when the Deity has bestowed on them everything they prayed for, discover, as a peculiar gift of Providence, some fault in the actions or opinions of a neighbour, and run it down, crying and shouting after it, with more alacrity and more clamour than boys would a leveret or a squirrel in the playground. Are our years and our intellects, and the word of God itself, given us for this, O Timotheus?

Timotheus. A certain latitude, a liberal construction....

Lucian. Ay, ay! These 'liberal constructions' let loose all the worst passions into those 'certain latitudes'. The priests themselves, who ought to be the poorest, are the richest; who ought to be the most obedient, are the most refractory and rebellious. All trouble and all piety are vicarious. They send missionaries, at the cost of others, into foreign lands, to teach observances which they supersede at home. I have ridiculed the puppets of all features, all colours, all sizes, by which an impudent and audacious set of impostors have been gaining an easy livelihood these two thousand years.

Timotheus. Gently! gently! Ours have not been at it yet two hundred. We abolish all idolatry. We know that Jupiter was not the father of gods and men: we know that Mars was not the Lord of Hosts: we know who is: we are quite at ease upon that question.

Lucian. Are you so fanatical, my good Timotheus, as to imagine that the Creator of the world cares a fig by what appellation you adore Him? whether you call Him on one occasion Jupiter, on another Apollo? I will not add Mars or Lord of Hosts; for, wanting as I may be in piety, I am not, and never was, so impious as to call the Maker the Destroyer; to call Him Lord of Hosts who, according to your holiest of books, declared so lately and so plainly that He permits no hosts at all; much less will He take the command of one against another. Would any man in his senses go down into the cellar, and seize first an amphora from the right, and then an amphora from the left, for the pleasure of breaking them in pieces, and of letting out the wine he had taken the trouble to put in? We are not contented with attributing to the gods our own infirmities; we make them even more wayward, even more passionate, even more exigent and more malignant: and then some of us try to coax and cajole them, and others run away from them outright.

Timotheus. No wonder: but only in regard to yours: and even those are types.

Lucian. There are honest men who occupy their lives in discovering types for all things.

Timotheus. Truly and rationally thou speakest now. Honest men and wise men above their fellows are they, and the greatest of all discoverers. There are many types above thy reach, O Lucian!

Lucian. And one which my mind, and perhaps yours also, can comprehend. There is in Italy, I hear, on the border of a quiet and beautiful lake, a temple dedicated to Diana; the priests of which temple have murdered each his predecessor for unrecorded ages.

Timotheus. What of that? They were idolaters.

Lucian. They made the type, however: take it home with you, and hang it up in your temple.

Timotheus. Why! you seem to have forgotten on a sudden that I am a Christian: you are talking of the heathens.

Lucian. True! true! I am near upon eighty years of age, and to my poor eyesight one thing looks very like another.

Timotheus. You are too indifferent.

Lucian. No indeed. I love those best who quarrel least, and who bring into public use the most civility and good humour.

Timotheus. Our holy religion inculcates this duty especially.

Lucian. Such being the case, a pleasant story will not be thrown away upon you. Xenophanes, my townsman of Samosata, was resolved to buy a new horse: he had tried him, and liked him well enough. I asked him why he wished to dispose of his old one, knowing how sure-footed he was, how easy in his paces, and how quiet in his pasture. 'Very true, O Lucian,' said he; 'the horse is a clever horse; noble eye, beautiful figure, stately step; rather too fond of neighing and of shuffling a little in the vicinity of a mare; but tractable and good tempered.' 'I would not have parted with him then,' said I. 'The fact is,' replied he, 'my grandfather, whom I am about to visit, likes no horses but what are **Saturnized**. To-morrow I begin my journey: come and see me set out.' I went at the hour appointed. The new purchase looked quiet and demure; but **he** also pricked up his ears, and gave sundry other tokens of equinity, when the more interesting part of his fellow-creatures came near him. As the morning oats began to operate, he grew more and more unruly, and snapped at one friend of Xenophanes, and sidled against another, and gave a kick at a third. 'All in play! all in play!' said Xenophanes; 'his nature is more of a lamb's than a horse's.' However, these mute salutations being over, away went Xenophanes. In the evening, when my lamp had just been replenished for the commencement of my studies, my friend came in striding as if he were still across the saddle. 'I am apprehensive, O Xenophanes,' said I, 'your new acquaintance has disappointed you.' 'Not in the least,' answered he. 'I do assure you, O Lucian! he is the very horse I was looking out for.' On my requesting him to be seated, he no more thought of doing so than if it had been in the presence of the Persian king. I then handed my lamp to him, telling him (as was true) it contained all the oil I had in the house, and protesting I should be happier to finish my Dialogue in the morning. He took the lamp into my bedroom, and appeared to be much refreshed on his return. Nevertheless, he treated his chair with great delicacy and circumspection, and evidently was afraid of breaking it by too sudden a descent. I did not revert to the horse: but he went on of his own accord. 'I declare to you, O Lucian! it is impossible for me to be mistaken in a palfrey. My new one is the only one in Samosata that could carry me at one stretch to my grandfather's.' 'But *has* he?' said I, timidly. 'No; he has not yet,' answered my friend. 'To-morrow, then, I am afraid, we really must lose you.' 'No,' said he; 'the horse does trot hard: but he is the better for that: I shall soon get used to him.' In fine, my worthy friend deferred his visit to his grandfather: his rides were neither long nor frequent: he was ashamed to part with his purchase, boasted of him everywhere, and, humane as he is by nature, could almost have broken on the cross the quiet contented owner of old Bucephalus.

Timotheus. Am I to understand by this, O Cousin Lucian, that I ought to be contented with the impurities of paganism?

Lucian. Unless you are very unreasonable. A moderate man finds plenty in it.

Timotheus. We abominate the Deities who patronize them, and we hurl down the images of the monsters.

Lucian. Sweet cousin! be tenderer to my feelings. In such a tempest as this, my spark of piety may be blown out. Hold your hand cautiously before it, until I can find my way. Believe me, no Deities (out of their own houses) patronize immorality; none patronize unruly passions, least of all the fierce and ferocious. In my opinion, you are wrong in throwing down the images of those among them who look on you benignly: the others I give up to your discretion. But I think it impossible to stand habitually in the presence of a sweet and open countenance, graven or depicted, without in some degree partaking of the character it expresses. Never tell any man that he can derive no good, in his devotions, from this or from that: abolish neither hope nor gratitude.

Timotheus. God is offended at vain efforts to represent Him.

Lucian. No such thing, my dear Timotheus. If you knew Him at all, you would not talk of Him so irreverently. He is pleased, I am convinced, at every effort to resemble Him, at every wish to remind both ourselves and others of His benefits. You cannot think so often of Him without an effigy.

Timotheus. What likeness is there in the perishable to the Unperishable?

Lucian. I see no reason why there may not be a similitude. All that the senses can comprehend may be represented by any material; clay or fig-tree, bronze or ivory, porphyry or gold. Indeed I have a faint remembrance that, according to your sacred volumes, man was made by God after His own image. If so, man's intellectual powers are worthily exercised in attempting to collect all that is beautiful, serene, and dignified, and to bring Him back to earth again by showing Him the noblest of His gifts, the work most like His own. Surely He cannot hate or abandon those who thus cherish His memory, and thus implore His regard. Perishable and imperfect is everything human: but in these very qualities I find the best reason for striving to attain what is least so. Would not any father be gratified by seeing his child attempt to delineate his features? And would not the gratification be rather increased than diminished by his incapacity? How long shall the narrow mind of man stand between goodness and omnipotence? Perhaps the effigy of your ancestor Isknos is unlike him; whether it is or no, you cannot tell; but you keep it in your hall, and would be angry if anybody broke it to pieces or defaced it. Be quite sure there are many who think as much of their gods as you think of your ancestor Isknos, and who see in their images as good a likeness. Let men have their own way, especially their way to the temples. It is easier to drive them out of one road than into another. Our judicious and good-humoured Trajan has found it necessary on many occasions to chastise the law-breakers of your sect, indifferent as he is what gods are worshipped, so long as their followers are orderly and decorous. The fiercest of the Dacians never knocked off Jupiter's beard, or broke an arm off Venus; and the emperor will hardly tolerate in those who have received a liberal education what he would punish in barbarians. Do not wear out his patience: try rather to imitate his equity, his equanimity, and forbearance.

Timotheus. I have been listening to you with much attention, O Lucian! for I seldom have heard you speak with such gravity. And yet, O Cousin Lucian! I really do find in you a sad deficiency of that wisdom which alone is of any value. You talk of Trajan! what is Trajan?

Lucian. A beneficent citizen, an impartial judge, a sagacious ruler; the comrade of every brave soldier, the friend and associate of every man eminent in genius, throughout his empire, the empire of the world. All arts, all sciences, all philosophies, all religions, are protected by him. Wherefore his name will flourish, when the proudest of these have perished in the land of Egypt. Philosophies and religions will strive, struggle, and suffocate one another. Priesthoods, I know not how many, are quarrelling and scuffling in the street at this instant, all calling on Trajan to come and knock an antagonist on the head; and the most peaceful of them, as it wishes to be thought, proclaiming him an infidel for turning a deaf ear to its imprecations. Mankind was never so happy as under his guidance; and he has nothing now to do but to put down the battles of the gods. If they must fight it out, he will insist on our neutrality.

Timotheus. He has no authority and no influence over us in matters of faith. A wise and upright man, whose serious thoughts lead him forward to religion, will never be turned aside from it by any worldly consideration or any human force.

Lucian. True: but mankind is composed not entirely of the upright and the wise. I suspect that we may find some, here and there, who are rather too fond of novelties in the furniture of temples; and I have observed that new sects are apt to warp, crack, and split, under the heat they generate. Our homely old religion has run into fewer quarrels, ever since the Centaurs and Lapiths (whose controversy was on a subject quite comprehensible), than yours has engendered in twenty years.

Timotheus. We shall obviate that inconvenience by electing a supreme Pontiff to decide all differences. It has been seriously thought about long ago: and latterly we have been making out an ideal series down to the present day, in order that our successors in the ministry may have stepping-stones up to the fountain-head. At first the disseminators of our doctrines were equal in their commission; we do not approve of this any longer, for reasons of our own.

Lucian. You may shut, one after another, all our other temples, but, I plainly see, you will never shut the temple of Janus. The Roman Empire will never lose its pugnacious character while your sect exists. The only danger is, lest the fever rage internally and consume the vitals. If you sincerely wish your religion to be long-lived, maintain in it the spirit of its constitution, and keep it patient, humble, abstemious, domestic, and zealous only in the services of humanity. Whenever the higher of your priesthood shall attain the riches they are aiming at, the people will envy their possessions and revolt from their impostures. Do not let them seize upon the palace, and shove their God again into the manger.

Timotheus. Lucian! Lucian! I call this impiety.

Lucian. So do I, and shudder at its consequences. Caverns which at first look inviting, the roof at the aperture green with overhanging ferns and clinging mosses, then glittering with native gems and with water as sparkling and pellucid, freshening the air all around; these caverns grow darker and closer, until you find yourself among animals that shun the daylight, adhering to the walls, hissing along the bottom, flapping, screeching, gaping, glaring, making you shrink at the sounds, and sicken at the smells, and afraid to advance or retreat.

Timotheus. To what can this refer? Our caverns open on verdure, and terminate in veins of gold.

Lucian. Veins of gold, my good Timotheus, such as your excavations have opened and are opening, in the spirit of avarice and ambition, will be washed (or as you would say, ***purified***) in streams of blood. Arrogance, intolerance, resistance to authority and contempt of law, distinguish your aspiring sectarians from the other subjects of the empire.

Timotheus. Blindness hath often a calm and composed countenance; but, my Cousin Lucian! it usually hath also the advantage of a cautious and a measured step. It hath pleased God to blind you, like all the other adversaries of our faith; but He has given you no staff to lean upon. You object against us the very vices from which we are peculiarly exempt.

Lucian. Then it is all a story, a fable, a fabrication, about one of your earlier leaders cutting off with his sword a servant's ear? If the accusation is true, the offence is heavy. For not only was the wounded man innocent of any provocation, but he is represented as being in the service of the high priest at Jerusalem. Moreover, from the direction and violence of the blow, it is evident that his life was aimed at. According to law, you know, my dear cousin, all the party might have been condemned to death, as accessories to an attempt at murder. I am unwilling to think so unfavourably of your sect; nor indeed do I see the possibility that, in such an outrage, the principal could be pardoned. For any man but a soldier to go about armed is against the Roman law, which, on that head, as on many others, is borrowed from the Athenian; and it is incredible that in any civilized country so barbarous a practice can be tolerated. Travellers do indeed relate that, in certain parts of India, there are princes at whose courts even civilians are armed. But ***traveller*** has occasionally the same signification as ***liar***, and ***India*** as ***fable***. However, if the practice really does exist in that remote and rarely visited country, it must be in some region of it very far beyond the Indus or the Ganges: for the nations situated between those rivers are, and were in the reign of Alexander, and some thousand years before his birth, as civilized as the Europeans; nay, incomparably more courteous, more industrious, and more pacific; the three grand criterions.

But answer my question: is there any foundation for so mischievous a report?

Timotheus. There was indeed, so to say, an ear, or something of the kind, absconded; probably by mistake. But high priests' servants are propense to follow the swaggering gait of their masters, and to carry things with a high hand, in such wise as to excite the choler of the most quiet. If you knew the character of the eminently holy man who punished the atrocious insolence of that bloody-minded wretch, you would be sparing of your animadversions. We take him for our model.

Lucian. I see you do.

Timotheus. We proclaim him Prince of the Apostles.

Lucian. I am the last in the world to question his princely qualifications; but, if I might advise you, it should be to follow in preference Him whom you acknowledge to be an unerring guide; who delivered to you His ordinances with His own hand, equitable, plain, explicit, compendious, and complete; who committed no violence, who countenanced no injustice, whose compassion was without weakness, whose love was without frailty, whose life was led in humility, in purity, in beneficence, and, at the end, laid down in obedience to His Father's will.

Timotheus. Ah, Lucian! what strangely imperfect notions! all that is little.

Lucian. Enough to follow.

Timotheus. Not enough to compel others. I did indeed hope, O Lucian! that you would again come forward with the irresistible arrows of your wit, and unite with us against our adversaries. By what you have just spoken, I doubt no longer that you approve of the doctrines inculcated by the blessed Founder of our religion.

Lucian. To the best of my understanding.

Timotheus. So ardent is my desire for the salvation of your precious soul, O my cousin! that I would devote many hours of every day to disputation with you on the principal points of our Christian controversy.

Lucian. Many thanks, my kind Timotheus! But I think the blessed Founder of your religion very strictly forbade that there should be *any* points of controversy. Not only has He prohibited them on the doctrines He delivered, but on everything else. Some of the most obstinate might never have doubted of His Divinity, if the conduct of His followers had not repelled them from the belief of it. How can they imagine you sincere when they see you disobedient? It is in vain for you to protest that you worship the God of Peace, when you are found daily in the courts and market-places with clenched fists and bloody noses. I acknowledge the full value of your offer; but really I am as anxious for the salvation of your precious time as you appear to be for the salvation of my precious soul, particularly since I am come to the conclusion that souls cannot be lost, and that time can.

Timotheus. We mean by *salvation* exemption from eternal torments.

Lucian. Among all my old gods and their children, morose as some of the senior are, and mischievous as are some of the junior, I have never represented the worst of them as capable of inflicting such atrocity. Passionate and capricious and unjust are several of them; but a skin stripped off the shoulder, and a liver tossed to a vulture, are among the worst of their inflictions.

Timotheus. This is scoffing.

Lucian. Nobody but an honest man has a right to scoff at anything.

Timotheus. And yet people of a very different cast are usually those who scoff the most.

Lucian. We are apt to push forward at that which we are without: the low-born at titles and distinctions, the silly at wit, the knave at the semblance of probity. But I was about to remark, that an honest man may fairly scoff at all philosophies and religions which are proud, ambitious, intemperate, and contradictory. The thing most adverse to the spirit and essence of them all is falsehood. It is the business of the philosophical to seek truth: it is the office of the religious to worship her; under what name is unimportant. The falsehood that the tongue commits is slight in comparison with what is conceived by the heart, and executed by the whole man, throughout life. If, professing love and charity to the human race at large, I quarrel day after day with my next neighbour; if, professing that the rich can never see God, I spend in the luxuries of my household a talent monthly; if, professing to place so much confidence in His word, that, in regard to wordly weal, I need take no care for to-morrow, I accumulate stores even beyond what would be necessary, though I quite distrusted both His providence and His veracity; if, professing that 'he who giveth to the poor lendeth to the Lord', I question the Lord's security, and haggle with Him about the amount of the loan; if, professing that I am their steward, I keep ninety-nine parts in the hundred as the emolument of my stewardship; how, when God hates liars and punishes defrauders, shall I, and other such thieves and hypocrites, fare hereafter?

Timotheus. Let us hope there are few of them.

Lucian. We cannot hope against what is: we may, however, hope that in future these will be fewer; but never while the overseers of a priesthood look for offices out of it, taking the lead in politics, in debate, and strife. Such men bring to ruin all religion, but their own first, and raise unbelievers not only in Divine Providence, but in human faith.

Timotheus. If they leave the altar for the market-place, the sanctuary for the senate-house, and agitate party questions instead of Christian verities, everlasting punishments await them.

Lucian. Everlasting?

Timotheus. Certainly: at the very least. I rank it next to heresy in the catalogue of sins; and the Church supports my opinion.

Lucian. I have no measure for ascertaining the distance between the opinions and practices of men; I only know that they stand widely apart in all countries on the most important occasions; but this newly-hatched word *heresy*, alighting on my ear, makes me rub it. A beneficent God descends on earth in the human form, to redeem us from the slavery of sin, from the penalty of our passions: can you imagine He will punish an error in opinion, or even an obstinacy in unbelief, with everlasting torments? Supposing it highly criminal to refuse to weigh a string of arguments, or to cross-question a herd of witnesses, on a subject which no experience has warranted and no sagacity can comprehend; supposing it highly criminal to be contented with the religion which our parents taught us, which they bequeathed to us as the most precious of possessions, and which it would have broken their hearts if they had foreseen we should cast aside; yet are eternal pains the just retribution of what at worst is but indifference and supineness?

Timotheus. Our religion has clearly this advantage over yours: it teaches us to regulate our passions.

Lucian. Rather say it *tells* us. I believe all religions do the same; some indeed more emphatically and primarily than others; but *that* indeed would be incontestably of Divine origin, and acknowledged at once by the most sceptical, which should thoroughly teach it. Now, my friend Timotheus, I think you are about seventy-five years of age.

Timotheus. Nigh upon it.

Lucian. Seventy-five years, according to my calculation, are equivalent to seventy-five gods and goddesses in regulating our passions for us, if we speak of the amatory, which are always thought in every stage of life the least to be pardoned.

Timotheus. Execrable!

Lucian. I am afraid the sourest hang longest on the tree. Mimnermus says:

> In early youth we often sigh
> Because our pulses beat so high;
> All this we conquer, and at last
> We sigh that we are grown so chaste.

Timotheus. Swine!

Lucian. No animal sighs oftener or louder. But, my dear cousin, the quiet swine is less troublesome and less odious than the grumbling and growling and fierce hyena, which will not let the dead rest in their graves. We may be merry with the follies and even the vices of men, without doing or wishing them harm; punishment should come from the magistrate, not from us. If we are to give pain to any one because he thinks differently from us, we ought to begin by inflicting a few smart stripes on ourselves; for both upon light and upon grave occasions, if we have thought much and often, our opinions must have varied. We are always fond of seizing and managing what appertains to others. In the savage state all belongs to all. Our neighbours the Arabs, who stand between barbarism and civilization, waylay travellers, and plunder their equipage and their gold. The wilier marauders in Alexandria start up from under the shadow of temples, force us to change our habiliments for theirs, and strangle us with fingers dipped in holy water if we say they sit uneasily.

Timotheus. This is not the right view of things.

Lucian. That is never the right view which lets in too much light. About two centuries have elapsed since your religion was founded. Show me the pride it has humbled; show me the cruelty it has mitigated; show me the lust it has extinguished or repressed. I have now been living ten years in Alexandria; and you never will accuse me, I think, of any undue partiality for the system in which I was educated; yet, from all my observation, I find no priest or elder, in your community, wise, tranquil, firm, and sedate as Epicurus, and Carneades, and Zeno, and Epictetus; or indeed in the same degree as some who were often called forth into political and military life; Epaminondas, for instance, and Phocion.

Timotheus. I pity them from my soul: they were ignorant of the truth: they are lost, my cousin! take my word for it, they are lost men.

Lucian. Unhappily, they are. I wish we had them back again; or that, since we have lost them, we could at least find among us the virtues they left for our example.

Timotheus. Alas, my poor cousin! you too are blind; you do not understand the plainest words, nor comprehend those verities which are the most evident and palpable. Virtues! if the poor wretches had any, they were false ones.

Lucian. Scarcely ever has there been a politician, in any free state, without much falsehood and duplicity. I have named the most illustrious exceptions. Slender and irregular lines of a darker colour run along the bright blade that decides the fate of nations, and may indeed be necessary to the perfection of its temper. The great warrior has usually his darker lines of character, necessary (it may be) to constitute his greatness. No two men possess the same quantity of the same virtues, if they have many or much. We want some which do not far outstep us, and which we may follow with the hope of reaching; we want others to elevate, and others to defend us. The order of things would be less beautiful without this variety. Without the ebb and flow of our passions, but guided and moderated by a beneficent light above, the ocean of life would stagnate; and zeal, devotion, eloquence, would become dead carcasses, collapsing and wasting on unprofitable sands. The vices of some men cause the virtues of others, as corruption is the parent of fertility.

Timotheus. O my cousin! this doctrine is diabolical.

Lucian. What is it?

Timotheus. Diabolical; a strong expression in daily use among us. We turn it a little from its origin.

Lucian. Timotheus, I love to sit by the side of a clear water, although there is nothing in it but naked stones. Do not take the trouble to muddy the stream of language for my benefit; I am not about to fish in it.

Timotheus. Well, we will speak about things which come nearer to your apprehension. I only wish you were somewhat less indifferent in your choice between the true and the false.

Lucian. We take it for granted that what is not true must be false.

Timotheus. Surely we do.

Lucian. This is erroneous.

Timotheus. Are you grown captious? Pray explain.

Lucian. What is not true, I need not say, must be untrue; but that alone is false which is intended to deceive. A witness may be mistaken, yet would not you call him a false witness unless he asserted what he knew to be false.

Timotheus. Quibbles upon words!

Lucian. On words, on quibbles, if you please to call distinctions so, rests the axis of the intellectual world. A winged word hath stuck ineradicably in a million hearts, and envenomed every hour throughout their hard pulsation. On a winged word hath hung the destiny of nations. On a winged word hath human wisdom been willing to cast the immortal soul, and to leave it dependent for all its future happiness. It is because a word is unsusceptible of explanation, or because they who employed it were impatient of any, that enormous evils have prevailed, not only against our common sense, but against our common humanity. Hence the most pernicious of absurdities, far exceeding in folly and mischief the worship of threescore gods; namely, that an implicit faith in what outrages our reason, which we know is God's gift, and bestowed on us for our guidance, that this weak, blind, stupid faith is surer of His favour than the constant practice of every human virtue. They at whose hands one prodigious lie, such as this, hath been accepted, may reckon on their influence in the dissemination of many smaller, and may turn them easily to their own account. Be sure they will do it sooner or later. The fly floats on the surface for a while, but up springs the fish at last and swallows it.

Timotheus. Was ever man so unjust as you are? The abominable old priesthoods are avaricious and luxurious: ours is willing to stand or fall by maintaining its ordinances of fellowship and frugality. Point out to me a priest of our religion whom you could, by any temptation or entreaty, so far mislead, that he shall reserve for his own consumption one loaf, one plate of lentils, while another poor Christian hungers. In the meanwhile the priests of Isis are proud and wealthy, and admit none of the indigent to their tables. And now, to tell you the whole truth, my Cousin Lucian, I come to you this morning to propose that we should lay our heads together and compose a merry dialogue on these said priests of Isis. What say you?

Lucian. These said priests of Isis have already been with me, several times, on a similar business in regard to yours.

Timotheus. Malicious wretches!

Lucian. Beside, they have attempted to persuade me that your religion is borrowed from theirs, altering a name a little and laying the scene of action in a corner, in the midst of obscurity and ruins.

Timotheus. The wicked dogs! the hellish liars! We have nothing in common with such vile impostors. Are they not ashamed of taking such unfair means of lowering us in the estimation of our fellow-citizens? And so, they artfully came to you, craving any spare jibe to throw against us! They lie open to these weapons; we do not: we stand above the malignity, above the strength, of man. You would do justly in turning their own devices against them: it would be amusing to see how they would look. If you refuse me, I am resolved to write a Dialogue of the Dead, myself, and to introduce these hypocrites in it.

Lucian. Consider well first, my good Timotheus, whether you can do any such thing with propriety; I mean to say judiciously in regard to composition.

Timotheus. I always thought you generous and open-hearted, and quite inaccessible to jealousy.

Lucian. Let nobody ever profess himself so much as that: for, although he may be insensible of the disease, it lurks within him, and only waits its season to break out. But really, my cousin, at present I feel no symptoms: and, to prove that I am ingenuous and sincere with you, these are my reasons for dissuasion. We believers in the Homeric family of gods and goddesses, believe also in the locality of Tartarus and Elysium. We entertain no doubt whatever that the passions of men and demigods and gods are nearly the same above ground and below; and that Achilles would dispatch his spear through the body of any shade who would lead Briseis too far among the myrtles, or attempt to throw the halter over the ears of any chariot horse belonging to him in the meads of asphodel. We admit no doubt of these verities, delivered down to us from the ages when Theseus and Hercules had descended into Hades itself. Instead of a few stadions in a cavern, with a bank and a bower at the end of it, under a very small portion of our diminutive Hellas, you Christians possess the whole cavity of the earth for punishment, and the whole convex of the sky for felicity.

Timotheus. Our passions are burnt out amid the fires of purification, and our intellects are elevated to the enjoyment of perfect intelligence.

Lucian. How silly then and incongruous would it be, not to say how impious, to represent your people as no better and no wiser than they were before, and discoursing on subjects which no longer can or ought to concern them. Christians must think your Dialogue of the Dead no less irreligious than their opponents think mine, and infinitely more absurd. If indeed you are resolved on this form of composition, there is no topic which may not, with equal facility, be discussed on earth; and you may intersperse as much ridicule as you please, without any fear of censure for inconsistency or irreverence. Hitherto such writers have confined their view mostly to speculative points, sophistic reasonings, and sarcastic interpellations.

Timotheus. Ha! you are always fond of throwing a little pebble at the lofty Plato, whom we, on the contrary, are ready to receive (in a manner) as one of ourselves.

Lucian. To throw pebbles is a very uncertain way of showing where lie defects. Whenever I have mentioned him seriously, I have brought forward, not accusations, but passages from his writings, such as no philosopher or scholar or moralist can defend.

Timotheus. His doctrines are too abstruse and too sublime for you.

Lucian. Solon, Anaxagoras, and Epicurus, are more sublime, if truth is sublimity.

Timotheus. Truth is, indeed; for God is truth.

Lucian. We are upon earth to learn what can be learnt upon earth, and not to speculate on what never can be. This you, O Timotheus, may call philosophy: to me it appears the idlest of curiosity; for every other kind may teach us something, and may lead to more beyond. Let men learn what benefits men; above all things, to contract their wishes, to calm their passions, and, more especially, to dispel their fears. Now these are to be dispelled, not by collecting clouds, but by piercing and scattering them. In the dark we may imagine depths and heights immeasurable, which, if a torch be carried right before us, we find it easy to leap across. Much of what we call sublime is only the residue of infancy, and the worst of it.

The philosophers I quoted are too capacious for schools and systems. Without noise, without ostentation, without mystery, not quarrelsome, not captious, not frivolous, their lives were commentaries on their doctrine. Never evaporating into mist, never stagnating into mire, their limpid and broad morality runs parallel with the lofty summits of their genius.

Timotheus. Genius! was ever genius like Plato's?

Lucian. The most admired of his Dialogues, his **Banquet**, is beset with such puerilities, deformed with such pedantry, and disgraced with such impurity, that none but the thickest beards, and chiefly of the philosophers and the satyrs, should bend over it. On a former occasion he has given us a specimen of history, than which nothing in our language is worse: here he gives us one of poetry, in honour of Love, for which the god has taken ample vengeance on him, by perverting his taste and feelings. The grossest of all the absurdities in this dialogue is, attributing to Aristophanes, so much of a scoffer and so little of a visionary, the silly notion of male and female having been originally complete in one person, and walking circuitously. He may be joking: who knows?

Timotheus. Forbear! forbear! do not call this notion a silly one: he took it from our Holy Scriptures, but perverted it somewhat. Woman was made from man's rib, and did not require to be cut asunder all the way down: this is no proof of bad reasoning, but merely of misinterpretation.

Lucian. If you would rather have bad reasoning, I will adduce a little of it. Farther on, he wishes to extol the wisdom of Agathon by attributing to him such a sentence as this:

'It is evident that Love is the most beautiful of the gods, ***because*** he is the youngest of them.'

Now, even on earth, the youngest is not always the most beautiful; how infinitely less cogent, then, is the argument when we come to speak of the Immortals, with whom age can have no concern! There was a time when Vulcan was the youngest of the gods: was he, also, at that time, and for that reason, the most beautiful? Your philosopher tells us, moreover, that 'Love is of all deities the most *liquid*; else he never could fold himself about everything, and flow into and out of men's souls.'

The three last sentences of Agathon's rhapsody are very harmonious, and exhibit the finest specimen of Plato's style; but we, accustomed as we are to hear him lauded for his poetical diction, should hold that poem a very indifferent one which left on the mind so superficial an impression. The garden of Academus is flowery without fragrance, and dazzling without warmth: I am ready to dream away an hour in it after dinner, but I think it insalutary for a night's repose. So satisfied was Plato with his **Banquet**, that he says of himself, in the person of Socrates, 'How can I or any one but find it difficult to speak after a discourse so eloquent? It would have been wonderful if the brilliancy of the sentences at the end of it, and the choice of expression throughout, had not astonished all the auditors. I, who can never say anything nearly so beautiful, would if possible have made my escape, and have fairly run off for shame.' He had indeed much better run off before he made so wretched a pun on the name of Gorgias. 'I dreaded,' says he, 'lest Agathon, measuring my discourse by the head of the eloquent Gorgias, should turn me to stone for inability of utterance.'

Was there ever joke more frigid? What painful twisting of unelastic stuff! If Socrates was the wisest man in the world, it would require another oracle to persuade us, after this, that he was the wittiest.

But surely a small share of common sense would have made him abstain from hazarding such failures. He falls on his face in very flat and very dry ground; and, when he gets up again, his quibbles are well-nigh as tedious as his witticisms. However, he has the presence of mind to throw them on the shoulders of Diotima, whom he calls a prophetess, and who, ten years before the plague broke out in Athens, obtained from the gods (he tells us) that delay. Ah! the gods were doubly mischievous: they sent her first. Read her words, my cousin, as delivered by Socrates; and if they have another plague in store for us, you may avert it by such an act of expiation.

Timotheus. The world will have ended before ten years are over.

Lucian. Indeed!

Timotheus. It has been pronounced.

Lucian. How the threads of belief and unbelief run woven close together in the whole web of human life! Come, come; take courage; you will have time for your Dialogue. Enlarge the circle; enrich it with a variety of matter, enliven it with a multitude of characters, occupy the intellect of the thoughtful, the imagination of the lively; spread the board with solid viands, delicate rarities, and sparkling wines; and throw, along the whole extent of it, geniality and festal crowns.

Timotheus. What writer of dialogues hath ever done this, or undertaken, or conceived, or hoped it?

Lucian. None whatever; yet surely you yourself may, when even your babes and sucklings are endowed with abilities incomparably greater than our niggardly old gods have bestowed on the very best of us.

Timotheus. I wish, my dear Lucian, you would let our babes and sucklings lie quiet, and say no more about them: as for your gods, I leave them at your mercy. Do not impose on me the performance of a task in which Plato himself, if he had attempted it, would have failed.

Lucian. No man ever detected false reasoning with more quickness; but unluckily he called in Wit at the exposure; and Wit, I am sorry to say, held the lowest place in his household. He sadly mistook the qualities of his mind in attempting the facetious; or, rather, he fancied he possessed one quality more than belonged to him. But, if he himself had not been a worse quibbler than any whose writings are come down to us, we might have been gratified by the exposure of wonderful acuteness wretchedly applied. It is no small service to the community to turn into ridicule the grave impostors, who are contending which of them shall guide and govern us, whether in politics or religion. There are always a few who will take the trouble to walk down among the seaweeds and slippery stones, for the sake of showing their credulous fellow-citizens that skins filled with sand, and set upright at the forecastle, are neither men nor merchandise.

Timotheus. I can bring to mind, O Lucian, no writer possessing so great a variety of wit as you.

Lucian. No man ever possessed any variety of this gift; and the holder is not allowed to exchange the quality for another. Banter (and such is Plato's) never grows large, never sheds its bristles, and never do they soften into the humorous or the facetious.

Timotheus. I agree with you that banter is the worst species of wit. We have indeed no correct idea what persons those really were whom Plato drags by the ears, to undergo slow torture under Socrates. One sophist, I must allow, is precisely like another: no discrimination of character, none of manner, none of language.

Lucian. He wanted the fancy and fertility of Aristophanes.

Timotheus. Otherwise, his mind was more elevated and more poetical.

Lucian. Pardon me if I venture to express my dissent in both particulars. Knowledge of the human heart, and discrimination of character, are requisites of the poet. Few ever have possessed them in an equal degree with Aristophanes: Plato has given no indication of either.

Timotheus. But consider his imagination.

Lucian. On what does it rest? He is nowhere so imaginative as in his *Polity*. Nor is there any state in the world that is, or would be, governed by it. One day you may find him at his counter in the midst of old-fashioned toys, which crack and crumble under his fingers while he exhibits and recommends them; another day, while he is sitting on a goat's bladder, I may discover his bald head surmounting an enormous mass of loose chaff and uncleanly feathers, which he would persuade you is the pleasantest and healthiest of beds, and that dreams descend on it from the gods.

> 'Open your mouth, and shut your eyes, and see what Zeus shall send you,'

says Aristophanes in his favourite metre. In this helpless condition of closed optics and hanging jaw, we find the followers of Plato. It is by shutting their eyes that they see, and by opening their mouths that they apprehend. Like certain broad-muzzled dogs, all stand equally stiff and staunch, although few scent the game, and their lips wag, and water, at whatever distance from the net. We must leave them with their hands hanging down before them, confident that they are wiser than we are, were it only for this attitude of humility. It is amusing to see them in it before the tall, well-robed Athenian, while he mis-spells the charms, and plays clumsily the tricks, he acquired from the conjurors here in Egypt. I wish you better success with the same materials. But in my opinion all philosophers should speak clearly. The highest things are the purest and brightest; and the best writers are those who render them the most intelligible to the world below. In the arts and sciences, and particularly in music and metaphysics, this is difficult: but the subjects not being such as lie within the range of the community, I lay little stress upon them, and wish authors to deal with them as they best may, only beseeching that they recompense us, by bringing within our comprehension the other things with which they are entrusted for us. The followers of Plato fly off indignantly from any such proposal. If I ask them the meaning of some obscure passage, they answer that I am unprepared and unfitted for it, and that his mind is so far above mine, I cannot grasp it. I look up into the faces of these worthy men, who mingle so much commiseration with so much calmness, and wonder at seeing them look no less vacant than my own.

Timotheus. You have acknowledged his eloquence, while you derided his philosophy and repudiated his morals.

Lucian. Certainly there was never so much eloquence with so little animation. When he has heated his oven, he forgets to put the bread into it; instead of which, he throws in another bundle of faggots. His words and sentences are often too large for the place they occupy. If a water-melon is not to be placed in an oyster-shell, neither is a grain of millet in a golden salver. At high festivals a full band may enter: ordinary conversation goes on better without it.

Timotheus. There is something so spiritual about him, that many of us Christians are firmly of opinion he must have been partially enlightened from above.

Lucian. I hope and believe we all are. His entire works are in our library. Do me the favour to point out to me a few of those passages where in poetry he approaches the spirit of Aristophanes, or where in morals he comes up to Epictetus.

Timotheus. It is useless to attempt it if you carry your prejudices with you. Beside, my dear cousin, I would not offend you, but really your mind has no point about it which could be brought to contact or affinity with Plato's.

Lucian. In the universality of his genius there must surely be some atom coincident with another in mine. You acknowledge, as everybody must do, that his wit is the heaviest and lowest: pray, is the specimen he has given us of history at all better?

Timotheus. I would rather look to the loftiness of his mind, and the genius that sustains him.

Lucian. So would I. Magnificent words, and the pomp and procession of stately sentences, may accompany genius, but are not always nor frequently called out by it. The voice ought not to be perpetually nor much elevated in the ethic and didactic, nor to roll sonorously, as if it issued from a mask in the theatre. The horses in the plain under Troy are not always kicking and neighing; nor is the dust always raised in whirlwinds on the banks of Simois and Scamander; nor are the rampires always in a blaze. Hector has lowered his helmet to the infant of Andromache, and Achilles to the embraces of Briseis. I do not blame the prose-writer who opens his bosom occasionally to a breath of poetry; neither, on the contrary, can I praise the gait of that pedestrian who lifts up his legs as high on a bare heath as in a cornfield. Be authority as old and obstinate as it may, never let it persuade you that a man is the stronger for being unable to keep himself on the ground, or the weaker for breathing quietly and softly on ordinary occasions. Tell me, over and over, that you find every great quality in Plato: let me only once ask you in return, whether he ever is ardent and energetic, whether he wins the affections, whether he agitates the heart. Finding him deficient in every one of these faculties, I think his disciples have extolled him too highly. Where power is absent, we may find the robes of genius, but we miss the throne. He would acquit a slave who killed another in self-defence, but if he killed any free man, even in self-defence; he was not only to be punished with death, but to undergo the cruel death of a parricide. This effeminate philosopher was more severe than the manly Demosthenes, who quotes a law against the striking of a slave: and Diogenes, when one ran away from him, remarked that it would be horrible if Diogenes could not do without a slave, when a slave could do without Diogenes.

Timotheus. Surely the allegories of Plato are evidences of his genius.

Lucian. A great poet in the hours of his idleness may indulge in allegory: but the highest poetical character will never rest on so unsubstantial a foundation. The poet must take man from God's hands, must look into every fibre of his heart and brain, must be able to take the magnificent work to pieces, and to reconstruct it. When this labour is completed, let him throw himself composedly on the earth, and care little how many of its ephemeral insects creep over him. In regard to these allegories of Plato, about which I have heard so much, pray what and where are they? You hesitate, my fair cousin Timotheus! Employ one morning in transcribing them, and another in noting all the passages which are of practical utility in the commerce of social life, or purify our affections at home, or excite and elevate our enthusiasm in the prosperity and glory of our country. Useful books, moral books, instructive books are easily composed: and surely so great a writer should present them to us without blot or blemish: I find among his many volumes no copy of a similar composition. My enthusiasm is not easily raised indeed; yet such a whirlwind of a poet must carry it away with him; nevertheless, here I stand, calm and collected, not a hair of my beard in commotion. Declamation will find its echo in vacant places: it beats ineffectually on the well-furnished mind. Give me proof; bring the work; show the passages; convince, confound, overwhelm me.

Timotheus. I may do that another time with Plato. And yet, what effect can I hope to produce on an unhappy man who doubts even that the world is on the point of extinction?

Lucian. Are there many of your association who believe that this catastrophe is so near at hand?

Timotheus. We all believe it; or rather, we all are certain of it.

Lucian. How so? Have you observed any fracture in the disk of the sun? Are any of the stars loosened in their orbits? Has the beautiful light of Venus ceased to pant in the heavens, or has the belt of Orion lost its gems?

Timotheus. Oh, for shame!

Lucian. Rather should I be ashamed of indifference on so important an occasion.

Timotheus. We know the fact by surer signs.

Lucian. These, if you could vouch for them, would be sure enough for me. The least of them would make me sweat as profusely as if I stood up to the neck in the hot preparation of a mummy. Surely no wise or benevolent philosopher could ever have uttered what he knew or believed might be distorted into any such interpretation. For if men are persuaded that they and their works are so soon about to perish, what provident care are they likely to take in the education and welfare of their families? What sciences will they improve, what learning will they cultivate, what monuments of past ages will they be studious to preserve, who are certain that there can be no future ones? Poetry will be censured as rank profaneness, eloquence will be converted into howls and execrations, statuary will exhibit only Midases and Ixions, and all the colours of painting will be mixed together to produce one grand conflagration: flammantia moenia mundi.

Timotheus. Do not quote an atheist; especially in Latin. I hate the language; the Romans are beginning to differ from us already.

Lucian. Ah! you will soon split into smaller fractions. But pardon me my unusual fault of quoting. Before I let fall a quotation I must be taken by surprise. I seldom do it in conversation, seldomer in composition; for it mars the beauty and unity of style, especially when it invades it from a foreign tongue. A quoter is either ostentatious of his acquirements or doubtful of his cause. And moreover, he never walks gracefully who leans upon the shoulder of another, however gracefully that other may walk. Herodotus, Plato, Aristoteles, Demosthenes, are no quoters. Thucydides, twice or thrice, inserts a few sentences of Pericles: but Thucydides is an emanation of Pericles, somewhat less clear indeed, being lower, although at no great distance from that purest and most pellucid source. The best of the Romans, I agree with you, are remote from such originals, if not in power of mind, or in acuteness of remark, or in sobriety of judgment, yet in the graces of composition. While I admired, with a species of awe such as not Homer himself ever impressed me with, the majesty and sanctimony of Livy, I have been informed by learned Romans that in the structure of his sentences he is often inharmonious, and sometimes uncouth. I can imagine such uncouthness in the goddess of battles, confident of power and victory, when part of her hair is waving round the helmet, loosened by the rapidity of her descent or the vibration of her spear. Composition may be too adorned even for beauty. In painting it is often requisite to cover a bright colour with one less bright; and, in language, to relieve the ear from the tension of high notes, even at the cost of a discord. There are urns of which the borders are too prominent and too decorated for use, and which appear to be brought out chiefly for state, at grand carousals. The author who imitates the artificers of these, shall never have my custom.

Timotheus. I think you judge rightly: but I do not understand languages: I only understand religion.

Lucian. He must be a most accomplished, a most extraordinary man, who comprehends them both together. We do not even talk clearly when we are walking in the dark.

Timotheus. Thou art not merely walking in the dark, but fast asleep.

Lucian. And thou, my cousin, wouldst kindly awaken me with a red-hot poker. I have but a few paces to go along the corridor of life: prithee let me turn into my bed again and lie quiet. Never was any man less an enemy to religion than I am, whatever may be said to the contrary: and you shall judge of me by the soundness of my advice. If your leaders are in earnest, as many think, do persuade them to abstain from quarrelsomeness and contention, and not to declare it necessary that there should perpetually be a religious as well as a political war between east and west. No honest and considerate man will believe in their doctrines, who, inculcating peace and good-will, continue all the time to assail their fellow-citizens with the utmost rancour at every divergency of opinion, and, forbidding the indulgence of the kindlier affections, exercise at full stretch the fiercer. This is certain: if they obey any commander, they will never sound a charge when his order is to sound a retreat: if they acknowledge any magistrate, they will never tear down the tablet of his edicts.

Timotheus. We have what is all-sufficient.

Lucian. I see you have.

Timotheus. You have ridiculed all religion and all philosophy.

Lucian. I have found but little of either. I have cracked many a nut, and have come only to dust or maggots.

Timotheus. To say nothing of the saints, are all philosophers fools or impostors? And, because you cannot rise to the ethereal heights of Plato, nor comprehend the real magnitude of a man so much above you, must he be a dwarf?

Lucian. The best sight is not that which sees best in the dark or the twilight; for no objects are then visible in their true colours, and just proportions; but it is that which presents to us things as they are, and indicates what is within our reach and what is beyond it. Never were any three writers, of high celebrity, so little understood in the main character, as Plato, Diogenes, and Epicurus. Plato is a perfect master of logic and rhetoric; and whenever he errs in either, as I have proved to you he does occasionally, he errs through perverseness, not through unwariness. His language often settles into clear and most beautiful prose, often takes an imperfect and incoherent shape of poetry, and often, cloud against cloud, bursts with a vehement detonation in the air. Diogenes was hated both by the vulgar and the philosophers. By the philosophers, because he exposed their ignorance, ridiculed their jealousies, and rebuked their pride:

by the vulgar, because they never can endure a man apparently of their own class who avoids their society and partakes in none of their humours, prejudices, and animosities. What right has he to be greater or better than they are? he who wears older clothes, who eats staler fish, and possesses no vote to imprison or banish anybody. I am now ashamed that I mingled in the rabble, and that I could not resist the childish mischief of smoking him in his tub. He was the wisest man of his time, not excepting Aristoteles; for he knew that he was greater than Philip or Alexander. Aristoteles did not know that he himself was, or knowing it, did not act up to his knowledge; and here is a deficiency of wisdom.

Timotheus. Whether you did or did not strike the cask, Diogenes would have closed his eyes equally. He would never have come forth and seen the truth, had it shone upon the world in that day. But, intractable as was this recluse, Epicurus, I fear, is quite as lamentable. What horrible doctrines!

Lucian. Enjoy, said he, the pleasant walks where you are: repose and eat gratefully the fruit that falls into your bosom: do not weary your feet with an excursion, at the end whereof you will find no resting-place: reject not the odour of roses for the fumes of pitch and sulphur. What horrible doctrines!

Timotheus. Speak seriously. He was much too bad for ridicule.

Lucian. I will then speak as you desire me, seriously. His smile was so unaffected and so graceful, that I should have thought it very injudicious to set my laugh against it. No philosopher ever lived with such uniform purity, such abstinence from censoriousness, from controversy, from jealousy, and from arrogance.

Timotheus. Ah, poor mortal! I pity him, as far as may be; he is in hell: it would be wicked to wish him out: we are not to murmur against the all-wise dispensations.

Lucian. I am sure he would not; and it is therefore I hope he is more comfortable than you believe.

Timotheus. Never have I defiled my fingers, and never will I defile them, by turning over his writings. But in regard to Plato, I can have no objection to take your advice.

Lucian. He will reward your assiduity: but he will assist you very little if you consult him principally (and eloquence for this should principally be consulted) to strengthen your humanity. Grandiloquent and sonorous, his lungs seem to play the better for the absence of the heart. His imagination is the most conspicuous, buoyed up by swelling billows over unsounded depths. There are his mild thunders, there are his glowing clouds, his traversing coruscations, and his shooting stars. More of true wisdom, more of trustworthy manliness, more of promptitude and power to keep you steady and straightforward on the perilous road of life, may be found in the little manual of Epictetus, which I could write in the palm of my left hand, than there is in all the rolling and redundant volumes of this mighty rhetorician, which you may begin to transcribe on the summit of the Great Pyramid, carry down over the Sphinx at the bottom, and continue on the sands half-way to Memphis. And indeed the materials are appropriate; one part being far above our sight, and the other on what, by the most befitting epithet, Homer calls the ***no-corn-bearing***.

Timotheus. There are many who will stand against you on this ground.

Lucian. With what perfect ease and fluency do some of the dullest men in existence toss over and discuss the most elaborate of all works! How many myriads of such creatures would be insufficient to furnish intellect enough for any single paragraph in them! Yet 'we think this', 'we advise that', are expressions now become so customary, that it would be difficult to turn them into ridicule. We must pull the creatures out while they are in the very act, and show who and what they are. One of these fellows said to Caius Fuscus in my hearing, that there was a time when it was permitted him to doubt occasionally on particular points of criticism, but that the time was now over.

Timotheus. And what did you think of such arrogance? What did you reply to such impertinence?

Lucian. Let me answer one question at a time. First: I thought him a legitimate fool, of the purest breed. Secondly: I promised him I would always be contented with the judgment he had rejected, leaving him and his friends in the enjoyment of the rest.

Timotheus. And what said he?

Lucian. I forget. He seemed pleased at my acknowledgment of his discrimination, at my deference and delicacy. He wished, however, I had studied Plato, Xenophon, and Cicero, more attentively; without which preparatory discipline, no two persons could be introduced advantageously into a dialogue. I agreed with him on this position, remarking that we ourselves were at that very time giving our sentence on the fact. He suggested a slight mistake on my side, and expressed a wish that he were conversing with a writer able to sustain the opposite part. With his experience and skill in rhetoric, his long habitude of composition, his knowledge of life, of morals, and of character, he should be less verbose than Cicero, less gorgeous than Plato, and less trimly attired than Xenophon.

Timotheus. If he spoke in that manner, he might indeed be ridiculed for conceitedness and presumption, but his language is not altogether a fool's.

Lucian. I deliver his sentiments, not his words: for who would read, or who would listen to me, if such fell from me as from him? Poetry has its probabilities, so has prose: when people cry out against the representation of a dullard, **Could he have spoken all that?** 'Certainly no,' is the reply: neither did Priam implore, in harmonious verse, the pity of Achilles. We say only what might be said, when great postulates are conceded.

Timotheus. We will pretermit these absurd and silly men: but, Cousin Lucian! Cousin Lucian! the name of Plato will be durable as that of Sesostris.

Lucian. So will the pebbles and bricks which gangs of slaves erected into a pyramid. I do not hold Sesostris in much higher estimation than those quieter lumps of matter. They, O Timotheus, who survive the wreck of ages, are by no means, as a body, the worthiest of our admiration. It is in these wrecks, as in those at sea, the best things are not always saved. Hen-coops and empty barrels bob upon the surface, under a serene and smiling sky, when the graven or depicted images of the gods are scattered on invisible rocks, and when those who most resemble them in knowledge and beneficence are devoured by cold monsters below.

Timotheus. You now talk reasonably, seriously, almost religiously. Do you ever pray?

Lucian. I do. It was no longer than five years ago that I was deprived by death of my dog Melanops. He had uniformly led an innocent life; for I never would let him walk out with me, lest he should bring home in his mouth the remnant of some god or other, and at last get bitten or stung by one. I reminded Anubis of this: and moreover I told him, what he ought to be aware of, that Melanops did honour to his relationship.

Timotheus. I cannot ever call it piety to pray for dumb and dead beasts.

Lucian. Timotheus! Timotheus! have you no heart? have you no dog? do you always pray only for yourself?

Timotheus. We do not believe that dogs can live again.

Lucian. More shame for you! If they enjoy and suffer, if they hope and fear, if calamities and wrongs befall them, such as agitate their hearts and excite their apprehensions; if they possess the option of being grateful or malicious, and choose the worthier; if they exercise the same sound judgment on many other occasions, some for their own benefit and some for the benefit of their masters, they have as good a chance of a future life, and a better chance of a happy one, than half the priests of all the religions in the world. Wherever there is the choice of doing well or ill, and that choice (often against a first impulse) decides for well, there must not only be a soul of the same nature as man's, although of less compass and comprehension, but, being of the same nature, the same immortality must appertain to it; for spirit, like body, may change, but cannot be annihilated.

It was among the prejudices of former times that pigs are uncleanly animals, and fond of wallowing in the mire for mire's sake. Philosophy has now discovered that when they roll in mud and ordure, it is only from an excessive love of cleanliness, and a vehement desire to rid themselves of scabs and vermin. Unfortunately, doubts keep pace with discoveries. They are like warts, of which the blood that springs from a great one extirpated, makes twenty little ones.

Timotheus. The Hydra would be a more noble simile.

Lucian. I was indeed about to illustrate my position by the old Hydra, so ready at hand and so tractable; but I will never take hold of a hydra, when a wart will serve my turn.

Timotheus. Continue then.

Lucian. Even children are now taught, in despite of Aesop, that animals never spoke. The uttermost that can be advanced with any show of confidence is, that if they spoke at all, they spoke in unknown tongues. Supposing the fact, is this a reason why they should not be respected? Quite the contrary. If the tongues were unknown, it tends to demonstrate ***our*** ignorance, not ***theirs***. If we could not understand them, while they possessed the gift, here is no proof that they did not speak to the purpose, but only that it was not to ***our*** purpose; which may likewise be said with equal certainty of the wisest men that ever existed. How little have we learned from them, for the conduct of life or the avoidance of calamity! Unknown tongues, indeed! yes, so are all tongues to the vulgar and the negligent.

Timotheus. It comforts me to hear you talk in this manner, without a glance at our gifts and privileges.

Lucian. I am less incredulous than you suppose, my cousin! Indeed I have been giving you what ought to be a sufficient proof of it.

Timotheus. You have spoken with becoming gravity, I must confess.

Lucian. Let me then submit to your judgment some fragments of history which have lately fallen into my hands. There is among them a ***hymn***, of which the metre is so incondite, and the phraseology so ancient, that the grammarians have attributed it to Linus. But the hymn will interest you less, and is less to our purpose, than the tradition; by which it appears that certain priests of high antiquity were of the brute creation.

Timotheus. No better, any of them.

Lucian. Now you have polished the palms of your hands, I will commence my narrative from the manuscript.

Timotheus. Pray do.

Lucian. There existed in the city of Nephosis a fraternity of priests, reverenced by the appellation of **Gasteres**. It is reported that they were not always of their present form, but were birds aquatic and migratory, a species of cormorant. The poet Linus, who lived nearer the transformation (if there indeed was any), sings thus, in his Hymn to Zeus:

'Thy power is manifest, O Zeus! in the Gasteres. Wild birds were they, strong of talon, clanging of wing, and clamorous of gullet. Wild birds, O Zeus! wild birds; now cropping the tender grass by the river of Adonis, and breaking the nascent reed at the root, and depasturing the sweet nymphaea; now again picking up serpents and other creeping things on each hand of old Aegyptos, whose head is hidden in the clouds.

'Oh that Mnemosyne would command the staidest of her three daughters to stand and sing before me! to sing clearly and strongly. How before thy throne, Saturnian! sharp voices arose, even the voices of Here and of thy children. How they cried out that innumerable mortal men, various-tongued, kid-roasters in tent and tabernacle, devising in their many-turning hearts and thoughtful minds how to fabricate well-rounded spits of beech-tree, how such men having been changed into brute animals, it behoved thee to trim the balance, and in thy wisdom to change sundry brute animals into men; in order that they might pour out flame-coloured wine unto thee, and sprinkle the white flower of the sea upon the thighs of many bulls, to pleasure thee. Then didst thou, O storm-driver! overshadow far lands with thy dark eyebrows, looking down on them, to accomplish thy will. And then didst thou behold the Gasteres, fat, tall, prominent-crested, purple-legged, daedal-plumed, white and black, changeable in colour as Iris. And lo! thou didst will it, and they were men.'

Timotheus. No doubt whatever can be entertained of this hymn's antiquity. But what farther says the historian?

Lucian. I will read on, to gratify you.

'It is recorded that this ancient order of a most lordly priesthood went through many changes of customs and ceremonies, which indeed they were always ready to accommodate to the maintenance of their authority and the enjoyment of their riches. It is recorded that, in the beginning, they kept various tame animals, and some wild ones, within the precincts of the temple: nevertheless, after a time, they applied to their own uses everything they could lay their hands on, whatever might have been the vow of those who came forward with the offering. And when it was expected of them to make sacrifices, they not only would make none, but declared it an act of impiety to expect it. Some of the people, who feared the Immortals, were dismayed and indignant at this backwardness; and the discontent at last grew universal. Whereupon, the two chief priests held a long conference together, and agreed that something must be done to pacify the multitude. But it was not until the greater of them, acknowledging his despondency, called on the gods to answer for him that his grief was only because he never could abide bad precedents: and the other, on his side, protested that he was overruled by his superior, and moreover had a serious objection (founded on principle) to be knocked on the head. Meanwhile the elder was looking down on the folds of his robe, in deep melancholy. After long consideration, he sprang upon his feet, pushing his chair behind him, and said, "Well, it is grown old, and was always too long for me: I am resolved to cut off a finger's breadth."

"'Having, in your wisdom and piety, well contemplated the bad precedent," said the other, with much consternation in his countenance at seeing so elastic a spring in a heel by no means bearing any resemblance to a stag's.... "I have, I have," replied the other, interrupting him; "say no more; I am sick at heart; you must do the same."

"'A cursed dog has torn a hole in mine," answered the other, "and, if I cut anywhere about it, I only make bad worse. In regard to its length, I wish it were as long again." "Brother! brother! never be worldly-minded," said the senior. "Follow my example: snip off it not a finger's breadth, half a finger's breadth."

"'But," expostulated the other, "will that satisfy the gods?" "Who talked about them?" placidly said the senior. "It is very unbecoming to have them always in our mouths: surely there are appointed times for them. Let us be contented with laying the snippings on the altar, and thus showing the people our piety and condescension. They, and the gods also, will be just as well satisfied, as if we offered up a buttock of beef, with a bushel of salt and the same quantity of wheaten flour on it."

"'Well, if that will do ... and you know best," replied the other, "so be it." Saying which words, he carefully and considerately snipped off as much in proportion (for he was shorter by an inch) as the elder had done, yet leaving on his shoulders quite enough of materials to make handsome cloaks for seven or eight stout-built generals. Away they both went, arm-in-arm, and then holding up their skirts a great deal higher than was necessary, told the gods what they two had been doing for them and their glory. About the court of the temple the sacred swine were lying in indolent composure: seeing which, the brotherly twain began to commune with themselves afresh: and the senior said repentantly, "What fools we have been! The populace will laugh outright at the curtailment of our vestures, but would gladly have seen these animals eat daily a quarter less of the lentils." The words were spoken so earnestly and emphatically that they were overheard by the quadrupeds. Suddenly there was a rising of all the principal ones in the sacred enclosure: and many that were in the streets took up, each according to his temperament and condition, the gravest or shrillest tone of reprobation. The thinner and therefore the more desperate of the creatures, pushing their snouts under the curtailed habiliments of the high priests, assailed them with ridicule and reproach. For it had pleased the gods to work a miracle in their behoof, and they became as loquacious as those who governed them, and who were appointed to speak in the high places. "Let the worst come to the worst, we at least have our tails to our hams," said they. "For how long?" whined others, piteously: others incessantly ejaculated tremendous imprecations: others, more serious and sedate, groaned inwardly; and, although under their hearts there lay a huge mass of indigestible sourness ready to rise up against the chief priests, they ventured no farther than expostulation. "We shall lose our voices," said they, "if we lose our complement of lentils; and then, most reverend lords, what will ye do for choristers?" Finally, one of grand dimensions, who seemed almost half-human, imposed silence on every debater. He lay stretched out apart from his brethren, covering with his side the greater portion of a noble dunghill, and all its verdure native and imported. He crushed a few measures of peascods to cool his tusks; then turned his pleasurable longitudinal eyes far toward the outer extremities of their sockets, and leered fixedly and sarcastically at the high priests, showing every tooth in each jaw. Other men might have feared them; the high priests envied them, seeing what order they were in, and what exploits they were capable of. A great painter, who flourished many olympiads ago, has, in his volume entitled the ***Canon***, defined the line of beauty. It was here in its perfection: it followed with winning obsequiousness every member, but delighted more especially to swim along that placid and pliant curvature on which Nature had ranged the implements of mastication. Pawing with his cloven hoof, he suddenly changed his countenance from the contemplative to the wrathful. At one effort he rose up to his whole length, breadth, and height: and they who had never seen him in earnest, nor separate from the common swine of the enclosure, with which he was in the habit of husking what was thrown to him, could form no idea what a prodigious beast he was. Terrible were the expressions of choler and comminations which burst forth from his fulminating tusks. Erimanthus would have hidden his puny offspring before them; and Hercules would have paused at the encounter. Thrice he called aloud to the high priests: thrice he swore in their own sacred language that they were a couple of thieves and impostors: thrice he imprecated the worst maledictions on his own head if they had not violated the holiest of their vows, and were not ready even to sell their gods. A tremor ran throughout the whole body of the united swine; so awful was the adjuration! Even the Gasteres themselves in some sort shuddered, not perhaps altogether at the solemn tone of its impiety; for they had much experience in these matters. But among them was a Gaster who was calmer than the swearer, and more prudent and conciliating than those he swore against. Hearing this objurgation, he went blandly up to the sacred porker, and, lifting the flap of his right ear between forefinger and thumb with all delicacy and gentleness, thus whispered into it: "You do not in your heart believe that any of us are such fools as to sell our gods, at least while we have such a reserve to fall back upon."

'"Are we to be devoured?" cried the noble porker, twitching his ear indignantly from under the hand of the monitor. "Hush!" said he, laying it again, most soothingly, rather farther from the tusks: "hush! sweet friend! Devoured? Oh, certainly not: that is to say, not ***all***: or, if all, not all at once. Indeed the holy men my brethren may perhaps be contented with taking a little blood from each of you, entirely for the advantage of your health and activity, and merely to compose a few slender black-puddings for the inferior monsters of the temple, who latterly are grown very exacting, and either are, or pretend to be, hungry after they have eaten a whole handful of acorns, swallowing I am ashamed to say what a quantity of water to wash them down. We do not grudge them it, as they well know: but they appear to have forgotten how recently no inconsiderable portion of this bounty has been conferred. If we, as they object to us, eat more, they ought to be aware that it is by no means for our gratification, since we have abjured it before the gods, but to maintain the dignity of the priesthood, and to exhibit the beauty and utility of subordination."

'The noble porker had beaten time with his muscular tail at many of these periods; but again his heart panted visibly, and he could bear no more.

'"All this for our good! for our activity! for our health! Let us alone: we have health enough; we want no activity. Let us alone, I say again, or by the Immortals!..." "Peace, my son! Your breath is valuable: evidently you have but little to spare: and what mortal knows how soon the gods may demand the last of it?"

'At the beginning of this exhortation, the worthy high priest had somewhat repressed the ebullient choler of his refractory and pertinacious disciple, by applying his flat soft palm to the signet-formed extremity of the snout.

'"We are ready to hear complaints at all times," added he, "and to redress any grievance at our own. But beyond a doubt, if you continue to raise your abominable outcries, some of the people are likely to hit upon two discoveries: first that your lentils would be sufficient to make daily for every poor family a good wholesome porridge; and secondly, that your flesh, properly cured, might hang up nicely against the forthcoming bean-season." Pondering these mighty words, the noble porker kept his eyes fixed upon him for some instants, then leaned forward dejectedly, then tucked one foot under him, then another, cautious to descend with dignity. At last he grunted (it must for ever be ambiguous whether with despondency or with resignation), pushed his wedgy snout far within the straw subjacent, and sank into that repose which is granted to the just.'

Timotheus. Cousin! there are glimmerings of truth and wisdom in sundry parts of this discourse, not unlike little broken shells entangled in dark masses of seaweed. But I would rather you had continued to adduce fresh arguments to demonstrate the beneficence of the Deity, proving (if you could) that our horses and dogs, faithful servants and companions to us, and often treated cruelly, may recognize us hereafter, and we them. We have no authority for any such belief.

Lucian. We have authority for thinking and doing whatever is humane. Speaking of humanity, it now occurs to me, I have heard a report that some well-intentioned men of your religion so interpret the words or wishes of its Founder, they would abolish slavery throughout the empire.

Timotheus. Such deductions have been drawn indeed from our Master's doctrine: but the saner part of us receive it metaphorically, and would only set men free from the bonds of sin. For if domestic slaves were manumitted, we should neither have a dinner dressed nor a bed made, unless by our own children: and as to labour in the fields, who would cultivate them in this hot climate? We must import slaves from Ethiopia and elsewhere, wheresoever they can be procured: but the hardship lies not on them; it lies on us, and bears heavily; for we must first buy them with our money, and then feed them; and not only must we maintain them while they are hale and hearty and can serve us, but likewise in sickness and (unless we can sell them for a trifle) in decrepitude. Do not imagine, my cousin, that we are no better than enthusiasts, visionaries, subverters of order, and ready to roll society down into one flat surface.

Lucian. I thought you were maligned: I said so.

Timotheus. When the subject was discussed in our congregation, the meaner part of the people were much in favour of the abolition: but the chief priests and ministers absented themselves, and gave no vote at all, deeming it secular, and saying that in such matters the laws and customs of the country ought to be observed.

Lucian. Several of these chief priests and ministers are robed in purple and fine linen, and fare sumptuously every day.

Timotheus. I have hopes of you now.

Lucian. Why so suddenly?

Timotheus. Because you have repeated those blessed words, which are only to be found in our Scriptures.

Lucian. There indeed I found them. But I also found in the same volume words of the same speaker, declaring that the rich shall never see His face in heaven.

Timotheus. He does not always mean what you think He does.

Lucian. How is this? Did He then direct His discourses to none but men more intelligent than I am?

Timotheus. Unless He gave you understanding for the occasion, they might mislead you.

Lucian. Indeed!

Timotheus. Unquestionably. For instance, He tells us to take no heed of to-morrow: He tells us to share equally all our worldly goods: but we know that we cannot be respected unless we bestow due care on our possessions, and that not only the vulgar but the well-educated esteem us in proportion to the gifts of fortune.

Lucian. The eclectic philosophy is most flourishing among you Christians. You take whatever suits your appetites, and reject the rest.

Timotheus. We are not half so rich as the priests of Isis. Give us their possessions; and we will not sit idle as they do, but be able and ready to do incalculable good to our fellow-creatures.

Lucian. I have never seen great possessions excite to great alacrity. Usually they enfeeble the sympathies, and often overlie and smother them.

Timotheus. Our religion is founded less on sympathies than on miracles. Cousin! you smile most when you ought to be most serious.

Lucian. I was smiling at the thought of one whom I would recommend to your especial notice, as soon as you disinherit the priests of

Isis. He may perhaps be refractory; for he pretends (the knave!) to work miracles.

Timotheus. Impostor! who is he?

Lucian. Aulus of Pelusium. Idle and dissolute, he never gained anything honestly but a scourging, if indeed he ever made, what he long merited, this acquisition. Unable to run into debt where he was known, he came over to Alexandria.

Timotheus. I know him: I know him well. Here, of his own accord, he has betaken himself to a new and regular life.

Lucian. He will presently wear it out, or make it sit easier on his shoulders. My metaphor brings me to my story. Having nothing to carry with him beside an empty valise, he resolved on filling it with something, however worthless, lest, seeing his utter destitution, and hopeless of payment, a receiver of lodgers should refuse to admit him into the hostelry. Accordingly, he went to a tailor's, and began to joke about his poverty. Nothing is more apt to bring people into good humour; for, if they are poor themselves, they enjoy the pleasure of discovering that others are no better off; and, if not poor, there is the consciousness of superiority.

'The favour I am about to ask of a man so wealthy and so liberal as you are,' said Aulus, 'is extremely small: you can materially serve me, without the slightest loss, hazard, or inconvenience. In few words, my valise is empty: and to some ears an empty valise is louder and more discordant than a bagpipe: I cannot say I like the sound of it myself. Give me all the shreds and snippings you can spare me. They will feel like clothes; not exactly so to me and my person, but to those who are inquisitive, and who may be importunate.'

The tailor laughed, and distended both arms of Aulus with his munificence. Soon was the valise well filled and rammed down. Plenty of boys were in readiness to carry it to the boat. Aulus waved them off, looking at some angrily, at others suspiciously. Boarding the skiff, he lowered his treasure with care and caution, staggering a little at the weight, and shaking it gently on deck, with his ear against it: and then, finding all safe and compact, he sat on it; but as tenderly as a pullet on her first eggs. When he was landed, his care was even greater, and whoever came near him was warned off with loud vociferations. Anxiously as the other passengers were invited by the innkeepers to give their houses the preference, Aulus was importuned most: the others were only beset; he was borne off in triumphant captivity. He ordered a bedroom, and carried his valise with him; he ordered a bath, and carried with him his valise. He started up from the company at dinner, struck his forehead, and cried out, 'Where is my valise?' 'We are honest men here,' replied the host. 'You have left it, sir, in your chamber: where else indeed should you leave it?'

'Honesty is seated on your brow,' exclaimed Aulus; 'but there are few to be trusted in the world we live in. I now believe I can eat.' And he gave a sure token of the belief that was in him, not without a start now and then and a finger at his ear, as if he heard somebody walking in the direction of his bedchamber. Now began his first miracle: for now he contrived to pick up, from time to time, a little money. In the presence of his host and fellow-lodgers, he threw a few obols, negligently and indifferently, among the beggars. 'These poor creatures,' said he, 'know a new-comer as well as the gnats do: in one half-hour I am half ruined by them; and this daily.'

Nearly a month had elapsed since his arrival, and no account of board and lodging had been delivered or called for. Suspicion at length arose in the host whether he really was rich. When another man's honesty is doubted, the doubter's is sometimes in jeopardy. The host was tempted to unsew the valise. To his amazement and horror he found only shreds within it. However, he was determined to be cautious, and to consult his wife, who, although a Christian like Aulus, and much edified by his discourses, might dissent from him in regard to a community of goods, at least in her own household, and might defy him to prove by any authority that the doctrine was meant for innkeepers. Aulus, on his return in the evening, found out that his valise had been opened. He hurried back, threw its contents into the canal, and, borrowing an old cloak, he tucked it up under his dress, and returned. Nobody had seen him enter or come back again, nor was it immediately that his host or hostess were willing to appear. But, after he had called them loudly for some time, they entered his apartment: and he thus addressed the woman:

'O Eucharis! no words are requisite to convince you (firm as you are in the faith) of eternal verities, however mysterious. But your unhappy husband has betrayed his incredulity in regard to the most awful. If my prayers, offered up in our holy temples all day long, have been heard, and that they have been heard I feel within me the blessed certainty, something miraculous has been vouchsafed for the conversion of this miserable sinner. Until the present hour, the valise before you was filled with precious relics from the apparel of saints and martyrs, fresh as when on them.' 'True, by Jove!' said the husband to himself. 'Within the present hour,' continued Aulus, 'they are united into one raiment, signifying our own union, our own restoration.'

He drew forth the cloak, and fell on his face. Eucharis fell also, and kissed the saintly head prostrate before her. The host's eyes were opened, and he bewailed his hardness of heart. Aulus is now occupied in strengthening his faith, not without an occasional support to the wife's: all three live together in unity.

Timotheus. And do you make a joke even of this? Will you never cease from the habitude?

Lucian. Too soon. The farther we descend into the vale of years, the fewer illusions accompany us: we have little inclination, little time, for jocularity and laughter. Light things are easily detached from us, and we shake off heavier as we can. Instead of levity, we are liable to moroseness: for always near the grave there are more briers than flowers, unless we plant them ourselves, or our friends supply them.

Timotheus. Thinking thus, do you continue to dissemble or to distort the truth? The shreds are become a cable for the faithful. That they were miraculously turned into one entire garment who shall gainsay? How many hath it already clothed with righteousness? Happy men, casting their doubts away before it! Who knows, O Cousin Lucian, but on some future day you yourself will invoke the merciful interposition of Aulus!

Lucian. Possibly: for if ever I fall among thieves, nobody is likelier to be at the head of them.

Timotheus. Uncharitable man! how suspicious! how ungenerous! how hardened in unbelief! Reason is a bladder on which you may paddle like a child as you swim in summer waters: but, when the winds rise and the waves roughen, it slips from under you, and you sink; yes, O Lucian, you sink into a gulf whence you never can emerge.

Lucian. I deem those the wisest who exert the soonest their own manly strength, now with the stream and now against it, enjoying the exercise in fine weather, venturing out in foul, if need be, yet avoiding not only rocks and whirlpools, but also shallows. In such a light, my cousin, I look on your dispensations. I shut them out as we shut out winds blowing from the desert; hot, debilitating, oppressive, laden with impalpable sands and pungent salts, and inflicting an incurable blindness.

Timotheus. Well, Cousin Lucian! I can bear all you say while you are not witty. Let me bid you farewell in this happy interval.

Lucian. Is it not serious and sad, O my cousin, that what the Deity hath willed to lie incomprehensible in His mysteries, we should fall upon with tooth and nail, and ferociously growl over, or ignorantly dissect?

Timotheus. Ho! now you come to be serious and sad, there are hopes of you. Truth always begins or ends so.

Lucian. Undoubtedly. But I think it more reverential to abstain from that which, with whatever effort, I should never understand.

Timotheus. You are lukewarm, my cousin, you are lukewarm. A most dangerous state.

Lucian. For milk to continue in, not for men. I would not fain be frozen or scalded.

Timotheus. Alas! you are blind, my sweet cousin!

Lucian. Well; do not open my eyes with pincers, nor compose for them a collyrium of spurge.

May not men eat and drink and talk together, and perform in relation one to another all the duties of social life, whose opinions are different on things immediately under their eyes? If they can and do, surely they may as easily on things equally above the comprehension of each party. The wisest and most virtuous man in the whole extent of the Roman Empire is Plutarch of Cheronaea: yet Plutarch holds a firm belief in the existence of I know not how many gods, every one of whom has committed notorious misdemeanours. The nearest to the Cheronaean in virtue and wisdom is Trajan, who holds all the gods dog-cheap. These two men are friends. If either of them were influenced by your religion, as inculcated and practised by the priesthood, he would be the enemy of the other, and wisdom and virtue would plead for the delinquent in vain. When your religion had existed, as you tell us, about a century, Caius Caecilius, of Novum Comum, was proconsul in Bithynia. Trajan, the mildest and most equitable of mankind, desirous to remove from them, as far as might be, the hatred and invectives of those whose old religion was assailed by them, applied to Caecilius for information on their behaviour as good citizens. The reply of Caecilius was favourable. Had Trajan applied to the most eminent and authoritative of the sect, they would certainly have brought into jeopardy all who differed in one tittle from any point of their doctrine or discipline. For the thorny and bitter aloe of dissension required less than a century to flower on the steps of your temple.

Timotheus. You are already half a Christian, in exposing to the world the vanities both of philosophy and of power.

Lucian. I have done no such thing: I have exposed the vanities of the philosophizing and the powerful. Philosophy is admirable; and Power may be glorious: the one conduces to truth, the other has nearly all the means of conferring peace and happiness, but it usually, and indeed almost always, takes a contrary direction. I have ridiculed the futility of speculative minds, only when they would pave the clouds instead of the streets. To see distant things better than near is a certain proof of a defective sight. The people I have held in derision never turn their eyes to what they can see, but direct them continually where nothing is to be seen. And this, by their disciples, is called the sublimity of speculation! There is little merit acquired, or force exhibited, in blowing off a feather that would settle on my nose: and this is all I have done in regard to the philosophers: but I claim for myself the approbation of humanity, in having shown the true dimensions of the great. The highest of them are no higher than my tunic; but they are high enough to trample on the necks of those wretches who throw themselves on the ground before them.

Timotheus. Was Alexander of Macedon no higher?

Lucian. What region of the earth, what city, what theatre, what library, what private study, hath he enlightened? If you are silent, I may well be. It is neither my philosophy nor your religion which casts the blood and bones of men in their faces, and insists on the most reverence for those who have made the most unhappy. If the Romans scourged by the hands of children the schoolmaster who would have betrayed them, how greatly more deserving of flagellation, from the same quarter, are those hundreds of pedagogues who deliver up the intellects of youth to such immoral revellers and mad murderers! They would punish a thirsty child for purloining a bunch of grapes from a vineyard, and the same men on the same day would insist on his reverence for the subverter of Tyre, the plunderer of Babylon, and the incendiary of Persepolis. And are these men teachers? are these men philosophers? are these men priests? Of all the curses that ever afflicted the earth, I think Alexander was the worst. Never was he in so little mischief as when he was murdering his friends.

Timotheus. Yet he built this very city; a noble and opulent one when Rome was of hurdles and rushes.

Lucian. He built it! I wish, O Timotheus! he had been as well employed as the stone-cutters or the plasterers. No, no: the wisest of architects planned the most beautiful and commodious of cities, by which, under a rational government and equitable laws, Africa might have been civilized to the centre, and the palm have extended her conquests through the remotest desert. Instead of which, a dozen of Macedonian thieves rifled a dying drunkard and murdered his children. In process of time, another drunkard reeled hitherward from Rome, made an easy mistake in mistaking a palace for a brothel, permitted a stripling boy to beat him soundly, and a serpent to receive the last caresses of his paramour.

Shame upon historians and pedagogues for exciting the worst passions of youth by the display of such false glories! If your religion hath any truth or influence, her professors will extinguish the promontory lights, which only allure to breakers. They will be assiduous in teaching the young and ardent that great abilities do not constitute great men, without the right and unremitting application of them; and that, in the sight of Humanity and Wisdom, it is better to erect one cottage than to demolish a hundred cities. Down to the present day we have been taught little else than falsehood. We have been told to do this thing and that: we have been told we shall be punished unless we do: but at the same time we are shown by the finger that prosperity and glory, and the esteem of all about us, rest upon other and very different foundations. Now, do the ears or the eyes seduce the most easily and lead the most directly to the heart? But both eyes and ears are won over, and alike are persuaded to corrupt us.

Timotheus. Cousin Lucian, I was leaving you with the strangest of all notions in my head. I began to think for a moment that you doubted my sincerity in the religion I profess; and that a man of your admirable good sense, and at your advanced age, could reject that only sustenance which supports us through the grave into eternal life.

Lucian. I am the most docile and practicable of men, and never reject what people set before me: for if it is bread, it is good for my own use; if bone or bran, it will do for my dog or mule. But, although you know my weakness and facility, it is unfair to expect I should have admitted at once what the followers and personal friends of your Master for a long time hesitated to receive. I remember to have read in one of the early commentators, that His disciples themselves could not swallow the miracle of the loaves; and one who wrote more recently says, that even His brethren did not believe in Him.

Timotheus. Yet, finally, when they have looked over each other's accounts, they cast them up, and make them all tally in the main sum; and if one omits an article, the next supplies its place with a commodity of the same value. What would you have? But it is of little use to argue on religion with a man who, professing his readiness to believe, and even his credulity, yet disbelieves in miracles.

Lucian. I should be obstinate and perverse if I disbelieved in the existence of a thing for no better reason than because I never saw it, and cannot understand its operations. Do you believe, O Timotheus, that Perictione, the mother of Plato, became his mother by the sole agency of Apollo's divine spirit, under the phantasm of that god?

Timotheus. I indeed believe such absurdities?

Lucian. You touch me on a vital part if you call an absurdity the religion or philosophy in which I was educated. Anaxalides, and Clearagus, and Speusippus, his own nephew, assert it. Who should know better than they?

Timotheus. Where are their proofs?

Lucian. I would not be so indelicate as to require them on such an occasion. A short time ago I conversed with an old centurion, who was in service by the side of Vespasian, when Titus, and many officers and soldiers of the army, and many captives, were present, and who saw one Eleazar put a ring to the nostril of a demoniac (as the patient was called) and draw the demon out of it.

Timotheus. And do you pretend to believe this nonsense?

Lucian. I only believe that Vespasian and Titus had nothing to gain or accomplish by the miracle; and that Eleazar, if he had been detected in a trick by two acute men and several thousand enemies, had nothing to look forward to but a cross--the only piece of upholstery for which Judea seems to have either wood or workmen, and which are as common in that country as direction-posts are in any other.

Timotheus. The Jews are a stiff-necked people.

Lucian. On such occasions, no doubt.

Timotheus. Would you, O Lucian, be classed among the atheists, like Epicurus?

Lucian. It lies not at my discretion what name shall be given me at present or hereafter, any more than it did at my birth. But I wonder at the ignorance and precipitancy of those who call Epicurus an atheist. He saw on the same earth with himself a great variety of inferior creatures, some possessing more sensibility and more thoughtfulness than others. Analogy would lead so contemplative a reasoner to the conclusion that if many were inferior and in sight, others might be superior and out of sight. He never disbelieved in the existence of the gods; he only disbelieved that they troubled their heads with our concerns. Have they none of their own? If they are happy, does their happiness depend on us, comparatively so imbecile and vile? He believed, as nearly all nations do, in different ranks and orders of superhuman beings; and perhaps he thought (but I never was in his confidence or counsels) that the higher were rather in communication with the next to them in intellectual faculties, than with the most remote. To me the suggestion appears by no means irrational, that if we are managed or cared for at all by beings wiser than ourselves (which in truth would be no sign of any great wisdom in them), it can only be by such as are very far from perfection, and who indulge us in the commission of innumerable faults and follies, for their own speculation or amusement.

Timotheus. There is only one such; and he is the devil.

Lucian. If he delights in our wickedness, which you believe, he must be incomparably the happiest of beings, which you do not believe. No god of Epicurus rests his elbow on his armchair with less energetic exertion or discomposure.

Timotheus. We lead holier and purer lives than such ignorant mortals as are not living under Grace.

Lucian. I also live under Grace, O Timotheus! and I venerate her for the pleasures I have received at her hands. I do not believe she has quite deserted me. If my grey hairs are unattractive to her, and if the trace of her fingers is lost in the wrinkles of my forehead, still I sometimes am told it is discernible even on the latest and coldest of my writings.

Timotheus. You are wilful in misapprehension. The Grace of which I speak is adverse to pleasure and impurity.

Lucian. Rightly do you separate impurity and pleasure, which indeed soon fly asunder when the improvident would unite them. But never believe that tenderness of heart signifies corruption of morals, if you happen to find it (which indeed is unlikely) in the direction you have taken; on the contrary, no two qualities are oftener found together, on mind as on matter, than hardness and lubricity.

Believe me, Cousin Timotheus, when we come to eighty years of age we are all Essenes. In our kingdom of heaven there is no marrying or giving in marriage; and austerity in ourselves, when Nature holds over us the sharp instrument with which Jupiter operated on Saturn, makes us austere to others. But how happens it that you, both old and young, break every bond which connected you anciently with the Essenes? Not only do you marry (a height of wisdom to which I never have attained, although in others I commend it), but you never share your substance with the poorest of your community, as they did, nor live simply and frugally, nor purchase nor employ slaves, nor refuse rank and offices in the State, nor abstain from litigation, nor abominate and execrate the wounds and cruelties of war. The Essenes did all this, and greatly more, if Josephus and Philo, whose political and religious tenets are opposite to theirs, are credible and trustworthy.

Timotheus. Doubtless you would also wish us to retire into the desert, and eschew the conversation of mankind.

Lucian. No, indeed; but I would wish the greater part of your people to eschew mine, for they bring all the worst of the desert with them whenever they enter; its smothering heats, its blinding sands, its sweeping suffocation. Return to the pure spirit of the Essenes, without their asceticism; cease from controversy, and drop party designations. If you will not do this, do less, and be merely what you profess to be, which is quite enough for an honest, a virtuous, and a religious man.

Timotheus. Cousin Lucian, I did not come hither to receive a lecture from you.

Lucian. I have often given a dinner to a friend who did not come to dine with me.

Timotheus. Then, I trust, you gave him something better for dinner than bay-salt and dandelions. If you will not assist us in nettling our enemies a little for their absurdities and impositions, let me entreat you, however, to let us alone, and to make no remarks on us. I myself run into no extravagances, like the Essenes, washing and fasting, and retiring into solitude. I am not called to them; when I am, I go.

Lucian. I am apprehensive the Lord may afflict you with deafness in that ear.

Timotheus. Nevertheless, I am indifferent to the world, and all things in it. This, I trust, you will acknowledge to be true religion and true philosophy.

Lucian. That is not philosophy which betrays an indifference to those for whose benefit philosophy was designed; and those are the whole human race. But I hold it to be the most unphilosophical thing in the world to call away men from useful occupations and mutual help, to profitless speculations and acrid controversies. Censurable enough, and contemptible, too, is that supercilious philosopher, sneeringly sedate, who narrates in full and flowing periods the persecutions and tortures of a fellow-man, led astray by his credulity, and ready to die in the assertion of what in his soul he believes to be the truth. But hardly less censurable, hardly less contemptible, is the tranquilly arrogant sectarian, who denies that wisdom or honesty can exist beyond the limits of his own ill-lighted chamber.

Timotheus. What! is he sanguinary?

Lucian. Whenever he can be, he is; and he always has it in his power to be even worse than that, for he refuses his custom to the industrious and honest shopkeeper who has been taught to think differently from himself in matters which he has had no leisure to study, and by which, if he had enjoyed that leisure, he would have been a less industrious and a less expert artificer.

Timotheus. We cannot countenance those hard-hearted men who refuse to hear the word of the Lord.

Lucian. The hard-hearted knowing this of the tender-hearted, and receiving the declaration from their own lips, will refuse to hear the word of the Lord all their lives.

Timotheus. Well, well; it cannot be helped. I see, cousin, my hopes of obtaining a little of your assistance in your own pleasant way are disappointed; but it is something to have conceived a better hope of saving your soul, from your readiness to acknowledge your belief in miracles.

Lucian. Miracles have existed in all ages and in all religions. Witnesses to some of them have been numerous; to others of them fewer. Occasionally, the witnesses have been disinterested in the result.

Timotheus. Now indeed you speak truly and wisely.

Lucian. But sometimes the most honest and the most quiescent have either been unable or unwilling to push themselves so forward as to see clearly and distinctly the whole of the operation; and have listened to some knave who felt a pleasure in deluding their credulity, or some other who himself was either an enthusiast or a dupe. It also may have happened in the ancient religions, of Egypt for instance, or of India, or even of Greece, that narratives have been attributed to authors who never heard of them; and have been circulated by honest men who firmly believed them; by half-honest, who indulged their vanity in becoming members of a novel and bustling society; and by utterly dishonest, who, having no other means of rising above the shoulders of the vulgar, threw dust into their eyes and made them stoop.

Timotheus. Ha! the rogues! It is nearly all over with them.

Lucian. Let us hope so. Parthenius and the Roman poet Ovidius Naso, have related the transformations of sundry men, women, and gods.

Timotheus. Idleness! Idleness! I never read such lying authors.

Lucian. I myself have seen enough to incline me toward a belief in them.

Timotheus. You? Why! you have always been thought an utter infidel; and now you are running, hot and heedless as any mad dog, to the opposite extreme!

Lucian. I have lived to see, not indeed one man, but certainly one animal turned into another; nay, great numbers. I have seen sheep with the most placid faces in the morning, one nibbling the tender herb with all its dew upon it; another, negligent of its own sustenance, and giving it copiously to the tottering lamb aside it.

Timotheus. How pretty! half poetical!

Lucian. In the heat of the day I saw the very same sheep tearing off each other's fleeces with long teeth and longer claws, and imitating so admirably the howl of wolves, that at last the wolves came down on them in a body, and lent their best assistance at the general devouring. What is more remarkable, the people of the villages seemed to enjoy the sport; and, instead of attacking the wolves, waited until they had filled their stomachs, ate the little that was left, said piously and from the bottom of their hearts what you call ***grace***, and went home singing and piping.

BISHOP SHIPLEY AND BENJAMIN FRANKLIN

Shipley. There are very few men, even in the bushes and the wilderness, who delight in the commission of cruelty; but nearly all, throughout the earth, are censurable for the admission. When we see a blow struck, we go on and think no more about it: yet every blow aimed at the most distant of our fellow-creatures, is sure to come back, some time or other, to our families and descendants. He who lights a fire in one quarter is ignorant to what other the winds may carry it, and whether what is kindled in the wood may not break out again in the cornfield.

Franklin. If we could restrain but one generation from deeds of violence, the foundation for a new and a more graceful edifice of society would not only have been laid, but would have been consolidated.

Shipley. We already are horrified at the bare mention of religious wars; we should then be horrified at the mention of political. Why should they who, when they are affronted or offended, abstain from inflicting blows, some from a sense of decorousness and others from a sense of religion, be forward to instigate the infliction of ten thousand, all irremediable, all murderous? Every chief magistrate should be arbitrator and umpire in all differences between any two, forbidding war. Much would be added to the dignity of the most powerful king by rendering him an efficient member of such a grand Amphictyonic council. Unhappily they are persuaded in childhood that a reign is made glorious by a successful war. What schoolmaster ever taught a boy to question it? or indeed any point of political morality, or any incredible thing in history? Caesar and Alexander are uniformly clement: Themistocles died by a draught of bull's blood: Portia by swallowing red-hot pieces of charcoal.

Franklin. Certainly no woman or man could perform either of these feats. In my opinion it lies beyond a doubt that Portia suffocated herself by the fumes of charcoal; and that the Athenian, whose stomach must have been formed on the model of other stomachs, and must therefore have rejected a much less quantity of blood than would have poisoned him, died by some chemical preparation, of which a bull's blood might, or might not, have been part. Schoolmasters who thus betray their trust, ought to be scourged by their scholars, like him of their profession who underwent the just indignation of the Roman Consul. You shut up those who are infected with the plague; why do you lay no coercion on those who are incurably possessed by the legion devil of carnage? When a creature is of intellect so perverted that he can discern no difference between a review and a battle, between the animating bugle and the dying groan, it were expedient to remove him, as quietly as may be, from his devastation of God's earth and his usurpation of God's authority. Compassion points out the cell for him at the bottom of the hospital, and listens to hear the key turned in the ward: until then the house is insecure.

Shipley. God grant our rulers wisdom, and our brethren peace!

Franklin. Here are but indifferent specimens and tokens. Those fellows throw stones pretty well: if they practise much longer, they will hit us: let me entreat you, my lord, to leave me here. So long as the good people were contented with hooting and shouting at us, no great harm was either done or apprehended: but now they are beginning to throw stones, perhaps they may prove themselves more dexterous in action than their rulers have done latterly in council.

Shipley. Take care, Doctor Franklin! *That* was very near being the philosopher's stone.

Franklin. Let me pick it up, then, and send it to London by the diligence. But I am afraid your ministers, and the nation at large, are as little in the way of wealth as of wisdom, in the experiment they are making.

Shipley. While I was attending to you, William had started. Look! he has reached them: they are listening to him. Believe me, he has all the courage of an Englishman and of a Christian; and, if the stoutest of them force him to throw off his new black coat, the blusterer would soon think it better to have listened to less polemical doctrine.

Franklin. Meantime a few of the town boys are come nearer, and begin to grow troublesome. I am sorry to requite your hospitality with such hard fare.

Shipley. True, these young bakers make their bread very gritty, but we must partake of it together so long as you are with us.

Franklin. Be pleased, my lord, to give us grace; our repast is over; this is my boat.

Shipley. We will accompany you as far as to the ship. Thank God! we are now upon the water, and all safe. Give me your hand, my good Doctor Franklin! and although you have failed in the object of your mission, yet the intention will authorize me to say, in the holy words of our Divine Redeemer, Blessed are the peacemakers!

Franklin. My dear lord! if God ever blessed a man at the

intercession of another, I may reasonably and confidently hope in such a benediction. Never did one arise from a warmer, a tenderer, or a purer heart.

Shipley. Infatuation! that England should sacrifice to her king so many thousands of her bravest men, and ruin so many thousands of her most industrious, in a vain attempt to destroy the very principles on which her strength and her glory are founded! The weakest prince that ever sat upon a throne, and the most needy and sordid Parliament that ever pandered to distempered power, are thrusting our blindfold nation from the pinnacle of prosperity.

Franklin. I believe *your* king (from this moment it is permitted me to call him *ours* no longer) to be as honest and as wise a man as any of those about him: but unhappily he can see no difference between a review and a battle. Such are the optics of most kings and rulers. His Parliament, in both Houses, acts upon calculation. There is hardly a family, in either, that does not anticipate the clear profit of several thousands a year, to itself and its connexions. Appointments to regiments and frigates raise the price of papers; and forfeited estates fly confusedly about, and darken the air from the Thames to the Atlantic.

Shipley. It is lamentable to think that war, bringing with it every species of human misery, should become a commercial speculation. Bad enough when it arises from revenge; another word for honour.

Franklin. A strange one indeed! but not more strange than fifty others that come under the same title. Wherever there is nothing of religion, nothing of reason, nothing of truth, we come at once to honour; and here we draw the sword, dispense with what little of civilization we ever pretended to, and murder or get murdered, as may happen. But these ceremonials both begin and end with an appeal to

God, who, before we appealed to Him, plainly told us we should do no such thing, and that He would punish us most severely if we did. And yet, my lord, even the gentlemen upon your bench turn a deaf ear to Him on these occasions: nay, they go further; they pray to Him for success in that which He has forbidden so strictly, and when they have broken His commandment, thank Him. Upon seeing these mockeries and impieties age after age repeated, I have asked myself whether the depositaries and expounders of religion have really any whatever of their own; or rather, like the lawyers, whether they do not defend professionally a cause that otherwise does not interest them in the least. Surely, if these holy men really believed in a just retributive God, they would never dare to utter the word *war*, without horror and deprecation.

Shipley. Let us attribute to infirmity what we must else attribute to wickedness.

Franklin. Willingly would I: but children are whipped severely for inobservance of things less evident, for disobedience of commands less audible and less awful. I am loath to attribute cruelty to your order: men so entirely at their ease have seldom any. Certain I am that several of the bishops would not have patted Cain upon the back while he was about to kill Abel; and my wonder is that the very same holy men encourage their brothers in England to kill their brothers in America; not one, not two nor three, but thousands, many thousands.

Shipley. I am grieved at the blindness with which God has afflicted us for our sins. These unhappy men are little aware what combustibles they are storing under the Church, and how soon they may explode. Even the wisest do not reflect on the most important and the most certain of things; which is, that every act of inhumanity and injustice goes far beyond what is apparent at the time of its commission; that these, and all other things, have their consequences; and that the consequences are infinite and eternal. If this one truth alone could be deeply impressed upon the hearts of men, it would regenerate the whole human race.

Franklin. In regard to politics, I am not quite certain whether a politician may not be too far-sighted: but I am quite certain that, if it be a fault, it is one into which few have fallen. The policy of the Romans in the time of the republic, seems to have been prospective. Some of the Dutch also, and of the Venetians, used the telescope. But in monarchies the prince, not the people, is consulted by the minister of the day; and what pleases the weakest supersedes what is approved by the wisest.

Shipley. We have had great statesmen: Burleigh, Cromwell, Marlborough, Somers: and whatever may have been in the eyes of a moralist the vices of Walpole, none ever understood more perfectly, or pursued more steadily, the direct and palpable interests of the country. Since his administration, our affairs have never been managed by men of business; and it was more than could have been expected that, in our war against the French in Canada, the appointment fell on an able commander.

Franklin. Such an anomaly is unlikely to recur. You have in the English Parliament (I speak of both Houses) only two great men; only two considerate and clear-sighted politicians; Chatham and Burke. Three or four can say clever things; several have sonorous voices; many vibrate sharp comminations from the embrasures of portentously slit sleeves; and there are those to be found who deliver their oracles out of wigs as worshipful as the curls of Jupiter, however they may be grumbled at by the flour-mills they have laid under such heavy contribution; yet nearly all of all parties want alike the sagacity to discover that in striking America you shake Europe; that kings will come out of the war either to be victims or to be despots;

and that within a quarter of a century they will be hunted down like vermin by the most servile nations, or slain in their palaces by their own courtiers. In a peace of twenty years you might have paid off the greater part of your National Debt, indeed as much of it as it would be expedient to discharge, and you would have left your old enemy France labouring and writhing under the intolerable and increasing weight of hers. This is the only way in which you can ever quite subdue her; and in this you subdue her without a blow, without a menace, and without a wrong. As matters now stand, you are calling her from attending to the corruptions of her court, and inviting her from bankruptcy to glory.

Shipley. I see not how bankruptcy can be averted by the expenditure of war.

Franklin. It cannot. But war and glory are the same thing to France, and she sings as shrilly and as gaily after a beating as before. With a subsidy to a less amount than she has lately been accustomed to squander in six weeks, and with no more troops than would garrison a single fortress, she will enable us to set you at defiance, and to do you a heavier injury in two campaigns than she has been able to do in two centuries, although your king was in her pay against you. She will instantly be our ally, and soon our scholar. Afterward she will sell her crown jewels and her church jewels, which cover the whole kingdom, and will derive unnatural strength from her vices and her profligacy. You ought to have conciliated us as your ally, and to have had no other, excepting Holland and Denmark. England could never have, unless by her own folly, more than one enemy. Only one is near enough to strike her; and that one is down. All her wars for six hundred years have not done this; and the first trumpet will untrance her. You leave your house open to incendiaries while you are running after a refractory child. Had you laid down the rod, the child would have come back. And because he runs away from the rod, you take up the poker.

Seriously, what means do you possess of enforcing your unjust claims and insolent authority? Never since the Norman Conquest had you an army so utterly inefficient, or generals so notoriously unskilful: no, not even in the reign of that venal traitor, that French stipendiary, the second Charles. Those were yet living who had fought bravely for his father, and those also who had vanquished him: and Victory still hovered over the mast that had borne the banners of our Commonwealth: *ours*, *ours*, my lord! the word is the right word here.

Shipley. I am depressed in spirit, and can sympathize but little in your exultation. All the crimes of Nero and Caligula are less afflicting to humanity, and consequently we may suppose will bring down on the offenders a less severe retribution, than an unnecessary and unjust war. And yet the authors and abettors of this most grievous among our earthly calamities, the enactors and applauders (on how vast a theatre!) of the first and greatest crime committed upon earth, are quiet complacent creatures, jovial at dinner, hearty at breakfast, and refreshed with sleep! Nay, the prime movers in it are called most religious and most gracious; and the hand that signs in cold blood the death-warrant of nations, is kissed by the kind-hearted, and confers distinction upon the brave! The prolongation of a life that shortens so many others, is prayed for by the conscientious and the pious! Learning is inquisitive in the research of phrases to celebrate him who has conferred such blessings, and the eagle of genius holds the thunderbolt by his throne! Philosophy, O my friend, has hitherto done little for the social state; and Religion has nearly all her work to do! She too hath but recently washed her hands from blood, and stands neutrally by, yes, worse than neutrally, while others shed it. I am convinced that no day of my life will be so censured by my own clergy, as this, the day on which the last hopes of peace have abandoned us, and the only true minister of it is pelted from our shores. Farewell, until better times! may the next generation be wiser! and wiser it surely will be, for the lessons of Calamity are far more impressive than those which repudiated Wisdom would have taught.

Franklin. Folly hath often the same results as Wisdom: but Wisdom would not engage in her schoolroom so expensive an assistant as Calamity. There are, however, some noisy and unruly children whom she alone has the method of rendering tame and tractable: perhaps it may be by setting them to their tasks both sore and supperless. The ship is getting under weigh. Adieu once more, my most reverend and noble friend! Before me in imagination do I see America, beautiful as Leda in her infant smiles, when her father Jove first raised her from the earth; and behind me I leave England, hollow, unsubstantial, and broken, as the shell she burst from.

Shipley. O worst of miseries, when it is impiety to pray that our country may be successful. Farewell! may every good attend you! with as little of evil to endure or to inflict, as national sins can expect from the Almighty.

SOUTHEY AND LANDOR

Southey. Of all the beautiful scenery round King's Weston the view from this terrace, and especially from this sundial, is the pleasantest.

Landor. The last time I ever walked hither in company (which, unless with ladies, I rarely have done anywhere) was with a just, a valiant, and a memorable man, Admiral Nichols, who usually spent his summer months at the village of Shirehampton, just below us. There, whether in the morning or evening, it was seldom I found him otherwise engaged than in cultivating his flowers.

Southey. I never had the same dislike to company in my walks and rambles as you profess to have, but of which I perceived no sign whatever when I visited you, first at Llanthony Abbey and afterward on the Lake of Como. Well do I remember our long conversations in the silent and solitary church of Sant' Abondio (surely the coolest spot in Italy), and how often I turned back my head toward the open door, fearing lest some pious passer-by, or some more distant one in the wood above, pursuing the pathway that leads to the tower of Luitprand, should hear the roof echo with your laughter, at the stories you had collected about the brotherhood and sisterhood of the place.

Landor. I have forgotten most of them, and nearly all: but I have not forgotten how we speculated on the possibility that Milton might once have been sitting on the very bench we then occupied, although we do not hear of his having visited that part of the country. Presently we discoursed on his poetry; as we propose to do again this morning.

Southey. In that case, it seems we must continue to be seated on the turf.

Landor. Why so?

Southey. Because you do not like to walk in company: it might disturb and discompose you: and we never lose our temper without losing at the same time many of our thoughts, which are loath to come forward without it.

Landor. From my earliest days I have avoided society as much as I could decorously, for I received more pleasure in the cultivation and improvement of my own thoughts than in walking up and down among the thoughts of others. Yet, as you know, I never have avoided the intercourse of men distinguished by virtue and genius; of genius, because it warmed and invigorated me by my trying to keep pace with it; of virtue, that if I had any of my own it might be called forth by such vicinity. Among all men elevated in station who have made a noise in the world (admirable old expression!) I never saw any in whose presence I felt inferiority, excepting Kosciusco. But how many in the lower paths of life have exerted both virtues and abilities which I never exerted, and never possessed! what strength and courage and perseverance in some, in others what endurance and forbearance! At the very moment when most, beside yourself, catching up half my words, would call and employ against me in its ordinary signification what ought to convey the most honorific, the term ***self-sufficiency***, I bow my head before the humble, with greatly more than their humiliation. You are better tempered than I am, and are readier to converse. There are half-hours when, although in good humour and good spirits, I would, not be disturbed by the necessity of talking, to be the possessor of all the rich marshes we see yonder. In this interval there is neither storm nor sunshine of the mind, but calm and (as the farmer would call it) ***growing*** weather, in which the blades of thought spring up and dilate insensibly. Whatever I do, I must do in the open air, or in the silence of night: either is sufficient: but I prefer the hours of exercise, or, what is next to exercise, of field-repose. Did you happen to know the admiral?

Southey. Not personally: but I believe the terms you have applied to him are well merited. After some experience, he contended that public men, public women, and the public press, may be all designated by one and the same trisyllable. He is reported to have been a strict disciplinarian. In the mutiny at the Nore he was seized by his crew, and summarily condemned by them to be hanged. Many taunting questions were asked him, to which he made no reply. When the rope was fastened round his neck, the ringleader cried, 'Answer this one thing, however, before you go, sir! What would you do with any of us, if we were in your power as you are now in ours?' The admiral, then captain, looked sternly and contemptuously, and replied, 'Hang you, by God!' Enraged at this answer, the mutineer tugged at the rope: but another on the instant rushed forward, exclaiming, 'No, captain!' (for thus he called the fellow) 'he has been cruel to us, flogging here and flogging there, but before so brave a man is hanged like a dog, you heave me overboard.' Others among the most violent now interceded: and an old seaman, not saying a single word, came forward with his knife in his hand, and cut the noose asunder. Nichols did not thank him, nor notice him, nor speak: but, looking round at the other ships, in which there was the like insubordination, he went toward his cabin slow and silent. Finding it locked, he called to a midshipman: 'Tell that man with a knife to come down and open the door.' After a pause of a few minutes, it was done: but he was confined below until the quelling of the mutiny.

Landor. His conduct as Controller of the Navy was no less magnanimous and decisive. In this office he presided at the trial of Lord Melville. His lordship was guilty, we know, of all the charges brought against him; but, having more patronage than ever minister had before, he refused to answer the questions which (to repeat his own expression) might incriminate him. And his refusal was given with a smile of indifference, a consciousness of security. In those days, as indeed in most others, the main use of power was promotion and protection: and **honest man** was never in any age among the titles of nobility, and has always been the appellation used toward the feeble and inferior by the prosperous. Nichols said on the present occasion, 'If this man is permitted to skulk away under such pretences, trial is here a mockery.' Finding no support, he threw up his office as Controller of the Navy, and never afterward entered the House of Commons. Such a person, it appears to me, leads us aptly and becomingly to that steadfast patriot on whose writings you promised me your opinion; not incidentally, as before, but turning page after page. It would ill beseem us to treat Milton with generalities. Radishes and salt are the picnic quota of slim spruce reviewers: let us hope to find somewhat more solid and of better taste. Desirous to be a listener and a learner when you discourse on his poetry, I have been more occupied of late in examining the prose.

Southey. Do you retain your high opinion of it?

Landor. Experience makes us more sensible of faults than of beauties. Milton is more correct than Addison, but less correct than Hooker, whom I wish he had been contented to receive as a model in style, rather than authors who wrote in another and a poorer language; such, I think, you are ready to acknowledge is the Latin.

Southey. This was always my opinion.

Landor. However, I do not complain that in oratory and history his diction is sometimes poetical.

Southey. Little do I approve of it in prose on any subject. Demosthenes and Aeschines, Lisias and Isaeus, and finally Cicero, avoided it.

Landor. They did: but Chatham and Burke and Grattan did not; nor indeed the graver and greater Pericles; of whom the most memorable sentence on record is pure poetry. On the fall of the young Athenians in the field of battle, he said, 'The year hath lost its spring.' But how little are these men, even Pericles himself, if you compare them as men of genius with Livy! In Livy, as in Milton, there are bursts of passion which cannot by the nature of things be other than poetical, nor (being so) come forth in other language. If Milton had executed his design of writing a history of England, it would probably have abounded in such diction, especially in the more turbulent scenes and in the darker ages.

Southey. There are quiet hours and places in which a taper may be carried steadily, and show the way along the ground; but you must stand a-tiptoe and raise a blazing torch above your head, if you would bring to our vision the obscure and time-worn figures depicted on the lofty vaults of antiquity. The philosopher shows everything in one clear light; the historian loves strong reflections and deep shadows, but, above all, prominent and moving characters. We are little pleased with the man who disenchants us: but whoever can make us wonder, must himself (we think) be wonderful, and deserve our admiration.

Landor. Believing no longer in magic and its charms, we still shudder at the story told by Tacitus, of those which were discovered in the mournful house of Germanicus.

Southey. Tacitus was also a great poet, and would have been a greater, had he been more contented with the external and ordinary appearances of things. Instead of which, he looked at a part of his pictures through a prism, and at another part through a camera obscura. If the historian were as profuse of moral as of political axioms, we should tolerate him less: for in the political we fancy a writer is but meditating; in the moral we regard him as declaiming. In history we desire to be conversant with only the great, according to our notions of greatness: we take it as an affront, on such an invitation, to be conducted into the lecture-room, or to be desired to amuse ourselves in the study.

Landor. Pray go on. I am desirous of hearing more.

Southey. Being now alone, with the whole day before us, and having carried, as we agreed at breakfast, each his Milton in his pocket, let us collect all the graver faults we can lay our hands upon, without a too minute and troublesome research; not in the spirit of Johnson, but in our own.

Landor. That is, abasing our eyes in reverence to so great a man, but without closing them. The beauties of his poetry we may omit to notice, if we can: but where the crowd claps the hands, it will be difficult for us always to refrain. Johnson, I think, has been charged unjustly with expressing too freely and inconsiderately the blemishes of Milton. There are many more of them than he has noticed.

Southey. If we add any to the number, and the literary world hears of it, we shall raise an outcry from hundreds who never could see either his excellences or his defects, and from several who never have perused the noblest of his writings.

Landor. It may be boyish and mischievous, but I acknowledge I have sometimes felt a pleasure in irritating, by the cast of a pebble, those who stretch forward to the full extent of the chain their open and frothy mouths against me. I shall seize upon this conjecture of yours, and say everything that comes into my head on the subject. Beside which, if any collateral thoughts should spring up, I may throw them in also; as you perceive I have frequently done in my Imaginary Conversations, and as we always do in real ones.

Southey. When we adhere to one point, whatever the form, it should rather be called a disquisition than a conversation. Most writers of dialogue take but a single stride into questions the most abstruse, and collect a heap of arguments to be blown away by the bloated whiffs of some rhetorical charlatan, tricked out in a multiplicity of ribbons for the occasion.

Before we open the volume of poetry, let me confess to you I admire his prose less than you do.

Landor. Probably because you dissent more widely from the opinions it conveys: for those who are displeased with anything are unable to confine the displeasure to one spot. We dislike everything a little when we dislike anything much. It must indeed be admitted that his prose is often too latinized and stiff. But I prefer his heavy cut velvet, with its ill-placed Roman fibula, to the spangled gauze and gummed-on flowers and puffy flounces of our present street-walking literature. So do you, I am certain.

Southey. Incomparably. But let those who have gone astray, keep astray, rather than bring Milton into disrepute by pushing themselves into his company and imitating his manner. Milton is none of these: and his language is never a patchwork. We find daily, in almost every book we open, expressions which are not English, never were, and never will be: for the writers are by no means of sufficiently high rank to be masters of the mint. To arrive at this distinction, it is not enough to scatter in all directions bold, hazardous, undisciplined thoughts: there must be lordly and commanding ones, with a full establishment of well-appointed expressions adequate to their maintenance.

Occasionally I have been dissatisfied with Milton, because in my opinion that is ill said in prose which can be said more plainly. Not so in poetry: if it were, much of Pindar and Aeschylus, and no little of Dante, would be censurable.

Landor. Acknowledge that he whose poetry I am holding in my hand is free from every false ornament in his prose, unless a few bosses of latinity may be called so; and I am ready to admit the full claims of your favourite South. Acknowledge that, heading all the forces of our language, he was the great antagonist of every great monster which infested our country; and he disdained to trim his lion-skin with lace. No other English writer has equalled Raleigh, Hooker, and Milton, in the loftier parts of their works.

Southey. But Hooker and Milton, you allow, are sometimes pedantic. In Hooker there is nothing so elevated as there is in Raleigh.

Landor. Neither he, however, nor any modern, nor any ancient, has attained to that summit on which the sacred ark of Milton strikes and rests. Reflections, such as we indulged in on the borders of the Larius, come over me here again. Perhaps from the very sod where you are sitting, the poet in his youth sate looking at the Sabrina he was soon to celebrate. There is pleasure in the sight of a glebe which never has been broken; but it delights me particularly in those places where great men have been before. I do not mean warriors: for extremely few among the most remarkable of them will a considerate man call great: but poets and philosophers and philanthropists, the ornaments of society, the charmers of solitude, the warders of civilization, the watchmen at the gate which Tyranny would batter down, and the healers of those wounds which she left festering in the field. And now, to reduce this demon into its proper toad-shape again, and to lose sight of it, open your ***Paradise Lost***.

THE EMPEROR OF CHINA AND TSING-TI

On the morrow I was received at the folding-doors by Pru-Tsi, and ushered by him into the presence of his majesty the Emperor, who was graciously pleased to inform me that he had rendered thanks to Almighty God for enlightening his mind, and for placing his empire far beyond the influence of the persecutor and fanatic. 'But,' continued his majesty, 'this story of the sorcerer's man quite confounds me. Little as the progress is which the Europeans seem to have made in the path of humanity, yet the English, we know, are less cruel than their neighbours, and more given to reflection and meditation. How then is it possible they should allow any portion of their fellow-citizens to be hoodwinked, gagged, and carried away into darkness, by such conspirators and assassins? Why didst thou not question the man thyself?'

Tsing-Ti. I did, O Emperor! and his reply was, 'We can bury such only as were in the household of the faith. It would be a mockery to bid those spirits go in peace which we know are condemned to everlasting fire.'

Emperor. Amazing! have they that? Who invented it? Everlasting fire! It surely might be applied to better purposes. And have those rogues authority to throw people into it? In what part of the kingdom is it? If natural, it ought to have been marked more plainly in the maps. The English, no doubt, are ashamed of letting it be known abroad that they have any such places in their country. If artificial, it is no wonder they keep such a secret to themselves. Tsing-Ti, I commend thy prudence in asking no questions about it; for I see we are equally at a loss on this curiosity.

Tsing-Ti. The sorcerer has a secret for diluting it. Oysters and the white of eggs, applied on lucky days, enter into the composition; but certain charms in a strange language must also be employed, and must be repeated a certain number of times. There are stones likewise, and wood cut into particular forms, good against this eternal fire, as they believe. The sorcerer has the power, they pretend, of giving the faculty of hearing and seeing to these stones and pieces of wood; and when he has given them the faculties, they become so sensible and grateful, they do whatever he orders. Some roll their eyes, some sweat, some bleed; and the people beat their breasts before them, calling themselves miserable sinners.

Emperor. *Sinners* is not the name I should have given them, although no doubt they are in the right.

Tsing-Ti. Sometimes, if they will not bleed freely, nor sweat, nor roll their eyes, the devouter break their heads with clubs, and look out for others who will.

Emperor. Take heed, Tsing-Ti! Take heed! I do believe thou art talking all the while of idols. Thou must be respectful; remember I am head of all the religions in the empire. We have something in our own country not very unlike them, only the people do not worship them; they merely fall down before them as representatives of a higher power. So they say.

Tsing-Ti. I do not imagine they go much farther in Europe, excepting the introduction of this club-law into their adoration.

Emperor. And difference enough, in all conscience. Our people is less ferocious and less childish. If any man break an idol here for not sweating, he himself would justly be condemned to sweat, showing him how inconvenient a thing it is when the sweater is not disposed. As for rolling the eyes, surely they know best whom they should ogle; as for bleeding, that must be regulated by the season of the year. Let every man choose his idol as freely as he chooses his wife; let him be constant if he can; if he cannot, let him at least be civil. Whoever dares to scratch the face of any one in my empire, shall be condemned to varnish it afresh, and moreover to keep it in repair all his lifetime.

Tsing-Ti. In Europe such an offence would be punished with the extremities of torture.

Emperor. Perhaps their idols cost more, and are newer. Is there no chance, in all their changes, that we may be called upon to supply them with a few?

Tsing-Ti. They have plenty for the present, and they dig up fresh occasionally.

Emperor. In regard to the worship of idols, they have not a great deal to learn from us; and what is deficient will come by degrees as they grow humaner. But how little care can any ruler have for the happiness and improvement of his people, who permits such ferocity in the priesthood. If its members are employed by the government to preside at burials, as according to thy discourse I suppose, a virtuous prince would order a twelvemonth's imprisonment, and spare diet, to whichever of them should refuse to perform the last office of humanity toward a fellow-creature. What separation of citizen from citizen, and necessarily what diminution of national strength, must be the consequence of such a system! A single act of it ought to be punished more severely than any single act of sedition, not only as being a greater distractor of civic union, but, in its cruel sequestration of the best affections, a fouler violator of domestic peace. I always had fancied, from the books in my library, that the Christian religion was founded on brotherly love and pure equality. I may calculate ill; but, in my hasty estimate, damnation and dog-burial stand many removes from these.

'Wait a little,' the Emperor continued: 'I wish to read in my library the two names that my father said are considered the two greatest in the West, and may vie nearly with the highest of our own country.'

Whereupon did his majesty walk forth into his library; and my eyes followed his glorious figure as he passed through the doorway, traversing the ***gallery of the peacocks***, so called because fifteen of those beautiful birds unite their tails in the centre of the ceiling, painted so naturally as to deceive the beholder, each carrying in his beak a different flower, the most beautiful in China, and bending his neck in such a manner as to present it to the passer below. Traversing this gallery, his majesty with his own hand drew aside the curtain of the library door. His majesty then entered; and, after some delay, he appeared with two long scrolls, and shook them gently over the fish-pond, in this dormitory of the sages. Suddenly there were so many splashes and plunges that I was aware of the gratification the fishes had received from the grubs in them, and the disappointment in the atoms of dust. His majesty, with his own right hand, drew the two scrolls trailing on the marble pavement, and pointing to them with his left, said:

'Here they are; Nhu-Tong: Pa-Kong. Suppose they had died where the sorcerer's men held firm footing, would the priests have refused them burial?'

I bowed my head at the question; for a single tinge of red, whether arising from such ultra-bestial cruelty in those who have the impudence to accuse the cannibals of theirs, or whether from abhorrent shame at the corroding disease of intractable superstition, hereditary in the European nations for fifteen centuries, a tinge of red came over the countenance of the emperor. When I raised up again my forehead, after such time as I thought would have removed all traces of it, still fixing my eyes on the ground, I answered:

'O Emperor! the most zealous would have done worse. They would have prepared these great men for burial, and then have left them unburied.'

Emperor. So! so! they would have embalmed them, in their reverence for meditation and genius, although their religion prohibits the ceremony of interring them.

Tsing-Ti. Alas, sire, my meaning is far different. They would have dislocated their limbs with pulleys, broken them with hammers, and then have burnt the flesh off the bones. This is called an act of faith.

Emperor. *Faith*, didst thou say? Tsing-Ti, thou speakest bad Chinese: thy native tongue is strangely occidentalized.

Tsing-Ti. So they call it.

Emperor. God hath not given unto all men the use of speech. Thou meanest to designate the ancient inhabitants of the country, not those who have lived there within the last three centuries.

Tsing-Ti. The Spaniards and Italians (such are the names of the nations who are most under the influence of the spells) were never so barbarous and cruel as during the first of the last three centuries. The milder of them would have refused two cubits of earth to the two philosophers; and not only would have rejected them from the cemetery of the common citizens, but from the side of the common hangman; the most ignorant priest thinking himself much wiser, and the most enlightened prince not daring to act openly as one who could think otherwise. The Italians had formerly two illustrious men among them; the earlier was a poet, the later a philosopher; one was exiled, the other was imprisoned, and both were within a span of being burnt alive.

Emperor. We have in Asia some odd religions and some barbarous princes, but neither are like the Europeans. In the name of God! do the fools think of their Christianity as our neighbours in Tartary (with better reason) think of their milk; that it will keep the longer for turning sour? or that it must be wholesome because it is heady? Swill it out, swill it out, say I, and char the tub.

LOUIS XVIII AND TALLEYRAND

Louis. M. Talleyrand! in common with all my family, all France, all Europe, I entertain the highest opinion of your abilities and integrity. You have convinced me that your heart, throughout the storms of the revolution, leaned constantly toward royalty; and that you permitted and even encouraged the caresses of the usurper, merely that you might strangle the more certainly and the more easily his new-born empire. After this, it is impossible to withhold my confidence from you.

Talleyrand. Conscious of the ridicule his arrogance and presumption would incur, the usurper attempted to silence and stifle it with other and far different emotions. Half his cruelties were perpetrated that his vanity might not be wounded: for scorn is superseded by horror. Whenever he committed an action or uttered a sentiment which would render him an object of derision, he instantly gave vent to another which paralysed by its enormous wickedness. He would extirpate a nation to extinguish a smile. No man alive could deceive your majesty: the extremely few who would wish to do it, lie under that vigilant and piercing eye, which discerned in perspective from the gardens of Hartwell those of the Tuileries and Versailles. As joy arises from calamity, so spring arises from the bosom of winter, purely to receive your majesty, inviting the august descendant of their glorious founder to adorn and animate them again with his beneficent and gracious presence. The waters murmur, in voices half-suppressed, the reverential hymn of peace restored: the woods bow their heads....

Louis. Talking of woods, I am apprehensive all the game has been woefully killed up in my forests.

Talleyrand. A single year will replenish them.

Louis. Meanwhile! M. Talleyrand! meanwhile!

Talleyrand. Honest and active and watchful gamekeepers, in sufficient number, must be sought; and immediately.

Louis. Alas! if the children of my nobility had been educated like the children of the English, I might have promoted some hundreds of them in this department. But their talents lie totally within the binding of their breviaries. Those of them who shoot, can shoot only with pistols; which accomplishment they acquired in England, that they might challenge any of the islanders who should happen to look with surprise or displeasure in their faces, expecting to be noticed by them in Paris, for the little hospitalities the proud young gentlemen, and their prouder fathers, were permitted to offer them in London and at their country-seats. What we call *reconnaissance*, they call *gratitude*, treating a recollector like a debtor. This is a want of courtesy, a defect in civilization, which it behoves us to supply. Our memories are as tenacious as theirs, and rather more eclectic.

Since my return to my kingdom I have undergone great indignities from this unreflecting people. One Canova, a sculptor at Rome, visited Paris in the name of the Pope, and in quality of his envoy, and insisted on the cession of those statues and pictures which were brought into France by the French armies. He began to remove them out of the gallery: I told him I would never give my consent: he replied, he thought it sufficient that he had Wellington's. Therefore, the next time Wellington presented himself at the Tuileries, I turned my back upon him before the whole court. Let the English and their allies be aware, that I owe my restoration not to them, but partly to God and partly to Saint Louis. They and their armies are only brute instruments in the hands of my progenitor and intercessor.

Talleyrand. Fortunate, that the conqueror of France bears no resemblance to the conqueror of Spain. Peterborough (I shudder at the idea) would have ordered a file of soldiers to seat your Majesty in your travelling carriage, and would have reinstalled you at Hartwell. The English people are so barbarous, that he would have done it not only with impunity, but with applause.

Louis. But the sovereign of his country ... would the sovereign suffer it?

Talleyrand. Alas! sire! Confronted with such men, what are sovereigns, when the people are the judges? Wellington can drill armies: Peterborough could marshal nations.

Louis. Thank God! we have no longer any such pests on earth. The most consummate general of our days (such is Wellington) sees nothing one single inch beyond the field of battle; and he is so observant of discipline, that if I ordered him to be flogged in the presence of the allied armies, he would not utter a complaint nor shrug a shoulder; he would only write a dispatch.

Talleyrand. But his soldiers would execute the Duke of Brunswick's manifesto, and Paris would sink into her catacombs. No man so little beloved was ever so well obeyed: and there is not a man in England, of either party, citizen or soldier, who would not rather die than see him disgraced. His firmness, his moderation, his probity, place him more opposite to Napoleon than he stood in the field of Waterloo.

These are his lofty lines of Torres Vedras, which no enemy dares assail throughout their whole extent.

Louis. M. Talleyrand! is it quite right to extol an enemy and an Englishman in this manner?

Talleyrand. Pardon! Sire! I stand corrected. Forgive me a momentary fit of enthusiasm, in favour of those qualities by which, although an Englishman's, I am placed again in your majesty's service.

Louis. We will now then go seriously to business. Wellington and the allied armies have interrupted and occupied us. I will instantly write, with my own hand, to the Marquis of Buckingham, desiring him to send me five hundred pheasants' eggs. I am restored to my throne, M. Talleyrand! but in what a condition! Not a pheasant on the table! I must throw myself on the mercy of foreigners, even for a pheasant! When I have written my letter, I shall be ready to converse with you on the business on which I desired your presence. [*Writes.*] Here; read it. Give me your opinion: is not the note a model?

Talleyrand. If the charms of language could be copied, it would be. But what is intended for delight may terminate in despair: and there are words which, unapproachable by distance and sublimity, may wither the laurels on the most exalted of literary brows.

Louis. There is grace in that expression of yours, M. Talleyrand! there is really no inconsiderable grace in it. Seal my letter: direct it to the Marquis of Buckingham at Stowe. Wait: open it again: no, no: write another in your own name: instruct him how sure you are it will be agreeable to me, if he sends at the same time fifty or a hundred brace of the birds as well as the eggs. At present I am desolate. My heart is torn, M. Talleyrand! it is almost plucked out of my bosom. I have no other care, no other thought, day or night, but the happiness of my people. The allies, who have most shamefully overlooked the destitution of my kitchen, seem resolved to turn a deaf ear to its cries evermore; nay, even to render them shriller and shriller. The allies, I suspect, are resolved to execute the design of the mischievous Pitt.

Talleyrand. May it please your majesty to inform me **which** of them; for he formed a thousand, all mischievous, but greatly more mischievous to England than to France. Resolved to seize the sword, in his drunkenness, he seized it by the edge, and struck at us with the hilt, until he broke it off and until he himself was exhausted by loss of breath and of blood. We owe alike to him the energy of our armies, the bloody scaffolds of public safety, the Reign of Terror, the empire of usurpation, and finally, as the calm is successor to the tempest, and sweet fruit to bitter kernel, the blessing of your majesty's restoration. Excepting in this one event, he was mischievous to our country; but in all events, and in all undertakings, he was pernicious to his own. No man ever brought into the world such enduring evil; few men such extensive.

Louis. His king ordered it. George III loved battles and blood.

Talleyrand. But he was prudent in his appetite for them.

Louis. He talked of peppering his people as I would talk of peppering a capon.

Talleyrand. Having split it. His subjects cut up by his subjects were only capers to his leg of mutton. From none of his palaces and parks was there any view so rural, so composing to his spirits, as the shambles. When these were not fresh, the gibbet would do.

I wish better luck to the pheasants' eggs than befell Mr. Pitt's designs. Not one brought forth anything.

Louis. No: but he declared in the face of his Parliament, and of Europe, that he would insist on indemnity for the past and security for the future. These were his words. Now, all the money and other wealth the French armies levied in Spain, Portugal, Italy, and everywhere else, would scarcely be sufficient for this indemnity.

Talleyrand. England shall never receive from us a tithe of that amount.

Louis. A tithe of it! She may demand a quarter or a third, and leave us wondering at her moderation and forbearance.

Talleyrand. The matter must be arranged immediately, before she has time for calculation or reflection. A new peace maddens England to the same paroxysm as a new war maddens France. She hath sent over hither her minister ... or rather her prime minister himself is come to transact all the business ... the most ignorant and most shortsighted man to be found in any station of any public office throughout the whole of Europe. He must be treated as her arbiter: we must talk to him of restoring her, of regenerating her, of preserving her, of guiding her, which (we must protest with our hands within our frills) he alone is capable of doing. We must enlarge on his generosity (and generous he indeed is), and there is nothing he will not concede.

Louis. But if they do not come over in a week, we shall lose the season. I ought to be eating a pheasant-poult by the middle of July. Oh, but you were talking to me about the other matter, and perhaps the weightier of the two; ay, certainly. If this indemnity is paid to England, what becomes of our civil list, the dignity of my family and household?

Talleyrand. I do assure your majesty, England shall never receive ... did I say a tithe?... I say she shall never receive a fiftieth of what she expended in the war against us. It would be out of all reason, and out of all custom in her to expect it. Indeed it would place her in almost as good a condition as ourselves. Even if she were beaten she could hardly hope *that*: she never in the last three centuries has demanded it when she was victorious. Of all the sufferers by the war, we shall be the best off.

Louis. The English are calculators and traders.

Talleyrand. Wild speculators, gamblers in trade, who hazard more ventures than their books can register. It will take England some years to cast up the amount of her losses.

Louis. But she, in common with her allies, will insist on our ceding those provinces which my predecessor Louis XIV annexed to his kingdom. Be quite certain that nothing short of Alsace, Lorraine, and Franc Comte, will satisfy the German princes. They must restore the German language in those provinces: for languages are the only true boundaries of nations, and there will always be dissension where there is difference of tongue. We must likewise be prepared to surrender the remainder of the Netherlands; not indeed to England, who refused them in the reign of Elizabeth: she wants only Dunkirk, and Dunkirk she will have.

Talleyrand. This seems reasonable: for which reason it must never be. Diplomacy, when she yields to such simple arguments as plain reason urges against her, loses her office, her efficacy, and her name.

Louis. I would not surrender our conquests in Germany, if I could help it.

Talleyrand. Nothing more easy. The Emperor Alexander may be persuaded that Germany united and entire, as she would then become, must be a dangerous rival to Russia.

Louis. It appears to me that Poland will be more so, with her free institutions.

Talleyrand. There is only one statesman in the whole number of those assembled at Paris, who believes that her institutions will continue free; and he would rather they did not; but he stipulates for it, to gratify and mystify the people of England.

Louis. I see this clearly. I have a great mind to send Blacas over to Stowe. I can trust to him to look to the crates and coops, and to see that the pheasants have enough of air and water, and that the Governor of Calais finds a commodious place for them to roost in, forbidding the drums to beat and disturb them, evening or morning. The next night, according to my calculation, they repose at Montreuil. I must look at them before they are let loose. I cannot well imagine why the public men employed by England are usually, indeed constantly so inferior in abilities to those of France, Prussia, Austria, and Russia. What say you, M. Talleyrand? I do not mean about the pheasants; I mean about the envoys.

Talleyrand. It can only be that I have considered the subject more frequently and attentively than suited the avocations of your majesty, that the reason comes out before me clearly and distinctly. The prime ministers, in all these countries, are independent, and uncontrolled in the choice of agents. A prime minister in France may perhaps be willing to promote the interests of his own family; and hence he may appoint from it one unworthy of the place. In regard to other families, he cares little or nothing about them, knowing that his power lies in the palace, and not in the club-room. Whereas in England he must conciliate the great families, the hereditary dependants of his faction, Whig or Tory. Hence even the highest commands have been conferred on such ignorant and worthless men as the Duke of York and the Earl of Chatham, although the minister was fully aware that the honour of his nation was tarnished, and that its safety was in jeopardy, by such appointments. Meanwhile he kept his seat however, and fed from it his tame creatures in the cub.

Louis. Do you apprehend any danger (talking of cubs) that my pheasants will be bruised against the wooden bars, or suffer by sea-sickness? I would not command my bishops to offer up public prayers against such contingencies: for people must never have positive evidence that the prayers of the Church can possibly be ineffectual: and we cannot pray for pheasants as we pray for fine weather, by the barometer. We must drop it. Now go on with the others, if you have done with England.

Talleyrand. A succession of intelligent men rules Prussia, Russia, and Austria; because these three are economical, and must get their bread by creeping, day after day, through the hedges next to them, and by filching a sheaf or two, early and late, from cottager or small farmer; that is to say, from free states and petty princes. Prussia, like a mongrel, would fly at the legs of Austria and Russia, catching them with the sack upon their shoulders, unless they untied it and tossed a morsel to her. These great powers take especial care to impose a protective duty on intellect; to let none enter the country, and none leave it, without a passport. Their diplomatists are as clever and conciliatory as those of England are ignorant and repulsive, who, while they offer an uncounted sum of secret-service money with the left hand, give a sounding slap on the face with the right.

Louis. We, by adopting a contrary policy, gain more information, raise more respect, inspire more awe, and exercise more authority. The weightiest of our disbursements are smiles and flatteries, with a ribbon and a cross at the end of them.

But, between the Duke of York and the Earl of Chatham, I must confess, I find very little difference.

Talleyrand. Some, however. The one was only drunk all the evening and all the night; the other was only asleep all the day. The accumulated fogs of Walcheren seemed to concentrate in his brain, puffing out at intervals just sufficient to affect with typhus and blindness four thousand soldiers. A cake of powder rusted their musket-pans, which they were too weak to open and wipe. Turning round upon their scanty and mouldy straw, they beheld their bayonets piled together against the green dripping wall of the chamber, which neither bayonet nor soldier was ever to leave again.

Louis. We suffer by the presence of the allied armies in our capital: but we shall soon be avenged: for the English minister in another fortnight will return and remain at home.

Talleyrand. England was once so infatuated as to give up Malta to us, although fifty Gibraltars would be of inferior value to her. Napoleon laughed at her: she was angry: she began to suspect she had been duped and befooled: and she broke her faith.

Louis. For the first time, M. Talleyrand, and with a man who never had any.

Talleyrand. We shall now induce her to evacuate Sicily, in violation of her promises to the people of that island. Faith, having lost her virginity, braves public opinion, and never blushes more.

Louis. Sicily is the key to India, Egypt is the lock.

Talleyrand. What, if I induce the minister to restore to us Pondicherry?

Louis. M. Talleyrand! you have done great things, and without boasting. Whenever you do boast, let it be that you will perform only the thing which is possible. The English know well enough what it is to allow us a near standing-place anywhere. If they permit a Frenchman to plant one foot in India, it will upset all Asia before the other touches the ground. It behoves them to prohibit a single one of us from ever landing on those shores. Improbable as it is that a man uniting to the same degree as Hyder-Ali did political and military genius, will appear in the world again for centuries; most of the princes are politic, some are brave, and perhaps no few are credulous. While England is confiding in our loyalty, we might expatiate on her perfidy, and our tears fall copiously on the broken sceptre in the dust of Delhi. Ignorant and stupid as the king's ministers may be, the East India Company is well-informed on its interests, and alert in maintaining them. I wonder that a republic so wealthy and so wise should be supported on the bosom of royalty. Believe me, her merchants will take alarm, and arouse the nation.

Talleyrand. We must do all we have to do, while the nation is feasting and unsober. It will awaken with sore eyes and stiff limbs.

Louis. Profuse as the English are, they will never cut the bottom of their purses.

Talleyrand. They have already done it. Whenever I look toward the shores of England, I fancy I descry the Danaids there, toiling at the replenishment of their perforated vases, and all the Nereids leering and laughing at them in the mischievous fullness of their hearts.

Louis. Certainly she can do me little harm at present, and for several years to come: but we must always have an eye upon her, and be ready to assert our superiority.

Talleyrand. We feel it. In fifty years, by abstaining from war, we may discharge our debt and replenish our arsenals. England will never shake off the heavy old man from her shoulders. Overladen and morose, she will be palsied in the hand she unremittingly holds up against Ireland. Proud and perverse, she runs into domestic warfare as blindly as France runs into foreign: and she refuses to her subject what she surrenders to her enemy.

Louis. Her whole policy tends to my security.

Talleyrand. We must now consider how your majesty may enjoy it at home, all the remainder of your reign.

Louis. Indeed you must, M. Talleyrand! Between you and me be it spoken, I trust but little my loyal people; their loyalty being so ebullient, that it often overflows the vessel which should contain it, and is a perquisite of scouts and scullions. I do not wish to offend you.

Talleyrand. Really I can see no other sure method of containing and controlling them, than by bastions and redoubts, the whole circuit of the city.

Louis. M. Talleyrand! I will not doubt your sincerity: I am confident you have reserved the whole of it for my service; and there are large arrears. But M. Talleyrand! such an attempt would be resisted by any people which had ever heard of liberty, and much more by a people which had ever dreamt of enjoying it.

Talleyrand. Forts are built in all directions above Genoa.

Louis. Yes; by her conqueror, not by her king.

Talleyrand. Your majesty comes with both titles, and rules, like your great progenitor,

> Et par droit de conquete et par droit de naissance.

Louis. True; my arms have subdued the rebellious; but not without great firmness and great valour on my part, and some assistance (however tardy) on the part of my allies. Conquerors must conciliate: fatherly kings must offer digestible spoon-meat to their ill-conditioned children. There would be sad screaming and kicking were I to swaddle mine in stone-work. No, M. Talleyrand; if ever Paris is surrounded by fortifications to coerce the populace, it must be the work of some democrat, some aspirant to supreme power, who resolves to maintain it, exercising a domination too hazardous for legitimacy. I will only scrape from the chambers the effervescence of superficial letters and corrosive law.

Talleyrand. Sire! under all their governments the good people of Paris have submitted to the *octroi*. Now, all complaints, physical or political, arise from the stomach. Were it decorous in a subject to ask a question (however humbly) of his king, I would beg permission to inquire of your majesty, in your wisdom, whether a bar across the shoulders is less endurable than a bar across the palate. Sire! the French can bear anything now they have the honour of bowing before your majesty.

Louis. The compliment is in a slight degree (a **very** slight degree) ambiguous, and (accept in good part my criticism, M. Talleyrand) not turned with your usual grace.

Announce it as my will and pleasure that the Duc de Blacas do superintend the debarkation of the pheasants; and I pray God, M. de Talleyrand, to have you in His holy keeping.

OLIVER CROMWELL AND SIR OLIVER CROMWELL

Sir Oliver. How many saints and Sions dost carry under thy cloak, lad? Ay, what dost groan at? What art about to be delivered of? Troth, it must be a vast and oddly-shapen piece of roguery which findeth no issue at such capacious quarters. I never thought to see thy face again. Prithee what, in God's name, hath brought thee to Ramsey, fair Master Oliver?

Oliver. In His name verily I come, and upon His errand; and the love and duty I bear unto my godfather and uncle have added wings, in a sort, unto my zeal.

Sir Oliver. Take 'em off thy zeal and dust thy conscience with 'em. I have heard an account of a saint, one Phil Neri, who in the midst of his devotions was lifted up several yards from the ground. Now I do suspect, Nol, thou wilt finish by being a saint of his order; and nobody will promise or wish thee the luck to come down on thy feet again, as he did. So! because a rabble of fanatics at Huntingdon have equipped thee as their representative in Parliament, thou art free of all men's houses, forsooth! I would have thee to understand, sirrah, that thou art fitter for the House they have chaired thee unto than for mine. Yet I do not question but thou wilt be as troublesome and unruly there as here. Did I not turn thee out of Hinchinbrook when thou wert scarcely half the rogue thou art latterly grown up to? And yet wert thou immeasurably too big a one for it to hold.

Oliver. It repenteth me, O mine uncle! that in my boyhood and youth the Lord had not touched me.

Sir Oliver. Touch thee! thou wast too dirty a dog by half.

Oliver. Yes, sorely doth it vex and harrow me that I was then of ill conditions, and that my name ... even your godson's ... stank in your nostrils.

Sir Oliver. Ha! polecat! it was not thy name, although bad enough, that stank first; in my house, at least. But perhaps there are worse maggots in stauncher mummeries.

Oliver. Whereas in the bowels of your charity you then vouchsafed me forgiveness, so the more confidently may I crave it now in this my urgency.

Sir Oliver. More confidently! What! hast got more confidence? Where didst find it? I never thought the wide circle of the world had within it another jot for thee. Well, Nol, I see no reason why shouldst stand before me with thy hat off, in the courtyard and in the sun, counting the stones in the pavement. Thou hast some knavery in thy head, I warrant thee. Come, put on thy beaver.

Oliver. Uncle Sir Oliver! I know my duty too well to stand covered in the presence of so worshipful a kinsman, who, moreover, hath answered at baptism for my good behaviour.

Sir Oliver. God forgive me for playing the fool before Him so presumptuously and unprofitably! Nobody shall ever take me in again to do such an absurd and wicked thing. But thou hast some left-handed business in the neighbourhood, no doubt, or thou wouldst never more have come under my archway.

Oliver. These are hard times for them that seek peace. We are clay in the hands of the potter.

Sir Oliver. I wish your potters sought nothing costlier, and dug in their own grounds for it. Most of us, as thou sayest, have been upon the wheel of these artificers; and little was left but rags when we got off. Sanctified folks are the cleverest skinners in all Christendom, and their Jordan tans and constringes us to the avoirdupois of mummies.

Oliver. The Lord hath chosen His own vessels.

Sir Oliver. I wish heartily He would pack them off, and send them anywhere on ass-back or cart (cart preferably), to rid our country of 'em. But now again to the point: for if we fall among the potsherds we shall hobble on but lamely. Since thou art raised unto a high command in the army, and hast a dragoon to hold thy solid and stately piece of horse-flesh, I cannot but take it into my fancy that thou hast some commission of array or disarray to execute hereabout.

Oliver. With a sad sinking of spirit, to the pitch well-nigh of swounding, and with a sight of bitter tears, which will not be put back nor stayed in any wise, as you bear testimony unto me, Uncle Oliver!

Sir Oliver. No tears, Master Nol, I beseech thee! Wet days, among those of thy kidney, portend the letting of blood. What dost whimper at?

Oliver. That I, that I, of all men living, should be put upon this work!

Sir Oliver. What work, prithee?

Oliver. I am sent hither by them who (the Lord in His loving kindness having pity, and mercy upon these poor realms) do, under His right hand, administer unto our necessities, and righteously command us, **by the aforesaid as aforesaid** (thus runs the commission), hither am I deputed (woe is me!) to levy certain fines in this county, or shire, on such as the Parliament in its wisdom doth style malignants.

Sir Oliver. If there is anything left about the house, never be over-nice: dismiss thy modesty and lay hands upon it. In this county or shire, we let go the civet-bag to save the weazon.

Oliver. O mine uncle and godfather! be witness for me.

Sir Oliver. Witness for thee! not I indeed. But I would rather be witness than surety, lad, where thou art docketed.

Oliver. From the most despised doth the Lord ever choose His servants.

Sir Oliver. Then, faith! thou art His first butler.

Oliver. Serving Him with humility, I may peradventure be found worthy of advancement.

Sir Oliver. Ha! now if any devil speaks from within thee, it is thy own: he does not snuffle: to my ears he speaks plain English. Worthy or unworthy of advancement, thou wilt attain it. Come in; at least for an hour's rest. Formerly thou knewest the means of setting the heaviest heart afloat, let it be sticking in what mud-bank it might: and my wet dock at Ramsey is pretty near as commodious as that over yonder at Hinchinbrook was erewhile. Times are changed, and places too! yet the cellar holds good.

Oliver. Many and great thanks! But there are certain men on the other side of the gate, who might take it ill if I turn away and neglect them.

Sir Oliver. Let them enter also, or eat their victuals where they are.

Oliver. They have proud stomachs: they are recusants.

Sir Oliver. Recusants of what? of beef and ale? We have claret, I trust, for the squeamish, if they are above the condition of tradespeople. But of course you leave no person of higher quality in the outer court.

Oliver. Vain are they and worldly, although such wickedness is the most abominable in their cases. Idle folks are fond of sitting in the sun: I would not forbid them this indulgence.

Sir Oliver. But who are they?

Oliver. The Lord knows. Maybe priests, deacons, and such-like.

Sir Oliver. Then, sir, they are gentlemen. And the commission you bear from the parliamentary thieves, to sack and pillage my mansion-house, is far less vexatious and insulting to me, than your behaviour in keeping them so long at my stable-door. With your permission, or without it, I shall take the liberty to invite them to partake of my poor hospitality.

Oliver. But, Uncle Sir Oliver! there are rules and ordinances whereby it must be manifested that they lie under displeasure ... not mine ... not mine ... but my milk must not flow for them.

Sir Oliver. You may enter the house or remain where you are, at your option; I make my visit to these gentlemen immediately, for I am tired of standing. If thou ever reachest my age,[12] Oliver! (but God will not surely let this be) thou wilt know that the legs become at last of doubtful fidelity in the service of the body.

Oliver. Uncle Sir Oliver! now that, as it seemeth, you have been taking a survey of the courtyard and its contents, am I indiscreet in asking your worship whether I acted not prudently in keeping the **men-at-belly** under the custody of the **men-at-arms**? This pestilence, like unto one I remember to have read about in some poetry of Master Chapman's,[13] began with the dogs and mules, and afterwards crope up into the breasts of men.

Sir Oliver. I call such treatment barbarous; their troopers will not let the gentlemen come with me into the house, but insist on sitting down to dinner with them. And yet, having brought them out of their colleges, these brutal half-soldiers must know that they are fellows.

Oliver. Yea, of a truth are they, and fellows well met. Out of their superfluities they give nothing to the Lord or His saints; no, not even stirrup or girth, wherewith we may mount our horses and go forth against those who thirst for our blood. Their eyes are fat, and they raise not up their voices to cry for our deliverance.

Sir Oliver. Art mad? What stirrups and girths are hung up in college halls and libraries? For what are these gentlemen brought hither?

Oliver. They have elected me, with somewhat short of unanimity, not indeed to be one of themselves, for of that distinction I acknowledge and deplore my unworthiness, nor indeed to be a poor scholar, to which, unless it be a very poor one, I have almost as small pretension, but simply to undertake a while the heavier office of bursar for them; to cast up their accounts; to overlook the scouring of their plate; and to lay a list thereof, with a few specimens, before those who fight the fight of the Lord, that His saints, seeing the abasement of the proud and the chastisement of worldly-mindedness, may rejoice.

Sir Oliver. I am grown accustomed to such saints and such rejoicings. But, little could I have thought, threescore years ago, that the hearty and jovial people of England would ever join in so filching and stabbing a jocularity. Even the petticoated torchbearers from rotten Rome, who lighted the faggots in Smithfield some years before, if more blustering and cocksy, were less bitter and vulturine. They were all intolerant, but they were not all hypocritical; they had not always '***the Lord***' in their mouth.

Oliver. According to their own notions, they might have had, at an outlay of a farthing.

Sir Oliver. Art facetious, Nol? for it is as hard to find that out as anything else in thee, only it makes thee look, at times, a little the grimmer and sourer.

But, regarding these gentlemen from Cambridge. Not being such as, by their habits and professions, could have opposed you in the field, I hold it unmilitary and unmanly to put them under any restraint, and to lead them away from their peaceful and useful occupations.

Oliver. I always bow submissively before the judgment of mine elders; and the more reverentially when I know them to be endowed with greater wisdom, and guided by surer experience than myself. Alas! these collegians not only are strong men, as you may readily see if you measure them round the waistband, but boisterous and pertinacious challengers. When we, who live in the fear of God, exhorted them earnestly unto peace and brotherly love, they held us in derision. Thus far indeed it might be an advantage to us, teaching us forbearance and self-seeking, but we cannot countenance the evil spirit moving them thereunto. Their occupations, as you remark most wisely, might have been useful and peaceful, and had formerly been so. Why then did they gird the sword of strife about their loins against the children of Israel? By their own declaration, not only are they our enemies, but enemies the most spiteful and untractable. When I came quietly, lawfully, and in the name of the Lord, for their plate, what did they? Instead of surrendering it like honest and conscientious men, they attacked me and my people on horseback, with syllogisms and enthymemes, and the Lord knows with what other such gimcracks; such venomous and rankling old weapons as those who have the fear of God before their eyes are fain to lay aside. Learning should not make folks mockers ... should not make folks malignants ... should not harden their hearts. We came with bowels for them.

Sir Oliver. That ye did! and bowels which would have stowed within them all the plate on board of a galleon. If tankards and wassail-bowls had stuck between your teeth, you would not have felt them.

Oliver. We did feel them; some at least: perhaps we missed too many.

Sir Oliver. How can these learned societies raise the money you exact from them, beside plate? dost think they can create and coin it?

Oliver. In Cambridge, Uncle Sir Oliver, and more especially in that college named in honour (as they profanely call it) of the Blessed Trinity, there are great conjurors or chemists. Now the said conjurors or chemists not only do possess the faculty of making the precious metals out of old books and parchments, but out of the skulls of young lordlings and gentlefolks, which verily promise less. And this they bring about by certain gold wires fastened at the top of certain caps. Of said metals, thus devilishly converted, do they make a vain and sumptuous use; so that, finally, they are afraid of cutting their lips with glass. But indeed it is high time to call them.

Sir Oliver. Well ... at last thou hast some mercy.

Oliver. [***Aloud.***] Cuffsatan Ramsbottom! Sadsoul Kiteclaw! advance! Let every gown, together with the belly that is therein, mount up behind you and your comrades in good fellowship. And forasmuch as you at the country places look to bit and bridle, it seemeth fair and equitable that ye should leave unto them, in full propriety, the mancipular office of discharging the account. If there be any spare beds at the inns, allow the doctors and dons to occupy the same ... they being used to lie softly; and be not urgent that more than three lie in each ... they being mostly corpulent. Let pass quietly and unreproved any light bubble of pride or impetuosity, seeing that they have not always been accustomed to the service of guards and ushers. The Lord be with ye!... Slow trot! And now, Uncle Sir Oliver, I can resist no longer your loving kindness. I kiss you, my godfather, in heart's and soul's duty; and most humbly and gratefully do I accept of your invitation to dine and lodge with you, albeit the least worthy of your family and kinsfolk. After the refreshment of needful food, more needful prayer, and that sleep which descendeth on the innocent like the dew of Hermon, to-morrow at daybreak I proceed on my journey Londonward.

Sir Oliver. [***Aloud.***] Ho, there! [***To a servant.***] Let dinner be prepared in the great dining-room; let every servant be in waiting, each in full livery; let every delicacy the house affords be placed upon the table in due courses; arrange all the plate upon the sideboard: a gentleman by descent ... a stranger ... has claimed my hospitality. [***Servant goes.***]

Sir! you are now master. Grant me dispensation, I entreat you, from a further attendance on you.

NOTES:

[12] Sir Oliver, who died in 1655, aged ninety-three, might, by possibility, have seen all the men of great genius, excepting Chaucer and Roger Bacon, whom England had produced from its first discovery down to our own times, Francis Bacon, Shakespeare, Milton, Newton, and the prodigious shoal that attended these leviathans through the intellectual deep. Newton was but in his thirteenth year at Sir Oliver's death. Raleigh, Spenser, Hooker, Eliot, Selden, Taylor, Hobbes, Sidney, Shaftesbury, and Locke, were existing in his lifetime; and several more, who may be compared with the smaller of these.

[13] Chapman's ***Homer***, first book.

THE COUNT GLEICHEM: THE COUNTESS: THEIR CHILDREN, AND ZAIDA.

Countess. Ludolph! my beloved Ludolph! do we meet again? Ah! I am jealous of these little ones, and of the embraces you are giving them.

Why sigh, my sweet husband?

Come back again, Wilhelm! Come back again, Annabella! How could you run away? Do you think you can see better out of the corner?

Annabella. Is this indeed our papa? What, in the name of mercy, can have given him so dark a colour? I hope I shall never be like that; and yet everybody tells me I am very like papa.

Wilhelm. Do not let her plague you, papa; but take me between your knees (I am too old to sit upon them), and tell me all about the Turks, and how you ran away from them.

Countess. Wilhelm! if your father had run away from the enemy, we should not have been deprived of him two whole years.

Wilhelm. I am hardly such a child as to suppose that a Christian knight would run away from a rebel Turk in battle. But even Christians are taken, somehow, by their tricks and contrivances, and their dog Mahomet. Beside, you know you yourself told me, with tear after tear, and scolding me for mine, that papa was taken by them.

Annabella. Neither am I, who am only one year younger, so foolish as to believe there is any dog Mahomet. And, if there were, we have dogs that are better and faithfuller and stronger.

Wilhelm. [*To his father.*] I can hardly help laughing to think what curious fancies girls have about Mahomet. We know that Mahomet is a dog-spirit with three horsetails.

Annabella. Papa! I am glad to see you smile at Wilhelm. I do assure you he is not half so bad a boy as he was, although he did point at me, and did tell you some mischief.

Count. I ought to be indeed most happy at seeing you all again.

Annabella. And so you are. Don't pretend to look grave now. I very easily find you out. I often look grave when I am the happiest. But forth it bursts at last: there is no room for it in tongue, or eyes, or anywhere.

Count. And so, my little angel, you begin to recollect me.

Annabella. At first I used to dream of papa, but at last I forgot how to dream of him: and then I cried, but at last I left off crying. And then, papa, who could come to me in my sleep, seldom came again.

Count. Why do you now draw back from me, Annabella?

Annabella. Because you really are so very very brown: just like those ugly Turks who sawed the pines in the saw-pit under the wood, and who refused to drink wine in the heat of summer, when Wilhelm and I brought it to them. Do not be angry; we did it only once.

Wilhelm. Because one of them stamped and frightened her when the other seemed to bless us.

Count. Are they still living?

Countess. One of them is.

Wilhelm. The fierce one.

Count. We will set him free, and wish it were the other.

Annabella. Papa! I am glad you are come back without your spurs.

Countess. Hush, child, hush.

Annabella. Why, mamma? Do not you remember how they tore my frock when I clung to him at parting? Now I begin to think of him again: I lose everything between that day and this.

Countess. The girl's idle prattle about the spurs has pained you: always too sensitive; always soon hurt, though never soon offended.

Count. O God! O my children! O my wife! it is not the loss of spurs I now must blush for.

Annabella. Indeed, papa, you never can blush at all, until you cut that horrid beard off.

Countess. Well may you say, my own Ludolph, as you do; for most gallant was your bearing in the battle.

Count. Ah! why was it ever fought?

Countess. Why were most battles? But they may lead to glory even through slavery.

Count. And to shame and sorrow.

Countess. Have I lost the little beauty I possessed, that you hold my hand so languidly, and turn away your eyes when they meet mine? It was not so formerly ... unless when first we loved.

That one kiss restores to me all my lost happiness.

Come; the table is ready: there are your old wines upon it: you must want that refreshment.

Count. Go, my sweet children! you must eat your supper before I do.

Countess. Run into your own room for it.

Annabella. I will not go until papa has patted me again on the shoulder, now I begin to remember it. I do not much mind the beard: I grow used to it already: but indeed I liked better to stroke and pat the smooth laughing cheek, with my arm across the neck behind. It is very pleasant even so. Am I not grown? I can put the whole length of my finger between your lips.

Count. And now, will not *you* come, Wilhelm?

Wilhelm. I am too tall and too heavy: she is but a child.
[*Whispers.*] Yet I think, papa, I am hardly so much of a man but you may kiss me over again ... if you will not let her see it.

Countess. My dears! why do not you go to your supper?

Annabella. Because he has come to show us what Turks are like.

Wilhelm. Do not be angry with her. Do not look down, papa!

Count. Blessings on you both, sweet children!

Wilhelm. We may go now.

Countess. And now, Ludolph, come to the table, and tell me all your sufferings.

Count. The worst begin here.

Countess. Ungrateful Ludolph!

Count. I am he: that is my name in full.

Countess. You have then ceased to love me?

Count. Worse; if worse can be: I have ceased to deserve your love.

Countess. No: Ludolph hath spoken falsely for once; but Ludolph is not false.

Count. I have forfeited all I ever could boast of, your affection and my own esteem. Away with caresses! Repulse me, abjure me; hate, and never pardon me. Let the abject heart lie untorn by one remorse. Forgiveness would split and shiver what slavery but abased.

Countess. Again you embrace me; and yet tell me never to pardon you! O inconsiderate man! O idle deviser of impossible things!

But you have not introduced to me those who purchased your freedom, or who achieved it by their valour.

Count. Mercy! O God!

Countess. Are they dead? Was the plague abroad.

Count. I will not dissemble ... such was never my intention ... that my deliverance was brought about by means of----

Countess. Say it at once ... a lady.

Count. It was.

Countess. She fled with you.

Count. She did.

Countess. And have you left her, sir?

Count. Alas! alas! I have not; and never can.

Countess. Now come to my arms, brave, honourable Ludolph! Did I not say thou couldst not be ungrateful? Where, where is she who has given me back my husband?

Count. Dare I utter it! in this house.

Countess. Call the children.

Count. No; they must not affront her: they must not even stare at her: other eyes, not theirs, must stab me to the heart.

Countess. They shall bless her; we will all. Bring her in.

[*Zaida is led in by the Count.*]

Countess. We three have stood silent long enough: and much there may be on which we will for ever keep silence. But, sweet young creature! can I refuse my protection, or my love, to the preserver of my husband? Can I think it a crime, or even a folly, to have pitied the brave and the unfortunate? to have pressed (but alas! that it ever should have been so here!) a generous heart to a tender one?

Why do you begin to weep?

Zaida. Under your kindness, O lady, lie the sources of these tears.

But why has he left us? He might help me to say many things which I want to say.

Countess. Did he never tell you he was married?

Zaida. He did indeed.

Countess. That he had children?

Zaida. It comforted me a little to hear it.

Countess. Why? prithee why?

Zaida. When I was in grief at the certainty of holding but the second place in his bosom, I thought I could at least go and play with them, and win perhaps their love.

Countess. According to our religion, a man must have only one wife.

Zaida. That troubled me again. But the dispenser of your religion, who binds and unbinds, does for sequins or services what our Prophet does purely through kindness.

Countess. We can love but one.

Zaida. We indeed can love only one: but men have large hearts.

Countess. Unhappy girl!

Zaida. The very happiest in the world.

Countess. Ah! inexperienced creature!

Zaida. The happier for that perhaps.

Countess. But the sin!

Zaida. Where sin is, there must be sorrow: and I, my sweet sister, feel none whatever. Even when tears fall from my eyes, they fall only to cool my breast: I would not have one the fewer: they all are for him: whatever he does, whatever he causes, is dear to me.

Countess. [*Aside.*] This is too much. I could hardly endure to have him so beloved by another, even at the extremity of the earth. [To Zaida.] You would not lead him into perdition?

Zaida. I have led him (Allah be praised!) to his wife and children. It was for those I left my father. He whom we love might have stayed with me at home: but there he would have been only half happy, even had he been free. I could not often let him see me through the lattice; I was too afraid; and I dared only once let fall the water-melon; it made such a noise in dropping and rolling on the terrace: but, another day, when I had pared it nicely, and had swathed it up well among vine-leaves, dipped in sugar and sherbet, I was quite happy. I leaped and danced to have been so ingenious. I wonder what creature could have found and eaten it. I wish he were here, that I might ask him if he knew.

Countess. He quite forgot home then!

Zaida. When we could speak together at all, he spoke perpetually of those whom the calamity of war had separated from him.

Countess. It appears that you could comfort him in his distress, and did it willingly.

Zaida. It is delightful to kiss the eye-lashes of the beloved: is it not? but never so delightful as when fresh tears are on them.

Countess. And even this too? you did this?

Zaida. Fifty times.

Countess. Insupportable!

He often then spoke about me?

Zaida. As sure as ever we met: for he knew I loved him the better when I heard him speak so fondly.

Countess. [*To herself.*] Is this possible? It may be ... of the absent, the unknown, the unfeared, the unsuspected.

Zaida. We shall now be so happy, all three.

Countess. How can we all live together?

Zaida. Now he is here, is there no bond of union?

Countess. Of union? of union? [*Aside*.] Slavery is a frightful thing! slavery for life, too! And she released him from it. What then? Impossible! impossible! [***To Zaida.***] We are rich....

Zaida. I am glad to hear it. Nothing anywhere goes on well without riches.

Countess. We can provide for you amply....

Zaida. Our husband....

Countess. Our!... husband!...

Zaida. Yes, yes; I know he is yours too; and you, being the elder and having children, are lady above all. He can tell you how little I want: a bath, a slave, a dish of pilau, one jonquil every morning, as usual; nothing more. But he must swear that he has kissed it first. No, he need not swear it; I may always see him do it, now.

Countess. [*Aside*.] She agonizes me. [***To Zaida.***] Will you never be induced to return to your own country? Could not Ludolph persuade you?

Zaida. He who could once persuade me anything, may now command me everything: when he says I must go, I go. But he knows what awaits me.

Countess. No, child! he never shall say it.

Zaida. Thanks, lady! eternal thanks! The breaking of his word would break my heart; and better *that* break first. Let the command come from you, and not from him.

Countess. [***Calling aloud.***] Ludolph! Ludolph! hither! Kiss the hand I present to you, and never forget it is the hand of a preserver.

THE PENTAMERON; OR,
INTERVIEWS OF MESSER GIOVANNI BOCCACCIO AND MESSER FRANCESCO PETRARCA WHEN SAID MESSER GIOVANNI LAY INFIRM AT HIS VILLETTA HARD BY CERTALDO;
AFTER WHICH THEY SAW NOT EACH OTHER ON OUR SIDE OF PARADISE.

FIRST DAY'S INTERVIEW

Boccaccio. Who is he that entered, and now steps so silently and softly, yet with a foot so heavy it shakes my curtains?

Frate Biagio! can it possibly be you?

No more physic for me, nor masses neither, at present.

Assunta! Assuntina! who is it?

Assunta. I cannot say, Signor Padrone! he puts his finger in the dimple of his chin, and smiles to make me hold my tongue.

Boccaccio. Fra Biagio! are you come from Samminiato for this? You need not put your finger there. We want no secrets. The girl knows her duty and does her business. I have slept well, and wake better.
[***Raising himself up a little.***]

Why? who are you? It makes my eyes ache to look aslant over the sheets; and I cannot get to sit quite upright so conveniently; and I must not have the window-shutters opened, they tell me.

Petrarca. Dear Giovanni! have you then been very unwell?

Boccaccio. O that sweet voice! and this fat friendly hand of thine, Francesco!

Thou hast distilled all the pleasantest flowers, and all the wholesomest herbs of spring, into my breast already.

What showers we have had this April, ay! How could you come along such roads? If the devil were my labourer, I would make him work upon these of Certaldo. He would have little time and little itch for mischief ere he had finished them, but would gladly fan himself with an Agnus-castus, and go to sleep all through the carnival.

Petrarca. Let us cease to talk both of the labour and the labourer. You have then been dangerously ill?

Boccaccio. I do not know: they told me I was: and truly a man might be unwell enough, who has twenty masses said for him, and fain sigh when he thinks what he has paid for them. As I hope to be saved, they cost me a lira each. Assunta is a good market-girl in eggs, and mutton, and cow-heel; but I would not allow her to argue and haggle about the masses. Indeed she knows best whether they were not fairly worth all that was asked for them, although I could have bought a winter cloak for less money. However, we do not want both at the same time. I did not want the cloak: I wanted ***them***, it seems. And yet I begin to think God would have had mercy on me, if I had begged it of him myself in my own house. What think you?

Petrarca. I think he might.

Boccaccio. Particularly if I offered him the sacrifice on which I wrote to you.

Petrarca. That letter has brought me hither.

Boccaccio. You do then insist on my fulfilling my promise, the moment I can leave my bed. I am ready and willing.

Petrarca. Promise! none was made. You only told me that, if it pleased God to restore you to your health again, you are ready to acknowledge His mercy by the holocaust of your ***Decameron***. What proof have you that God would exact it? If you could destroy the ***Inferno*** of Dante, would you?

Boccaccio. Not I, upon my life! I would not promise to burn a copy of it on the condition of a recovery for twenty years.

Petrarca. You are the only author who would not rather demolish another's work than his own; especially if he thought it better: a thought which seldom goes beyond suspicion.

Boccaccio. I am not jealous of any one: I think admiration pleasanter. Moreover, Dante and I did not come forward at the same time, nor take the same walks. His flames are too fierce for you and me: we had trouble enough with milder. I never felt any high gratification in hearing of people being damned; and much less would I toss them into the fire myself. I might indeed have put a nettle under the nose of the learned judge in Florence, when he banished you and your family; but I hardly think I could have voted for more than a scourging to the foulest and fiercest of the party.

Petrarca. Be as compassionate, be as amiably irresolute, toward your own *Novelle*, which have injured no friend of yours, and deserve more affection.

Boccaccio. Francesco! no character I ever knew, ever heard of, or ever feigned, deserves the same affection as you do; the tenderest lover, the truest friend, the firmest patriot, and, rarest of glories! the poet who cherishes another's fame as dearly as his own.

Petrarca. If aught of this is true, let it be recorded of me that my exhortations and entreaties have been successful, in preserving the works of the most imaginative and creative genius that our Italy, or indeed our world, hath in any age beheld.

Boccaccio. I would not destroy his poems, as I told you, or think I told you. Even the worst of the Florentines, who in general keep only one of God's commandments, keep it rigidly in regard to Dante--

Love them who curse you.

He called them all scoundrels, with somewhat less courtesy than cordiality, and less afraid of censure for veracity than adulation: he sent their fathers to hell, with no inclination to separate the child and parent: and now they are hugging him for it in his shroud! Would you ever have suspected them of being such lovers of justice?

You must have mistaken my meaning; the thought never entered my head: the idea of destroying a single copy of Dante! And what effect would that produce? There must be fifty, or near it, in various parts of Italy.

Petrarca. I spoke of you.

Boccaccio. Of me! My poetry is vile; I have already thrown into the fire all of it within my reach.

Petrarca. Poetry was not the question. We neither of us are such poets as we thought ourselves when we were younger, and as younger men think us still. I meant your **Decameron**; in which there is more character, more nature, more invention, than either modern or ancient Italy, or than Greece, from whom she derived her whole inheritance, ever claimed or ever knew. Would you consume a beautiful meadow because there are reptiles in it; or because a few grubs hereafter may be generated by the succulence of the grass?

Boccaccio. You amaze me: you utterly confound me.

Petrarca. If you would eradicate twelve or thirteen of the **Novelle**, and insert the same number of better, which you could easily do within as many weeks, I should be heartily glad to see it done. Little more than a tenth of the **Decameron** is bad: less than a twentieth of the **Divina Commedia** is good.

Boccaccio. So little?

Petrarca. Let me never seem irreverent to our master.

Boccaccio. Speak plainly and fearlessly, Francesco! Malice and detraction are strangers to you.

Petrarca. Well then: at least sixteen parts in twenty of the *Inferno* and ***Purgatorio*** are detestable, both in poetry and principle: the higher parts are excellent indeed.

Boccaccio. I have been reading the ***Paradiso*** more recently. Here it is, under the pillow. It brings me happier dreams than the others, and takes no more time in bringing them. Preparation for my lectures made me remember a great deal of the poem. I did not request my auditors to admire the beauty of the metrical version:

> Osanna sanctus deus Sabbaoth,
> Super-illustrans charitate tua
> Felices ignes horum Malahoth,

nor these, with a slip of Italian between two pales of Latin:

> Modicum,[14] et non videbitis me,
> Et iterum, sorelle mie dilette,
> Modicum, et vos videbitis me.

I dare not repeat all I recollect of

> Pepe Setan, Pepe Setan, aleppe,

as there is no holy-water-sprinkler in the room: and you are aware that other dangers awaited me, had I been so imprudent as to show the Florentines the allusion of our poet. His ***gergo*** is perpetually in play, and sometimes plays very roughly.

Petrarca. We will talk again of him presently. I must now rejoice with you over the recovery and safety of your prodigal son, the

Decameron.

Boccaccio. So then, you would preserve at any rate my favourite volume from the threatened conflagration.

Petrarca. Had I lived at the time of Dante, I would have given him the same advice in the same circumstances. Yet how different is the tendency of the two productions! Yours is somewhat too licentious; and young men, in whose nature, or rather in whose education and habits, there is usually this failing, will read you with more pleasure than is commendable or innocent. Yet the very time they occupy with you, would perhaps be spent in the midst of those excesses or irregularities, to which the moralist, in his utmost severity, will argue that your pen directs them. Now there are many who are fond of standing on the brink of precipices, and who nevertheless are as cautious as any of falling in. And there are minds desirous of being warmed by description, which without this warmth might seek excitement among the things described.

I would not tell you in health what I tell you in convalescence, nor urge you to compose what I dissuade you from cancelling. After this avowal, I do declare to you, Giovanni, that in my opinion, the very idlest of your tales will do the world as much good as evil; not reckoning the pleasure of reading, nor the exercise and recreation of the mind, which in themselves are good. What I reprove you for, is the indecorous and uncleanly; and these, I trust, you will abolish. Even these, however, may repel from vice the ingenuous and graceful spirit, and can never lead any such toward them. Never have you taken an inhuman pleasure in blunting and fusing the affections at the furnace of the passions; never, in hardening by sour sagacity and ungenial strictures, that delicacy which is more productive of innocence and happiness, more estranged from every track and tendency of their opposites, than what in cold, crude systems hath holden the place and dignity of the highest virtue. May you live, O my friend, in the enjoyment of health, to substitute the facetious for the licentious, the simple for the extravagant, the true and characteristic for the indefinite and diffuse.

* * * * *

Boccaccio. And after all this, can you bear to think what I am?

Petrarca. Complacently and joyfully; venturing, nevertheless, to offer you a friend's advice.

Enter into the mind and heart of your own creatures: think of them long, entirely, solely: never of style, never of self, never of critics, cracked or sound. Like the miles of an open country, and of an ignorant population, when they are correctly measured they become smaller. In the loftiest rooms and richest entablatures are suspended the most spider-webs; and the quarry out of which palaces are erected is the nursery of nettle and bramble.

Boccaccio. It is better to keep always in view such writers as Cicero, than to run after those idlers who throw stones that can never reach us.

Petrarca. If you copied him to perfection, and on no occasion lost sight of him, you would be an indifferent, not to say a bad writer.

Boccaccio. I begin to think you are in the right. Well then, retrenching some of my licentious tales, I must endeavour to fill up the vacancy with some serious and some pathetic.

Petrarca. I am heartily glad to hear of this decision; for, admirable as you are in the jocose, you descend from your natural position when you come to the convivial and the festive. You were placed among the Affections, to move and master them, and gifted with the rod that sweetens the fount of tears. My nature leads me also to the pathetic; in which, however, an imbecile writer may obtain celebrity. Even the hard-hearted are fond of such reading, when they are fond of any; and nothing is easier in the world than to find and accumulate its sufferings. Yet this very profusion and luxuriance of misery is the reason why few have excelled in describing it. The eye wanders over the mass without noticing the peculiarities. To mark them distinctly is the work of genius; a work so rarely performed, that, if time and space may be compared, specimens of it stand at wider distances than the trophies of Sesostris. Here we return again to the *Inferno* of Dante, who overcame the difficulty. In this vast desert are its greater and its less oasis; Ugolino and Francesca di Rimini. The peopled region is peopled chiefly with monsters and moschitoes: the rest for the most part is sand and suffocation.

Boccaccio. Ah! had Dante remained through life the pure solitary lover of Bice, his soul had been gentler, tranquiller, and more generous. He scarcely hath described half the curses he went through, nor the roads he took on the journey: theology, politics, and that barbican of the *Inferno*, marriage, surrounded with its

Selva selvaggia ed aspra e forte.

Admirable is indeed the description of Ugolino, to whoever can endure the sight of an old soldier gnawing at the scalp of an old archbishop.

Petrarca. The thirty lines from

Ed io sentii,

are unequalled by any other continuous thirty in the whole dominions of poetry.

Boccaccio. Give me rather the six on Francesca: for if in the former I find the simple, vigorous, clear narration, I find also what I would not wish, the features of Ugolino reflected full in Dante. The two characters are similar in themselves; hard, cruel, inflexible, malignant, but, whenever moved, moved powerfully. In Francesca, with the faculty of divine spirits, he leaves his own nature (not indeed the exact representative of theirs) and converts all his strength into tenderness. The great poet, like the original man of the Platonists, is double, possessing the further advantage of being able to drop one half at his option, and to resume it. Some of the tenderest on paper have no sympathies beyond; and some of the austerest in their intercourse with their fellow-creatures have deluged the world with tears. It is not from the rose that the bee gathers her honey, but often from the most acrid and the most bitter leaves and petals:

> Quando leggemmo il disiato viso
>   Esser baciato di cotanto amante,
> Questi, chi mai da me non sia diviso!
>   La bocca mi bacio tutto tremante ...
> **Galeotto** fu il libro, e chi lo scrisse ...
>   Quel giorno piu non vi leggemmo avante.

In the midst of her punishment, Francesca, when she comes to the tenderest part of her story, tells it with complacency and delight; and, instead of naming Paolo, which indeed she never has done from the beginning, she now designates him as

> Questi chi mai da me non sia diviso!

Are we not impelled to join in her prayer, wishing them happier in their union?

Petrarca. If there be no sin in it.

Boccaccio. Ay, and even if there be ... God help us!

What a sweet aspiration in each cesura of the verse! three love-sighs fixed and incorporate! Then, when she hath said

    La bocca mi bacio, tutto tremante,

she stops: she would avert the eyes of Dante from her: he looks for the sequel: she thinks he looks severely: she says: '***Galeotto*** is the name of the book,' fancying by this timorous little flight she has drawn him far enough from the nest of her young loves. No, the eagle beak of Dante and his piercing eyes are yet over her.

'***Galeotto*** is the name of the book.'

'What matters that?'

'And of the writer.'

'Or that either?'

At last she disarms him: but how?

'***That*** day we read no more.'

Such a depth of intuitive judgment, such a delicacy of perception, exists not in any other work of human genius; and from an author who, on almost all occasions, in this part of the work, betrays a deplorable want of it.

Petrarca. Perfection of poetry! The greater is my wonder at discovering nothing else of the same order or cast in this whole section of the poem. He who fainted at the recital of Francesca,

> And he who fell as a dead body falls,

would exterminate all the inhabitants of every town in Italy! What execrations against Florence, Pistoia, Siena, Pisa, Genoa! what hatred against the whole human race! what exultation and merriment at eternal and immitigable sufferings! Seeing this, I cannot but consider the ***Inferno*** as the most immoral and impious book that ever was written. Yet, hopeless that our country shall ever see again such poetry, and certain that without it our future poets would be more feebly urged forward to excellence, I would have dissuaded Dante from cancelling it, if this had been his intention. Much however as I admire his vigour and severity of style in the description of Ugolino, I acknowledge with you that I do not discover so much imagination, so much creative power, as in the Francesca. I find indeed a minute detail of probable events: but this is not all I want in a poet: it is not even all I want most in a scene of horror. Tribunals of justice, dens of murderers, wards of hospitals, schools of anatomy, will afford us nearly the same sensations, if we hear them from an accurate observer, a clear reporter, a skilful surgeon, or an attentive nurse. There is nothing of sublimity in the horrific of Dante, which there always is in Aeschylus and Homer. If you, Giovanni, had described so nakedly the reception of Guiscardo's heart by Gismonda, or Lorenzo's head by Lisabetta, we could hardly have endured it.

Boccaccio. Prithee, dear Francesco, do not place me over Dante: I stagger at the idea of approaching him.

Petrarca. Never think I am placing you blindly or indiscriminately. I have faults to find with you, and even here. Lisabetta should by no means have been represented cutting off the head of her lover, 'as well as she could,' with a clasp-knife. This is shocking and improbable. She might have found it already cut off by her brothers, in order to bury the corpse more commodiously and expeditiously. Nor indeed is it likely that she should have entrusted it to her waiting-maid, who carried home in her bosom a treasure so dear to her, and found so unexpectedly and so lately.

Boccaccio. That is true: I will correct the oversight. Why do we never hear of our faults until everybody knows them, and until they stand in record against us?

Petrarca. Because our ears are closed to truth and friendship for some time after the triumphal course of composition. We are too sensitive for the gentlest touch; and when we really have the most infirmity, we are angry to be told that we have any.

Boccaccio. Ah, Francesco! thou art poet from scalp to heel: but what other would open his breast as thou hast done! They show ostentatiously far worse weaknesses; but the most honest of the tribe would forswear himself on this. Again, I acknowledge it, you have reason to complain of Lisabetta and Gismonda.

* * * * *

Petrarca. In my delight to listen to you after so long an absence, I have been too unwary; and you have been speaking too much for one infirm. Greatly am I to blame, not to have moderated my pleasure and your vivacity. You must rest now: to-morrow we will renew our conversation.

Boccaccio. God bless thee, Francesco! I shall be talking with thee all night in my slumbers. Never have I seen thee with such pleasure as to-day, excepting when I was deemed worthy by our fellow-citizens of bearing to thee, and of placing within this dear hand of thine, the sentence of recall from banishment, and when my tears streamed over the ordinance as I read it, whereby thy paternal lands were redeemed from the public treasury.

Again God bless thee! Those tears were not quite exhausted: take the last of them.

NOTE:

[14] It may puzzle an Englishman to read the lines beginning with 'Modicum', so as to give the metre. The secret is, to draw out *et* into a disyllable, et-te, as the Italians do, who pronounce Latin verse, if possible, worse than we, adding a syllable to such as end with a consonant.

THIRD DAY'S INTERVIEW

It being now the Lord's day, Messer Francesco thought it meet that he should rise early in the morning and bestir himself, to hear mass in the parish church at Certaldo. Whereupon he went on tiptoe, if so weighty a man could indeed go in such a fashion, and lifted softly the latch of Ser Giovanni's chamber door, that he might salute him ere he departed, and occasion no wonder at the step he was about to take. He found Ser Giovanni fast asleep, with the missal wide open across his nose, and a pleasant smile on his genial, joyous mouth. Ser Francesco leaned over the couch, closed his hands together, and looking with even more than his usual benignity, said in a low voice:

'God bless thee, gentle soul! the mother of purity and innocence protect thee!'

He then went into the kitchen, where he found the girl Assunta, and mentioned his resolution. She informed him that the horse had eaten his two beans,[15] and was as strong as a lion and as ready as a lover. Ser Francesco patted her on the cheek, and called her *semplicetta*! She was overjoyed at this honour from so great a man, the bosom friend of her good master, whom she had always thought the greatest man in the world, not excepting Monsignore, until he told her he was only a dog confronted with Ser Francesco. She tripped alertly across the paved court into the stable, and took down the saddle and bridle from the farther end of the rack. But Ser Francesco, with his natural politeness, would not allow her to equip his palfrey.

'This is not the work for maidens,' said he; 'return to the house, good girl!'

She lingered a moment, then went away; but, mistrusting the dexterity of Ser Francesco, she stopped and turned back again, and peeped through the half-closed door, and heard sundry sobs and wheezes round about the girth. Ser Francesco's wind ill seconded his intention; and, although he had thrown the saddle valiantly and stoutly in its station, yet the girths brought him into extremity. She entered again, and dissembling the reason, asked him whether he would not take a small beaker of the sweet white wine before he set out, and offered to girdle the horse while his Reverence bitted and bridled him. Before any answer could be returned, she had begun. And having now satisfactorily executed her undertaking, she felt irrepressible delight and glee at being able to do what Ser Francesco had failed in. He was scarcely more successful with his allotment of the labour; found unlooked-for intricacies and complications in the machinery, wondered that human wit could not simplify it, and declared that the animal had never exhibited such restiveness before. In fact, he never had experienced the same grooming. At this conjuncture, a green cap made its appearance, bound with straw-coloured ribbon, and surmounted with two bushy sprigs of hawthorn, of which the globular buds were swelling, and some bursting, but fewer yet open. It was young Simplizio Nardi, who sometimes came on the Sunday morning to sweep the courtyard for Assunta.

'Oh! this time you are come just when you were wanted,' said the girl.

'Bridle, directly, Ser Francesco's horse, and then go away about your business.'

The youth blushed, and kissed Ser Francesco's hand, begging his permission. It was soon done. He then held the stirrup; and Ser Francesco, with scarcely three efforts, was seated and erect on the saddle. The horse, however, had somewhat more inclination for the stable than for the expedition; and, as Assunta was handing to the rider his long ebony staff, bearing an ivory caduceus, the quadruped turned suddenly round. Simplizio called him **bestiaccia**! and then, softening it, **poco garbato**! and proposed to Ser Francesco that he should leave the bastone behind, and take the crab-switch he presented to him, giving at the same time a sample of its efficacy, which covered the long grizzle hair of the worthy quadruped with a profusion of pink blossoms, like embroidery. The offer was declined; but Assunta told Simplizio to carry it himself, and to walk by the side of Ser Canonico quite up to the church porch, having seen what a sad, dangerous beast his reverence had under him.

With perfect good will, partly in the pride of obedience to Assunta, and partly to enjoy the renown of accompanying a canon of Holy Church, Simplizio did as she enjoined.

And now the sound of village bells, in many hamlets and convents and churches out of sight, was indistinctly heard, and lost again; and at last the five of Certaldo seemed to crow over the faintness of them all. The freshness of the morning was enough of itself to excite the spirits of youth; a portion of which never fails to descend on years that are far removed from it, if the mind has partaken in innocent mirth while it was its season and its duty to enjoy it. Parties of young and old passed the canonico and his attendant with mute respect, bowing and bare-headed; for that ebony staff threw its spell over the tongue, which the frank and hearty salutation of the bearer was inadequate to break. Simplizio, once or twice, attempted to call back an intimate of the same age with himself; but the utmost he could obtain was a **riveritissimo**! and a genuflexion to the rider. It is reported that a heart-burning rose up from it in the breast of a cousin, some days after, too distinctly apparent in the long-drawn appellation of **Gnor**[16] Simplizio.

Ser Francesco moved gradually forward, his steed picking his way along the lane, and looking fixedly on the stones with all the sobriety of a mineralogist. He himself was well satisfied with the pace, and told Simplizio to be sparing of the switch, unless in case of a hornet or a gadfly. Simplizio smiled, toward the hedge, and wondered at the condescension of so great a theologian and astrologer, in joking with him about the gadflies and hornets in the beginning of April. 'Ah! there are men in the world who can make wit out of anything!' said he to himself.

As they approached the walls of the town, the whole country was pervaded by a stirring and diversified air of gladness. Laughter and songs and flutes and viols, inviting voices and complying responses, mingled with merry bells and with processional hymns, along the woodland paths and along the yellow meadows. It was really the Lord's Day, for He made His creatures happy in it, and their hearts were thankful. Even the cruel had ceased from cruelty; and the rich man alone exacted from the animal his daily labour. Ser Francesco made this remark, and told his youthful guide that he had never been before where he could not walk to church on a Sunday; and that nothing should persuade him to urge the speed of his beast, on the seventh day, beyond his natural and willing foot's-pace. He reached the gates of Certaldo more than half an hour before the time of service, and he found laurels suspended over them, and being suspended; and many pleasant and beautiful faces were protruded between the ranks of gentry and clergy who awaited him. Little did he expect such an attendance; but Fra Biagio of San Vivaldo, who himself had offered no obsequiousness or respect, had scattered the secret of his visit throughout the whole country. A young poet, the most celebrated in the town, approached the canonico with a long scroll of verses, which fell below the knee, beginning:

How shall we welcome our illustrious guest?

To which Ser Francesco immediately replied: 'Take your favourite maiden, lead the dance with her, and bid all your friends follow; you have a good half-hour for it.'

Universal applauses succeeded, the music struck up, couples were instantly formed. The gentry on this occasion led out the cittadinanza, as they usually do in the villeggiatura, rarely in the carnival, and never at other times. The elder of the priests stood round in their sacred vestments, and looked with cordiality and approbation on the youths, whose hands and arms could indeed do much, and did it, but whose active eyes could rarely move upward the modester of their partners.

While the elder of the clergy were thus gathering the fruits of their liberal cares and paternal exhortations, some of the younger looked on with a tenderer sentiment, not unmingled with regret. Suddenly the bells ceased; the figure of the dance was broken; all hastened into the church; and many hands that joined on the green, met together at the font, and touched the brow reciprocally with its lustral waters, in soul-devotion.

After the service, and after a sermon a good church-hour in length to gratify him, enriched with compliments from all authors, Christian and Pagan, informing him at the conclusion that, although he had been crowned in the Capitol, he must die, being born mortal, Ser Francesco rode homeward. The sermon seemed to have sunk deeply into him, and even into the horse under him, for both of them nodded, both snorted, and one stumbled. Simplizio was twice fain to cry:

'Ser Canonico! Riverenza! in this country if we sleep before dinner it does us harm. There are stones in the road, Ser Canonico, loose as eggs in a nest, and pretty nigh as thick together, huge as mountains.'

'Good lad!' said Ser Francesco, rubbing his eyes, 'toss the biggest of them out of the way, and never mind the rest.'

The horse, although he walked, shuffled almost into an amble as he approached the stable, and his master looked up at it with nearly the same contentment. Assunta had been ordered to wait for his return, and cried:

'O Ser Francesco! you are looking at our long apricot, that runs the whole length of the stable and barn, covered with blossoms as the old white hen is with feathers. You must come in the summer, and eat this fine fruit with Signor Padrone. You cannot think how ruddy and golden and sweet and mellow it is. There are peaches in all the fields, and plums, and pears, and apples, but there is not another apricot for miles and miles. Ser Giovanni brought the stone from Naples before I was born: a lady gave it to him when she had eaten only half the fruit off it: but perhaps you may have seen her, for you have ridden as far as Rome, or beyond. Padrone looks often at the fruit, and eats it willingly; and I have seen him turn over the stones in his plate, and choose one out from the rest, and put it into his pocket, but never plant it.'

'Where is the youth?' inquired Ser Francesco.

'Gone away,' answered the maiden.

'I wanted to thank him,' said the Canonico.

'May I tell him so?' asked she.

'And give him ...' continued he, holding a piece of silver.

'I will give him something of my own, if he goes on and behaves well,' said she; 'but Signor Padrone would drive him away for ever, I am sure, if he were tempted in an evil hour to accept a quattrino for any service he could render the friends of the house.'

Ser Francesco was delighted with the graceful animation of this ingenuous girl, and asked her, with a little curiosity, how she could afford to make him a present.

'I do not intend to make him a present,' she replied: 'but it is better he should be rewarded by me,' she blushed and hesitated, 'or by Signor Padrone,' she added, 'than by your reverence. He has not done half his duty yet; not half. I will teach him: he is quite a child; four months younger than me.'

Ser Francesco went into the house, saying to himself at the doorway:

'Truth, innocence, and gentle manners have not yet left the earth. There are sermons that never make the ears weary. I have heard but few of them, and come from church for this.'

Whether Simplizio had obeyed some private signal from Assunta, or whether his own delicacy had prompted him to disappear, he was now again in the stable, and the manger was replenished with hay. A bucket was soon after heard ascending from the well; and then two words: 'Thanks, Simplizio.'

When Petrarca entered the chamber, he found Boccaccio with his breviary in his hand, not looking into it indeed, but repeating a thanksgiving in an audible and impassioned tone of voice. Seeing Ser

Francesco, he laid the book down beside him, and welcomed him.

'I hope you have an appetite after your ride,' said he, 'for you have sent home a good dinner before you.'

Ser Francesco did not comprehend him, and expressed it not in words but in looks.

'I am afraid you will dine sadly late to-day: noon has struck this half-hour, and you must wait another, I doubt. However, by good luck, I had a couple of citrons in the house, intended to assuage my thirst if the fever had continued. This being over, by God's mercy, I will try (please God!) whether we two greyhounds cannot be a match for a leveret.'

'How is this?' said Ser Francesco.

'Young Marc-Antonio Grilli, the cleverest lad in the parish at noosing any wild animal, is our patron of the feast. He has wanted for many a day to say something in the ear of Matilda Vercelli. Bringing up the leveret to my bedside, and opening the lips, and cracking the knuckles, and turning the foot round to show the quality and quantity of the hair upon it, and to prove that it really and truly was a leveret, and might be eaten without offence to my teeth, he informed me that he had left his mother in the yard, ready to dress it for me; she having been cook to the prior. He protested he owed the crowned martyr a forest of leverets, boars, deers, and everything else within them, for having commanded the most backward girls to dance directly. Whereupon he darted forth at Matilda, saying, "The **crowned martyr** orders it," seizing both her hands, and swinging her round before she knew what she was about. He soon had an opportunity of applying a word, no doubt as dexterously as hand or foot; and she said submissively, but seriously, and almost sadly, "Marc-Antonio, now all the people have seen it, they will think it."

'And after a pause:

'"I am quite ashamed: and so should you be: are not you now?"

'The others had run into the church. Matilda, who scarcely had noticed it, cried suddenly:

'"O Santissima! we are quite alone."

'"Will you be mine?" cried he, enthusiastically.

'"Oh! they will hear you in the church," replied she.

'"They shall, they shall," cried he again, as loudly.

'"If you will only go away."

'"And then?"

'"Yes, yes, indeed."

'"The Virgin hears you: fifty saints are witnesses."

'"Ah! they know you made me: they will look kindly on us."

'He released her hand: she ran into the church, doubling her veil (I will answer for her) at the door, and kneeling as near it as she could find a place.

'"By St. Peter," said Marc-Antonio, "if there is a leveret in the wood, the **crowned martyr** shall dine upon it this blessed day." And he bounded off, and set about his occupation. I inquired what induced him to designate you by such a title. He answered, that everybody knew you had received the crown of martyrdom at Rome, between the pope and antipope, and had performed many miracles, for which they had canonized you, and that you wanted only to die to become a saint.'

The leveret was now served up, cut into small pieces, and covered with a rich tenacious sauce, composed of sugar, citron, and various spices. The appetite of Ser Francesco was contagious. Never was dinner more enjoyed by two companions, and never so much by a greater number. One glass of a fragrant wine, the colour of honey, and unmixed with water, crowned the repast. Ser Francesco then went into his own chamber, and found, on his ample mattress, a cool, refreshing sleep, quite sufficient to remove all the fatigues of the morning; and Ser Giovanni lowered the pillow against which he had seated himself, and fell into his usual repose. Their separation was not of long continuance: and, the religious duties of the Sabbath having been performed, a few reflections on literature were no longer interdicted.

*   *   *   *   *

Petrarca. The land, O Giovanni, of your early youth, the land of my only love, fascinates us no longer. Italy is our country; and not ours only, but every man's, wherever may have been his wanderings, wherever may have been his birth, who watches with anxiety the recovery of the Arts, and acknowledges the supremacy of Genius. Besides, it is in Italy at last that all our few friends are resident. Yours were left behind you at Paris in your adolescence, if indeed any friendship can exist between a Florentine and a Frenchman: mine at Avignon were Italians, and older for the most part than myself. Here we know that we are beloved by some, and esteemed by many. It indeed gave me pleasure the first morning as I lay in bed, to overhear the fondness and earnestness which a worthy priest was expressing in your behalf.

Boccaccio. In mine?

Petrarca. Yes indeed: what wonder?

Boccaccio. A worthy priest?

Petrarca. None else, certainly.

Boccaccio. Heard in bed! dreaming, dreaming; ay?

Petrarca. No indeed: my eyes and ears were wide open.

Boccaccio. The little parlour opens into your room. But what priest could that be? Canonico Casini? He only comes when we have a roast of thrushes, or some such small matter, at table: and this is not the season; they are pairing. Plover eggs might tempt him hitherward. If he heard a plover he would not be easy, and would fain make her drop her oblation before she had settled her nest.

Petrarca. It is right and proper that you should be informed who the clergyman was, to whom you are under an obligation.

Boccaccio. Tell me something about it, for truly I am at a loss to conjecture.

Petrarca. He must unquestionably have been expressing a kind and ardent solicitude for your eternal welfare. The first words I heard on awakening were these:

'Ser Giovanni, although the best of masters ...'

Boccaccio. Those were Assuntina's.

Petrarca. '... may hardly be quite so holy (not being priest or friar) as your Reverence.'

She was interrupted by the question: 'What conversation holdeth he?'

She answered:

'He never talks of loving our neighbour with all our heart, all our soul, and all our strength, although he often gives away the last loaf in the pantry.'

Boccaccio. It was she! Why did she say that? the slut!

Petrarca. 'He doth well,' replied the confessor. 'Of the Church, of the brotherhood, that is, of me, what discourses holdeth he?'

I thought the question an indiscreet one; but confessors vary in their advances to the seat of truth.

She proceeded to answer:

'He never said anything about the power of the Church to absolve us, if we should happen to go astray a little in good company, like your Reverence.'

Here, it is easy to perceive, is some slight ambiguity. Evidently she meant to say, by the seduction of 'bad' company, and to express that his Reverence had asserted his power of absolution; which is undeniable.

Boccaccio. I have my version.

Petrarca. What may yours be?

Boccaccio. Frate Biagio; broad as daylight; the whole frock round!

I would wager a flask of oil against a turnip, that he laid another trap for a penance. Let us see how he went on. I warrant, as he warmed, he left off limping in his paces, and bore hard upon the bridle.

Petrarca. 'Much do I fear,' continued the expositor, 'he never spoke to thee, child, about another world.'

There was a silence of some continuance.

'Speak!' said the confessor.

'No indeed he never did, poor Padrone!' was the slow and evidently reluctant avowal of the maiden; for, in the midst of the acknowledgment her sighs came through the crevices of the door: then, without any farther interrogation, and with little delay, she added:

'But he often makes this look like it.'

Boccaccio. And now, if he had carried a holy scourge, it would not have been on his shoulders that he would have laid it.

Petrarca. Zeal carries men often too far afloat; and confessors in general wish to have the sole steerage of the conscience. When she told him that your benignity made this world another heaven, he warmly and sharply answered:

'It is only we who ought to do that.'

'Hush,' said the maiden; and I verily believe she at that moment set her back against the door, to prevent the sounds from coming through the crevices, for the rest of them seemed to be just over my night-cap. 'Hush,' said she, in the whole length of that softest of all articulations. 'There is Ser Francesco in the next room: he sleeps long into the morning, but he is so clever a clerk, he may understand you just the same. I doubt whether he thinks Ser Giovanni in the wrong for making so many people quite happy; and if he should, it would grieve me very much to think he blamed Ser Giovanni.'

'Who is Ser Francesco?' he asked, in a low voice.

'Ser Canonico,' she answered.

'Of what Duomo?' continued he.

'Who knows?' was the reply; 'but he is Padrone's heart's friend, for certain.'

'Cospetto di Bacco! It can then be no other than Petrarca. He makes rhymes and love like the devil. Don't listen to him, or you are undone. Does he love you too, as well as Padrone?' he asked, still lowering his voice.

'I cannot tell that matter,' she answered, somewhat impatiently; 'but I love him.'

'To my face!' cried he, smartly.

'To the Santissima!' replied she, instantaneously; 'for have not I told your Reverence he is Padrone's true heart's friend! And are not you my confessor, when you come on purpose?'

'True, true!' answered he; 'but there are occasions when we are shocked by the confession, and wish it made less daringly.'

'I was bold; but who can help loving him who loves my good Padrone?' said she, much more submissively.

Boccaccio. Brave girl, for that!

Dog of a Frate! They are all of a kidney; all of a kennel. I would dilute their meal well and keep them low. They should not waddle and wallop in every hollow lane, nor loll out their watery tongues at every wash-pool in the parish. We shall hear, I trust, no more about Fra Biagio in the house while you are with us. Ah! were it then for life.

Petrarca. The man's prudence may be reasonably doubted, but it were uncharitable to question his sincerity. Could a neighbour, a religious one in particular, be indifferent to the welfare of Boccaccio, or any belonging to him?

Boccaccio. I do not complain of his indifference. Indifferent! no, not he. He might as well be, though. My villetta here is my castle: it was my father's; it was his father's. Cowls did not hang to dry upon the same cord with caps in their podere; they shall not in mine. The girl is an honest girl, Francesco, though I say it. Neither she nor any other shall be befooled and bamboozled under my roof. Methinks Holy Church might contrive some improvement upon confession.

Petrarca. Hush! Giovanni! But, it being a matter of discipline, who knows but she might.

Boccaccio. Discipline! ay, ay, ay! faith and troth there are some who want it.

Petrarca. You really terrify me. These are sad surmises.

Boccaccio. Sad enough: but I am keeper of my handmaiden's probity.

Petrarca. It could not be kept safer.

Boccaccio. I wonder what the Frate would be putting into her head?

Petrarca. Nothing, nothing: be assured.

Boccaccio. Why did he ask her all those questions?

Petrarca. Confessors do occasionally take circuitous ways to arrive at the secrets of the human heart.

Boccaccio. And sometimes they drive at it, me thinks, a whit too directly. He had no business to make remarks about me.

Petrarca. Anxiety.

Boccaccio. 'Fore God, Francesco, he shall have more of that; for I will shut him out the moment I am again up and stirring, though he stand but a nose's length off. I have no fear about the girl; no suspicion of her. He might whistle to the moon on a frosty night, and expect as reasonably her descending. Never was a man so entirely at his ease as I am about that; never, never. She is adamant; a bright sword now first unscabbarded; no breath can hang about it. A seal of beryl, of chrysolite, of ruby; to make impressions (all in good time and proper place though) and receive none: incapable, just as they are, of splitting, or cracking, or flawing, or harbouring dirt. Let him mind that. Such, I assure you, is that poor little wench, Assuntina.

Petrarca. I am convinced that so well-behaved a young creature as Assunta----

Boccaccio. Right! Assunta is her name by baptism; we usually call her Assuntina, because she is slender, and scarcely yet full-grown, perhaps: but who can tell?

As for those friars, I never was a friend to impudence: I hate loose suggestions. In girls' minds you will find little dust but what is carried there by gusts from without. They seldom want sweeping; when they do, the broom should be taken from behind the house door, and the master should be the sacristan.

... Scarcely were these words uttered when Assunta was heard running up the stairs; and the next moment she rapped. Being ordered to come in, she entered with a willow twig in her hand, from the middle of which willow twig (for she held the two ends together) hung a fish, shining with green and gold.

'What hast there, young maiden?' said Ser Francesco.

'A fish, Riverenza!' answered she. 'In Tuscany we call it ***tinca***.'

Petrarca. I too am a little of a Tuscan.

Assunta. Indeed! well, you really speak very like one, but only more sweetly and slowly. I wonder how you can keep up with Signor Padrone--he talks fast when he is in health; and you have made him so. Why did not you come before? Your Reverence has surely been at Certaldo in time past.

Petrarca. Yes, before thou wert born.

Assunta. Ah, sir! it must have been long ago then.

Petrarca. Thou hast just entered upon life.

Assunta. I am no child.

Petrarca. What then art thou?

Assunta. I know not: I have lost both father and mother; there is a name for such as I am.

Petrarca. And a place in heaven.

Boccaccio. Who brought us that fish, Assunta? hast paid for it? there must be seven pounds: I never saw the like.

Assunta. I could hardly lift up my apron to my eyes with it in my hand. Luca, who brought it all the way from the Padule, could scarcely be entreated to eat a morsel of bread or sit down.

Boccaccio. Give him a flask or two of our wine; he will like it better than the sour puddle of the plain.

Assunta. He is gone back.

Boccaccio. Gone! who is he, pray?

Assunta. Luca, to be sure.

Boccaccio. What Luca?

Assunta. Dominedio! O Riverenza! how sadly must Ser Giovanni, my poor Padrone, have lost his memory in this cruel long illness! he cannot recollect young Luca of the Bientola, who married Maria.

Boccaccio. I never heard of either, to the best of my knowledge.

Assunta. Be pleased to mention this in your prayers to-night, Ser Canonico! May Our Lady soon give him back his memory! and everything else she has been pleased (only in play, I hope) to take away from him! Ser Francesco, you must have heard all over the world how Maria Gargarelli, who lived in the service of our paroco, somehow was outwitted by Satanasso. Monsignore thought the paroco had not done all he might have done against his wiles and craftiness, and sent his Reverence over to the monastery in the mountains, Laverna yonder, to make him look sharp; and there he is yet.

And now does Signor Padrone recollect?

Boccaccio. Rather more distinctly.

Assunta. Ah me! Rather more distinctly! have patience, Signor Padrone! I am too venturous, God help me! But, Riverenza, when Maria was the scorn or the abhorrence of everybody else, excepting poor Luca Sabbatini, who had always cherished her, and excepting Signor Padrone, who had never seen her in his lifetime ... for paroco Snello said he desired no visits from any who took liberties with Holy Church ... as if Padrone did! Luca one day came to me out of breath, with money in his hand for our duck. Now it so happened that the duck, stuffed with noble chestnuts, was going to table at that instant. I told Signor Padrone....

Boccaccio. Assunta, I never heard thee repeat so long and tiresome a story before, nor put thyself out of breath so. Come, we have had enough of it.

Petrarca. She is mortified: pray let her proceed.

Boccaccio. As you will.

Assunta. I told Signor Padrone how Luca was lamenting that Maria was seized with an *imagination*.

Petrarca. No wonder then she fell into misfortune, and her neighbours and friends avoided her.

Assunta. Riverenza! how can you smile? Signor Padrone! and you too? You shook your head and sighed at it when it happened. The Demonio, who had caused all the first mischief, was not contented until he had given her the *imagination*.

Petrarca. He could not have finished his work more effectually.

Assunta. He was balked, however. Luca said:

'She shall not die under her wrongs, please God!'

I repeated the words to Signor Padrone.... He seems to listen, Riverenza! and will remember presently ... and Signor Padrone cut away one leg for himself, clean forgetting all the chestnuts inside, and said sharply, 'Give the bird to Luca; and, hark ye, bring back the minestra.'

Maria loved Luca with all her heart, and Luca loved Maria with all his: but they both hated paroco Snello for such neglect about the evil one. And even Monsignore, who sent for Luca on purpose, had some difficulty in persuading him to forbear from choler and discourse. For Luca, who never swears, swore bitterly that the devil should play no such tricks again, nor alight on girls napping in the parsonage.

Monsignore thought he intended to take violent possession, and to keep watch there himself without consent of the incumbent. 'I will have no scandal,' said Monsignore; so there was none. Maria, though she did indeed, as I told your Reverence, love her Luca dearly, yet she long refused to marry him, and cried very much at last on the wedding day, and said, as she entered the porch:

'Luca! it is not yet too late to leave me.'

He would have kissed her, but her face was upon his shoulder.

Pievano Locatelli married them, and gave them his blessing: and going down from the altar, he said before the people, as he stood on the last step: 'Be comforted, child! be comforted! God above knows that thy husband is honest, and that thou art innocent.' Pievano's voice trembled, for he was an aged and holy man, and had walked two miles on the occasion. Pulcheria, his governante, eighty years old, carried an apronful of lilies to bestrew the altar; and partly from the lilies, and partly from the blessed angels who (although invisible) were present, the church was filled with fragrance. Many who heretofore had been frightened at hearing the mention of Maria's name, ventured now to walk up toward her; and some gave her needles, and some offered skeins of thread, and some ran home again for pots of honey.

Boccaccio. And why didst not thou take her some trifle?

Assunta. I had none.

Boccaccio. Surely there are always such about the premises.

Assunta. Not mine to give away.

Boccaccio. So then at thy hands, Assunta, she went off not overladen. Ne'er a bone-bodkin out of thy bravery, ay?

Assunta. I ran out knitting, with the woodbine and syringa in the basket for the parlour. I made the basket ... I and ... but myself chiefly, for boys are loiterers.

Boccaccio. Well, well: why not bestow the basket, together with its rich contents?

Assunta. I am ashamed to say it ... I covered my half-stocking with them as quickly as I could, and ran after her, and presented it. Not knowing what was under the flowers, and never minding the liberty I had taken, being a stranger to her, she accepted it as graciously as possible, and bade me be happy.

Petrarca. I hope you have always kept her command.

Assunta. Nobody is ever unhappy here, except Fra Biagio, who frets sometimes: but that may be the walk; or he may fancy Ser Giovanni to be worse than he really is.

... Having now performed her mission and concluded her narrative, she bowed, and said:

'Excuse me, Riverenza! excuse me, Signor Padrone! my arm aches with this great fish.'

Then, bowing again, and moving her eyes modestly toward each, she added, 'with permission!' and left the chamber.

'About the sposina,' after a pause began Ser Francesco: 'about the sposina, I do not see the matter clearly.'

'You have studied too much for seeing all things clearly,' answered Ser Giovanni; 'you see only the greatest. In fine, the devil, on this count, is acquitted by acclamation; and the paroco Snello eats lettuce and chicory up yonder at Laverna. He has mendicant friars for his society every day; and snails, as pure as water can wash and boil them, for his repast on festivals. Under this discipline, if they keep it up, surely one devil out of legion will depart from him.'

NOTES:

[15] Literally, *due fave*, the expression on such occasions to signify a small quantity.

[16] Contraction of *signor*, customary in Tuscany.

FOURTH DAY'S INTERVIEW

Petrarca. Giovanni, you are unsuspicious, and would scarcely see a monster in a minotaur. It is well, however, to draw good out of evil, and it is the peculiar gift of an elevated mind. Nevertheless, you must have observed, although with greater curiosity than concern, the slipperiness and tortuousness of your detractors.

Boccaccio. Whatever they detract from me, they leave more than they can carry away. Beside, they always are detected.

Petrarca. When they are detected, they raise themselves up fiercely, as if their nature were erect and they could reach your height.

Boccaccio. Envy would conceal herself under the shadow and shelter of contemptuousness, but she swells too huge for the den she creeps into. Let her lie there and crack, and think no more about her. The people you have been talking of can find no greater and no other faults in my writings than I myself am willing to show them, and still more willing to correct. There are many things, as you have just now told me, very unworthy of their company.

Petrarca. He who has much gold is none the poorer for having much silver too. When a king of old displayed his wealth and magnificence before a philosopher, the philosopher's exclamation was:

'How many things are here which I do not want!'

Does not the same reflection come upon us, when we have laid aside our compositions for a time, and look into them again more leisurely? Do we not wonder at our own profusion, and say like the philosopher:

'How many things are here which I do not want!'

It may happen that we pull up flowers with weeds; but better this than rankness. We must bear to see our first-born dispatched before our eyes, and give them up quietly.

Boccaccio. The younger will be the most reluctant. There are poets among us who mistake in themselves the freckles of the hay-fever for beauty-spots. In another half-century their volumes will be inquired after; but only for the sake of cutting out an illuminated letter from the title-page, or of transplanting the willow at the end, that hangs so prettily over the tomb of Amaryllis. If they wish to be healthy and vigorous, let them open their bosoms to the breezes of Sunium; for the air of Latium is heavy and overcharged. Above all, they must remember two admonitions; first, that sweet things hurt digestion; secondly, that great sails are ill adapted to small vessels. What is there lovely in poetry unless there be moderation and composure? Are they not better than the hot, uncontrollable harlotry of a flaunting, dishevelled enthusiasm? Whoever has the power of creating, has likewise the inferior power of keeping his creation in order. The best poets are the most impressive, because their steps are regular; for without regularity there is neither strength nor state. Look at Sophocles, look at Aeschylus, look at Homer.

Petrarca. I agree with you entirely to the whole extent of your observations; and, if you will continue, I am ready to lay aside my Dante for the present.

Boccaccio. No, no; we must have him again between us: there is no danger that he will sour our tempers.

Petrarca. In comparing his and yours, since you forbid me to declare all I think of your genius, you will at least allow me to congratulate you as being the happier of the two.

Boccaccio. Frequently, where there is great power in poetry, the imagination makes encroachments on the heart, and uses it as her own. I have shed tears on writings which never cost the writer a sigh, but which occasioned him to rub the palms of his hands together, until they were ready to strike fire, with satisfaction at having overcome the difficulty of being tender.

Petrarca. Giovanni! are you not grown satirical?

Boccaccio. Not in this. It is a truth as broad and glaring as the eye of the Cyclops. To make you amends for your shuddering, I will express my doubt, on the other hand, whether Dante felt all the indignation he threw into his poetry. We are immoderately fond of warming ourselves; and we do not think, or care, what the fire is composed of. Be sure it is not always of cedar, like Circe's. Our Alighieri had slipped into the habit of vituperation; and he thought it fitted him; so he never left it off.

Petrarca. Serener colours are pleasanter to our eyes and more becoming to our character. The chief desire in every man of genius is to be thought one; and no fear or apprehension lessens it. Alighieri, who had certainly studied the gospel, must have been conscious that he not only was inhumane, but that he betrayed a more vindictive spirit than any pope or prelate who is enshrined within the fretwork of his golden grating.

Boccaccio. Unhappily, his strong talon had grown into him, and it would have pained him to suffer amputation. This eagle, unlike Jupiter's, never loosened the thunderbolt from it under the influence of harmony.

Petrarca. The only good thing we can expect in such minds and tempers is good poetry: let us at least get that; and, having it, let us keep and value it. If you had never written some wanton stories, you would never have been able to show the world how much wiser and better you grew afterward.

Boccaccio. Alas! if I live, I hope to show it. You have raised my spirits: and now, dear Francesco! do say a couple of prayers for me, while I lay together the materials of a tale; a right merry one, I promise you. Faith! it shall amuse you, and pay decently for the prayers; a good honest litany-worth. I hardly know whether I ought to have a nun in it: do you think I may?

Petrarca. Cannot you do without one?

Boccaccio. No; a nun I must have: say nothing against her; I can more easily let the abbess alone. Yet Frate Biagio ... that Frate Biagio, who never came to visit me but when he thought I was at extremities or asleep.... Assuntina! are you there?

Petrarca. No; do you want her?

Boccaccio. Not a bit. That Frate Biagio has heightened my pulse when I could not lower it again. The very devil is that Frate for heightening pulses. And with him I shall now make merry ... God willing ... in God's good time ... should it be His divine will to restore me! which I think He has begun to do miraculously. I seem to be within a frog's leap of well again; and we will presently have some rare fun in my *Tale of the Frate*.

Petrarca. Do not openly name him.

Boccaccio. He shall recognize himself by one single expression. He said to me, when I was at the worst:

'Ser Giovanni! it would not be much amiss (with permission!) if you begin to think (at any spare time), just a morsel, of eternity.'

'Ah! Fra Biagio!' answered I, contritely, 'I never heard a sermon of yours but I thought of it seriously and uneasily, long before the discourse was over.'

'So must all,' replied he, 'and yet few have the grace to own it.'

Now mind, Francesco! if it should please the Lord to call me unto Him, I say, *The Nun and Fra Biagio* will be found, after my decease, in the closet cut out of the wall, behind yon Saint Zacharias in blue and yellow.

Well done! well done! Francesco. I never heard any man repeat his prayers so fast and fluently. Why! how many (at a guess) have you repeated? Such is the power of friendship, and such the habit of religion! They have done me good: I feel myself stronger already. To-morrow I think I shall be able, by leaning on that stout maple stick in the corner, to walk half over my podere.

Have you done? have you done?

Petrarca. Be quiet: you may talk too much.

Boccaccio. I cannot be quiet for another hour; so, if you have any more prayers to get over, stick the spur into the other side of them: they must verily speed, if they beat the last.

Petrarca. Be more serious, dear Giovanni.

Boccaccio. Never bid a convalescent be more serious: no, nor a sick man neither. To health it may give that composure which it takes away from sickness. Every man will have his hours of seriousness; but, like the hours of rest, they often are ill-chosen and unwholesome. Be assured, our heavenly Father is as well pleased to see His children in the playground as in the schoolroom. He has provided both for us, and has given us intimations when each should occupy us.

Petrarca. You are right, Giovanni! but we know which bell is heard the most distinctly. We fold our arms at the one, try the cooler part of the pillow, and turn again to slumber; at the first stroke of the other, we are beyond our monitors. As for you, hardly Dante himself could make you grave.

Boccaccio. I do not remember how it happened that we slipped away from his side. One of us must have found him tedious.

Petrarca. If you were really and substantially at his side, he would have no mercy on you.

Boccaccio. In sooth, our good Alighieri seems to have had the appetite of a dogfish or shark, and to have bitten the harder the warmer he was. I would not voluntarily be under his manifold rows of dentals. He has an incisor to every saint in the calendar. I should fare, methinks, like Brutus and the archbishop. He is forced to stretch himself, out of sheer listlessness, in so idle a place as Purgatory: he loses half his strength in Paradise: Hell alone makes him alert and lively: there he moves about and threatens as tremendously as the serpent that opposed the legions on their march in Africa. He would not have been contented in Tuscany itself, even had his enemies left him unmolested. Were I to write on his model a tripartite poem, I think it should be entitled, Earth, Italy, and Heaven.

Petrarca. You will never give yourself the trouble.

Boccaccio. I should not succeed.

Petrarca. Perhaps not: but you have done very much, and may be able to do very much more.

Boccaccio. Wonderful is it to me, when I consider that an infirm and helpless creature, as I am, should be capable of laying thoughts up in their cabinets of words, which Time, as he rushes by, with the revolutions of stormy and destructive years, can never move from their places. On this coarse mattress, one among the homeliest in the fair at Impruneta, is stretched an old burgess of Certaldo, of whom perhaps more will be known hereafter than we know of the Ptolemies and the Pharaohs; while popes and princes are lying as unregarded as the fleas that are shaken out of the window. Upon my life, Francesco! to think of this is enough to make a man presumptuous.

Petrarca. No, Giovanni! not when the man thinks justly of it, as such a man ought to do, and must. For so mighty a power over Time, who casts all other mortals under his, comes down to us from a greater; and it is only if we abuse the victory that it were better we had encountered a defeat. Unremitting care must be taken that nothing soil the monuments we are raising: sure enough we are that nothing can subvert, and nothing but our negligence, or worse than negligence, efface them. Under the glorious lamp entrusted to your vigilance, one among the lights of the world, which the ministering angels of our God have suspended for His service, let there stand, with unclosing eyes, Integrity, Compassion, Self-denial.

Boccaccio. These are holier and cheerfuller images than Dante has been setting up before us. I hope every thesis in dispute among his theologians will be settled ere I set foot among them. I like Tuscany well enough: it answers all my purposes for the present: and I am without the benefit of those preliminary studies which might render me a worthy auditor of incomprehensible wisdom.

Petrarca. I do not wonder you are attached to Tuscany. Many as have been your visits and adventures in other parts, you have rendered it pleasanter and more interesting than any: and indeed we can scarcely walk in any quarter from the gates of Florence without the recollection of some witty or affecting story related by you. Every street, every farm, is peopled by your genius: and this population cannot change with seasons or with ages, with factions or with incursions. Ghibellines and Guelphs will have been contested for only by the worms, long before the **Decameron** has ceased to be recited on our banks of blue lilies and under our arching vines. Another plague may come amidst us; and something of a solace in so terrible a visitation would be found in your pages, by those to whom letters are a refuge and relief.

Boccaccio. I do indeed think my little bevy from Santa Maria Novella would be better company on such an occasion, than a devil with three heads, who diverts the pain his claws inflicted, by sticking his fangs in another place.

Petrarca. This is atrocious, not terrific nor grand. Alighieri is grand by his lights, not by his shadows; by his human affections, not by his infernal. As the minutest sands are the labours of some profound sea, or the spoils of some vast mountain, in like manner his horrid wastes and wearying minutenesses are the chafings of a turbulent spirit, grasping the loftiest things and penetrating the deepest, and moving and moaning on the earth in loneliness and sadness.

Boccaccio. Among men he is what among waters is

   The strange, mysterious, solitary Nile.

Petrarca. Is that his verse? I do not remember it.

Boccaccio. No, it is mine for the present: how long it may continue mine I cannot tell. I never run after those who steal my apples: it would only tire me: and they are hardly worth recovering when they are bruised and bitten, as they are usually. I would not stand upon my verses: it is a perilous boy's trick, which we ought to leave off when we put on square shoes. Let our prose show what we are, and our poetry what we have been.

Petrarca. You would never have given this advice to Alighieri.

Boccaccio. I would never plough porphyry; there is ground fitter for grain. Alighieri is the parent of his system, like the sun, about whom all the worlds are but particles thrown forth from him. We may write little things well, and accumulate one upon another; but never will any be justly called a great poet unless he has treated a great subject worthily. He may be the poet of the lover and of the idler, he may be the poet of green fields or gay society; but whoever is this can be no more. A throne is not built of birds'-nests, nor do a thousand reeds make a trumpet.

Petrarca. I wish Alighieri had blown his on nobler occasions.

Boccaccio. We may rightly wish it: but, in regretting what he wanted, let us acknowledge what he had: and never forget (which we omitted to mention) that he borrowed less from his predecessors than any of the Roman poets from theirs. Reasonably may it be expected that almost all who follow will be greatly more indebted to antiquity, to whose stores we, every year, are making some addition.

Petrarca. It can be held no flaw in the title-deeds of genius, if the same thoughts reappear as have been exhibited long ago. The indisputable sign of defect should be looked for in the proportion they bear to the unquestionably original. There are ideas which necessarily must occur to minds of the like magnitude and materials, aspect and temperature. When two ages are in the same phasis, they will excite the same humours, and produce the same coincidences and combinations. In addition to which, a great poet may really borrow: he may even condescend to an obligation at the hand of an equal or inferior: but he forfeits his title if he borrows more than the amount of his own possessions. The nightingale himself takes somewhat of his song from birds less glorified: and the lark, having beaten with her wing the very gates of heaven, cools her breast among the grass. The lowlier of intellect may lay out a table in their field, at which table the highest one shall sometimes be disposed to partake: want does not compel him. Imitation, as we call it, is often weakness, but it likewise is often sympathy.

Boccaccio. Our poet was seldom accessible in this quarter. Invective picks up the first stone on the wayside, and wants leisure to consult a forerunner.

Petrarca. Dante (original enough everywhere) is coarse and clumsy in this career. Vengeance has nothing to do with comedy, nor properly with satire. The satirist who told us that Indignation made his verses for him, might have been told in return that she excluded him thereby from the first class, and thrust him among the rhetoricians and declaimers. Lucretius, in his vituperation, is graver and more dignified than Alighieri. Painful; to see how tolerant is the atheist, how intolerant the Catholic: how anxiously the one removes from among the sufferings of Mortality, her last and heaviest, the fear of a vindictive Fury pursuing her shadow across rivers of fire and tears; how laboriously the other brings down Anguish and Despair, even when Death has done his work. How grateful the one is to that beneficent philosopher who made him at peace with himself, and tolerant and kindly toward his fellow-creatures! how importunate the other that God should forgo His divine mercy, and hurl everlasting torments both upon the dead and the living!

Boccaccio. I have always heard that Ser Dante was a very good man and sound Catholic: but Christ forgive me if my heart is oftener on the side of Lucretius![17] Observe, I say, my heart; nothing more. I devoutly hold to the sacraments and the mysteries: yet somehow I would rather see men tranquillized than frightened out of their senses, and rather fast asleep than burning. Sometimes I have been ready to believe, as far as our holy faith will allow me, that it were better our Lord were nowhere, than torturing in His inscrutable wisdom, to all eternity, so many myriads of us poor devils, the creatures of His hands. Do not cross thyself so thickly, Francesco! nor hang down thy nether lip so loosely, languidly, and helplessly; for I would be a good Catholic, alive or dead. But, upon my conscience, it goes hard with me to think it of Him, when I hear that woodlark yonder, gushing with joyousness, or when I see the beautiful clouds, resting so softly one upon another, dissolving ... and not damned for it. Above all, I am slow to apprehend it, when I remember His great goodness vouchsafed to me, and reflect on my sinful life heretofore, chiefly in summer time, and in cities, or their vicinity. But I was tempted beyond my strength; and I fell as any man might do. However, this last illness, by God's grace, has well-nigh brought me to my right mind again in all such matters: and if I get stout in the present month, and can hold out the next without sliding, I do verily think I am safe, or nearly so, until the season of beccaficoes.

Petrarca. Be not too confident!

Boccaccio. Well, I will not be.

Petrarca. But be firm.

Boccaccio. Assuntina! what! are you come in again?

Assunta. Did you or my master call me, Riverenza?

Petrarca. No, child!

Boccaccio. Oh! get you gone! Get you gone! you little rogue you!

Francesco, I feel quite well. Your kindness to my playful creatures in the **Decameron** has revived me, and has put me into good humour with the greater part of them. Are you quite certain the Madonna will not expect me to keep my promise? You said you were: I need not ask you again. I will accept the whole of your assurances, and half your praises.

Petrarca. To represent so vast a variety of personages so characteristically as you have done, to give the wise all their wisdom, the witty all their wit, and (what is harder to do advantageously) the simple all their simplicity, requires a genius such as you alone possess. Those who doubt it are the least dangerous of your rivals.

NOTE:

[17] Qy. How much of Lucretius (or Petronius or Catullus, before cited) was then known?

FIFTH DAY'S INTERVIEW

It being now the last morning that Petrarca could remain with his friend, he resolved to pass early into his bedchamber. Boccaccio had risen and was standing at the open window, with his arms against it. Renovated health sparkled in the eyes of the one; surprise and delight and thankfulness to Heaven filled the other's with sudden tears. He clasped Giovanni, kissed his flaccid and sallow cheek, and falling on his knees, adored the Giver of life, the source of health to body and soul. Giovanni was not unmoved: he bent one knee as he leaned on the shoulder of Francesco, looking down into his face, repeating his words, and adding:

'Blessed be Thou, O Lord! who sendest me health again! and blessings on Thy messenger who brought it.'

He had slept soundly; for ere he closed his eyes he had unburdened his mind of its freight, not only by employing the prayers appointed by Holy Church, but likewise by ejaculating; as sundry of the fathers did of old. He acknowledged his contrition for many transgressions, and chiefly for uncharitable thoughts of Fra Biagio: on which occasion he turned fairly round on his couch, and leaning his brow against the wall, and his body being in a becomingly curved position, and proper for the purpose, he thus ejaculated:

'Thou knowest, O most Holy Virgin! that never have I spoken to handmaiden at this villetta, or within my mansion at Certaldo, wantonly or indiscreetly, but have always been, inasmuch as may be, the guardian of innocence; deeming it better, when irregular thoughts assailed me, to ventilate them abroad than to poison the house with them. And if, sinner as I am, I have thought uncharitably of others, and more especially of Fra Biagio, pardon me, out of thy exceeding great mercies! And let it not be imputed to me, if I have kept, and may keep hereafter, an eye over him, in wariness and watchfulness; not otherwise. For thou knowest, O Madonna! that many who have a perfect and unwavering faith in thee, yet do cover up their cheese from the nibblings of vermin.'

Whereupon, he turned round again, threw himself on his back at full length, and feeling the sheets cool, smooth, and refreshing, folded his arms, and slept instantaneously. The consequence of his wholesome slumber was a calm alacrity: and the idea that his visitor would be happy at seeing him on his feet again, made him attempt to get up: at which he succeeded, to his own wonder. And it was increased by the manifestation of his strength in opening the casement, stiff from being closed, and swelled by the continuance of the rains. The morning was warm and sunny: and it is known that on this occasion he composed the verses below:

> My old familiar cottage-green!
> I see once more thy pleasant sheen;
> The gossamer suspended over
> Smart celandine by lusty clover;
> And the last blossom of the plum
> Inviting her first leaves to come;
> Which hang a little back, but show
> 'Tis not their nature to say no.
> I scarcely am in voice to sing
> How graceful are the steps of Spring;
> And ah! it makes me sigh to look

> How leaps along my merry brook,
> The very same to-day as when
> He chirrupt first to maids and men.

Petrarca. I can rejoice at the freshness of your feelings: but the sight of the green turf reminds me rather of its ultimate use and destination.

> For many serves the parish pall,
> The turf in common serves for all.

Boccaccio. Very true; and, such being the case, let us carefully fold it up, and lay it by until we call for it.

Francesco, you made me quite light-headed yesterday. I am rather too old to dance either with Spring, as I have been saying, or with Vanity: and yet I accepted her at your hand as a partner. In future, no more of comparisons for me! You not only can do me no good, but you can leave me no pleasure: for here I shall remain the few days I have to live, and shall see nobody who will be disposed to remind me of your praises. Beside, you yourself will get hated for them. We neither can deserve praise nor receive it with impunity.

Petrarca. Have you never remarked that it is into quiet water that children throw pebbles to disturb it? and that it is into deep caverns that the idle drop sticks and dirt? We must expect such treatment.

Boccaccio. Your admonition shall have its wholesome influence over me, when the fever your praises have excited has grown moderate.

... After the conversation on this topic and various others had continued some time, it was interrupted by a visitor. The clergy and monkery at Certaldo had never been cordial with Messer Giovanni, it being suspected that certain of his *Novelle* were modelled on originals in their orders. Hence, although they indeed both professed and felt esteem for Canonico Petrarca, they abstained from expressing it at the villetta. But Frate Biagio of San Vivaldo was (by his own appointment) the friend of the house; and, being considered as very expert in pharmacy, had, day after day, brought over no indifferent store of simples, in ptisans, and other refections, during the continuance of Ser Giovanni's ailment. Something now moved him to cast about in his mind whether it might not appear dutiful to make another visit. Perhaps he thought it possible that, among those who peradventure had seen him lately on the road, one or other might expect from him a solution of the questions, What sort of person was the ***crowned martyr***? whether he carried a palm in his hand? whether a seam was visible across the throat? whether he wore a ring over his glove, with a chrysolite in it, like the bishops, but representing the city of Jerusalem and the judgment-seat of Pontius Pilate? Such were the reports; but the inhabitants of San Vivaldo could not believe the Certaldese, who, inhabiting the next township to them, were naturally their enemies. Yet they might believe Frate Biagio, and certainly would interrogate him accordingly. He formed his determination, put his frock and hood on, and gave a curvature to his shoe, to evince his knowledge of the world, by pushing the extremity of it with his breast-bone against the corner of his cell. Studious of his figure and of his attire, he walked as much as possible on his heels, to keep up the reformation he had wrought in the workmanship of the cordwainer. On former occasions he had borrowed a horse, as being wanted to hear confession or to carry medicines, which might otherwise be too late. But, having put on an entirely new habiliment, and it being the season when horses are beginning to do the same, he deemed it prudent to travel on foot. Approaching the villetta, his first intention was to walk directly into his patient's room: but he found it impossible to resist the impulses of pride, in showing Assunta his rigid and stately frock, and shoes rather of the equestrian order than the monastic. So he went into the kitchen where the girl was at work, having just taken away the remains of the breakfast.

'Frate Biagio!' cried she, 'is this you? Have you been sleeping at Conte Jeronimo's?'

'Not I,' replied he.

'Why!' said she, 'those are surely his shoes! Santa Maria! you must have put them on in the dusk of the morning, to say your prayers in! Here! here! take these old ones of Signor Padrone, for the love of God! I hope your Reverence met nobody.'

Frate. What dost smile at?

Assunta. Smile at! I could find in my heart to laugh outright, if I only were certain that nobody had seen your Reverence in such a funny trim. Riverenza! put on these.

Frate. Not I indeed.

Assunta. Allow me then?

Frate. No, nor you.

Assunta. Then let me stand upon yours, to push down the points.

... Frate Biagio now began to relent a little, when Assunta, who had made one step toward the project, bethought herself suddenly, and said:

'No; I might miss my footing. But, mercy upon us! what made you cramp your Reverence with those ox-yoke shoes? and strangle your Reverence with that hangdog collar?'

'If you must know,' answered the Frate, reddening, 'it was because I am making a visit to the Canonico of Parma. I should like to know something about him: perhaps you could tell me?'

Assunta. Ever so much.

Frate. I thought no less: indeed I knew it. Which goes to bed first?

Assunta. Both together.

Frate. Demonio! what dost mean?

Assunta. He tells me never to sit up waiting, but to say my prayers and dream of the Virgin.

Frate. As if it was any business of his! Does he put out his lamp himself?

Assunta. To be sure he does: why should not he? what should he be afraid of? It is not winter: and beside, there is a mat upon the floor, all round the bed, excepting the top and bottom.

Frate. I am quite convinced he never said anything to make you blush. Why are you silent?

Assunta. I have a right.

Frate. He did then? ay? Do not nod your head: that will never do. Discreet girls speak plainly.

Assunta. What would you have?

Frate. The truth; the truth; again, I say, the truth.

Assunta. He ***did*** then.

Frate. I knew it! The most dangerous man living!

Assunta. Ah! indeed he is! Signor Padrone said so.

Frate. He knows him of old: he warned you, it seems.

Assunta. Me! He never said it was I who was in danger.

Frate. He might: it was his duty.

Assunta. Am I so fat? Lord! you may feel every rib. Girls who run about as I do, slip away from apoplexy.

Frate. Ho! ho! that is all, is it?

Assunta. And bad enough too! that such good-natured men should ever grow so bulky; and stand in danger, as Padrone said they both do, of such a seizure?

Frate. What? and art ready to cry about it? Old folks cannot die easier: and there are always plenty of younger to run quick enough for a confessor. But I must not trifle in this manner. It is my duty to set your feet in the right way: it is my bounden duty to report to Ser Giovanni all irregularities I know of, committed in his domicile. I could indeed, and would, remit a trifle, on hearing the worst. Tell me now, Assunta! tell me, you little angel! did you ... we all may, the very best of us may, and do ... sin, my sweet?

Assunta. You may be sure I did not: for whenever I sin I run into church directly, although it snows or thunders: else I never could see again Padrone's face, or any one's.

Frate. You do not come to me.

Assunta. You live at San Vivaldo.

Frate. But when there is sin so pressing I am always ready to be found. You perplex, you puzzle me. Tell me at once how he made you blush.

Assunta. Well then!

Frate. Well then! you did not hang back so before him. I lose all patience.

Assunta. So famous a man!...

Frate. No excuse in that.

Assunta. So dear to Padrone....

Frate. The more shame for him!

Assunta. Called me....

Frate. And **called** you, did he! the traitorous swine!

Assunta. Called me ... **good girl**.

Frate. Psha! the wenches, I think, are all mad: but few of them in this manner.

* * * * *

... Without saying another word, Fra Biagio went forward and opened the bedchamber door, saying briskly:

'Servant! Ser Giovanni! Ser Canonico! most devoted! most obsequious! I venture to incommode you. Thanks to God, Ser Canonico, you are looking well for your years. They tell me you were formerly (who would believe it?) the handsomest man in Christendom, and worked your way glibly, yonder at Avignon.

'Capperi! Ser Giovanni! I never observed that you were sitting bolt-upright in that long-backed armchair, instead of lying abed. Quite in the right. I am rejoiced at such a change for the better. Who advised it?'

Boccaccio. So many thanks to Fra Biagio! I not only am sitting up, but have taken a draught of fresh air at the window, and every leaf had a little present of sunshine for me.

There is one pleasure, Fra Biagio, which I fancy you never have experienced, and I hardly know whether I ought to wish it you; the first sensation of health after a long confinement.

Frate. Thanks! infinite! I would take any man's word for that, without a wish to try it. Everybody tells me I am exactly what I was a dozen years ago; while, for my part, I see everybody changed: those who ought to be much about my age, even those.... Per Bacco! I told them my thoughts when they had told me theirs; and they were not so agreeable as they used to be in former days.

Boccaccio. How people hate sincerity!

Cospetto! why, Frate! what hast got upon thy toes? Hast killed some Tartar and tucked his bow into one, and torn the crescent from the vizier's tent to make the other match it? Hadst thou fallen in thy mettlesome expedition (and it is a mercy and a miracle thou didst not) those sacrilegious shoes would have impaled thee.

Frate. It was a mistake in the shoemaker. But no pain or incommodity whatsoever could detain me from paying my duty to Ser Canonico, the first moment I heard of his auspicious arrival, or from offering my congratulations to Ser Giovanni, on the annunciation that he was recovered and looking out of the window. All Tuscany was standing on the watch for it, and the news flew like lightning. By this time it is upon the Danube.

And pray, Ser Canonico, how does Madonna Laura do?

Petrarca. Peace to her gentle spirit! she is departed.

Frate. Ay, true. I had quite forgotten: that is to say, I recollect it. You told us as much, I think, in a poem on her death. Well, and do you know! our friend Giovanni here is a bit of an author in his way.

Boccaccio. Frate! you confuse my modesty.

Frate. Murder will out. It is a fact, on my conscience. Have you never heard anything about it, Canonico! Ha! we poets are sly fellows: we can keep a secret.

Boccaccio. Are you quite sure you can?

Frate. Try, and trust me with any. I am a confessional on legs: there is no more a whisper in me than in a woolsack.

I am in feather again, as you see; and in tune, as you shall hear.

April is not the month for moping. Sing it lustily.

Boccaccio. Let it be your business to sing it, being a Frate; I can only recite it.

Frate. Pray do, then.

Boccaccio.

> Frate Biagio! sempre quando
> Qua tu vieni cavalcando,
> Pensi che le buone strade
> Per il mondo sien ben rade;
> E, di quante sono brutte,
> La piu brutta e tua di tutte.
> Badi, non cascare sulle
> Graziosissime fanciulle,
> Che con capo dritto, alzato,
> Uova portano al mercato.
> Pessima mi pare l'opra
> Rovesciarle sottosopra.
> Deh! scansando le erte e sassi,
> Sempre con premura passi.
> Caro amico! Frate Biagio!
> Passi pur, ma passi adagio.

Frate. Well now really, Canonico, for one not exactly one of us, that canzone of Ser Giovanni has merit; has not it? I did not ride, however, to-day; as you may see by the lining of my frock. But plus non vitiat; ay, Canonico! About the roads he is right enough; they are the devil's own roads; that must be said for them.

Ser Giovanni! with permission; your mention of eggs in the canzone has induced me to fancy I could eat a pair of them. The hens lay well now: that white one of yours is worth more than the goose that laid the golden: and you have a store of others, her equals or betters: we have none like them at poor St. Vivaldo. A riverderci, Ser Giovanni! Schiavo! Ser Canonico! mi commandino.

* * * * *

… Fra Biagio went back into the kitchen, helped himself to a quarter of a loaf, ordered a flask of wine, and, trying several eggs against his lips, selected seven, which he himself fried in oil, although the maid offered her services. He never had been so little disposed to enter into conversation with her; and on her asking him how he found her master, he replied, that in bodily health Ser Giovanni, by his prayers and ptisans, had much improved, but that his faculties were wearing out apace. 'He may now run in the same couples with the Canonico: they cannot catch the mange one of the other: the one could say nothing to the purpose, and the other nothing at all. The whole conversation was entirely at my charge,' added he. 'And now, Assunta, since you press it, I will accept the service of your master's shoes. How I shall ever get home I don't know.' He took the shoes off the handles of the bellows, where Assunta had placed them out of her way, and tucking one of his own under each arm, limped toward St. Vivaldo.

The unwonted attention to smartness of apparel, in the only article wherein it could be displayed, was suggested to Frate Biagio by hearing that Ser Francesco, accustomed to courtly habits and elegant society, and having not only small hands, but small feet, usually wore red slippers in the morning. Fra Biagio had scarcely left the outer door, than he cordially cursed Ser Francesco for making such a fool of him, and wearing slippers of black list. 'These canonicoes,' said he, 'not only lie themselves, but teach everybody else to do the same. He has lamed me for life: I burn as if I had been shod at the blacksmith's forge.'

The two friends said nothing about him, but continued the discourse which his visit had interrupted.

Petrarca. Turn again, I entreat you, to the serious; and do not imagine that because by nature you are inclined to playfulness, you must therefore write ludicrous things better. Many of your stories would make the gravest men laugh, and yet there is little wit in them.

Boccaccio. I think so myself; though authors, little disposed as they are to doubt their possession of any quality they would bring into play, are least of all suspicious on the side of wit. You have convinced me. I am glad to have been tender, and to have written tenderly: for I am certain it is this alone that has made you love me with such affection.

Petrarca. Not this alone, Giovanni! but this principally. I have always found you kind and compassionate, liberal and sincere, and when Fortune does not stand very close to such a man, she leaves only the more room for Friendship.

Boccaccio. Let her stand off then, now and for ever! To my heart, to my heart, Francesco! preserver of my health, my peace of mind, and (since you tell me I may claim it) my glory.

Petrarca. Recovering your strength you must pursue your studies to complete it. What can you have been doing with your books? I have searched in vain this morning for the treasury. Where are they kept? Formerly they were always open. I found only a short manuscript, which I suspect is poetry, but I ventured not on looking into it, until I had brought it with me and laid it before you.

Boccaccio. Well guessed! They are verses written by a gentleman who resided long in this country, and who much regretted the necessity of leaving it. He took great delight in composing both Latin and Italian, but never kept a copy of them latterly, so that these are the only ones I could obtain from him. Read: for your voice will improve them:

TO MY CHILD CARLINO

Carlino! what art thou about, my boy?
Often I ask that question, though in vain,
For we are far apart: ah! therefore 'tis
I often ask it; not in such a tone
As wiser fathers do, who know too well.
Were we not children, you and I together?
Stole we not glances from each other's eyes?
Swore we not secrecy in such misdeeds?
Well could we trust each other. Tell me then
What thou art doing. Carving out thy name,
Or haply mine, upon my favourite seat,
With the new knife I sent thee over sea?
Or hast thou broken it, and hid the hilt
Among the myrtles, starr'd with flowers, behind?
Or under that high throne whence fifty lilies
(With sworded tuberoses dense around)
Lift up their heads at once, not without fear
That they were looking at thee all the while.

  Does Cincirillo follow thee about?
Inverting one swart foot suspensively,
And wagging his dread jaw at every chirp
Of bird above him on the olive-branch?
Frighten him then away! 'twas he who slew
Our pigeons, our white pigeons peacock-tailed,

That fear'd not you and me ... alas, nor him!
I flattened his striped sides along my knee,
And reasoned with him on his bloody mind,
Till he looked blandly, and half-closed his eyes
To ponder on my lecture in the shade.
I doubt his memory much, his heart a little,
And in some minor matters (may I say it?)
Could wish him rather sager. But from thee
God hold back wisdom yet for many years!
Whether in early season or in late
It always comes high-priced. For thy pure breast
I have no lesson; it for me has many.
Come throw it open then! What sports, what cares
(Since there are none too young for these) engage
Thy busy thoughts? Are you again at work,
Walter and you, with those sly labourers,
Geppo, Giovanni, Cecco, and Poeta,
To build more solidly your broken dam
Among the poplars, whence the nightingale
Inquisitively watch'd you all day long?
I was not of your council in the scheme,
Or might have saved you silver without end,
And sighs too without number. Art thou gone
Below the mulberry, where that cold pool
Urged to devise a warmer, and more fit
For mighty swimmers, swimming three abreast?
Or art thou panting in this summer noon
Upon the lowest step before the hall,
Drawing a slice of water-melon, long
As Cupid's bow, athwart thy wetted lips
(Like one who plays Pan's pipe) and letting drop
The sable seeds from all their separate cells,
And leaving bays profound and rocks abrupt,

Redder than coral round Calypso's cave?

Petrarca. There have been those anciently who would have been pleased with such poetry, and perhaps there may be again. I am not sorry to see the Muses by the side of childhood, and forming a part of the family. But now tell me about the books.

Boccaccio. Resolving to lay aside the more valuable of those I had collected or transcribed, and to place them under the guardianship of richer men, I locked them up together in the higher story of my tower at Certaldo. You remember the old tower?

Petrarca. Well do I remember the hearty laugh we had together (which stopped us upon the staircase) at the calculation we made, how much longer you and I, if we continued to thrive as we had thriven latterly, should be able to pass within its narrow circle. Although I like this little villa much better, I would gladly see the place again, and enjoy with you, as we did before, the vast expanse of woodlands and mountains and maremma; frowning fortresses inexpugnable; and others more prodigious for their ruins; then below them, lordly abbeys, overcanopied with stately trees and girded with rich luxuriance; and towns that seem approaching them to do them honour, and villages nestling close at their sides for sustenance and protection.

Boccaccio. My disorder, if it should keep its promise of leaving me at last, will have been preparing me for the accomplishment of such a project. Should I get thinner and thinner at this rate, I shall soon be able to mount not only a turret or a belfry, but a tube of macarone, while a Neapolitan is suspending it for deglutition.

What I am about to mention will show you how little you can rely on me! I have preserved the books, as you desired, but quite contrary to my resolution: and, no less contrary to it, by your desire I shall now preserve the ***Decameron***. In vain had I determined not only to mend in future, but to correct the past; in vain had I prayed most fervently for grace to accomplish it, with a final aspiration to Fiametta that she would unite with your beloved Laura, and that, gentle and beatified spirits as they are, they would breathe together their purer prayers on mine. See what follows.

Petrarca. Sigh not at it. Before we can see all that follows from their intercession, we must join them again. But let me hear anything in which they are concerned.

Boccaccio. I prayed; and my breast, after some few tears, grew calmer. Yet sleep did not ensue until the break of morning, when the dropping of soft rain on the leaves of the fig-tree at the window, and the chirping of a little bird, to tell another there was shelter under them, brought me repose and slumber. Scarcely had I closed my eyes, if indeed time can be reckoned any more in sleep than in heaven, when my Fiametta seemed to have led me into the meadow. You will see it below you: turn away that branch: gently! gently! do not break it; for the little bird sat there.

Petrarca. I think, Giovanni, I can divine the place. Although this fig-tree, growing out of the wall between the cellar and us, is fantastic enough in its branches, yet that other which I see yonder, bent down and forced to crawl along the grass by the prepotency of the young shapely walnut-tree, is much more so. It forms a seat, about a cubit above the ground, level and long enough for several.

Boccaccio. Ha! you fancy it must be a favourite spot with me, because of the two strong forked stakes wherewith it is propped and supported!

Petrarca. Poets know the haunts of poets at first sight; and he who loved Laura.... O Laura! did I say he who **loved** thee? ... hath whisperings where those feet would wander which have been restless after Fiametta.

Boccaccio. It is true, my imagination has often conducted her thither; but there in this chamber she appeared to me more visibly in a dream.

'Thy prayers have been heard, O Giovanni,' said she.

I sprang to embrace her.

'Do not spill the water! Ah! you have spilt a part of it.'

I then observed in her hand a crystal vase. A few drops were sparkling on the sides and running down the rim: a few were trickling from the base and from the hand that held it.

'I must go down to the brook,' said she, 'and fill it again as it was filled before.'

What a moment of agony was this to me! Could I be certain how long might be her absence? She went: I was following: she made a sign for me to turn back: I disobeyed her only an instant: yet my sense of disobedience, increasing my feebleness and confusion, made me lose sight of her. In the next moment she was again at my side, with the cup quite full. I stood motionless: I feared my breath might shake the water over. I looked her in the face for her commands ... and to see it ... to see it so calm, so beneficent, so beautiful. I was forgetting what I had prayed for, when she lowered her head, tasted of the cup, and gave it me. I drank; and suddenly sprang forth before me many groves and palaces and gardens, and their statues and their avenues, and their labyrinths of alaternus and bay, and alcoves of citron, and watchful loopholes in the retirements of impenetrable pomegranate. Farther off, just below where the fountain slipped away from its marble hall and guardian gods, arose, from their beds of moss and drosera and darkest grass, the sisterhood of oleanders, fond of tantalizing with their bosomed flowers and their moist and pouting blossoms the little shy rivulet, and of covering its face with all the colours of the dawn. My dream expanded and moved forward. I trod again the dust of Posilipo, soft as the feathers in the wings of Sleep. I emerged on Baia; I crossed her innumerable arches; I loitered in the breezy sunshine of her mole; I trusted the faithful seclusion of her caverns, the keepers of so many secrets; and I reposed on the buoyancy of her tepid sea. Then Naples, and her theatres and her churches, and grottoes and dells and forts and promontories, rushed forward in confusion, now among soft whispers, now among sweetest sounds, and subsided, and sank, and disappeared. Yet a memory seemed to come fresh from every one: each had time enough for its tale, for its pleasure, for its reflection, for its pang. As I mounted with silent steps the narrow staircase of the old palace, how distinctly did I feel against the palm of my hand the coldness of that smooth stone-work, and the greater of the cramps of iron in it!

'Ah me! is this forgetting?' cried I anxiously to Fiametta.

'We must recall these scenes before us,' she replied: 'such is the punishment of them. Let us hope and believe that the apparition, and the compunction which must follow it, will be accepted as the full penalty, and that both will pass away almost together.'

I feared to lose anything attendant on her presence: I feared to approach her forehead with my lips: I feared to touch the lily on its long wavy leaf in her hair, which filled my whole heart with fragrance. Venerating, adoring, I bowed my head at last to kiss her snow-white robe, and trembled at my presumption. And yet the effulgence of her countenance vivified while it chastened me. I loved her ... I must not say *more* than ever ... **better** than ever; it was Fiametta who had inhabited the skies. As my hand opened toward her:

'Beware!' said she, faintly smiling; 'beware, Giovanni! Take only the crystal; take it, and drink again.'

'Must all be then forgotten?' said I sorrowfully.

'Remember your prayer and mine, Giovanni. Shall both have been granted ... oh, how much worse than in vain?'

I drank instantly; I drank largely. How cool my bosom grew; how could it grow so cool before her! But it was not to remain in its quiescency; its trials were not yet over. I will not, Francesco! no, I may not commemorate the incidents she related to me, nor which of us said, 'I blush for having loved *first*;' nor which of us replied, 'Say *least*, say *least*, and blush again.'

The charm of the words (for I felt not the encumbrance of the body nor the acuteness of the spirit) seemed to possess me wholly. Although the water gave me strength and comfort, and somewhat of celestial pleasure, many tears fell around the border of the vase as she held it up before me, exhorting me to take courage, and inviting me with more than exhortation to accomplish my deliverance. She came nearer, more tenderly, more earnestly; she held the dewy globe with both hands, leaning forward, and sighed and shook her head, drooping at my pusillanimity. It was only when a ringlet had touched the rim, and perhaps the water (for a sunbeam on the surface could never have given it such a golden hue), that I took courage, clasped it, and exhausted it. Sweet as was the water, sweet as was the serenity it gave me ... alas! that also which it moved away from me was sweet!

'This time you can trust me alone,' said she, and parted my hair, and kissed my brow. Again she went toward the brook: again my agitation, my weakness, my doubt, came over me: nor could I see her while she raised the water, nor knew I whence she drew it. When she returned, she was close to me at once: she smiled: her smile pierced me to the bones: it seemed an angel's. She sprinkled the pure water on me; she looked most fondly; she took my hand; she suffered me to press hers to my bosom; but, whether by design I cannot tell, she let fall a few drops of the chilly element between.

'And now, O my beloved!' said she, 'we have consigned to the bosom of God our earthly joys and sorrows. The joys cannot return, let not the sorrows. These alone would trouble my repose among the blessed.'

'Trouble thy repose! Fiametta! Give me the chalice!' cried I ... 'not a drop will I leave in it, not a drop.'

'Take it!' said that soft voice. 'O now most dear Giovanni! I know thou hast strength enough; and there is but little ... at the bottom lies our first kiss.'

'Mine! didst thou say, beloved one? and is that left thee still?'

'*Mine*,' said she, pensively; and as she abased her head, the broad leaf of the lily hid her brow and her eyes; the light of heaven shone through the flower.

'O Fiametta! Fiametta!' cried I in agony, 'God is the God of mercy, God is the God of love ... can I, can I ever?' I struck the chalice against my head, unmindful that I held it; the water covered my face and my feet. I started up, not yet awake, and I heard the name of Fiametta in the curtains.

Petrarca. Love, O Giovanni, and life itself, are but dreams at best. I do think

> Never so gloriously was Sleep attended
> As with the pageant of that heavenly maid.

But to dwell on such subjects is sinful. The recollection of them, with all their vanities, brings tears into my eyes.

Boccaccio. And into mine too ... they were so very charming.

Petrarca. Alas, alas! the time always comes when we must regret the enjoyments of our youth.

Boccaccio. If we have let them pass us.

Petrarca. I mean our indulgence in them.

Boccaccio. Francesco! I think you must remember Raffaellino degli Alfani.

Petrarca. Was it Raffaellino who lived near San Michele in Orto?

Boccaccio. The same. He was an innocent soul, and fond of fish. But whenever his friend Sabbatelli sent him a trout from Pratolino, he always kept it until next day or the day after, just long enough to render it unpalatable. He then turned it over in the platter, smelt at it closer, although the news of its condition came undeniably from a distance, touched it with his forefinger, solicited a testimony from the gills which the eyes had contradicted, sighed over it, and sent it for a present to somebody else. Were I a lover of trout as Raffaellino was, I think I should have taken an opportunity of enjoying it while the pink and crimson were glittering on it.

Petrarca. Trout, yes.

Boccaccio. And all other fish I could encompass.

Petrarca. O thou grave mocker! I did not suspect such slyness in thee: proof enough I had almost forgotten thee.

Boccaccio. Listen! listen! I fancied I caught a footstep in the passage. Come nearer; bend your head lower, that I may whisper a word in your ear. Never let Assunta hear you sigh. She is mischievous: she may have been standing at the door: not that I believe she would be guilty of any such impropriety: but who knows what girls are capable of! She has no malice, only in laughing; and a sigh sets her windmill at work, van over van, incessantly.

Petrarca. I should soon check her. I have no notion....

Boccaccio. After all, she is a good girl ... a trifle of the wilful. She must have it that many things are hurtful to me ... reading in particular ... it makes people so odd. Tina is a small matter of the madcap ... in her own particular way ... but exceedingly discreet, I do assure you, if they will only leave her alone.

I find I was mistaken, there was nobody.

Petrarca. A cat, perhaps.

Boccaccio. No such thing. I order him over to Certaldo while the birds are laying and sitting: and he knows by experience, favourite as he is, that it is of no use to come back before he is sent for. Since the first impetuosities of youth, he has rarely been refractory or disobliging. We have lived together now these five years, unless I miscalculate; and he seems to have learnt something of my manners, wherein violence and enterprise by no means predominate. I have watched him looking at a large green lizard; and, their eyes being opposite and near, he has doubted whether it might be pleasing to me if he began the attack; and their tails on a sudden have touched one another at the decision.

Petrarca. Seldom have adverse parties felt the same desire of peace at the same moment, and none ever carried it more simultaneously and promptly into execution.

Boccaccio. He enjoys his **otium cum dignitate** at Certaldo: there he is my castellan, and his chase is unlimited in those domains. After the doom of relegation is expired, he comes hither at midsummer. And then if you could see his joy! His eyes are as deep as a well, and as clear as a fountain: he jerks his tail into the air like a royal sceptre, and waves it like the wand of a magician. You would fancy that, as Horace with his head, he was about to smite the stars with it. There is ne'er such another cat in the parish; and he knows it, a rogue! We have rare repasts together in the bean-and-bacon time, although in regard to the bean he sides with the philosopher of Samos; but after due examination. In cleanliness he is a very nun; albeit in that quality which lies between cleanliness and godliness, there is a smack of Fra Biagio about him. What is that book in your hand?

Petrarca. My breviary.

Boccaccio. Well, give me mine too ... there, on the little table in the corner, under the glass of primroses. We can do nothing better.

Petrarca. What prayer were you looking for? let me find it.

Boccaccio. I don't know how it is: I am scarcely at present in a frame of mind for it. We are of one faith: the prayers of the one will do for the other: and I am sure, if you omitted my name, you would say them all over afresh. I wish you could recollect in any book as dreamy a thing to entertain me as I have been just repeating. We have had enough of Dante: I believe few of his beauties have escaped us: and small faults, which we readily pass by, are fitter for small folks, as grubs are the proper bait for gudgeons.

Petrarca. I have had as many dreams as most men. We are all made up of them, as the webs of the spider are particles of her own vitality. But how infinitely less do we profit by them! I will relate to you, before we separate, one among the multitude of mine, as coming the nearest to the poetry of yours, and as having been not totally useless to me. Often have I reflected on it; sometimes with pensiveness, with sadness never.

Boccaccio. Then, Francesco, if you had with you as copious a choice of dreams as clustered on the elm-trees where the Sibyl led Aeneas, this, in preference to the whole swarm of them, is the queen dream for me.

Petrarca. When I was younger I was fond of wandering in solitary places, and never was afraid of slumbering in woods and grottoes. Among the chief pleasures of my life, and among the commonest of my occupations, was the bringing before me such heroes and heroines of antiquity, such poets and sages, such of the prosperous and the unfortunate, as most interested me by their courage, their wisdom, their eloquence, or their adventures. Engaging them in the conversation best suited to their characters, I knew perfectly their manners, their steps, their voices: and often did I moisten with my tears the models I had been forming of the less happy.

Boccaccio. Great is the privilege of entering into the studies of the intellectual; great is that of conversing with the guides of nations, the movers of the mass, the regulators of the unruly will, stiff, in its impurity and rust, against the finger of the Almighty Power that formed it: but give me, Francesco, give me rather the creature to sympathize with; apportion me the sufferings to assuage. Ah, gentle soul! thou wilt never send them over to another; they have better hopes from thee.

Petrarca. We both alike feel the sorrows of those around us. He who suppresses or allays them in another, breaks many thorns off his own; and future years will never harden fresh ones.

My occupation was not always in making the politician talk politics, the orator toss his torch among the populace, the philosopher run down from philosophy to cover the retreat or the advances of his sect; but sometimes in devising how such characters must act and discourse, on subjects far remote from the beaten track of their career. In like manner the philologist, and again the dialectician, were not indulged in the review and parade of their trained bands, but, at times, brought forward to show in what manner and in what degree external habits had influenced the conformation of the internal man. It was far from unprofitable to set passing events before past actors, and to record the decisions of those whose interests and passions are unconcerned in them.

Boccaccio. This is surely no easy matter. The thoughts are in fact your own, however you distribute them.

Petrarca. All cannot be my own; if you mean by ***thoughts*** the opinions and principles I should be the most desirous to inculcate. Some favourite ones perhaps may obtrude too prominently, but otherwise no misbehaviour is permitted them: reprehension and rebuke are always ready, and the offence is punished on the spot.

Boccaccio. Certainly you thus throw open, to its full extent, the range of poetry and invention; which cannot but be very limited and sterile, unless where we find displayed much diversity of character as disseminated by nature, much peculiarity of sentiment as arising from position, marked with unerring skill through every shade and gradation; and finally and chiefly, much intertexture and intensity of passion. You thus convey to us more largely and expeditiously the stores of your understanding and imagination, than you ever could by sonnets or canzonets, or sinewless and sapless allegories.

But weightier works are less captivating. If you had published any such as you mention, you must have waited for their acceptance. Not only the fame of Marcellus, but every other,

> Crescit occulto velut arbor aevo;

and that which makes the greatest vernal shoot is apt to make the least autumnal. Authors in general who have met celebrity at starting, have already had their reward; always their utmost due, and often much beyond it. We cannot hope for both celebrity and fame: supremely fortunate are the few who are allowed the liberty of choice between them. We two prefer the strength that springs from exercise and toil, acquiring it gradually and slowly: we leave to others the earlier blessing of that sleep which follows enjoyment. How many at first sight are enthusiastic in their favour! Of these how large a portion come away empty-handed and discontented! like idlers who visit the seacoast, fill their pockets with pebbles bright from the passing wave, and carry them off with rapture. After a short examination at home, every streak seems faint and dull, and the whole contexture coarse, uneven, and gritty: first one is thrown away, then another; and before the week's end the store is gone, of things so shining and wonderful.

Petrarca. Allegory, which you named with sonnets and canzonets, had few attractions for me, believing it to be the delight in general of idle, frivolous, inexcursive minds, in whose mansions there is neither hall nor portal to receive the loftier of the Passions. A stranger to the Affections, she holds a low station among the handmaidens of Poetry, being fit for little but an apparition in a mask. I had reflected for some time on this subject, when, wearied with the length of my walk over the mountains, and finding a soft old molehill, covered with grey grass, by the wayside, I laid my head upon it and slept. I cannot tell how long it was before a species of dream or vision came over me.

Two beautiful youths appeared beside me; each was winged; but the wings were hanging down, and seemed ill adapted to flight. One of them, whose voice was the softest I ever heard, looking at me frequently, said to the other:

'He is under my guardianship for the present: do not awaken him with that feather.'

Methought, hearing the whisper, I saw something like the feather on an arrow; and then the arrow itself; the whole of it, even to the point; although he carried it in such a manner that it was difficult at first to discover more than a palm's length of it: the rest of the shaft, and the whole of the barb, was behind his ankles.

'This feather never awakens any one,' replied he, rather petulantly; 'but it brings more of confident security, and more of cherished dreams, than you without me are capable of imparting.'

'Be it so!' answered the gentler ... 'none is less inclined to quarrel or dispute than I am. Many whom you have wounded grievously, call upon me for succour. But so little am I disposed to thwart you, it is seldom I venture to do more for them than to whisper a few words of comfort in passing. How many reproaches on these occasions have been cast upon me for indifference and infidelity! Nearly as many, and nearly in the same terms, as upon you!'

'Odd enough that we, O Sleep! should be thought so alike,' said Love, contemptuously. 'Yonder is he who bears a nearer resemblance to you: the dullest have observed it.' I fancied I turned my eyes to where he was pointing, and saw at a distance the figure he designated. Meanwhile the contention went on uninterruptedly. Sleep was slow in asserting his power or his benefits. Love recapitulated them; but only that he might assert his own above them. Suddenly he called on me to decide, and to choose my patron. Under the influence, first of the one, then of the other, I sprang from repose to rapture, I alighted from rapture on repose ... and knew not which was sweetest. Love was very angry with me, and declared he would cross me throughout the whole of my existence. Whatever I might on other occasions have thought of his veracity, I now felt too surely the conviction that he would keep his word. At last, before the close of the altercation, the third Genius had advanced, and stood near us. I cannot tell how I knew him, but I knew him to be the Genius of Death. Breathless as I was at beholding him, I soon became familiar with his features. First they seemed only calm; presently they grew contemplative; and lastly beautiful: those of the Graces themselves are less regular, less harmonious, less composed. Love glanced at him unsteadily, with a countenance in which there was somewhat of anxiety, somewhat of disdain; and cried: 'Go away! go away! nothing that thou touchest, lives.'

'Say rather, child!' replied the advancing form, and advancing grew loftier and statelier, 'say rather that nothing of beautiful or of glorious lives its own true life until my wing hath passed over it.'

Love pouted, and rumpled and bent down with his forefinger the stiff short feathers on his arrow-head; but replied not. Although he frowned worse than ever, and at me, I dreaded him less and less, and scarcely looked toward him. The milder and calmer Genius, the third, in proportion as I took courage to contemplate him, regarded me with more and more complacency. He held neither flower nor arrow, as the others did; but, throwing back the clusters of dark curls that overshadowed his countenance, he presented to me his hand, openly and benignly. I shrank on looking at him so near, and yet I sighed to love him. He smiled, not without an expression of pity, at perceiving my diffidence, my timidity: for I remembered how soft was the hand of Sleep, how warm and entrancing was Love's. By degrees, I became ashamed of my ingratitude; and turning my face away, I held out my arms, and felt my neck within his. Composure strewed and allayed all the throbbings of my bosom; the coolness of freshest morning breathed around: the heavens seemed to open above me; while the beautiful cheek of my deliverer rested on my head. I would now have looked for those others; but knowing my intention by my gesture, he said, consolatorily:

'Sleep is on his way to the Earth, where many are calling him; but it is not to these he hastens; for every call only makes him fly farther off. Sedately and gravely as he looks, he is nearly as capricious and volatile as the more arrogant and ferocious one.'

'And Love!' said I, 'whither is he departed? If not too late, I would propitiate and appease him.'

'He who cannot follow me, he who cannot overtake and pass me,' said the Genius, 'is unworthy of the name, the most glorious in earth or heaven. Look up! Love is yonder, and ready to receive thee.'
I looked: the earth was under me: I saw only the clear blue sky, and something brighter above it.

POEMS

I

She I love (alas in vain!)
  Floats before my slumbering eyes:
When she comes she lulls my pain,
  When she goes what pangs arise!
Thou whom love, whom memory flies,
  Gentle Sleep! prolong thy reign!
If even thus she soothe my sighs,
  Never let me wake again!

II

Pleasure! why thus desert the heart
    In its spring-tide?
I could have seen her, I could part,
    And but have sigh'd!

O'er every youthful charm to stray,
    To gaze, to touch....
Pleasure! why take so much away,
    Or give so much?

III

Past ruin'd Ilion Helen lives,
  Alcestis rises from the shades;
Verse calls them forth; 'tis verse that gives
  Immortal youth to mortal maids.

Soon shall Oblivion's deepening veil
  Hide all the peopled hills you see,
The gay, the proud, while lovers hail
  These many summers you and me.

IV

Ianthe! you are call'd to cross the sea!
  A path forbidden *me*!
Remember, while the Sun his blessing sheds
  Upon the mountain-heads,
How often we have watcht him laying down
  His brow, and dropt our own
Against each other's, and how faint and short
  And sliding the support!
What will succeed it now? Mine is unblest,
  Ianthe! nor will rest
But on the very thought that swells with pain.
  O bid me hope again!
O give me back what Earth, what (without you)
  Not Heaven itself can do,
One of the golden days that we have past;
  And let it be my last!
Or else the gift would be, however sweet,
  Fragile and incomplete.

V

 The gates of fame and of the grave
 Stand under the same architrave.

VI

 Twenty years hence my eyes may grow
 If not quite dim, yet rather so,
 Still yours from others they shall know
   Twenty years hence.
 Twenty years hence tho' it may hap
 That I be call'd to take a nap
 In a cool cell where thunder-clap
   Was never heard,
 There breathe but o'er my arch of grass
 A not too sadly sigh'd *Alas*,
 And I shall catch, ere you can pass,
   That winged word.

VII

 Here, ever since you went abroad,
  If there be change, no change I see,
 I only walk our wonted road,
  The road is only walkt by me.

 Yes; I forgot; a change there is;
  Was it of *that* you bade me tell?
 I catch at times, at times I miss
  The sight, the tone, I know so well.

Only two months since you stood here!
  Two shortest months! then tell me why
Voices are harsher than they were,
  And tears are longer ere they dry.

VIII

Tell me not things past all belief;
  One truth in you I prove;
The flame of anger, bright and brief,
  Sharpens the barb of Love.

IX

Proud word you never spoke, but you will speak
  Four not exempt from pride some future day.
Resting on one white hand a warm wet cheek
  Over my open volume you will say,
'This man loved *me*!' then rise and trip away.

X
FIESOLE IDYL

Here, where precipitate Spring, with one light bound
Into hot Summer's lusty arms, expires,
And where go forth at morn, at eve, at night,
Soft airs that want the lute to play with 'em,
And softer sighs that know not what they want,
Aside a wall, beneath an orange-tree,
Whose tallest flowers could tell the lowlier ones

Of sights in Fiesole right up above,
While I was gazing a few paces off
At what they seem'd to show me with their nods,
Their frequent whispers and their pointing shoots,
A gentle maid came down the garden-steps
And gathered the pure treasure in her lap.
I heard the branches rustle, and stept forth
To drive the ox away, or mule, or goat,
Such I believed it must be. How could I
Let beast o'erpower them? When hath wind or rain
Borne hard upon weak plant that wanted me,
And I (however they might bluster round)
Walkt off? 'Twere most ungrateful: for sweet scents
Are the swift vehicles of still sweeter thoughts,
And nurse and pillow the dull memory
That would let drop without them her best stores.
They bring me tales of youth and tones of love,
And 'tis and ever was my wish and way
To let all flowers live freely, and all die
(Whene'er their Genius bids their souls depart)
Among their kindred in their native place.
I never pluck the rose; the violet's head
Hath shaken with my breath upon its bank
And not reproacht me; the ever-sacred cup
Of the pure lily hath between my hands
Felt safe, unsoil'd, nor lost one grain of gold.
I saw the light that made the glossy leaves
More glossy; the fair arm, the fairer cheek
Warmed by the eye intent on its pursuit;
I saw the foot that, although half-erect
From its grey slipper, could not lift her up
To what she wanted: I held down a branch
And gather'd her some blossoms; since their hour

Was come, and bees had wounded them, and flies
Of harder wing were working their way thro'
And scattering them in fragments under-foot.
So crisp were some, they rattled unevolved,
Others, ere broken off, fell into shells,
For such appear the petals when detacht,
Unbending, brittle, lucid, white like snow,
And like snow not seen thro', by eye or sun:
Yet every one her gown received from me
Was fairer than the first. I thought not so,
But so she praised them to reward my care.
I said, 'You find the largest.'
      'This indeed,'
Cried she, 'is large and sweet.' She held one forth,
Whether for me to look at or to stake
She knew not, nor did I; but taking it
Would best have solved (and this she felt) her doubt.
I dared not touch it; for it seemed a part
Of her own self; fresh, full, the most mature
Of blossoms, yet a blossom; with a touch
To fall, and yet unfallen. She drew back
The boon she tender'd, and then, finding not
The ribbon at her waist to fix it in,
Dropt it, as loath to drop it, on the rest.

XI

Ah what avails the sceptred race,
 Ah what the form divine!
What every virtue, every grace!
 Rose Aylmer, all were thine.
Rose Aylmer, whom these wakeful eyes

    May weep, but never see,
A night of memories and of sighs
    I consecrate to thee.

XII

With rosy hand a little girl prest down
A boss of fresh-cull'd cowslips in a rill:
Often as they sprang up again, a frown
Show'd she disliked resistance to her will:
But when they droopt their heads and shone much less,
She shook them to and fro, and threw them by,
And tript away. 'Ye loathe the heaviness
Ye love to cause, my little girls!' thought I,
'And what had shone for you, by you must die.'

XIII

    Ternissa! you are fled!
    I say not to the dead,
But to the happy ones who rest below:
    For, surely, surely, where
    Your voice and graces are,
Nothing of death can any feel or know.
    Girls who delight to dwell
    Where grows most asphodel,
Gather to their calm breasts each word you speak:
    The mild Persephone
    Places you on her knee,
And your cool palm smooths down stern Pluto's cheek.

XIV

    Various the roads of life; in one
      All terminate, one lonely way
    We go; and 'Is he gone?'
      Is all our best friends say.

XV

    Yes; I write verses now and then,
    But blunt and flaccid is my pen,
    No longer talkt of by young men
            As rather clever:

    In the last quarter are my eyes,
    You see it by their form and size;
    Is it not time then to be wise?
            Or now or never.

    Fairest that ever sprang from Eve!
    While Time allows the short reprieve,
    Just look at me! would you believe
            'Twas once a lover?

    I cannot clear the five-bar gate,
    But, trying first its timber's state,
    Climb stiffly up, take breath, and wait
            To trundle over.

    Thro' gallopade I cannot swing
    The entangling blooms of Beauty's spring:
    I cannot say the tender thing,

> Be 't true or false,

And am beginning to opine
Those girls are only half-divine
Whose waists yon wicked boys entwine
> In giddy waltz.

I fear that arm above that shoulder,
I wish them wiser, graver, older,
Sedater, and no harm if colder
> And panting less.

Ah! people were not half so wild
In former days, when, starchly mild,
Upon her high-heel'd Essex smiled
> The brave Queen Bess.

XVI
ON SEEING A HAIR OF LUCRETIA BORGIA

Borgia, thou once wert almost too august
And high for adoration; now thou'rt dust.
All that remains of thee these plaits unfold,
Calm hair, meandering in pellucid gold.

XVII

Once, and once only, have I seen thy face,
Elia! once only has thy tripping tongue
Run o'er my breast, yet never has been left
Impression on it stronger or more sweet.

Cordial old man! what youth was in thy years,
What wisdom in thy levity, what truth
In every utterance of that purest soul!
Few are the spirits of the glorified
I'd spring to earlier at the gate of Heaven.

XVIII
TO WORDSWORTH

  Those who have laid the harp aside
    And turn'd to idler things,
  From very restlessness have tried
    The loose and dusty strings.
  And, catching back some favourite strain,
  Run with it o'er the chords again.

  But Memory is not a Muse,
    O Wordsworth! though 'tis said
  They all descend from her, and use
    To haunt her fountain-head:
  That other men should work for me
  In the rich mines of Poesie,
  Pleases me better than the toil
    Of smoothing under hardened hand,
  With Attic emery and oil,
    The shining point for Wisdom's wand,
  Like those thou temperest 'mid the rills
  Descending from thy native hills.

  Without his governance, in vain
    Manhood is strong, and Youth is bold
  If oftentimes the o'er-piled strain

Clogs in the furnace, and grows cold
Beneath his pinions deep and frore,
And swells and melts and flows no more,
That is because the heat beneath
  Pants in its cavern poorly fed.
Life springs not from the couch of Death,
  Nor Muse nor Grace can raise the dead;
Unturn'd then let the mass remain,
Intractable to sun or rain.

A marsh, where only flat leaves lie,
And showing but the broken sky,
Too surely is the sweetest lay
That wins the ear and wastes the day,
Where youthful Fancy pouts alone
And lets not Wisdom touch her zone.

He who would build his fame up high,
The rule and plummet must apply,
Nor say, 'I'll do what I have plann'd,'
Before he try if loam or sand
Be still remaining in the place
Delved for each polisht pillar's base.
With skilful eye and fit device
Thou raisest every edifice,
Whether in sheltered vale it stand
Or overlook the Dardan strand,
Amid the cypresses that mourn
Laodameia's love forlorn.

We both have run o'er half the space
Listed for mortal's earthly race;
We both have crost life's fervid line,

And other stars before us shine:
May they be bright and prosperous
As those that have been stars for us!
Our course by Milton's light was sped,
And Shakespeare shining overhead:
Chatting on deck was Dryden too,
The Bacon of the rhyming crew;
None ever crost our mystic sea
More richly stored with thought than he;
Tho' never tender nor sublime,
He wrestles with and conquers Time.
To learn my lore on Chaucer's knee,
I left much prouder company;
Thee gentle Spenser fondly led,
But me he mostly sent to bed.

I wish them every joy above
That highly blessed spirits prove,
Save one: and that too shall be theirs,
But after many rolling years,
When 'mid their light thy light appears.

XIX
TO CHARLES DICKENS

Go then to Italy; but mind
To leave the pale low France behind;
Pass through that country, nor ascend
The Rhine, nor over Tyrol wend:
Thus all at once shall rise more grand
The glories of the ancient land.
  Dickens! how often, when the air

Breath'd genially, I've thought me there,
And rais'd to heaven my thankful eyes
To see three spans of deep blue skies.
  In Genoa now I hear a stir,
A shout ... **Here comes the Minister!**
Yes, thou art he, although not sent
By cabinet or parliament:
Yes, thou art he. Since Milton's youth
Bloom'd in the Eden of the South,
Spirit so pure and lofty none
Hath heavenly Genius from his throne
Deputed on the banks of Thames
To speak his voice and urge his claims.
Let every nation know from thee
How less than lovely Italy
Is the whole world beside; let all
Into their grateful breasts recall
How Prospero and Miranda dwelt
In Italy: the griefs that melt
The stoniest heart, each sacred tear
One lacrymatory gathered here;
All Desdemona's, all that fell
In playful Juliet's bridal cell.
  Ah! could my steps in life's decline
Accompany or follow thine!
But my own vines are not for me
To prune, or from afar to see.
I miss the tales I used to tell
With cordial Hare and joyous Gell,
And that good old Archbishop whose
Cool library, at evening's close
(Soon as from Ischia swept the gale
And heav'd and left the dark'ning sail),

Its lofty portal open'd wide
To me, and very few beside:
Yet large his kindness. Still the poor
Flock round Taranto's palace door,
And find no other to replace
The noblest of a noble race.
Amid our converse you would see
Each with white cat upon his knee,
And flattering that grand company:
For Persian kings might proudly own
Such glorious cats to share the throne.
  Write me few letters: I'm content
With what for all the world is meant;
Write then for all: but, since my breast
Is far more faithful than the rest,
Never shall any other share
With little Nelly nestling there.

XX
TO BARRY CORNWALL

Barry! your spirit long ago
Has haunted me; at last I know
The heart it sprung from: one more sound
Ne'er rested on poetic ground.
But, Barry Cornwall! by what right
Wring you my breast and dim my sight,
And make me wish at every touch
My poor old hand could do as much?
No other in these later times
Has bound me in so potent rhymes.
I have observed the curious dress

And jewelry of brave Queen Bess,
But always found some o'ercharged thing,
Some flaw in even the brightest ring,
Admiring in her men of war,
A rich but too argute guitar.
Our foremost now are more prolix,
And scrape with three-fell fiddlesticks,
And, whether bound for griefs or smiles,
Are slow to turn as crocodiles.
Once, every court and country bevy
Chose the gallant of loins less heavy,
And would have laid upon the shelf
Him who could talk but of himself.
Reason is stout, but even Reason
May walk too long in Rhyme's hot season.
I have heard many folks aver
They have caught horrid colds with her.
Imagination's paper kite,
Unless the string is held in tight,
Whatever fits and starts it takes,
Soon bounces on the ground, and breaks.
You, placed afar from each extreme,
Nor dully drowse nor wildly dream,
But, ever flowing with good-humour,
Are bright as spring and warm as summer.
Mid your Penates not a word
Of scorn or ill-report is heard;
Nor is there any need to pull
A sheaf or truss from cart too full,
Lest it o'erload the horse, no doubt,
Or clog the road by falling out.
We, who surround a common table,
And imitate the fashionable,

Wear each two eyeglasses: ***this*** lens
Shows us our faults, ***that*** other men's.
We do not care how dim may be
 This by whose aid our own we see,
But, ever anxiously alert
That all may have their whole desert,
We would melt down the stars and sun
In our heart's furnace, to make one
Thro' which the enlighten'd world might spy
A mote upon a brother's eye.

XXI
TO ROBERT BROWNING

There is delight in singing, tho' none hear
Beside the singer: and there is delight
In praising, tho' the praiser sit alone
And see the prais'd far off him, far above.
Shakespeare is not our poet, but the world's,
Therefore on him no speech! and brief for thee,
Browning! Since Chaucer was alive and hale,
No man hath walkt along our roads with step
So active, so inquiring eye, or tongue
So varied in discourse. But warmer climes
Give brighter plumage, stronger wing: the breeze
Of Alpine highths thou playest with, borne on
Beyond Sorrento and Amalfi, where
The Siren waits thee, singing song for song.

XXII
AGE

Death, tho' I see him not, is near
And grudges me my eightieth year.
Now, I would give him all these last
For one that fifty have run past.
Ah! he strikes all things, all alike,
But bargains: those he will not strike.

XXIII

Leaf after leaf drops off, flower after flower,
Some in the chill, some in the warmer hour:
Alike they flourish and alike they fall,
And Earth who nourisht them receives them all.
Should we, her wiser sons, be less content
To sink into her lap when life is spent?

XXIV

Well I remember how you smiled
  To see me write your name upon
The soft sea-sand--' ***O! what a child!***
  You think you're writing upon stone!'
I have since written what no tide
  Shall ever wash away, what men
Unborn shall read o'er ocean wide
  And find Ianthe's name again.

XXV

    I strove with none, for none was worth my strife.
    Nature I loved, and, next to Nature, Art;
    I warmed both hands before the fire of Life;
    It sinks, and I am ready to depart.

XXVI

    Death stands above me, whispering low
      I know not what into my ear:
    Of his strange language all I know
      Is, there is not a word of fear.

XXVII

A PASTORAL

    Damon was sitting in the grove
    With Phyllis, and protesting love;
    And she was listening; but no word
    Of all he loudly swore she heard.
    How! was she deaf then? no, not she,
    Phyllis was quite the contrary.
    Tapping his elbow, she said, 'Hush!
    O what a darling of a thrush!
    I think he never sang so well
    As now, below us, in the dell.'

XXVIII
THE LOVER

   Now thou art gone, tho' not gone far,
     It seems that there are worlds between us;
   Shine here again, thou wandering star!
     Earth's planet! and return with Venus.

   At times thou broughtest me thy light
     When restless sleep had gone away;
   At other times more blessed night
     Stole over, and prolonged thy stay.

XXIX
THE POET WHO SLEEPS

   One day, when I was young, I read
   About a poet, long since dead,
   Who fell asleep, as poets do
   In writing--and make others too.
   But herein lies the story's gist,
   How a gay queen came up and kist
   The sleeper.
            'Capital!' thought I.
   'A like good fortune let me try.'
   Many the things we poets feign.
   I feign'd to sleep, but tried in vain.
   I tost and turn'd from side to side,
   With open mouth and nostrils wide.
   At last there came a pretty maid,
   And gazed; then to myself I said,
   'Now for it!' She, instead of kiss,

Cried, 'What a lazy lout is this!'

XXX
DANIEL DEFOE

Few will acknowledge what they owe
To persecuted, brave Defoe.
Achilles, in Homeric song,
May, or he may not, live so long
As Crusoe; few their strength had tried
Without so staunch and safe a guide.
What boy is there who never laid
Under his pillow, half afraid,
That precious volume, lest the morrow
For unlearnt lessons might bring sorrow?
But nobler lessons he has taught
Wide-awake scholars who fear'd naught:
A Rodney and a Nelson may
Without him not have won the day.

XXXI
IDLE WORDS

They say that every idle word
Is numbered by the Omniscient Lord.
O Parliament! 'tis well that He
Endureth for Eternity,
And that a thousand Angels wait
To write them at thy inner gate.

XXXII
TO THE RIVER AVON

    Avon! why runnest thou away so fast?
Rest thee before that Chancel where repose
The bones of him whose spirit moves the world.
I have beheld thy birthplace, I have seen
Thy tiny ripples where they play amid
The golden cups and ever-waving blades.
I have seen mighty rivers, I have seen
Padus, recovered from his fiery wound,
And Tiber, prouder than them all to bear
Upon his tawny bosom men who crusht
The world they trod on, heeding not the cries
Of culprit kings and nations many-tongued.
What are to me these rivers, once adorn'd
With crowns they would not wear but swept away?
Worthier art thou of worship, and I bend
My knees upon thy bank, and call thy name,
And hear, or think I hear, thy voice reply.

www.bookjungle.com email: sales@bookjungle.com fax: 630-214-0564 mail: Book Jungle PO Box 2226 Champaign, IL 61825

The Codes Of Hammurabi And Moses
W. W. Davies

QTY

The discovery of the Hammurabi Code is one of the greatest achievements of archaeology, and is of paramount interest, not only to the student of the Bible, but also to all those interested in ancient history...

Religion ISBN: *1-59462-338-4* Pages:132 MSRP *$12.95*

The Theory of Moral Sentiments
Adam Smith

QTY

This work from 1749. contains original theories of conscience amd moral judgment and it is the foundation for systemof morals.

Philosophy ISBN: *1-59462-777-0* Pages:536 MSRP *$19.95*

Jessica's First Prayer
Hesba Stretton

QTY

In a screened and secluded corner of one of the many railway-bridges which span the streets of London there could be seen a few years ago, from five o'clock every morning until half past eight, a tidily set-out coffee-stall, consisting of a trestle and board, upon which stood two large tin cans, with a small fire of charcoal burning under each so as to keep the coffee boiling during the early hours of the morning when the work-people were thronging into the city on their way to their daily toil...

Childrens ISBN: *1-59462-373-2* Pages:84 MSRP *$9.95*

My Life and Work
Henry Ford

QTY

Henry Ford revolutionized the world with his implementation of mass production for the Model T automobile. Gain valuable business insight into his life and work with his own auto-biography... "We have only started on our development of our country we have not as yet, with all our talk of wonderful progress, done more than scratch the surface. The progress has been wonderful enough but..."

Biographies/ ISBN: *1-59462-198-5* Pages:300 MSRP *$21.95* www.bookjungle.com *email: sales@bookjungle.com fax: 630-214-0564 mail: Book Jungle PO Box 2226 Champaign, IL 61825*

The Art of Cross-Examination
Francis Wellman

QTY

I presume it is the experience of every author, after his first book is published upon an important subject, to be almost overwhelmed with a wealth of ideas and illustrations which could readily have been included in his book, and which to his own mind, at least, seem to make a second edition inevitable. Such certainly was the case with me; and when the first edition had reached its sixth impression in five months, I rejoiced to learn that it seemed to my publishers that the book had met with a sufficiently favorable reception to justify a second and considerably enlarged edition. ...

Reference   ISBN: *1-59462-647-2*   Pages:412   MSRP $19.95

On the Duty of Civil Disobedience
Henry David Thoreau

QTY

Thoreau wrote his famous essay, On the Duty of Civil Disobedience, as a protest against an unjust but popular war and the immoral but popular institution of slave-owning. He did more than write—he declined to pay his taxes, and was hauled off to gaol in consequence. Who can say how much this refusal of his hastened the end of the war and of slavery ?

Law   ISBN: *1-59462-747-9*   Pages:48   MSRP $7.45

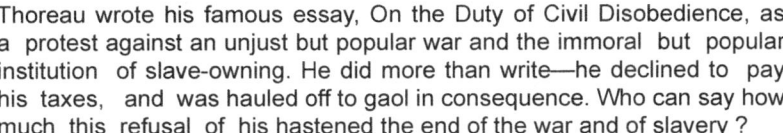

Dream Psychology Psychoanalysis for Beginners
Sigmund Freud

QTY

Sigmund Freud, born Sigismund Schlomo Freud (May 6, 1856 - September 23, 1939), was a Jewish-Austrian neurologist and psychiatrist who co-founded the psychoanalytic school of psychology. Freud is best known for his theories of the unconscious mind, especially involving the mechanism of repression; his redefinition of sexual desire as mobile and directed towards a wide variety of objects; and his therapeutic techniques, especially his understanding of transference in the therapeutic relationship and the presumed value of dreams as sources of insight into unconscious desires.

Psychology   ISBN: *1-59462-905-6*   Pages:196   MSRP $15.45

The Miracle of Right Thought
Orison Swett Marden

QTY

Believe with all of your heart that you will do what you were made to do. When the mind has once formed the habit of holding cheerful, happy, prosperous pictures, it will not be easy to form the opposite habit. It does not matter how improbable or how far away this realization may see, or how dark the prospects may be, if we visualize them as best we can, as vividly as possible, hold tenaciously to them and vigorously struggle to attain them, they will gradually become actualized, realized in the life. But a desire, a longing without endeavor, a yearning abandoned or held indifferently will vanish without realization.

Self Help   ISBN: *1-59462-644-8*   Pages:360   MSRP $25.45

www.bookjungle.com email: sales@bookjungle.com fax: 630-214-0564 mail: Book Jungle PO Box 2226 Champaign, IL 61825

QTY

☐ **The Rosicrucian Cosmo-Conception Mystic Christianity** by *Max Heindel* ISBN: *1-59462-188-8* **$38.95**
The Rosicrucian Cosmo-conception is not dogmatic, neither does it appeal to any other authority than the reason of the student. It is: not controversial, but is: sent forth in the, hope that it may help to clear... *New Age/Religion Pages 646*

☐ **Abandonment To Divine Providence** by *Jean-Pierre de Caussade* ISBN: *1-59462-228-0* **$25.95**
"The Rev. Jean Pierre de Caussade was one of the most remarkable spiritual writers of the Society of Jesus in France in the 18th Century. His death took place at Toulouse in 1751. His works have gone through many editions and have been republished... *Inspirational/Religion Pages 400*

☐ **Mental Chemistry** by *Charles Haanel* ISBN: *1-59462-192-6* **$23.95**
Mental Chemistry allows the change of material conditions by combining and appropriately utilizing the power of the mind. Much like applied chemistry creates something new and unique out of careful combinations of chemicals the mastery of mental chemistry... *New Age Pages 354*

☐ **The Letters of Robert Browning and Elizabeth Barret Barrett 1845-1846 vol II** ISBN: *1-59462-193-4* **$35.95**
by *Robert Browning* and *Elizabeth Barrett*
Biographies Pages 596

☐ **Gleanings In Genesis (volume I)** by *Arthur W. Pink* ISBN: *1-59462-130-6* **$27.45**
Appropriately has Genesis been termed "the seed plot of the Bible" for in it we have, in germ form, almost all of the great doctrines which are afterwards fully developed in the books of Scripture which follow... *Religion/Inspirational Pages 420*

☐ **The Master Key** by *L. W. de Laurence* ISBN: *1-59462-001-6* **$30.95**
In no branch of human knowledge has there been a more lively increase of the spirit of research during the past few years than in the study of Psychology, Concentration and Mental Discipline. The requests for authentic lessons in Thought Control, Mental Discipline and... *New Age/Business Pages 422*

☐ **The Lesser Key Of Solomon Goetia** by *L. W. de Laurence* ISBN: *1-59462-092-X* **$9.95**
This translation of the first book of the "Lernegton" which is now for the first time made accessible to students of Talismanic Magic was done, after careful collation and edition, from numerous Ancient Manuscripts in Hebrew, Latin, and French... *New Age/Occult Pages 92*

☐ **Rubaiyat Of Omar Khayyam** by *Edward Fitzgerald* ISBN: *1-59462-332-5* **$13.95**
Edward Fitzgerald, whom the world has already learned, in spite of his own efforts to remain within the shadow of anonymity, to look upon as one of the rarest poets of the century, was born at Bredfield, in Suffolk, on the 31st of March, 1809. He was the third son of John Purcell... *Music Pages 172*

☐ **Ancient Law** by *Henry Maine* ISBN: *1-59462-128-4* **$29.95**
The chief object of the following pages is to indicate some of the earliest ideas of mankind, as they are reflected in Ancient Law, and to point out the relation of those ideas to modern thought. *Religion/History Pages 452*

☐ **Far-Away Stories** by *William J. Locke* ISBN: *1-59462-129-2* **$19.45**
"Good wine needs no bush, but a collection of mixed vintages does. And this book is just such a collection. Some of the stories I do not want to remain buried for ever in the museum files of dead magazine-numbers an author's not unpardonable vanity..." *Fiction Pages 272*

☐ **Life of David Crockett** by *David Crockett* ISBN: *1-59462-250-7* **$27.45**
"Colonel David Crockett was one of the most remarkable men of the times in which he lived. Born in humble life, but gifted with a strong will, an indomitable courage, and unremitting perseverance... *Biographies/New Age Pages 424*

☐ **Lip-Reading** by *Edward Nitchie* ISBN: *1-59462-206-X* **$25.95**
Edward B. Nitchie, founder of the New York School for the Hard of Hearing, now the Nitchie School of Lip-Reading, Inc, wrote "LIP-READING Principles and Practice". The development and perfecting of this meritorious work on lip-reading was an undertaking... *How-to Pages 400*

☐ **A Handbook of Suggestive Therapeutics, Applied Hypnotism, Psychic Science** ISBN: *1-59462-214-0* **$24.95**
by *Henry Munro*
Health/New Age/Health/Self-help Pages 376

☐ **A Doll's House: and Two Other Plays** by *Henrik Ibsen* ISBN: *1-59462-112-8* **$19.95**
Henrik Ibsen created this classic when in revolutionary 1848 Rome. Introducing some striking concepts in playwriting for the realist genre, this play has been studied the world over. *Fiction/Classics/Plays 308*

☐ **The Light of Asia** by *sir Edwin Arnold* ISBN: *1-59462-204-3* **$13.95**
In this poetic masterpiece, Edwin Arnold describes the life and teachings of Buddha. The man who was to become known as Buddha to the world was born as Prince Gautama of India but he rejected the worldly riches and abandoned the reigns of power when... *Religion/History/Biographies Pages 170*

☐ **The Complete Works of Guy de Maupassant** by *Guy de Maupassant* ISBN: *1-59462-157-8* **$16.95**
"For days and days, nights and nights, I had dreamed of that first kiss which was to consecrate our engagement, and I knew not on what spot I should put my lips..." *Fiction/Classics Pages 240*

☐ **The Art of Cross-Examination** by *Francis L. Wellman* ISBN: *1-59462-309-0* **$26.95**
Written by a renowned trial lawyer, Wellman imparts his experience and uses case studies to explain how to use psychology to extract desired information through questioning. *How-to/Science/Reference Pages 408*

☐ **Answered or Unanswered?** by *Louisa Vaughan* ISBN: *1-59462-248-5* **$10.95**
Miracles of Faith in China
Religion Pages 112

☐ **The Edinburgh Lectures on Mental Science (1909)** by *Thomas* ISBN: *1-59462-008-3* **$11.95**
This book contains the substance of a course of lectures recently given by the writer in the Queen Street Hall, Edinburgh. Its purpose is to indicate the Natural Principles governing the relation between Mental Action and Material Conditions... *New Age/Psychology Pages 148*

☐ **Ayesha** by *H. Rider Haggard* ISBN: *1-59462-301-5* **$24.95**
Verily and indeed it is the unexpected that happens! Probably if there was one person upon the earth from whom the Editor of this, and of a certain previous history, did not expect to hear again... *Classics Pages 380*

☐ **Ayala's Angel** by *Anthony Trollope* ISBN: *1-59462-352-X* **$29.95**
The two girls were both pretty, but Lucy who was twenty-one who supposed to be simple and comparatively unattractive, whereas Ayala was credited, as her Bombwhat romantic name might show, with poetic charm and a taste for romance. Ayala when her father died was nineteen... *Fiction Pages 484*

☐ **The American Commonwealth** by *James Bryce* ISBN: *1-59462-286-8* **$34.45**
An interpretation of American democratic political theory. It examines political mechanics and society from the perspective of Scotsman James Bryce
Politics Pages 572

☐ **Stories of the Pilgrims** by *Margaret P. Pumphrey* ISBN: *1-59462-116-0* **$17.95**
This book explores pilgrims religious oppression in England as well as their escape to Holland and eventual crossing to America on the Mayflower, and their early days in New England... *History Pages 268*

www.bookjungle.com email: sales@bookjungle.com fax: 630-214-0564 mail: Book Jungle PO Box 2226 Champaign, IL 61825

QTY

The Fasting Cure by *Sinclair Upton* ISBN: *1-59462-222-1* $13.95
In the Cosmopolitan Magazine for May, 1910, and in the Contemporary Review (London) for April, 1910, I published an article dealing with my experiences in fasting. I have written a great many magazine articles, but never one which attracted so much attention... *New Age/Self Help/Health Pages 164*

Hebrew Astrology by *Sepharial* ISBN: *1-59462-308-2* $13.45
In these days of advanced thinking it is a matter of common observation that we have left many of the old landmarks behind and that we are now pressing forward to greater heights and to a wider horizon than that which represented the mind-content of our progenitors... *Astrology Pages 144*

Thought Vibration or The Law of Attraction in the Thought World ISBN: *1-59462-127-6* $12.95
by *William Walker Atkinson* *Psychology/Religion Pages 144*

Optimism by *Helen Keller* ISBN: *1-59462-108-X* $15.95
Helen Keller was blind, deaf, and mute since 19 months old, yet famously learned how to overcome these handicaps, communicate with the world, and spread her lectures promoting optimism. An inspiring read for everyone... *Biographies/Inspirational Pages 84*

Sara Crewe by *Frances Burnett* ISBN: *1-59462-360-0* $9.45
In the first place, Miss Minchin lived in London. Her home was a large, dull, tall one, in a large, dull square, where all the houses were alike, and all the sparrows were alike, and where all the door-knockers made the same heavy sound... *Childrens/Classic Pages 88*

The Autobiography of Benjamin Franklin by *Benjamin Franklin* ISBN: *1-59462-135-7* $24.95
The Autobiography of Benjamin Franklin has probably been more extensively read than any other American historical work, and no other book of its kind has had such ups and downs of fortune. Franklin lived for many years in England, where he was agent... *Biographies/History Pages 332*

Name	
Email	
Telephone	
Address	
City, State ZIP	

☐ Credit Card   ☐ Check / Money Order

Credit Card Number	
Expiration Date	
Signature	

Please Mail to: Book Jungle
PO Box 2226
Champaign, IL 61825
or Fax to: 630-214-0564

ORDERING INFORMATION

web: *www.bookjungle.com*
email: *sales@bookjungle.com*
fax: *630-214-0564*
mail: *Book Jungle PO Box 2226 Champaign, IL 61825*
or PayPal *to sales@bookjungle.com*

Please contact us for bulk discounts

DIRECT-ORDER TERMS

**20% Discount if You Order
Two or More Books**
Free Domestic Shipping!
Accepted: Master Card, Visa,
Discover, American Express

www.ingramcontent.com/pod-product-compliance
Lightning Source LLC
Chambersburg PA
CBHW080721230426
43665CB00020B/2572